*Feminist Coalitions*

WOMEN IN AMERICAN HISTORY

*Series Editors*
Anne Firor Scott
Susan Armitage
Susan K. Cahn
Deborah Gray White

*A list of books in the series appears*
*at the end of this book.*

# Feminist Coalitions

## Historical Perspectives on Second-Wave Feminism in the United States

Edited by
STEPHANIE GILMORE

Foreword by
SARA M. EVANS

*University of Illinois Press*
URBANA AND CHICAGO

Library of Congress Cataloging-in-Publication Data
Feminist coalitions : historical perspectives on second-wave
feminism in the United States / edited by Stephanie Gilmore ;
foreword by Sara M. Evans.
p.   cm. — (Women in American history)
Includes bibliographical references and index.
ISBN 978-0-252-03328-5 (cloth : alk. paper)
ISBN 978-0-252-07539-1 (pbk. : alk. paper)
1. Feminism—United States—History—20th century.
2. Women—United States—History—20th century.
3. Women's rights—United States—History—20th century.
I. Gilmore, Stephanie.
HQ1421.F47    2008
305.420973—dc22    2008002165

# Contents

# Foreword

## SARA M. EVANS

The essays in this collection offer irrefutable evidence that feminists in the 1970s formed numerous and highly diverse coalitions across lines of race, class, and political ideology. They shatter the stereotype of a white, middle-class, politically rigid movement and in doing so they make us wonder why that stereotype has had such power across the decades. These stories are not the first to offer a more complex version of that turbulent time, though they add a wonderful richness because of their reach. Yet, as the editor points out, the narrative of the women's movement as composed predominantly of white and middle-class women prevails and persists in spite of volumes of scholarship to the contrary. This narrative suspends the women's movement and its actors in what she calls "historical—or rather, *ahistorical*—amber"—a useful metaphor.

Many who were active in the seventies have known all along that the stereotype was fundamentally wrong. Not only did it erase the activism of women of color, religious women, and working-class women, but it also presumed that the white, middle-class members of a movement inspired into being by the black freedom movement were not concerned about race or class. It is a relief to find a new generation of scholars eager to challenge the standard narrative and retrieve the complexity of the second wave, but the very need for a book such as this one poses the question of why the stereotype has been so persistent.

I started writing the history of the second wave as a graduate student in the early 1970s when the movement itself was very young. My dissertation, which became my first book, focused on the origin of the younger, radical branch of feminism, born in the late 1960s.[1] I was aware that early academic papers incorrectly described the women's liberation movement as split-off from National Organization for Women, failing to perceive the linkages between feminism, the black freedom movement, and the student-led New Left. Influenced by theories of collective behavior, I also wanted to understand how women came to see themselves as a group with the capacity to act. Sisterhood was not a foregone conclusion, I argued, but rather a construct that developed through a set of shared experiences. In tracing the evolution of that *we*, however, I had neither the questions nor the conceptual tools to grapple with the complexities of differences *among* women beyond recognizing the historically specific circumstances that made cross-racial alliances very difficult in the late 1960s. Writing against the backdrop of a movement growing in complexity and torn by factionalism, I was reluctant to move my analysis beyond 1968, when the movement was taking off. I actually drafted a chapter analyzing the early evolution of groups in different parts of the country (the so-called politico-feminist split) but found that I was at the beginning of another story, not the end of the one I was telling. At that point, none of us could yet describe the trajectory of the movement once it was launched. When I returned to that project in the 1990s, to my delight, I was in the company of a growing number of historians—several of whom are in this volume—committed to recovering the history of that era in all of its complexity.

In my experience, the homogenized narrative we now struggle to complicate became fixed as "common knowledge" sometime in the 1980s, a decade in which feminist scholarship and theorizing flourished. I have a hunch that this amber congealed (fossilized?) in those debates. What led us down that path? My argument is that the central focus of the 1980s feminist debates—and the generational perspectives linked to them—used this stereotype as a foil (they were wrong and we are right), but very few were engaged in historical research.[2] Those same debates, however, laid crucial conceptual groundwork for the task now assumed by the authors of this volume who represent yet another generation of feminist scholarship.

In the late 1970s and early 1980s, there was a growing recognition that the theoretical frameworks available for analyzing race, class, and gender each reified particular identities in ways that obscured or even obliterated the others. The voices of feminists of color (bell hooks, Gloria Anzaldúa, Alice Walker, Toni Morrison, Cherríe Moraga, Bernice Johnson Reagon, Patricia Collins, and Barbara Smith—to name only a few) made a compelling case that in reality human beings always embody multiple sources of identity—not only race, class, and gender but also an endless list including religion, ethnicity, region, and family. Their work echoed Sojourner Truth's reputed cry, "aren't I a woman?" in demanding a more capacious understanding of gender capable of incorporating diversity. This conundrum quickly became central to feminist debate and theory, drawing additional intellectual energy from postmodernist challenges to the very idea of fixed identities and the theoretical focus on intersectionality and social construction.

That very enterprise, however, may well have helped to suspend the activism of the 1970s in ahistorical amber by presuming that theoretical dilemmas inherited from that decade were direct reflections of organizational behavior. A new generation of feminist scholars critiqued a variety of theoretical writings from the 1970s and took the lapses in those for descriptions of the movement itself. Those writings were struggling with the problem of collective identity: Who are women? Why and how are they oppressed? What is the path to their liberation? What are effective strategies of collective action? Debates on these questions raged across what seemed at the time, very deep divides: There was the politico-feminist split, the gay-straight split, the radical-cultural feminist split, the chasm between liberals and radicals, the so-called sex wars, and a plethora of personalized battles within organizations over strategic and ideological choices. At least some of those early differences, in retrospect, were not as sharp as participants believed and others offer vibrant evidence of diversity. However, most of them shared the assumption that identity is unified, fixed.

Gilmore points out that if we are to dislodge feminists from that ahistorical amber, "*we must embrace a capacious definition of feminism* [my emphasis]." In the maelstrom of the 1970s, however, when virtually every group sought to claim its point of view as "true feminism," much of the rhetoric of the movement itself obscured the coalitions that existed. In a time of extreme political polarization and identity politics, coalitions were real but so was fragmentation. The sharpness of the debates, however, meant that the latter was theorized more often than the former, and a capacious definition of feminism was hard to hold onto. Thus, the theoretical debates in the 1970s may also have made it more likely that the multiplicity of feminisms in that turbulent era would be lost in the subsequent telling of the story.

For a time, then, second-wave feminism in the 1970s served as a foil for the academic project of theorizing diversity and beginning to challenge the underpinnings of identity politics. Most of us who taught women's history or women's studies in the 1980s recall students who were sharply critical of feminists in the previous decade who, they believed, were not only all white and middle class but also utterly unconcerned about diversity. Theirs was a generation in which "lipstick lesbians" criticized "granola lesbians" who led the early battles, created public spaces (coffee houses, bookstores, music festivals), and articulated a lesbian feminist perspective. The restlessness of a younger generation that wants to explore new freedoms and is impatient with their elders who are forever marked by their battle scars is hardly unique. At that point, recent history tends to polarize into a foil or a golden age. Neither, of course, does justice to the complexity of the time nor does it yield a usable story of the past, but then, for a time, hardly anyone was actually doing historical research. I suspect that it took another generational turn, and scholars equipped with new theoretical tools and freed of necessity to either criticize or romanticize, to bring us back to doing that essential groundwork. Now, more than ever, we need these stories.

Social movements, in general, are somewhat miraculous. It is always remarkable when people outside centers of power develop the capacity to engage actively in reshaping social structures and public policy. If human identities are both multiple and fluid, the human communities generated by grassroots organizing are similarly never fixed and always filled with competing perspectives and interests. Such an insight—a gift of several decades of theoretical and historical research—makes it possible to pay attention to the complexity of the second wave in the 1970s. We no longer need to use that history as a foil; nor is it useful to see it as a golden age of activism to be treated with reverent nostalgia. Every version of feminism in the 1970s aspired to building a movement that crossed lines of race and class. The stories told here make it clear that there were many on-the-ground efforts that did so with varying degrees of success and, at the same time, that the coalitions they created were always fraught. This unromanticized history in *Feminist Coalitions* is a rich inheritance, moving us toward an honest and usable past.

## Notes

1. *Personal Politics: The Roots of Women's Liberation in the Civil Rights Movement and the New Left* (New York: Knopf, 1979).
2. We should be clear here that the stereotype that pervades feminist scholarship is quite different from the stereotypes created by right-wing backlash that pervade American popular culture.

# 1. Thinking about Feminist Coalitions

## STEPHANIE GILMORE

Conventional wisdom about feminism and the postwar U.S. women's movement suggests that it was composed predominantly of white and middle-class women. This often replicated narrative of a homogeneous social movement has tremendous staying power: it shapes the way scholars have defined and teach about feminism and its "waves," framed by woman's suffrage and women's liberation.[1] The scholarly story of feminism was the production of feminist activists who entered the academy; according to feminist activist and historian Eileen Boris, it "came out of the search for identity and struggles of some women in the late 1960s, their need for a sisterhood that was powerful."[2] Even more, this wisdom permeates popular culture: feminism in the past, even the recent past, was white and middle class, and exaggerated, even cartoonish, images of hairy-legged, braless, angry, white feminists still exist in the minds of many people. Both within and beyond scholarly treatments, the women's movement suffers from this standard narrative, which fuels discontent but also serves to further marginalize the women's movement. In spite of the fact that the women's movement was the largest and farthest-reaching social movement of the era, feminism and women's activism are often relegated to a sidebar of social movement histories of the 1960s and 1970s. In scholarly overviews of these decades, women are not major actors and their feminist activism is not considered as important as or connected to other social and political change. There are often indexed references for "women" and "feminism" but not for "men" in these books which speaks further to the secondary treatment women and their feminist activisms receive in the historical record.[3] This status within scholarly work, coupled with a short-sighted and inaccurate view of the women's movement, one whose origins are tied to discontent in the civil rights and New Left movements but quickly detached from these and other movements to focus on women's oppressions and equality, remains dominant.[4] As a result, the movement and its actors are suspended in historical—or rather, *ahistorical*—amber, unable to move or be moved.

Still, we *know* from various scholarly rejoinders and our own lived experiences that the movement was diverse, multifaceted, and spoke to and for many women. Sara Evans, Dorothy Sue Cobble, Ruth Rosen, Kimberly Springer, Benita Roth, Premilla Nadasen, Annelise Orleck, Susan Hartmann, and Becky Thompson have penned outstanding books that allow us to see the activism of women who are not white and/or middle class in the larger context of the women's movement, and they point us toward some of the cross-racial and cross-class alliances that some women forged as they built and sustained a feminist women's movement.[5] Feminist scholar Chandra Talpade Mohanty has asserted that "sisterhood cannot be assumed on the basis of gender; it must be formed in concrete, historical and political practice and analysis. . . ."[6] So too must feminist coalitions, and the chapters in this book move us in this practical and analytical direction, exploring how women came to work together in pursuit of feminist goals. The scholars whose chapters appear in this book have sought to explore how feminists during the women's movement of the 1970s looked to move "beyond the lines that separate us" and into "the fissures which make us who we are . . . in the discordance of our many-hued voices."[7]

Exploring how people come together in coalitions—feminist or otherwise, in face-to-face meetings or in virtual coalitions, in very short-lived alliances or in longer, more sustained ones—requires significant attention to lived experiences of the people involved. It moves us necessarily, although not exclusively, away from movement leaders and "stars" and into neighborhoods, community centers, and other local sites of day-to-day, grassroots activism—where coalitions most often take place. As historian Estelle Freedman observed, "facing common oppression and learning to trust across difference, though never an easy task, helped sustain grassroots feminism in the face of opposition."[8] As she articulates—and the chapters in this book make clear—coalitions, especially feminist coalitions, were necessary and beneficial to the longevity and scope of the movement as well as to the individual women involved in it.

The women whose lives and activisms are analyzed in the pages of this book operated from a worldview constructed out of their daily lives. Their political positions were based on a material understanding of the intersecting hierarchies in their lives. They brought multiple consciousness to their coalition work, and in these coalitions, they incorporated, or at least sought and tried to incorporate, many perspectives and experiences into their activism on a number of issues. They faced common oppression and discrimination *as women,* even if this oppression was mediated by other social and cultural factors. After all, "all women don't have the same gender."[9] Still, they did learn to trust one another. Sometimes that trust led to betrayal and distance.[10] Sometimes that trust led to long-term alliances. However, what requires our attention is how feminist coalitions emerged—who initiated them, for what reasons, why they lasted as long as they did, and what they achieved. Through a feminist lens, we see that the women featured in the following chapters were feminist activists, even if not exclusively so. When we take seriously feminist scholars' calls to expand definitions of women's experiences to include non–white, middle-class women, we also have to contemplate "expanding the boundaries of the women's movement."[11] Part of this expansion process demands attention to *how* women struggled to include and represent numbers of diverse women at all levels of the movement.[12]

The goal of this book is to explore the range of feminist activisms and coalitions that took place in the United States during the era of second-wave feminism. The chapters in this book reveal much that we do not know about the women's movement—the serious attempts, both successful and not, to build coalitions is one of them. They also bring to light a number of activists committed to feminist, antiracist, and egalitarian struggles. Their coalitions were imperfect and tenuous; most did not last very long, and some did not achieve their goals. In thinking about such feminist activism, I have been inspired by and draw upon feminist scholarship that traces feminist activisms in the larger context of other social justice movements—much of that scholarship has explored a variety of feminisms outside of the United States. This body of work underscores the impossibilities of conceptualizing a singular feminism in, say, Latin America, Europe, Africa, or Asia, or among transnational groups of women, such as the Third World.[13] As such, it has much to teach us about feminism in the United States, indicating that we can find various feminist activisms in places we do not expect and among women who do not necessarily embrace the term but who do the work of feminism.

Many of us who study and write about social movement activism tend to look at individuals and organizations in the context of distinct social movements. Even the handful of monographs and edited collections that speak to postwar social movement activism, such as *America Divided, Social Movements of the 1960s,* or *The World the 60s Made* make sense of this era by dividing the movements into comprehensible and discrete units of black freedom, antiwar, New Left, feminism, gay and lesbian liberation, and labor activisms.[14] Such an approach is quite logical as it allows us to go deep into a particular movement, finding and analyzing various individuals and organizations that mobilized and defined different movements. In monographs, for example, Barbara Ransby has captured the forceful impact of one woman, Ella Baker, on the development of the civil rights movement, and Belinda Robnett and Bettye Collier-Thomas and V. P. Franklin turned our attention to the role of women in the wider movement for black freedom.[15] Maryann Barakso focused on National Organization for Women (NOW) in her analysis of feminist organizational continuity, underscoring NOW's participation in a number of formal, national coalitions.[16] Kimberly Springer and Benita Roth have written important texts on black and Chicana women's organizations in the larger women's movement, training their—and our—attention to the various organizations that women founded to speak, act, and identify as feminists and to the racial and ethnic diversity of the women's movement.[17] Adding local depth and dimension to what we know about social movements, some scholars are turning to the importance of geographical location in understanding the full breadth and depth of social movement activism. Judith Ezekiel, Anne Valk, John Howard, Kimberly Dugan, Susan Freeman, Charles Payne, and others have written impressive histories of feminist, gay and lesbian, and civil rights movement activisms in the heartland, the nation's capital, and the U.S. South.[18] These outstanding works—examples that merely scratch the surface—provide analytical depth and dimension to twentieth-century social movements, but we still rarely see attention to coalitions *across* differences.

We have, then, tremendous knowledge about the histories of social movements, feminist and otherwise, but it is vital to integrate this information, weaving a more complex history of our recent activist past. We can use these scholarly works to explore coalitions and alliances within and between organizations, geographical locations, and movements. In Ransby's compelling narrative, for example, we see Baker as a connective thread weaving her way through a number of organizations, reaching all the way to Mississippi and into the very homes of people discussed in Payne's book; Baker is a central figure in Robnett's and Collier-Thomas and Franklin's work. Women in Ezekiel's history of women's liberation in Dayton appeared in the newsletters of the Columbus NOW chapter and subsequently in my own writing on NOW chapters; those same Dayton women likely visited the nearest feminist bookstore in Cincinnati, which appears prominently in Freeman's history of Cincinnati's lesbian feminist community. Indeed, some women from Cincinnati's lesbian feminist community in the 1970s were also active in the city's "face off" over gay, lesbian, and bisexual rights, as Dugan illustrates. Women from the Memphis and Columbus chapters of NOW, along with feminists from Dayton, traveled to Washington, D.C., for national demonstrations, encountering feminists in the women's liberation movement whose histories are analyzed in Valk's work. The men in John Howard's queer history of Mississippi may well have known (and perhaps even been intimate with) men from the families featured in Payne's study: the civil rights movement figures prominently in Howard's construction of a Southern queer history. We will not have definitive answers to such queries until we look beyond the bindings of our own books and start looking for such connections.

However, once we do, we realize they are everywhere. They may not always be at the more obvious organizational level, and they may not be formal or sustained; they may not be what feminist theorist María Lugones calls deep coalitions that "go beyond short-term interest-based alliances."[19] But what is worth noting—and what we know intuitively from our own experiences but rarely acknowledge in the lives we study historically—is how often people travel in many circles at the same time.[20] Doing so illuminates how the markers of difference, such as class, race, gender, ethnicity, religion, and other differences, do not operate independently of one another but instead intersect in people's lives.[21] Long a part of the theoretical discourse of feminism, intersectionality has not been fully integrated into our historical analyses of people's social movement activism. It is germane to understanding coalition building because we see intersectionality not only at the individual level but also at the interpersonal or group level. How people draw attention to and speak about their awareness of difference and multiple lived experiences through gender, race, class, ethnicity, religion, and other differences is at the core of understanding coalitions—and of *Feminist Coalitions*.

To dislodge the women's movement and its activists from that ahistorical amber and appreciate their complexities and nuances, we must embrace a capacious definition of feminism. Many of the women whose histories are shared here were those who "deemed the issues of race and class to be as crucial as that of gender." Following Dorothy Sue Cobble, I and the authors in this book explicitly or implicitly agree that feminism "need not require an unwavering single focus on gender, nor does gender-conscious reform reside only in all-female organizations."[22] Although most of the coalitions discussed in *Feminist Coalitions* were all-woman by design or default, many women involved in them were also connected to mixed-sex institutions, including labor unions, government, places of work and worship, and activist/feminist organizations such as NOW or National Welfare Rights Organization (NWRO).

In the pages that follow, we find Washington, D.C., feminists involved in both women's liberation groups and Citywide Welfare Alliance; in Chicago, NOW feminists joined Women Employed (WE); in cities across the country, black, white, and Chicana women joined one another and male allies in NWRO chapters. We also find numerous single- and mixed-sex organizations that operated simultaneously within the liberal and feminist establishments—NOW, NWRO, Daughters of Bilitis, National Women's Political Caucus, and United Auto Workers joined the Women's Action Alliance (WAA); many also spoke on behalf of women in the full employment campaign of the 1970s. Many of these women did not necessarily articulate their concerns as feminist ones nor did they analyze the disadvantages they suffered as women in an explicitly feminist framework, and some might argue that without this consciousness, we cannot claim them as feminists. However, I am more inclined to agree with Denise Riley, whose insightful analysis of feminism suggests that some of the most beneficial social movements for women "did not speak the name of woman."[23] They may not have operated in the name of feminism; indeed, many were uncomfortable with the label—understandable given that most women whose activism is recounted here were not white and/or middle class; they would not be represented in the contemporary media presentations or the historical tropes of feminism.[24] However, they did the work of feminism, whether they embraced or eschewed the label.[25] In all cases, they brought with them their overlapping networks and immediate common concerns to build feminist coalitions. Their feminist activism helped create and sustain a large-scale, wide-reaching movement through both national, organizational coalitions and grassroots agitation for feminist change in their workplaces, hospitals, churches, and communities.

So calling them "feminist" is one thing, but what makes them coalitions? Following Jill Bystydzienski and Stephen Schacht, I use coalitions and alliances interchangeably, although some distinguish between coalitions as short-term efforts around single issues and alliances as long-term efforts based on deep knowledge of others.[26] Their theoretical definition of coalitions—one of the most comprehensive—is "fluid sites of collective behavior where the blending of multiple personal identities with political activism interacts with structural conditions to influence the development of commitments, strategies, and specific actions."[27] As the following chapters make clear, feminists in the 1970s were creating these sites, blending identities and activism, and mobilizing for meaningful and significant change. Bystydzienski and Schacht identify the bottom-line goal of coalitions or alliances as changing "interpersonal relations and social structures in order to eradicate all forms of oppression."[28] Clearly, not all coalitions have this agenda as their goal; a number of contemporary coalitions operate with the goal of maintaining discrimination and oppression. However, feminists have historically sought to eradicate all forms of oppression, even if assigning priority to particular forms of discrimination. Although not wholly successful in the 1970s in *eliminating* classism, sexism, racism, homophobia, economic disparities, uneven political representation, and other forms of discrimination, the coalition activists whose histories are recounted here certainly addressed them head on, envisioning a future where these oppressions would disappear. In the meantime, though, they had hard work to do, and they banded together to do it.

Various scholars have criticized what has become known as *identity politics,* a framework and basis for activism and the pursuit of cultural and/or political change that is rooted in the interests of a particular group in society that shares experiences of real or perceived oppression. In *The Twilight of Common Dreams,* sociologist and leftist activist Todd Gitlin criticizes identity politics as "an American tragedy" and "a very bad turn, a detour into quicksand"; political activist and Green Party presidential candidate in 2000 Ralph Nader famously referred to identity politics as "gonadal politics" that are little more than a "trivializing distraction from the genuinely important agenda of economic issues."[29] Feminist scholar Nira Yuval-Davis has suggested that identity politics tend to "homogenize and naturalize social categories and groupings, denying shifting boundaries and internal power differences and conflicts of interest."[30] However, far from homogenizing experiences based on similarities or differences, the coalition politics of feminists moved beyond simple identity politics based on being women. Activists within feminist coalitions were aware of their larger social difference from men but also that these differences were mediated by other forms of oppression. They worked together in spite of differences, while never ignoring or minimizing them— indeed, building coalitions across significant differences between women is a hallmark of feminist activism in communities across the country. Chappell's chapter offers a pointed rejoinder to criticisms of identity politics, but this entire collection serves to examine historical perspectives on coalition building among feminists who, like all of us, had many different identities at the same time.

In his visionary work on the future of political activism in the United States, sociologist William Julius Wilson suggests that "in order to clear the path for the formation of a national, progressive, multiracial political coalition, proponents of social equality must pursue policies that unite rather than divide racial groups."[31] Wilson's volume offers a critical directive for the future, but it is important for us as scholars and activists to recognize that such work has also taken place in our recent past. Women's feminist activism offers an important vantage point from which to examine and analyze the historical foundations of such a national, political coalition, which in turn can also inform our present and our future.

*Feminist Coalitions,* then, explores and reflects the complexities of the women's movement. Taken as a whole, the chapters of this book describe, analyze, and offer a conceptual framework for feminist coalition building in the past. Bystydzienski and Schacht argue that coalition building always involves negotiations across difference; these negotiations are essential to collective action.[32] In the 1970s, some feminists entered into an alliance with keen awareness of difference, looking to negotiate among themselves in order to mobilize collectively. Cynthia Harrison's chapter opens this book with such an analysis, looking specifically at how a wide range of feminist organizations and individuals mobilized to create the WAA and the National Women's Agenda. It underscores the truth that feminists tackled a wide range of feminist issues, from health and poverty to education and government representation, and that the organized movement represented and spoke for a wide range of women. It also highlights how even the most politically connected feminists were never handmaidens of the liberal political establishment, but instead that they represented, in some ways, the "radical flank" of government action on women's issues—after all, the WAA was not the government-appointed International Women's Year Commission. As such, this chapter captures the breadth of the movement in its heyday—and the full force of feminist coalition building at a formal, national level.

In addition to building national coalitions such as the WAA, feminists also built long-standing institutions that served to mobilize feminists in various ways. Women's studies programs brought activism from the streets into the ivory tower; feminist music festivals, bookstores, and other public spaces also made feminism visible in women's day-to-day lives.[33] Publications also mobilized feminists, bringing different issues, insights, and analyses into women's homes; *Ms.* magazine is one of the most recognized publications of the women's movement. In her chapter, Amy Farrell demonstrates how feminists engaged with *Ms.,* often challenging the universal "sisterhood" made implicit and explicit in the pages of the magazine. She further illustrates how *Ms.* allowed people to connect easily with others without the geographical limitations inherent in a music festival, feminist bookstore, or women's studies classroom, all of which require the ability to meet in those spaces.[34]

Like Farrell, Wendy Kline also turns our attention to a feminist institution—*Our Bodies, Ourselves.* The feminist women's health bible, *Our Bodies, Ourselves* was a response to inadequate or insufficient attention to women's bodies and health; Kline observes that it "ignited the grassroots-based women's health movement" of the 1970s. Much like *Ms.* readers, women sought to find themselves represented in the pages of *Our Bodies, Ourselves.* They often confronted the editors when they found information lacking or incomplete or when their particular health and body concerns were not represented, as well as when the book offered the precise information readers had been seeking but could not find within the medical establishment.

Neither publication could possibly be everything to everybody, but *Ms.* and *Our Bodies, Ourselves* expanded their respective scopes to incorporate and represent as many women as possible. This did not happen because of the foresight of a handful of women; instead, it happened because of the *virtual* coalition building of readers who wrote to the publication editors. In the absence of the ability to research a subject on the Internet, readers of *Ms.* and *Our Bodies, Ourselves* took it upon themselves to push the women's movement to *include* them.

Moving from the virtual coalitions to face-to-face alliances, Andrea Estepa and Caryn Neumann turn our attention to places where we find women's activism but might not necessarily expect to find feminists. In Women Strike for Peace (WSP) and Church Women United (CWU), feminism emerged in the larger context of antiwar and interfaith coalition building. WSP developed in the late 1960s and early 1970s in the obvious context of the war in Vietnam, but, as Estepa demonstrates, WSP began to understand peace as a domestic issue and grew increasingly concerned with economic and racial justice. These middle-aged, middle-class, white (and white-gloved) women built likely and unlikely alliances with people from different races, generations, and socioeconomic backgrounds. Their feminist activism was tied to their identities as mothers, much like women in NWRO and the Poor People's Campaign; this identity shaped their feminist analysis of the war and of civil rights, broadly defined. They abandoned their ladylike image and linked arms with various people to bring about social justice and feminist change.

Neumann traces the development of CWU, an ecumenical coalition of women who sought to challenge the subordination of women who "served as the spine but not the head" of the church. Moving beyond the walls of the church and taking their mandate of active participation in the world seriously, they also became forceful civil rights and feminist activists, tackling poverty, segregation, and the "feminine mystique," not as separate issues but as integrated ones. These two chapters explore the origins of feminist activism among women we might not necessarily consider when we think of "feminists." Moreover, they highlight how many white, middle-class women moved beyond outreach programs and into diverse networks of activists.

Indeed, these networks helped sustain feminists as they confronted a number of issues and made the personal political, or at least public. Abortion, forced sterilization, and rape had long been political issues in the sense that there were laws mandating their legal parameters—criminalizing abortion, requiring forced sterilization, or, through law or practice, not intervening in the "domestic" matters of rape. Feminists get much, and much-deserved, credit for putting heretofore private issues of sexuality into the public discourse. However, the issues are often segregated—white feminists pursued antirape legislation and abortion rights and women of color pursued the end of forced sterilization. How feminists worked across differences of race, class, and political perspective to change laws and practices needs further exploration.

Creating some of the earliest stirrings of reproductive rights, white women liberationists and mostly black activists in Citywide Welfare Alliance mobilized together in Washington, D.C., to call for abortion as a health right, the subject of Anne Valk's chapter. Both groups charged that the city's D.C. General Hospital often denied poor black women legal abortions and pushed them toward illegal procedures; moreover, the hospital also often sterilized women without consent, leaving them unable to control their own reproduction. These groups worked together, albeit not easily, to confront the hospital's policy on therapeutic abortion as well as its shameful record of forced sterilization of black and Hispanic women, but in doing so, created the historical foundations for longer, sustained feminist activism in the context of reproductive rights.

Maria Bevacqua explores coalition politics in the antirape movement, exploring how feminists moved across racial and political lines to bring the issue of rape to the public fore. Rather than seeing only "separate roads to feminism," Bevacqua suggests that feminists met and coalesced at important intersections. Rape was one of these points—an issue that affected all women irrespective of race, class, or political perspective. Neither of these chapters paints a rosy picture of coalition building; indeed, feminists rarely saw eye to eye on issues of bodies and sexuality. Yet, both of these pieces push us to reconsider what we know about feminism and women's sexualities in the 1970s.

Women were often at the hands of men, quite literally, and feminists fought for women to gain control over their own bodies, whether obtaining abortion, preventing sterilization, or prosecuting or disarming rapists. But women also faced tremendous oppression from men—or rather, who NWRO activist Johnnie Tillmon famously referred to as "the man"[35]—when it came to economic autonomy. Moreover, when facing the state or employers, women often banded together, finding strength in numbers—and strength across racial and class boundaries. In her chapter on cross-race coalitions among welfare rights activists, Premilla Nadasen makes the case that the women in the NWRO did not see welfare as black, Chicana, or white problems; instead, "welfare's a green problem." Rather than turn our attention to alliances between middle-class whites and the predominantly black constituency of the welfare rights movement, Nadasen focuses instead on coalitions among women receiving welfare—the group with the most to say about life on welfare but whose experiences are most often ignored in histories of public assistance.

Tamar Carroll explores the multiracial women's movement that grew up in the Brooklyn-based National Congress of Neighborhood Women (NCNW). Through activists' own words, Carroll traces the early history of NCNW, focusing in particular on how women in this working-class feminist organization crossed racial, ethnic, and class lines to confront racial segregation in public housing and local economic stratification. She also suggests that their own form of consciousness-raising helped women move beyond the limits of what we typically call "identity politics" and focus instead on intersectionality.

Welfare and housing discrimination were not the only economic issues that mobilized women to create feminist change; on-the-job treatment and issues of economic equity also brought feminists together. Although *EEOC v. Sears* ultimately divided feminists, Emily Zuckerman explores the cooperative origins of the case. In particular, women's groups tried to force corporate employers, using Sears as the legal example, to change discriminatory hiring and promotion practices and bring widespread changes to the workplace. Looking specifically at NOW and WE in Chicago, Zuckerman explores and analyzes how feminists targeted issues of class; indeed, for the feminists involved in the origins of the Sears case, economic parity was their main concern. The coalition that emerged around this case brought together a wide range of allies across racial and ethnic lines.

In her chapter, Marisa Chappell addresses the full employment campaign of the 1970s, looking in particular at how feminists demanded attention to the special needs of women. She challenges the idea that identity politics fragmented social movements of the 1960s and 1970s. In terms of the full employment legislation that Congress debated in the mid-to-late 1970s, women's organizations repeatedly demanded attention to the "special needs of women"—and a wide range of feminist and women's groups articulated this position, from such groups as NOW and NWRO to the Young Women's Christian Association and League of Women Voters. Chappell notes that historians have focused on the racial and class differences that "consistently bedeviled attempts at unity among those committed to gender equity," yet demonstrates that nothing could be further from the truth. Women had to challenge the family wage ideal *as women* because the ideal was constructed on a male-breadwinner model, a model that did not reflect more and more women's lived experiences. Rather than divide feminists by race, class, and other social divisions, this politics of recognition was necessary because, in her words, "recognition was the only route to redistribution" of economic wealth and income.

In the final chapter of this book, Elizabeth Kaminski offers insight into what we can learn from these feminist coalitions, pointing specifically how coalition-based activism can be highly instructive to bridging our scholarly literatures and disciplines. Using the distinct literatures around resource mobilization, political process, and collective identity that frame how we understand social movement activism, she points to ways that we can move beyond the limitations of each theoretical framework by exploring the ways in which these literatures overlap. She also highlights the importance of emotion—which scholars often overlook when it comes to understanding how social movements coalesce—to building feminist coalitions. In her analysis, coalitions, especially feminist coalitions, direct us to undertake pursuits that bridge divides in our scholarly frameworks as we consider new directions for our work as activists and academics.

Within these pages, the grassroots work of the women's movement comes to life, as do the pitfalls and promises of such work. Many of the coalitions discussed in this book happen at the local level, revealing various ways that the movement unfolded in women's day-to-day lives. However, they do more than provide local nuances to a national story of a women's movement that washed in waves from the East Coast. Grassroots feminist coalitions such as the ones explored here add a new dimension to the national narrative by examining the various forces that create political, social, and cultural change, whether it is on a picket line in front of a hospital or between the covers of a new feminist magazine. They also illustrate the ways in which feminists both responded to and created political opportunities for further social justice work, be it in Brooklyn's housing projects or on the steps of the nation's capitol. The scholarship here provides grounded historical analysis about how feminists mobilized in the fertile context of the larger civil rights movements and in response to the political opportunities created by a more liberal federal government. Historian Nancy MacLean remarked on the symbiotic relationship between society and politics in this era, noting that "legal change invited social action, which itself altered ideas and institutions."[36] The work of feminist coalitions was possible because of a broadening government but their work also pushed the government to expand its laws and protections to women, not only responding to political opportunities but also creating them.

Although this book brings to light examples of coalition work, it does not minimize racism, classism, homophobia, and other oppressions that existed in the women's movement and still exist today. As the chapters herein make clear, these problems plagued the various coalitions and in some cases, tore them apart. Moreover, in the movement, they sometimes served to marginalize or exclude altogether many women (and feminist men). However, we must move beyond the point where we focus only on fractures and divides, the moments where the movement, or rather activists in the movement, let people down and pushed them aside. The pitfalls are real, and many chapters in this book do not tell happy stories of rainbow coalition politics. The successes are also real, as are the lessons that coalitions offer.

Furthermore, the coalitions discussed in this book were not the only feminist coalitions that existed during the heyday of the women's movement and, in some cases, exist today. Several vital coalitions are not represented within the pages of *Feminist Coalitions* but whose histories are told, or at least referenced, elsewhere. For example, the Committee for Abortion Rights and Against Sterilization Abuse was a vibrant and vital coalition of black, Puerto Rican, and white feminists in the 1960s and 1970s; its history provides another important and illuminating example of coalition building across racial and class lines.[37] Sociologist Winifred Breines elaborates on the Boston-based Coalition for Women's Safety and other "emergency" cross-racial efforts that women created in response to violence against women, and Annelise Orleck traces the long and difficult work of Operation Life, a grassroots welfare rights organization in Las Vegas. Both provide important examples of how white and black feminists worked both "apart and together."[38] In a compelling study of feminist coalition building among lesbians and gay men, Jennifer Brier has written how people living with acquired immunodeficiency syndrome (AIDS) (both men contracting the disease and women giving care to their dying friends) came together to construct a feminist response to the AIDS epidemic in the early 1980s. In an effort to produce "healthy and politicized communities," activists merged feminist and gay concepts of liberation, indicating how the personal was political but also how the political is personal.[39]

There were also critical alliances among women in and beyond the United States, and while some historical research exists on them, much more remains to be done. Kimberly Springer, for example, traces the history of Third World Women Alliance, a black feminist organization that sought to align physically and philosophically with women of color in so-called Third World countries around the world, arguing that U.S. women of color shared more with them than with white U.S. women.[40] Similarly, many U.S. women worked in vital formal coalitions with women around the world through the U.N. meetings on the global rights of women. Without vital coalition work initiated by Laura X, "marital rape" would not exist in our legal, political, and public vocabulary. As founder and director of the National Clearinghouse on Marital and Date Rape in Berkeley, California, Laura X organized with feminists in forty-five states and around the world to give women the right to say "no," and scholars should take up this important activism in future research. The absence of these and other coalitions does not imply their relative unimportance; instead, this collection invites further historical research on feminist coalition building, including especially scholarship on those not represented here or elsewhere.

There is far too little research that examines the prevalence of cross-movement coalitions or the factors that encourage their occurrence.[41] This book helps remedy this problem in the scholarship. As these chapters suggest, feminists forged numerous cross-movement coalitions and did so across differences of race, class, sexual identity, religion, political perspective, and other real distinctions in lived experiences. In many cases, the relationships in these alliances were tenuous and difficult. Most were not sustained, many fell apart, and some did not achieve their articulated goals. To be fair, however, they were not designed to be harmoniously integrated organizations. Instead, feminists in the coalitions explored here were well aware of the problems and pitfalls—as well as the potentials—for banding together to create feminist change. Rather than join each other blindly, they interrogated and investigated one another, bringing all of their cultural baggage, their suspicions, their uncertainties, and their visions of a better world—however small the orbit of that world— to the coalition. They were certainly aware, as June Jordan keenly noted, that "race and class and gender remain as real as the weather."[42] But in terms of individuals connecting with one another to create necessary feminist change, coalitions are "like the weather, not predictable."[43] Whether it was about gaining access to reproductive health care or to decent living conditions, calling for an end to the countless deaths of mothers' boys in Vietnam, or challenging sexist workplace practices at Sears, Roebuck Co., women did what some may see as the unpredictable—they pursued collective action across myriad differences and forged coalitions to make this change real.

Coalitions helped women identify and actualize solutions to problems in their immediate lives; feminist coalitions put those solutions into a larger framework of inequality based on gender and male supremacy. Black Panther and feminist Kathleen Cleaver once suggested that the women's liberation movement was best understood as a universal movement of women against a male-dominated society. She stated: "In order for women to obtain liberation, the struggles are going to have to be united on the basis of being women, not on the basis of being Black women or White women. . . . the relationship will have to be on a *coalition* basis and not on an integrated basis [because] the problems of Black women and the problems of White women are so completely diverse, they cannot possibly be solved in the same type of organization nor met by the same type of activity."[44] Cleaver is right in the sense that coalitions were—and are—necessary to achieve women's liberation in the grandest sense of the concept. She also rightly noted that women's problems are as diverse as the women who have them. As to why people enter into such coalitions in spite of these fundamentally different perspectives on their problems, perhaps Bernice Johnson Reagon said it best—people enter into coalitions for survival. For feminist poet Audre Lorde, survival meant "learning how to take our differences and make them strengths."[45] That is certainly true for the women whose histories are uncovered here—they needed a job, an abortion, a roof overhead, a space to come out as lesbian, a welfare check, a sense of freedom from the fear of rape, a child not to go to war. They needed one another—women from all walks of life and with different perspectives on these issues and reasons for getting involved to create change.

## Notes

1. See Premilla Nadasen, "Black Feminism: Waves, Rivers, and Still Waters"; Eileen Boris, "Feminism's Histories"; and Stephanie Gilmore, "Feminist Waves, Feminist Groundswells," all presented at the American Historical Association meeting, January 6, 2006, Philadelphia, Pa.

2. Boris, "Feminism's Histories."

3. *America Divided: The Civil War of the 1960s* is a well-written and useful history, yet women appear sporadically in the text and *feminism* is referenced only three times. For a direct criticism of histories of the left that denigrate feminist activism as divisive, see Amy Kesselman, "Women's Liberation and the Left in New Haven, Connecticut, 1968–1972," *Radical History Review* 81 (2001): 15–33.

4. For more on this standard, if inaccurate, narrative, see Alice Echols, "We Gotta Get Out of This Place: Notes Toward a Remapping of the Sixties," *Socialist Review* 22, no. 2 (1992): 11; Kesselman, "Women's Liberation and the Left in New Haven, Connecticut, 1968–1972."

5. Sara Evans, *Tidal Wave: How Women Changed America at Century's End* (New York: Free Press, 2003); Dorothy Sue Cobble, *The Other Women's Movement: Workplace Justice and Social Rights in Modern America* (Princeton, N.J.: Princeton University Press, 2005); Kimberly Springer, *Living for the Revolution: Black Feminist Organizations, 1968–1980* (Durham, N.C.: Duke University Press, 2005); Benita Roth, *Separate Roads to Feminism: Black, Chicana, and White Feminist Movements in America's Second Wave* (Cambridge: Cambridge University Press, 2004); Premilla Nadasen, *Welfare Warriors: The Welfare Rights Movement in the United States* (New York: Routledge Press, 2004); Annelise Orleck, *Storming Caesar's Palace: How Black Mothers Fought Their Own War on Poverty* (New

York: Beacon Press, 2005); Susan Hartmann, *The Other Feminists: Activists in the Liberal Establishment* (New Haven, Conn.: Yale University Press, 1998); and Becky Thompson, *A Promise and a Way of Life: White Antiracist Activism* (Minneapolis: University of Minnesota Press, 2001).

6. Chandra Talpade Mohanty, "Under Western Eyes: Feminist Scholarship and Colonial Discourses," *Feminist Review* 30 (Autumn 1988): 61–88.

7. Myriam J. A. Chancy, "Editor's Farewell: Still in Search of Safe Places," *Meridians: Feminism, Race, Transnationalism* 5 (2004): v-x, quotation on ix-x.

8. Estelle Freedman, *No Turning Back: The History of Feminism and the Future of Women* (New York: Ballantine Books, 2000), 92–93.

9. Elsa Barkley Brown, "What Has Happened Here: The Politics of Difference in Women's History and Feminist Politics," *Feminist Studies* 18, no. 2 (Summer 1992), 295–312.

10. Ellen K. Scott, "Creating Partnerships for Change: Alliances and Betrayals in the Racial Politics of Two Feminist Organizations," *Gender and Society* 12 (August 1998): 400–423.

11. Premilla Nadasen, "Expanding the Boundaries of the Women's Movement: Black Feminism and the Struggle for Welfare Rights," *Feminist Studies* 28 (Summer 2002): 271–301.

12. Scott, "Creating Partnerships for Change," esp. 401.

13. See, for example, Jacqui Alexander and Chandra Talpade Mohanty, *Feminist Genealogies, Colonial Legacies, Democratic Futures* (New York: Routlege, 1997); Kathleen Blee and France Winddance Twine, eds., *Feminism and Antiracism: International Struggles for Justice* (New York: NYU Press, 2001); Amrita Basu, *The Challenge of Local Feminisms: Women's Movements in Global Perspectives* (Boulder, Colo.: Westview Press, 1995); Chandra Talpade Mohanty, Ann Russo, and Lourdes Torres, eds., *Third World Women and the Politics of Feminism* (Bloomington: Indiana University Press, 1991); Karen Offen, *European Feminisms, 1750–1900* (Stanford, Calif.: Stanford University Press, 1999); and Raka Ray, *Fields of Protest: Women's Movements in India* (Minneapolis: University of Minnesota Press).

14. Maurice Isserman and Michael Kazin, *America Divided: The Civil War of the 1960s*, 2nd ed. (New York: Oxford University Press, 2003); Stewart Burns, *Social Movements of the 1960s* (Boston: Twayne Publishers, 1990); and Van Gosse and Richard Moser, eds., *The World the Sixties Made: Politics and Culture in Recent America* (Philadelphia: Temple University Press, 2003).

15. Barbara Ransby, *Ella Baker and the Black Freedom Movement: A Radical Democratic Vision* (Chapel Hill: University of North Carolina Press, 2002); Belinda Robnett, *How Long, How Long? African American Women in the Civil Rights Struggle*, new ed. (New York: Oxford University Press, 2000); and Bettye Collier-Thomas and V. P. Franklin, eds., *Sisters in the Struggle: African-American Women in the Civil Rights–Black Power Movement* (New York: NYU Press, 2001).

16. Maryann Barakso, *Governing NOW: Grassroots Activism in the National Organization for Women* (Ithaca, N.Y.: Cornell University Press, 2005). See also Stephanie Gilmore, review of *Governing NOW: Grassroots Activism in the National Organization for Women*, http://scholar.alexanderstreet.com/x/QQc, April 2006.

17. Kimberly Springer, *Living for the Revolution: Black Feminist Organizations, 1968–1980* (Durham, N.C.: Duke University Press, 2005); and Benita Roth, *Separate Roads to Feminism: Black, Chicana, and White Feminist Movements in America's Second Wave* (New York: Cambridge University Press, 2003).

18. Judith Ezekiel, *Feminism in the Heartland* (Columbus: Ohio State University Press, 2002); Anne Valk, *Sisterhood and Separatism: Feminism and Racial Liberation in Washington, D.C.* (Urbana: University of Illinois Press, 2008); John Howard, *Men Like That: A Southern Queer History* (Chicago: University of Chicago Press, 2001); Kimberly Dugan, *The Struggle over Gay, Lesbian, and Bisexual Rights: Facing Off in Cincinnati* (New York: Routledge, 2005); Susan Kathleen Freeman, "From the Lesbian Nation to the Cincinnati Lesbian Community: Toward a Politics of Location," *Journal of the History of Sexuality* 9 (January/April 2000): 104–29; and Charles Payne, *I've Got the Light of Freedom: The Organizing Tradition and the Mississippi Freedom Struggle* (Berkeley: University of California Press, 1997).

19. Maria Lugones, *Pilgramages/Peregrinajes: Theorizing Coalition against Multiple Oppressions* (Latham, Md.: Rowman and Littlefield Publishers, 2003); see also Cricket Keating, "Building Coalitional Consciousness," *NWSA Journal* 17 (Summer 2005): 86–103.

20. Ransby's biography of Ella Baker does this kind of analysis, but focuses only on one woman's activism. It is incredibly instructive and useful for my own thinking about this book, and I am grateful to Ransby for her sharp and well-developed text.

21. Patricia Hill Collins, *Black Feminist Thought: Knowledge, Consciousness, and the Politics of Empowerment* (New York: Routledge, 1990); Gloria Anzaldua, ed., *Making Faces/Making Soul: Creative and Critical Perspectives by Women of Color* (San Francisco: Aunt Lute Publishers, 1990); and Barbara Smith, ed., *Home Girls: A Black Feminist Anthology* (Boston: Kitchen Table Press, 1983) have been instrumental to the development of intersectionality theories.

22. Cobble, *The Other Women's Movement*, 8.

23. Denise Riley, *Am I That Name? Feminism and the Category of Women in History* (Minneapolis: University of Minnesota Press, 2003).

24. See, for example, Freedman, *No Turning Back*, 10–12.

25. Others who find feminist work among activists who did not embrace or openly rejected the label of feminism include Cobble, *The Other Women's Movement*; Nadasen, *Welfare Warriors*; Riley, *Am I That Name?*; and Roth, *Separate Roads to Feminism*. Many feminists in the movement defined their feminism in different ways. See Esther Ngan-Ling Chow, Doris Wilkinson, and Maxine Baca Zinn, eds., *Common Bonds, Different Voices: Race, Class, and Gender* (New York: Sage Publications, 1996); Gloria Anzaldúa, *Making Face, Making Soul/Haciendo Caras: Creative and Critical Perspectives by Feminists of Color* (San Francisco: Aunt Lute Books, 1990); and Smith, ed., *Home Girls: A Black Feminist Anthology.*

26. Jill Bystydzienski and Stephen Schacht, *Forging Radical Alliances across Difference: Coalition Politics for a New Millennium* (Latham, Md.: Rowman and Littlefield Publishers, 2001), esp. 14. See also Lisa Albrecht and Rose M. Brewer, eds., *Bridges of Power: Women's Multicultural Alliances* (Philadelphia: New Society Publishers, 1990); Jeremy Brecher and Tim Costello, eds., *Building Bridges: The Emerging Grassroots Coalition of Labor and Community* (New York: Monthly Review Press, 1990); and Reagon, "Coalition Politics."

27. Bystydzienski and Schacht, *Forging Radical Alliances across Difference*, 2.

28. Ibid., 1.

29. Todd Gitlin, *The Twilight of Common Dreams* (1995). Nader made the reference to "gonadal politics" in his 1996 campaign for the presidency. On this comment, see Martin Duberman, "In Defense of Identity Politics," InTheseTimes.com, July 9, 2001. http://www.inthesetimes.com/issue/25/16/duberman2516.html.

30. Nira Yural-Davis, *Gender and Nation* (London: Sage, 1997), 3.

31. William Julius Wilson, *The Bridge over the Racial Divide: Rising Inequality and Coalition Politics* (Berkeley: University of California Press, 1999): 117.

32. Bystydzienski and Schacht, *Forging Radical Alliances across Difference*, 7.

33. Anne Enke, *Finding the Movement: Sexuality, Contested Space, and Feminist Activism* (Durham, N.C.: Duke University Press, 2007).

34. For more on feminist geographies and space, see Anne Enke, "Smuggling Sex through the Gate: Race, Sexuality, and Contested Space in Second Wave Feminism," *American Quarterly* 55, no. 4 (2003): 635–67; and Nancy Whittier, *Feminist Generations* (Philadelphia: Temple University Press, 1997).

35. Johnnie Tillmon likened a woman going onto welfare as trading in a man for the man, referring to the power of the state to determine a woman's day-to-day life, from work, to sexual behavior, to childrearing. Johnnie Tillmon, "Welfare Is a Woman's Issue," *Ms.* 1 (July 1972), 42.

36. Nancy MacLean, *Freedom is Not Enough: The Opening of the American Workplace* (New York: Russell Sage Foundation, 2006), 4.

37. On CASARA, see Jennifer Nelson, *Women of Color and the Reproductive Rights Movement* (New York: NYU Press, 2003).

38. Winifred Breines, *The Trouble between Us: An Uneasy History of White and Black Women in the Feminist Movement* (New York: Oxford University Press, 2006), esp. chap. 5, the title of which is "Apart and Together: Boston, Race, and Feminism in the 1970s and Early 1980s." Annelise Orleck, *Storming Caesar's Palace: How Black Mothers Fought Their Own War on Poverty* (Boston: Beacon Press, 2006).

39. Jennifer Brier, "Locating Lesbian-Feminist Responses to AIDS, 1982–1984," *Women's Studies Quarterly* (forthcoming); and Jennifer Brier, "Infectious Ideas: AIDS and U.S. Politics, 1980–2000" (unpublished manuscript in process).

40. Springer, *Living for the Revolution*.

41. Nella Van Dyke, "Crossing Movement Boundaries: Factors that Facilitate Coalition Protest by American College Students, 1930–1990," *Social Problems* 50, no. 2 (2003): 226–50.

42. June Jordan, "Report from the Bahamas," in *On Call: Political Essays* (Boston: South End Press, 1985), 46.

43. Ibid.

44. Cleaver quoted in Paula Giddings, *When and Where I Enter: The Impact of Black Women on Race and Sex in America* (New York: Harper Collins), 311.

45. Audre Lorde, "The Master's Tools Will Never Dismantle the Master's House," *Sister Outsider* (Freedom, Calif.: Crossing Press, 1984), 112.

## 2. Creating a National Feminist Agenda

### *Coalition Building in the 1970s*

CYNTHIA HARRISON

In 1971, a group of feminists in New York, led by Brenda Feigen Fasteau and Gloria Steinem, created the Women's Action Alliance (WAA) to provide information to, practice advocacy for, and offer services in the cause of the young but growing feminist movement.[1] It considered its constituency the new, small feminist groups springing up across the country that needed to know what other feminists were doing to combat the sexism they faced in their own communities. In performing this informational function, the new organization wanted to act out its commitment to feminist principles of collective rather than hierarchical decision making. In 1975, in conjunction with International Women's Year, an initiative of the United Nations, the WAA decided to connect with the traditional women's organizations formed decades earlier. The goal was to create a comprehensive women's agenda that all could work toward and, by doing so, to strengthen the movement by bringing these older groups under the feminist umbrella.[2] The results were frustrating for two reasons: (1) crafting a unified agenda that compelled both the ideological commitment and the resources of a large number of diverse women's organizations was no easy feat; and (2) as before, the WAA had a competitor in the creation of a national agenda—the federal government, which had allocated funds for a national women's conference to be held in Houston, Texas, precisely to establish a new set of goals to improve the status of women.

On January 9, 1975, in response to the United Nations' declaration of International Women's Year, President Gerald Ford established the National Commission on the Observance of International Women's Year (IWY Commission),[3] the latest in a line of federal commissions on women that President

John Kennedy had inaugurated in 1961 with the President's Commission on the Status of Women. Each such body had issued reports that had served as goads for federal and state action, both public and private. However, after 1966, with the creation of the National Organization for Women (NOW), independent feminist groups had pushed hard from the outside to ensure that the government's cautious advocacy for women did not remain the only vehicle to improve women's status and expand their opportunities. Motivated by the same objective, Congresswoman Bella Abzug (D-N.Y.) had, within days of Ford's executive order, introduced legislation to fund state and national women's conferences in 1976. The bill, however, did not pass until late in the year, on December 23.[4]

During 1975, concerned about government control of the national response to the United Nations and the possibility of a timid national plan, and in response to a "huge amount of mail" from women,[5] the WAA mobilized to preempt it and to substitute the views of nongovernmental women's organizations. Moreover, the WAA sought to create an ongoing coalition of women's organizations that would manage the agenda of the women's movement indefinitely. WAA leaders believed that their coalition of feminist groups was the logical organization to perform this function. "When the United Nations declared 1975 International Women's Year and the beginning of a Decade on Women," WAA staff asserted, "the only group available to bring together women's groups to coordinate a National Women's Agenda was the Alliance. . . . Unlike every other women's group, the Alliance has no agenda except to strengthen the hand of other women's groups."[6] Of particular urgency was the need to get the views of U.S. nongovernmental women's organizations (NGOs) to the official government commission before the international meeting in Mexico City in June 1975 by which the United Nations would mark International Women's Year. After the Mexico City meeting, the WAA hoped to host a national convention for U.S. organizations to begin to implement the goals laid out in an action plan.[7] The proposal attracted the support of the Rockefeller Family Fund, and in March 1975, the planning committee met in New York at the fund's headquarters.[8]

About a dozen leaders of important national women's organizations—feminist and traditional, representing an array of different and diverse constituencies—attended that first meeting, including the National Women's Political Caucus (NWPC), the Girl Scouts, the National Conference of Puerto Rican Women, the National Council of Jewish Women (NCJW), the National Council of Negro Women, the Young Women's Christian Association (YWCA), the Women's Equity Action League (WEAL), and the Women's Committee of the United Automobile, Aerospace and Agricultural Implement Workers of America (UAW). Afterward, by letter, WAA invited more than a hundred national organizations, women's caucuses within national organizations, and special interest women's groups with a national scope to set forth their priorities. By May, seventy organizations had responded (eventually another two dozen would participate) and WAA staff collated their responses into a draft of what they called the National Women's Agenda (NWA). Objectives were revised in consultation with "diverse groups of women's organizations."[9] The working committee, consisting chiefly of those organizations at the first meeting in March, developed a preamble to the agenda.

The preamble spoke explicitly to the need for both unity and the recognition of diversity:

> In creating the first National Women's Agenda, we are making explicit demands on our Government and on the private sector as well. Firm policies and programs must be developed and implemented at all levels in order to eliminate those inequities that still stand as barriers to the full participation by women of every race and group. For too long, the nation has been deprived of women's insights and abilities. It is imperative that women be integrated into national life now. . . . Diverse as we are, we are united by the deep and common experience of womanhood. As we work toward our common goals, we insist upon the protection of this diversity, and call for the simultaneous elimination of all the insidious forms of discrimination, not only those based on gender, but also on race, creed, ethnicity, class, lifestyle, sexual preference, and age.[10]

The agenda reflected many and various concerns. One issue had attracted the interest of traditional women's organizations since suffrage and had received renewed attention from feminist groups—more women in positions of influence and authority. The agenda included this item under the rubric of "Fair Representation and Participation in the Political Process." Virtually all women's organizations supported greater access to education and to training programs, covered under "Equal Education and Training," and including admissions, financial aid and the enforcement of antidiscrimination laws. The influence of the new feminist groups could be seen in the demand for the "elimination of sex role, racial and cultural stereotyping at every level of the educational system, and in educational materials" as well as in workplace materials. Concern about the images of women emerged also in a section on "Fair Treatment by and Equal Access to Media and the Arts," which endorsed the elimination of stereotypes of women and girls. Insistence that attention be paid to women's issues in politics, in education, and in the media reappeared throughout the document, a commitment of women's advocacy organizations since the nineteenth century. A more modern focus on the availability of continuing education programs to enable women to obtain suitable education at all stages of life reflected interests of homemakers' reentering the labor force. Attention to homemakers was visible as well in the demand that the homemaker be legally recognized as a worker whose labor had economic value.[11]

Working women's needs were manifest in the section on "Meaningful Work and Adequate Compensation," where the NWA emphasized extension and enforcement of antidiscrimination laws; the expansion of labor laws to cover large numbers of additional women (and men) workers, including domestic workers and farm laborers; affirmative action; flexible work schedules; and accommodation of pregnant workers by construing the disabilities of pregnancy "as normal, temporary employment disabilities." The agenda demanded more women in unions and union leadership; and "equal pay for comparable work, that is, work frequently performed by women . . . equivalent to work performed by men, but for which women receive less pay."[12]

The agenda also addressed the circumstances of the most vulnerable women in a section titled "Equal Access to Economic Power." Here the NWA offered strategies to end poverty and to allow women to generate wealth. The agenda supported a guaranteed minimum income, a platform of the National Welfare Rights Organization (NWRO), although one that had already met congressional defeat in 1972. The establishment of such a program in addition to "other social benefits for low income and disadvantaged persons" would "respect the individual rights and dignity of all women." The need for adequate housing, subsidized by public funding was taken up in "Adequate Housing." Although the agenda demanded medical and mental health services available to all without regard to ability to pay (under "Quality Health Care and Services"), the proposal for "Quality Child Care for All Children," which sought "a comprehensive and adequate system of child care," failed to address its funding except for a tax deduction for child care payments.[13]

The NWA championed another group of vulnerable women, those caught in the criminal justice system. Under "Just and Humane Treatment in the Criminal Justice System," the agenda asked for humane treatment for prisoners and special accommodations for women in prison. The agenda also sought better treatment for rape victims and "re-examination of laws pertaining to victimless crimes"—that is, prostitution. For women in more privileged circumstances, the agenda proposed changes to the income tax code; social security coverage for homemakers; equal access to credit; elimination of discrimination in insurance, benefit, and pension plans; equal inheritance laws; and revision of laws affecting the family.

Bodily integrity, privacy, and sexual autonomy were dealt with in several places in the agenda. The Supreme Court had apparently settled the question of a woman's right to control reproductive decisions, which the agenda endorsed, but it further asserted the need for medical research specific to women and informed consent as "the right of every patient"—this last a key issue for women of color too often sterilized without their consent. Sex education provided "throughout the educational process" would ensure that women could not be victimized out of ignorance. Under "Physical Safety," the NWA asked for "recognition of and respect for the autonomy and dignity of the female person," including the recognition of rape as a violent crime against women and the reform of laws that unduly protect rapists and revictimize rape survivors, who should be served by specific support programs. Finally, the NWA took up the question of gay rights, supporting the "protection of the right to privacy of relationships between consenting adults" and a bar against discrimination based on "affectional or sexual preference." The agenda concluded with the demand for "recognition that women are individuals with full rights to make choices affecting their lives."[14] This attempt to craft a comprehensive agenda, sensitive to the needs of specific groups of women as well as of the mostly privileged women who ran the major national women's organizations, spoke to the desire of second-wave feminists to establish sisterhood among all women in the face of significant difference.

The chiefly white feminists who had founded the WAA had tried from the beginning to make it a cross-racial organization. Gloria Steinem drew from her network to make up the board of the new group, ensuring representation from black as well as white women. The board included Brenda Feigen Fasteau, vice-president for legislation of NOW and cofounder of the NWPC; Bella Abzug, elected in 1970 to the U.S. Congress; and Ruth Bader Ginsburg, among other white women, as well as Eleanor Holmes Norton, then chair of the New York City Commission on Human Rights; Yvonne Braithwaite Burke, Shirley Chisholm, and Patsy Mink, also members of Congress; Johnnie Tillmon, head of the NWRO; and Jane Galvin Lewis, founder of the National Black Feminist Organization, among other women of color. Another founder and board member of WAA, Dorothy Pitman Hughes asserted the utility of the WAA to breach racial divisions: "With Gloria's name attached, the Women's Action Alliance could help African American women who were in business but who couldn't get loans, credit lines, or contracts and who were just not treated well. The alliance was a way for us to talk with white women and find out how they were getting past these barriers." But, Hughes observed, Steinem was unusual in her commitment toward eliminating racism among women.[15]

Evidence indicates that, despite Steinem's personal qualities, problems existed internally in the WAA. In January 1977, Barbara Omolade, a black woman, was hired to direct the Non-Sexist Child Development Project. Despite her own success, in 1980 she resigned, writing:

> [R]acism at the Alliance is pervasive, subtle, and devious, permeating policy directions, program implementations, and interpersonal relationships. It makes effective work from Black women a minor miracle. It means every aspect of the work is a battle ground for inclusion. . . . The same old girl network permeates every program area: white, middle class women who have limited family or cultural obligations. The hiring practices of the last six months have been the same kind of woman—white. There is little reason to think this will change, especially since I am the only Black woman on the staff.[16]

She noted that in previous years when there had been other black women employees they had "laughed at the hypocrisy and cried at the insults of being Black and female in a white feminist organization."[17]

The organizers of the agenda project wanted to reach across racial and class barriers. As the content of the agenda revealed, privileged feminist leaders highlighted the needs of the poorest, most vulnerable women and the need to eliminate racism. Difficulties arose between privileged feminists and feminists acting from minority communities not from white disinterest, but in part from the tin ear some white privileged feminists brought to collaborative work and the blind eye to what only later came to be understood as white privilege. Lacking entree to the organizations founded by women of color and by women in the labor movement, white feminists took on the role of "leaders" and reproduced the very hierarchies they desired so ardently to dismantle. Doris Davenport, a black feminist, expressed the view of some of her colleagues about the feminist movement generally: "[W]e experience white feminists and their organizations as elitist, crudely insensitive and condescending. . . ."[18] The authors of *This Bridge Called My Back* put it this way: "We have had it with the word "*out*reach" referring to our joining racist white women's organizations. The question keeps coming up—where exactly then, is *in*? It smells white to us. We have had it."[19] Outreach, nevertheless, was the main tool of the WAA and such sentiments would have appalled the white women who conducted it.

The alliance did not resolve the problems in cross-racial organizing, although women's organizations of every stripe endorsed the agenda, ninety-four in all. Signers included traditional women's organizations: the American Association of University Women (AAUW); the National Federation of Business and Professional Women's Clubs; Lutheran Church Women; Girls Clubs; Planned Parenthood; the National Association of Social Workers; the National Association for Women Deans, Administrators, and Counselors; the

Women's International League for Peace and Freedom; Future Homemakers of America; the NCJW; the National Coalition of American Nuns; Women Strike for Peace; and the YWCA; labor unions: the Amalgamated Clothing Workers; American Federation of State, County, and Municipal Employees (AFSCME); feminist organizations: NOW, the National Abortion Rights Action League, the NWPC, the National Association of Commissions for Women, the Citizens' Advisory Council on the Status of Women, the Feminist Press, the Women's Legal Defense Fund, Federally Employed Women; gay rights groups: the National Gay Task Force, Lesbian Feminist Liberation, the Mattachine Society; groups representing women of color: the National Council of Negro Women, the National Conference of Puerto Rican Women, the National Black Feminist Organization, National Institute of Spanish-Speaking Women, Mujer Integrate Ahora (MIA); groups concerned with working class and poor women: the National Committee on Household Employment (NCHE), and the National Congress of Neighborhood Women.

Bella Abzug, WAA board member and a representative to Congress from New York City, waxed enthusiastic over the wide-ranging coalition that embraced the NWA. "The Women's Action Alliance has accomplished the impossible. . . . Nothing like it has ever happened before in the women's movement," she exclaimed. She noted that the WAA hoped for a national conference to ratify the NWA and that her proposed legislation would achieve that end.[20]

If Abzug saw herself as an ally of the WAA, President Gerald Ford took a more distanced position. He rebuffed several requests to discuss the agenda, understanding that the NWA coalition paralleled his own more conservative group and preferring to wait for its proposals.[21] The WAA responded in a letter signed by officers of sixteen participating organizations that the women's community, not the government, should chart the course for women: "Although we applaud the establishment of a Presidential Commission on the Observance of IWY, we cannot accept the idea that it will be the only voice speaking to the President of the United States on behalf of the diverse range of women in this country. While a government commission is useful, its activities and recommendations cannot be viewed as a substitute for those originating directly from women's organizations in this country." His commission would not address as wide a range of concerns as the NWA did. Although the signers to the request to the president represented a cross-section of women—church groups, the National Conference of Puerto Rican Women, the NCHE, the National Council of Negro Women, National Gay Task Force Women's Committee, the NWPC, the UAW, WEAL, YWCA, NOW, and the Association of Women Business Owners—Ford stuck to his guns and declined a meeting.[22]

Spurned by Ford, the WAA named December 2, 1975, "National Women's Agenda Day." Fifty national women's leaders gathered on the steps of the U.S. capitol and presented the agenda to Congress, while women's organizations in forty-five states did likewise in the state capitals. Mayors and governors received the agenda at their national meetings.[23]

Seeking publicly both to recognize the importance of diversity and to present a racially and ethnically diverse image to the public, the NWA gave women of color prominent roles. Paquita Vivo, of the National Conference of Puerto Rican Women, spoke to public officials in Washington on National Women's Agenda Day, emphasizing the layered oppression confronting women of color as well as the commitment of the women's movement to serve all women:

> We gather today to call upon the nation and the Congress to respond now to the challenge laid before you by the U.S. National Women's Agenda. . . . The National Conference of Puerto Rican Women looks forward to its participation in the work of implementing the agenda goals. Daily bearing the burden of racial and sexual prejudice, we are heartened that the women of our nation so clearly perceive the intimate and odious connection between the oppression of sexism and all other forms of discrimination.
>
> The Women's Movement is a movement for civil rights. Today black women stand beside Latin [sic] women, stand beside white women, to confirm the common denominator which unites us all. Today voluntary and service organizations stand beside political organizations in a strong show of the compatibility of goals and the ability of our women's movement to encompass many styles and to include many strategies. . . . Together we make the largest and strongest and most integrated force for social change this nation has ever seen.[24]

Edith Barksdale Sloan spoke on behalf of the agenda for low-waged women workers and for the unwaged homemaker, identifying the relationship between the two, based on the low valuation of women's work in the home and in the workforce:

> The NCHE whose constituencies represent one of the most oppressed groups of women—household workers—join hands with all women to achieve our common goals. The National Women's Agenda calls for the extension of the basic workers' benefits to women not now covered. One such uncovered group is household workers.
>
> It is important to point out that in our agenda, women are also expressing clear, unequivocal support for the homemaker. Listed here, most appropriately, under the worker section of the agenda, we call for the legal and economic recognition of her contribution to the general social welfare. Household work-

ers have much to gain if the homemaker's contribution is recognized; and the reverse is equally true. For such recognition will end the economic and social strangulation imposed by the denigration of so-called "women's work."[25]

The event sparked widespread and favorable press coverage, and the media noticed the participation of women of color. The *New York Times* observed editorially that the agenda demonstrated that "the women's movement is neither enfeebled nor weary." The coalition, the *Times* noted, was "remarkable both for the breadth of the issues addressed and for the diversity of the groups which have joined the effort," identifying specifically the presence of the Gray Panthers, the Junior League, and the NCHE. "It is so inclusive," the editors continued, "that it makes the old notions of the women's movement outmoded." The newly mature women's movement was taking its place as "a strong general force for social change."[26] Newspapers in Kentucky, Texas, North Carolina, Iowa, Illinois, Wisconsin, Colorado, Wyoming, and elsewhere covered the local presentation to state legislators. Almost all the stories commented on the size of the coalition and its representation of diverse groups.[27] In fact, showing her solidarity with the women's movement despite her connection to the Ford administration, Jill Ruckelshaus, the Republican head of the IWY Commission, appeared at the Washington rally, recommending that women keep the pressure on legislators "until the last item on the agenda is realized."[28] Representatives Patricia Schroeder (D-Colo.) and Elizabeth Holtzman (D-N.Y.) promised to shepherd the agenda through Congress.[29]

The WAA next took up the challenge of turning the agenda into "the first Women's Plan of Action for the Decade," referring to the United Nation's declaration of "the decade for women" to take place from 1975 to 1985. It created ten task forces, consisting of organization members and experts. Each met at least once between January and October 1976. Although many of the groups involved had long histories—the AAUW, for example, had been founded in 1881—the WAA saw them as needing instruction in understanding their particular issues from a feminist standpoint. A WAA staff member observed (with less than complete accuracy): "It . . . became clear that by and large women's organizations in this country had not viewed their issues from a woman's perspective before. They had, after all, been historically formed in order to give women a voice on fundamental social issues. But they had not been created and were only now beginning to understand their self-interest and self-relationship to these issues as women." The work of the task forces lagged ostensibly because "by and large, women have not engaged in strategy, they have not thought of themselves as policy makers or implementers nor as people with power."[30] The task forces were to work throughout 1976 and come together in October at a national conference—ostensibly, if not accurately— "the first time since Suffrage that the leadership of the major women's organization have gathered to discuss long-range goals and strategies." The WAA hoped the conference would result in the formation of a national coalition of women's organizations, cementing the relationship among feminist and traditional women's organizations and transferring ownership of the NWA to the organizations that participated in its creation.[31] The WAA would act as coordinator.[32]

The conference took place October 1 and 2, 1976 and in preparation for it, WAA Executive Director Ruth Abram sent letters to leaders of organizations not yet connected to the NWA. In her August invitation, she explained to Brenda Eichelberger, executive director of the Chicago-based National Alliance of Black Feminists:

> The leadership of more than 100 very diverse national women's organizations will meet to discuss long rang goals and strategies and to explore the formation of a national coalition of women's organizations. . . . The issues facing American women today are more complex and difficult [than they had been in 1920], and not all women share the same goals. . . . It is fundamental for the idea of the coalition that no organization need support all of the Agenda's goals. It is equally important that we represent as many different women's perspectives as there are in this country. We are very eager, therefore, to have you join us in October. Although the National Alliance of Black Feminists is not affiliated with the Agenda, we are confident that you have invaluable knowledge and experience to bring to bear on its issues.[33]

Abram asked if she might meet with Eichelberger in September to plan for the conference. Similar letters went to Olga Madar, of the Coalition of Labor Union Women; Ada R. Pena, with the Women's Affairs Division of the League of United Latin American Citizens; and Vang Elizonda of the Mexican American Women's Association, among others.[34]

Support beyond the community of feminist and women's organizations was widespread. Representatives attended the conference from the Rockefeller Family Fund, the U.S. Commission on Civil Rights, the Daycare and Child Development Council of America, the Congressional Clearinghouse on Women's Rights, the National Black Women's Agenda, the U.S. Department of Justice, the U.S. Women's Bureau, and the National Advisory Council on Women's Educational Programs. Notable individuals sponsored the agenda conference in October 1976, including prominent entertainers (Alan Alda, Ellen Burstyn, Valerie Harper, Cloris Leachman, Shirley MacLaine, Helen

Reddy, Robert Redford, Cybil Sheppard, Barbra Streisand, Marlo Thomas, and Dennis Weaver), as did major corporations—Avon, Bristol Myers, Dannon Milk, Johnson & Johnson, McCall's, and Redbook.[35]

Abram invited Eleanor Holmes Norton, a black civil rights attorney who was then commissioner on the New York City Human Rights Commission, to address the meeting. Abram emphasized the diversity of the groups already involved: "Representatives of women's organizations ranging from the Junior Leagues to the Household Workers actually worked together in countless meetings to hammer out this statement. In joining together in this way, they discovered the commonality of concerns and, I believe, redefined the boundaries of the women's movement today. It has touched the hearts of countless women—rich, poor, black, brown, white, service and politically-oriented. A look at the range of contributing groups makes this point clearly." However, Abram acknowledged the impossibility of melding all these groups into one entity: "The challenge before us now is to take advantage of the consensus while maintaining the integrity, autonomy, character and style of each of the organizations." The new coalition would serve as a guide and clearinghouse, "[defining] the general goals of the women's movement [and issuing] annual statements on our collective progress toward achieving these goals." Statewide coalitions would, she hoped, support the national effort. The first day of the conference would hear the task force reports and "affirm the concepts of both the Plan of Action and the National Women's Agenda Coalition." On the second day, the WAA would offer workshops on coalition building. Abram wanted Norton to remind the participants "in no uncertain terms— that we are not going to win unless we work as a coalition." She suggested that Norton recall the women's coalitions of the Progressive era, which won gains in labor laws, consumer safety laws, and suffrage. "The time is ripe," Abram concluded, "for a renewed effort by a much expanded, increasingly sophisticated women's movement. . . . [W]e can achieve most anything if we can see our way clear to join forces."[36] Agreement about the NWA, Steinem observed a few weeks later, was "deafening." However, her optimism was tempered: despite heightened consciousness, she concluded that "reality has budged very little."[37]

Reality appeared to have moved a bit because Jimmy Carter, the Democratic presidential candidate, chose to address the group and to unveil his own program for women a month before the election when publicity would be at its height. According to Madeline Lee, the director of the National Women's Agenda Project, Jimmy Carter at this meeting "delivered the major policy speech of his campaign on issues affecting over 50 per cent of the population of the country."[38] Ruth Abram noted that Carter's appearance marked "the first time that a presidential candidate has felt that he had to respond to a women's agenda."[39]

In his thirty-minute speech, Carter accused President Ford of neglecting women's issues, which he labeled a "terrible indictment of the Ford and Nixon administrations." He offered his own "complete sympathy" with the agenda and promised strong action on behalf of women in "politics, education, employment, health care, housing and justice," along with renewed efforts to ratify the Equal Rights Amendment (ERA). His proposed program included comprehensive child care; renewed federal antidiscrimination efforts; more women appointed to high-level posts; flextime and part-time work schedules for parents of school-age children; and pursuit of equality in credit, insurance, and education.[40] The candidate's appearance generated newspaper coverage but, to the frustration of WAA staff, little attention from the electronic media.[41]

After Carter's appearance, feminists set to work. Conference discussion about task force reports and workshops on coalition building occupied most of the conference meeting time. On the first day, the conference considered "draft plans of action" (a necessity because the WAA did not finish the plans of action in time). The task forces engaged their issues, although the tension between old and new organizations appeared in each one. In the Child Care Task Force, the issue emerged in conference discussions. One participant commented from the floor that "the problem of feminist versus traditional views of child care must be addressed." Other issues included the child care legislation that Richard Nixon had vetoed and the need for twenty-four-hour care. Some proposed connection to the public schools; others averred that day care should be responsibility of the private sector and unions. Though not unified, the task force members were optimistic, overly so as it turned out: "It was felt that it will take about five years to bring about a system of federally-funded day care. The bill for child care introduced five years ago is dead; many groups had put much energy into it and may be active again if a new, strong bill that held promise was introduced."[42] Feminist support for subsidized child care remained a permanent item on the agenda.

The Economic Power Task Force met twice in 1976 before the October conference. Its members came to the conference prepared to discuss poverty and the increasing number of women threatened:

> Although overall poverty in this country has declined, there has been an increase in poverty among women, specifically single female heads of households. Women and their dependents comprise an extremely disproportionate number of the poor in this country. The present income maintenance system excludes

many of the needy, especially the working poor. Earnings of welfare recipients are "taxed" 100 percent since whatever they may earn is deducted from the welfare check. Therefore, there is little incentive to work. Also the break-up of families is encouraged by the economics of some programs which will only provide assistance to single-parent households. Present "full employment" legislation is inadequate. There are not enough jobs for people who need or want to work. Women, who are most affected by unemployment, when they do have paying jobs, earn only about 57% of a man's income. . . . Research must be conducted into what elements comprise an adequate "health and decency" income. This includes estimation of the comparative cost to the public of pro-vision of such support, and the connection to a policy of full employment. . . . [N]ational legislation is needed to ensure that every person receives a health and decency income. A likely mechanism for this would be a negative income tax package. . . . The Task Force plans to look into the issue of provision of an adequate living standard versus retention of work incentives. This will involve a discussion of minimum wage issues, support and benefits for homemakers, retired persons and others not in the work force.[43]

Its recommendations for action included welfare reform to make it easier for families to qualify and to receive benefits and to be treated respectfully by welfare administrators.[44]

At the conference, the group considered whether or not to work within the existing economic structure or to pursue "radical economic concepts." Members noted the inadequate system to provide benefits to poor families and the lack of power among unorganized recipients. "There is less need for research dealing with the redistribution of income than for education as to what adequate income is," the task force reported. "There is not enough attention given to the low-income woman. The constituency to be reached must include the recipients of social services. Recipients of social services must be included in both the coalition and the Plans of Action."[45]

The Education Task Force, convened by Joy Simonson, executive director of the National Advisory Council on Women's Educational Programs, estab-lished "key objectives" that did not challenge existing political or economic structures: enforcement of sex discrimination laws guaranteeing equal access to women; more women at all management levels in education; "realistic" sex and health education beginning "at a very young age"; continuing education with tuition assistance (including retention of unemployment benefits); flex-ible programs; child care; and bilingual/bicultural education. Again, the task force proposed outreach to rural women and advised that "special attention should be given to minority and ethnic women."[46]

Both during the conference and after, the problem of the distinction—or connection—between the National Women's Agenda Coalition (NWAC) and the IWY Commission remained unclear. Efforts of WAA staff to establish a firm role for the NWA with the IWY Commission had failed. Ruth Abram had spoken before the commission on July 18, 1975, presenting the NWA. She proposed that the NWA become the agenda for the national conference proposed (although not yet authorized) in Abzug's legislation. In fact, the WAA suggested that the IWY Commission Conference "contract out" the national conference to the NWA, arguing that they could then "assure that the conference is indeed an expression from the private sector." Abram was adamant that the national women's conference be a private sector event, not one sponsored by the government: "It should provide an opportunity for women to present their own Agenda to the government rather than vice versa."[47] Noting that Abzug's legislation still hung fire, Abram reported that "if the bill is not passed, we will sponsor our own National Conference on Women."[48] IWY Commission Chair Jill Ruckelshaus thanked her and promised that IWY Commission would carefully consider the agenda's findings and recommendations as it proceeded "with its own task of examining the issues which are of priority and importance to all American women."[49]

In response to an inquiry from a participating organization, Abram explained further that the IWY Commission was not the right entity to hold a national conference for women, partly because it did not satisfy the need for diversity: "That Commission is by no means in touch with the broad spectrum of women represented by the organizations who helped create the Agenda. If the Commission contracted the planning out to the [NWA,] it would insure a conference which was enriched by input from women in Appalachia, in unions, in household work, in ethnic organizations, in religious organizations as well as in the network of established, mainstream women's groups."[50] Nevertheless, when Bella Abzug's bill passed in December 1975, it named the IWY Commission as the organizer of the national conference.[51]

Thus, in May 1976, NWA Project Director Catherine Samuels sent Jill Ruckelshaus an unsolicited memorandum, offering suggestions on organizing the state conferences provided for in the Abzug bill. Samuels emphasized the need to *ask* women, rather than *tell* them, what their priorities should be. She pointed out that the federal commission might attract women "who feel threatened by 'women's lib.'" The state conferences could thus draw them in, educate them, "feed" them into existing projects and organizations, and help women's organizations recruit new members. She went on to map out the conference program and organization. Finally, she laid out what she saw as the role of the NWA groups, saying that she understood that the IWY Commission had "committed itself" to presenting the agenda at all the conferences, for which the NWA would provide speakers; that state NWA members would serve on state conference coordinating committees; and, to avoid duplication, "no new Women's Agenda will be created since several hundreds of women's groups are already working to implement the National Women's Agenda and to create a *Women's Plan of Action for the Decade.*" She offered to have the NWA conduct training sessions at each conference. Finally, she revealed some frustration, pointing out that she had other suggestions to offer, but "we have no way of knowing how far you are in your planning, nor what your present assumption or plans are."[52]

In September and again in October 1976, Ruth Abram wrote to IWY Commission members asking for clarification of the role of the NWA. Referring to the 115 recommendations contained in the IWY Commission's report of July 1976, "... *To Form a More Perfect Union* ...": *Justice for American Women; Report of the National Commission on the Observance of International Women's Year,* Abram observed that they complemented the NWA. The agenda task forces were now creating a "Women's Plan of Action for the Decade"; she asked for assurance that the commission would not duplicate or oppose its work and that NWA members would have a role in the state conferences. More important, she wanted the commission to make a statement that the state conferences would not come up with new items to add to the NWA but would instead offer recommendations. Ruckelshaus demurred; the commission insisted on its responsibility to draft its own documents.[53]

Abram pointed out that the NWA and the IWY commission shared the goal of creating a far-reaching agenda but she noted that one is a government group and the other private. Her exasperation over the commission's unwillingness to collaborate with the NWA flared at the NWA October 1976 conference: "Who appointed this [IWY] commission? A man. If we allow all our hopes, unity, strength to be handed over, intrusted [*sic*] to a commission set up by a man, we're surrendering all we have."[54]

To be fair, the government commission had a strong feminist component, which strengthened after Carter's election. Jill Ruckelshaus, a well-respected Republican feminist, chaired the group during the Ford administration. Its members included, among others, Alan Alda, whose feminist activism was widely visible; Barbara Bergmann, a well-known feminist economist; Patricia Carbine, publisher and editor-in-chief of *Ms.* magazine; Audrey Rowe Colom, a black woman and president of the NWPC; Ella Grasso, Democratic governor of Connecticut; Martha Griffiths, who had been a Democratic member of the House of Representatives for twenty years, during which time she had introduced the ERA and successfully discharged the Judiciary Committee to secure its approval by Congress; Katharine Hepburn, whose mother had been a well-known suffragist; Senator Birch Bayh, a sponsor of the ERA; and Bella Abzug, a founder of the WAA and author of the legislation to create and fund the National Women's Conference in Houston. Commission staff included Deputy Coordinator Catherine East, whom Betty Friedan later denominated the midwife of the women's movement.[55] East had been actively engaged in feminist pursuits since 1962, and she was nobody's handmaiden, least of all Gerald Ford's. Other feminists who served included Kathy Bonk, from the Department of Justice; Joan Goodin, from the American Federation of Labor and Congress of Industrial Organizations; and Joy Simonson, of the Civil Service Commission and the National Advisory Council on Women's Educational Programs; all had impeccable feminist credentials.

The commission's lack of enthusiasm for WAA suggestions may have reflected the confidence of its members that they could pursue their mandate without help from the WAA. Once Jimmy Carter succeeded Gerald Ford as president, Abzug took over as the presiding officer. Carter added more liberal commissioners, including Abram herself and WAA founder Gloria Steinem. He also appointed Alice Rossi, a feminist sociologist; Eleanor Smeal, then president of NOW; LaDonna Harris, a Native American activist; civil rights activist Coretta Scott King; and labor unionists Addie Wyatt and Dorothy Haener. By then, however, the process was established and the commission continued pretty much as before.[56] The state conferences received for debate 14 "core" resolutions taken from the 115 recommendations in the IWY Commission's first report. Adoption by a dozen state conferences placed an issue in the plan of action for Houston.

The WAA had to respond repeatedly to inquiries about the overlap between the two groups. WAA women insisted that it had maintained close ties to the IWY Commission and that the commission viewed the NWA task forces as "the vehicle for achieving its recommendations for U.S. women."[57] According to the WAA, the commission would confer with local coalitions as it planned for 1977 women's conference.[58] Despite its efforts, WAA staff noted with annoyance that the presidents of the major women's organizations went to the U.S. commission meetings but sent staff to the NWA meetings. It seemed an irrational choice because, as the WAA pointed out, the IWY Commission would be going out of business but a coalition of independent organizations could be permanent. Staff attributed the problem to women's socialization: "[W]omen are confused as to what real power is and see anything with a government [imprimatur] as power. They do not see themselves or their organizations as power."[59]

To the WAA, the benefits of an independent nongovernmental commission seemed indisputable. Such a coalition could produce an annual agenda to reflect the current shared concerns about women's issues. A coalition would encourage all women's organizations to mobilize around feminist issues, "especially the older, richer, and larger ones, [who] have never looked at themselves as organizations defending or promoting the rights of all people." It would also assist the newer feminist organizations to develop the structures they needed to remain viable. Finally, it would create a central focus that would generate attention by the media. One WAA staffer declared: "Women's organizations are, [at] this point in time, basically considered [peripheral] if not ridiculous. Their goals and issuances and statements except for NOW are rarely attended by the press. An example of that surely is the National Women's Agenda conference. Through creating a coalition which acts on issues of common concern, we can indeed end this ridicule and non-attention."[60]

Many of the organizations that had supported the creation of the NWA remained unconvinced about the need to establish another entity. The older groups, with decades of experience, believed that they already knew how to mobilize their members and effect their own goals. The president of the General Federation of Women's Clubs informed the WAA that it had "spelled out and achieved measurable goals for women since 1889." Its executive committee had concluded that the federation did not need another coalition: "We already have the capabilities for making public statements, coordinating activities, focusing national attention on women's issues, developing positions on current and national events, and issuing statement on behalf of the organization."[61] Responding to a proposed coalition structure early in 1977, smaller organizations voiced dismay at the dues structure, initially set at $100. Carmen Delgado Votaw of the National Conference of Puerto Rican Women pointed out that "small groups such as ours have very limited resources—both human and economic. . . . A $100 fee for an organization such as ours which has a budget of less that $1,000 annually represents a contribution of 10 percent or more."[62] One organization observed that nonprofit organizations would be unable to afford such a membership fee.[63] NOW resisted joining the NWA Coalition, citing previous experience in coalitions where NOW had contributed more money and more workers than the other organizations but had not had entrée to the decision-making process and had not gotten credit for its efforts.[64] WAA staff noted with disappointment that the agenda remained the WAA agenda and had not become the agenda for the women's movement.

By the time of the Houston meeting in November 1977, the WAA had become a key supporter of the IWY Commission. The NWA staffed an office in Houston to encourage passage of the IWY National Plan of Action by the conferees, merging with other groups to create the "Pro-Plan Caucus." The action arose chiefly out of concern about conservative women delegates who opposed the ERA and abortion rights and who had worked effectively in the preparatory state conferences.[65] Many progressive delegates also wanted to amend the plan, but so many proposed changes that the conference schedule did not permit discussion on all or even most of them. Many of the issues were therefore negotiated in advance with different groups of advocates, in particular a comprehensive minority women's plank.

The National Plan of Action, emerging from the National Women's Conference in Houston, swamped the WAA National Women's Agenda.[66] The resulting plan now had the stamp of approval from the two thousand delegates elected to represent their states at the first federally funded national women's conference, many of them already members of the organizations that the WAA was trying to corral. Nevertheless, the WAA characterized the outcome of the Houston conference as an endorsement of its National Women's Agenda, which it maintained the National Plan of Action incorporated. WAA materials began to describe the Houston National Plan of Action and the National Women's Agenda as "parallel." In March 1978, NWA Program Coordinator Anne Bowen responded to an inquiry about the NWA conference: "the National Plan of Action and the National Women's Agenda (which . . . was written before the Plan) define the same issues, even if they differ in the specifics of language."[67] Ruth Abram told supporters, "the Houston Conference confirmed for us that the goals of the Agenda are indeed broadly supported."[68]

An item-to-item comparison indicated a great deal of overlap. The preamble to the Houston Plan, entitled "Declaration of American Women," contained somewhat more expansive language than the NWA's preamble:

> We are here to move history forward. We are women from every State and Territory in the Nation. We are women of different ages, beliefs and lifestyles. We are women of many economic, social, political, racial, ethnic, cultural, educational and religious backgrounds. We are married, single, widowed and divorced. We are mothers and daughters. We are sisters. We speak in varied accents and languages but we share the common language and experience of American women who throughout our National's life have been denied the opportunities, rights, privileges and responsibilities accorded to men. . . .
>
> We are poorer than men. And those of us who are minority women—Blacks, Hispanic Americans, Native Americans and Asian Americans—must overcome the double burden of discrimination based on race and sex. . . .
>
> We seek these rights for all women, whether or not they choose as individuals to use them.[69]

The NWA preamble was terser:

> We, women of the United States of America, join together to challenge our Nation to complete the unfinished work of achieving a free and democratic society, begun long ago by our Founding Mothers and Fathers. . . . It is impera-

tive that women be integrated into national life now. . . . Diverse as we are, we are united by the deep and common experience of womanhood. As we work toward our common goals, we insist upon the protection of this diversity, and call for the simultaneous elimination of all the insidious forms of discrimination, not only those based on gender, but also on race, creed, ethnicity, class, lifestyle, sexual preference, and age."[70]

In the specific planks, both programs took pains to acknowledge the differing needs of women depending on their specific circumstances, especially of race and class. The Houston plan tended more often to specify minority women but the NWA had a clearer statement on a welfare program, supporting "establishment of a minimum standard of income and other social benefits for low income and disadvantaged persons, which protect their equity and respect the individual rights and dignity of all women." The National Plan of Action offered support for "a welfare reform program developed from on-going consultation with persons who will be impacted."[71] The NWA plan offered a more definitive statement on health care, proposing the development of "medical and mental health services available to all without regard to ability to pay."[72] The Houston plan spoke less precisely about federal legislation "to establish a national health security program." However, the Houston plan offered a clearer statement on abortion, asserting support for the Supreme Court decisions and proposing inclusion of abortion in all plans to provide health care.[73] Specific planks in the Houston plan that were not in the NWA included "minority women," "rural women," "battered women," and "disabled women."[74]

A dramatic event, the Houston conference would have meaning only insofar as its recommendations were implemented. Jimmy Carter created yet another governmental group to follow the IWY Commission: a National Advisory Committee for Women (NACW).[75] Established in April 1978, Carter named Bella Abzug and Carmen Delgado Votaw to cochair it. Despite such estimable leadership, the WAA objected to its role overseeing implementation. Unless Carter were reelected, the NACW would go out of business in 1980. The WAA noted that it lacked funds, staff, and access to the president. Carter had also created an Interdepartmental Task Force on Women to follow up on the IWY Commission, but it could focus only on internal federal matters and it would also fold in 1980 if Carter were replaced. Feminists, moreover, viewed these groups as part of the administration, loyal to the president rather than to the constituency of women.

The Carter administration quickly came under attack from advocates. The president had submitted legislative proposals in July 1978 to implement the plan of action and later released a report noting "progress." Carol Burris, a feminist lobbyist, observed that the administration's report on the status of the IWY resolutions served simply "to justify the President's views" without creating new programs or supplying new resources.[76] When NWA staff met with Sarah Weddington, head of Carter's Interdepartmental Task Force on IWY, in November 1978, she said she was also going to work on implementing the Houston plan, focusing "particular[ly] on economic issues."[77] In general, though, Weddington was more cautious than enthusiastic. She reiterated that her office was unsettled and her staffing limited, apparently seeking to keep expectations low.

Feminist objections peaked in January 1979. Abzug and Delgado Votaw issued a statement critical of the president on many fronts, especially faulting his economic program. In response to this public embarrassment, Carter fired Bella Abzug immediately and publicly. In support of Abzug, twenty-three of the forty committee members resigned.[78] Carter replaced the NACW with the President's Advisory Committee for Women, chaired by the more politic Lynda Johnson Robb. It was set to expire on December 31, 1980.[79] In October 1978, the WAA insisted with reason that "little has changed since Houston."[80]

Even without Carter's groups, other competitors also existed for the role of monitoring implementation of the National Plan of Action. First, Abzug's statute, P.L. 94–167, which had authorized money for the original national conference, anticipated a continuing committee and a second conference. The Houston conference had passed a resolution to establish a "Continuing Committee" and the IWY Commission intended to create it and lead it. According to the resolution, the Continuing Committee would consist of all the present IWY commissioners, representatives from each state and territorial delegation to the Houston conference, representatives of major national women's organizations, representatives of "special interest" caucuses formed at the conference, and additional members to ensure that the committee comprised "persons of diverse ages, and racial, ethnic, religious, economic, political, social and geographic backgrounds."[81] Abzug saw implementation of the Houston plan as one of the responsibilities of Carter's NACW, but Abzug supported an independent, nongovernmental continuing committee with its own leadership and, an important feature, its own outside funding. Carter's group, as was typical of government committees on women, had little financial assistance to disburse. Abzug advocated that the two groups work closely together, with the NACW's monitoring governmental implementation of the National Plan of Action on both the federal and state levels and the private group monitoring nongovernmental actors.[82] The 470–member Continuing Committee met for the first time on March 22, 1978, and again in June 1978.[83]

In the meantime, the agenda coalition forged ahead, determined to become the primary overseer of implementation of the plans approved by the Houston conferees and by the NWAC. In March 1978, seventy participants from a variety of organizations convened in Washington, D.C., under the aegis of the NWAC to attend workshops on lobbying, fund-raising, and press relations. Speakers addressed women regarding household employment, gay rights, reproductive rights, child care, treatment of women in the criminal justice system, "meaningful work and adequate compensation," and the ERA.[84]

They also formally convened the NWAC, adopting a structure and dues. Membership consisted of about two dozen women's organizations able to afford the dues of $100 a year, including the AAUW, the Association for Voluntary Sterilization Women's Caucus, Catalyst, Church Women United, Federally Employed Women, Federation of Organizations for Professional Women, Gay Rights National Lobby Women's Caucus, Girls Clubs, Leadership Conference of Women Religious, National Associations of Commissions for Women, National Association of Women Business Owners, NCHE, National Council on Alcoholism Office on Women, NCJW, National Gay Task Force Women's Caucus, NWPC, Pioneer Women, Planned Parenthood Federation of America—Women's Rights Project, Screen Actors Guild Women's Conference Committee, Unitarian Universalist Women's Federation, UAW Women's Department, Women's Institute for Freedom of the Press, and the YWCA.[85] Poorer organizations were perforce excluded. The National Congress of Neighborhood Women responded to the dues schedule: "[W]e do not have any [such] funds at our disposal."[86]

At a meeting in December, with fifteen organizations represented, the NWAC considered and rejected a resolution to substitute the Houston plan for the NWA. Although "there was substantial coincidence of issues, and . . . the Plan was a nationally recognized instrument, . . . the Agenda was developed out of the member organizations own processes and goals, and has been formally endorsed/adopted by official policymaking bodies of the member organizations." Despite the rejection, the body noted that implementation of the Houston plan would further the achievement of agenda goals.[87]

In some instances, the members affirmed the superiority of the agenda. Anita Shelton, a black woman from the NCHE, commented: "The NCHE has reviewed the National Plan of Action and found it inadequate in dealing with issues affecting low-income women. As a document dealing with the needs of low-income women, the Agenda speaks more directly to the issues."[88]

However, the Wages for Housework Campaign, a group representing many local organizations of poor women, had a much different experience with the NWA. Their letter to the NWAC criticized the agenda coalition for going forward with implementation without the voices of grassroots women's groups. The cost of the NWAC December 1978 conference ($50 fee plus $18–$30 per night for housing) would put it beyond the means of their membership. Their letter emphasized that the National Women's Conference, by statute, had placed "special emphasis on the representation of low-income women, members of diverse racial, ethnic, and religious groups, and women of all ages." The signers observed that:

> All 26 resolutions in the National Plan of Action amount to a call for more money and resources to be put at women's disposal. But the extra initiative and determination that it took for grassroots women of all ages, races, regions and nationalities to get to Houston and to organize and lobby at the National Women's conference is most reflected in the resolutions on Women, Welfare and Poverty, Rape and Battered Women, Rural Women, Reproductive Freedom, Childcare, Health, Homemakers, Disabled and Older Women, Sexual Preference, Offenders, Education, Employment and Minority Women. For it is these resolutions which bring into focus most clearly the fact that the fundamental problem women face is poverty: that our lack of money is the first barrier against our organizing together as women and that our first need is for more money, services and other resources.

Implementation, they warned, "is impossible without organizing ways to include the participation of all sectors of women—despite the barriers of age, race, religion, nationality *and money* which have so long divided women from each other and from men."[89]

They asked what the NWAC planned to do about these resolutions without poor women's participating in discussions and decision making, and they specifically requested scholarships to attend the conference, the provision of child care, and low-cost housing to facilitate the attendance of poor women.[90] The signers included (among others) Black Women for Wages for Housework; Bronx Household Technicians (New York City); Massachusetts Welfare Recipients for Welfare Reform; New York Prostitutes Collective; New York State Coalition of Household Technicians; Sisterhood of Black Single Mothers—New York City; Wages Due Lesbians; Wages for Housework Committees (seven cities); Working Group on Battered Women; and Joan Adler of Women against Sterilization Abuse (Philadelphia); Frankie Mae Jeter, president of the NWRO of Allegheny County; Lilly Landrum, president of Massachusetts Welfare Recipients for Welfare Reform; Beulah Sanders, former president of the NWRO; and Deborah Gutierrez, coordinator of Lesbians of Color (California).

Anne Bowen, NWAC program coordinator, sent a five-page response to the signers.[91] She began with a brief history of the NWA, distinguishing it from the National Plan of Action. However, she then went on to explain that the NWAC was not the right group for these women to join. "This, then, should provide you with some sense of what the National Women's Agenda Coalition is and is not: 1) it *is* a formal standing multi-issue coalition of national women's organizations and women's caucuses (or projects) of national organizations. It does not, in its present structure, include regional, state, or local organizations. . . . The Coalition is a group of women's organizations—some quite traditional, some more radical—who share a certain perspective on issues of concern to women, and who have a history of working together on those issues." When she addressed the issue of expense, she noted that the conference fees had decreased each time, from $100 to $85 to $50. Partial registrations and some fee reductions had been offered but not for meals. The NWA had provided child care for the first two conferences but no one requested it so they dropped the service. She pointed out that their representatives could attend and speak, although they could not vote. Her invitation was ambiguous, perhaps even a rebuke: "The Coalition can speak for one viewpoint, you can speak for another. Together we can speak for many, but none of [us] can presume to speak for all women."[92] Such a response to a group of poor women betrayed the insensitivity to issues of race and class that bedeviled many white feminist organizations.

However, the women activists in the Wages for Housework Campaign were also feminists, part of a plainly identifiable women's movement, united by core beliefs, encompassing women from all quarters. Mary Burke of the Leadership Conference of Women Religious observed: "Women's organizations who felt uncomfortable before are now able to see themselves as part of the women's movement."[93] Responding to a national consensus, reflected in the multitude of organizations advocating for women, Congress gave feminists many legislative victories in the wake of the NWA and the Houston Conference.[94]

The sense of broad movement participation did not translate into support for the WAA NWAC. At the NWAC founding meeting in March 1978, twenty-three organizations joined; in December 1978, it consisted of twenty-nine groups, not including major organizations, such as NOW or the National Federation of Business and Professional Women's Clubs. In December, seeking to enlarge the NWAC, Anne Bowen, program coordinator, did more outreach. In letters to various organizations, she wrote: "I urge you to consider how this Coalition, both in its educational and activist functions, can best be of use to your organization."[95] However, the expense of participation kept some groups from joining the coalition and attending its meetings; membership rules kept others out. By 1979, it was down again to twenty-three groups.

With the NWAC faltering for lack of money and support, the WAA made a last ditch effort for outside funding to support an implementation group, which it called the Women's Action Network.[96] Despite the best efforts of the WAA, the National Women's Agenda Project folded in 1980, although the alliance continued for almost another two decades to serve as a resource for women's organizations, especially women's centers.

However, the Houston agenda served the feminist community well enough as a blueprint and the nongovernmental National Women's Conference Continuing Committee endured, held together by a few dedicated women including Sarah Harder at the University of Wisconsin-Eau Claire and Mal Johnson in Washington. In 1988 and in 1997, it published assessments of progress made toward implementing the various plans created by the United Nations' conferences on women. In 2003, it claimed five hundred members and thirty-five chapters.[97]

The need for a coalition not simply to implement but to create new agendas, especially in the hostile environment of the Reagan Revolution, generated new efforts. In 1985, the presidents of leading national women's organizations formalized a small working group by creating the Council of Presidents (COP). This group, which grew to comprise some eighty national organizations (representing, it claimed, 10 million grassroots citizens), met every two months in Washington, D.C., discussing public policy issues and strategies to achieve shared legislative ends. The COP adopted an annual women's agenda to influence Congress and guide activists. Respecting organizational autonomy, the COP created no governing structure, hired no staff, and raised no money. In 1988, the COP held a Women's Agenda Conference in Des Moines just before the Iowa presidential primary in an attempt to mobilize more feminist support for the election. The 1992 Women's Agenda focused on the national budget; global peace; "comprehensive health care for all women"; the elimination of racism, sexism, and violence; legal equality; economic equity, including adequate wages and training, family and medical leave, affordable housing, and care for children and elders.[98] Member groups included modern feminist organizations, older progressive women's organizations, groups of professional women, groups representing ethnicities and racial communities, legal organizations, research organizations, labor groups, educational associations, reproductive rights, religious groups, and the WAA.

As the COP matured and expanded, attendance of the presidents became less a priority. The COP changed its name in 1983 to the National Council of Women's Organizations (NCWO), reflecting the attendance of representatives rather than presidents. By 2005, NCWO counted almost two hundred member groups. Its strength, it asserts, lies in its function as a "coalescing force uniting member organizations around a common agenda." The most recent women's movement agenda can be found at its Web site: http://www.womensorganizations.org.

The NCWO is the heir to the feminist coalitions developed in the 1970s. By the end of that decade, the older women's organizations that had held watch over women's interests for almost a century and the plethora of new feminist groups that had appeared in the turmoil of the 1960s and 1970s had, if imperfectly, melded into a determined, fractious, legion dedicated to making the nation and the world work better for all women.

Moreover, the contest with the entities created by the federal government proved productive. The two agendas—one created by independent women's organizations in the WAA and the other drafted by a federal committee and modified and adopted by individual women from all over the country at the Houston convention—mirrored and reinforced each other, providing rolling publicity and legitimacy for subsequent legislative campaigns.

Still, the achievement of measures improving the status of women depends as much on political will as on feminist activism. Looking back, we see that policy makers in Washington proved more amenable to passing measures in support of formal equality than to enacting social programs needed to ameliorate the situation of the most vulnerable women. The feminist agenda was inclusive; the nation's political agenda was not.

## Notes

I would like to acknowledge the archivists at the Sophia Smith Collection, Smith College, Northampton, Massachusetts, which holds the papers of the Women's Action Alliance, and especially of Marla Miller, who constructed the finding aid for the collection. Thanks also to Brenda Feigen for permission to cite and quote from the collection.

1. "WAA: Agenda, Advice and Toys," *Majority Report,* September 20, 1975, clipping in box 192, file 5, WAA papers, Sophia Smith Collection, Smith College, Northampton, Mass. [hereafter WAA papers]; Brenda Feigen, *Not One of the Boys: Living Life as a Feminist* (New York: Knopf, 2000), 43–44.

2. Telephone interview, Ruth Abram, July 12, 2005.

3. Executive Order no. 11832.

4. Public Law 94–167.

5. "WAA: Agenda, Advice and Toys," *Majority Report,* September 20, 1975, clipping in box 192, file 5, WAA papers.

6. "Proposal, Women's Action Network, A Project of the Women's Action Alliance, Inc.," October 1978, p. 10, box 188, file 7, WAA papers.

7. Ruth J. Abram to Marilyn Levy, Rockefeller Family Fund, January 23, 1975, box 196, file 2, WAA papers.

8. "Individuals Invited to Attend the Monday, March 31 Meeting . . . ," WAA, box 198, file 11, WAA papers.

9. "Memorandum/Subject: The National Women's Agenda Organizing Problems; Draft Dictated 28 October 1976," p. 1, box 198, file 10, WAA papers.

10. Invitation and program for Oct. 1–2, 1976, conference—"By invitation only"— "Beyond Suffrage" The U.S. National Women's Agenda Conference, [National 4–H Center in Washington, D.C.]; National Women's Agenda, box 192, file 15, WAA papers.

11. Ibid.

12. Ibid.

13. Ibid.

14. Ibid.

15. "Steinem to Receive AAUW Educational Foundation Achievement Award" at http://www.aauw.org/outlook/gloria.cfm, accessed July 13, 2005.

16. Barbara Omolade, "Sisterhood in Black and White," in *The Feminist Memoir Project: Voices from Women's Liberation, ed.* Rachel Blau duPlessis and Ann Snitow (New York: Three Rivers Press [Crown Publishers], 1998), 387.

17. Ibid., 387–88.

18. "The Pathology of Racism: A Conversation with Third World Wimmin," in *This Bridge Called My Back: Writings by Radical Women of Color, ed.* Cheríe Moraga & Gloria Anzaldúa (New York: Kitchen Table: Women of Color Press, 1983), 86.

19. Ibid., 61.

20. "The U.S. National Women's Agenda by Bella Abzug for Ms. Magazine, December 1975 issue," file "Women, Abzug—Statements and Releases," box 599, Abzug papers, Columbia University, New York, New York [hereafter Abzug papers].

21. Patricia S. Lindh (special assistant to the president) to Ms. Abram, October 9, 1975; attached to Catherine Samuels to agenda participant, November 4, 1975, box 192, file 2, WAA papers.

22. Mary King et al., Women's Action Alliance, to Gerald Ford, November 11, 1975, box 192, file 6, WAA papers.

23. "Memorandum/Subject: The National Women's Agenda Organizing Problems; Draft Dictated 28 October 1976," p. 2, box 198, file 10, WAA papers.

24. Paquita Vivo (author), no title, n.d. [December 2, 1975], pp. 1–2, box 192, file 8, WAA papers.

25. Edith Barksdale Sloan, no title, n.d. [December 2, 1975], box 192, file 8, WAA papers.

26. *New York Times,* December 6, 1975, clipping, box 193, file 11, WAA papers.

27. See clips in box 193, file 11, WAA papers.

28. *Washington Star,* December 2, 1975, p. A7, clipping in box 193, file 11, WAA papers.

29. Ibid.

30. "Memorandum/Subject: The National Women's Agenda Organizing Problems; Draft Dictated 28 October 1976," [author not identified], p. 3, box 198, file 10, WAA papers.

31. Ibid.

32. Ruth J. Abram to Bess Meyerson, September 7, 1976, box 192, file 9, WAA papers.

33. Ruth Abram to Brenda Eichelberger, August 25, 1976, box 192, file 9, WAA papers.

34. Ruth Abram to Brenda Eichelberger, August 25, 1976; Abram to Olga Madar, August 26, 1976; Abram to Ada R. Pena, August 26, 1976; Abram to Vang Elizonda, August 31, 1976, box 192, file 9, WAA papers.

35. Ibid.

36. Abram to Eleanor Holmes Norton, September 9, 1976, box 192, file 11, WAA papers.

37. "Feminism: Expectations Raised Greatly, Reality Budged Very Little," *Valley News Dispatch* (Tarentum, PA), November 18, 1976, clipping from Gannet News Service, box 193, file 6, WAA papers.

38. "Reader's Forum" [newspaper illegible (N.J.)] October 21, 1976, clipping, box 193, file 6, WAA papers.

39. Cover letter with conference report, Ruth J. Abram, December 27, 1976, box 192, file 12, WAA papers.

40. "Carter Vows to Push for ERA," *San Diego Union*, October 3, 1976, clipping, box 193, file 6; "51.3%: Speech Given before the U.S. National Women's Agenda Conference, October 2, 1976, Washington, D.C., by Governor Jimmy Carter," box 193, file7, WAA papers.

41. "Reader's Forum" [newspaper illegible (N.J.)] October 21, 1976, clipping, box 193, file 6, WAA papers.

42. "Minutes, Task Force on Child Care," panel presentation, October 1, 1976, U.S. National Women's Agenda Conference, Sherley Koteen (convener), pp. 1–2, box 193, file 3, WAA papers.

43. "Minutes, Task Force on Economic Power," panel presentation, October 1, 1976, U.S. National Women's Agenda Conference, Irene Murphy (coconvener), p. 67, box 193, file 3, WAA papers.

44. Ibid., 71.

45. Ibid., 1.

46. "Minutes, Task Force on Equal Education and Training," panel presentation, October 1, 1976, U.S. National Women's Agenda Conference, Joy Simonson (convener), box 193, file 3, WAA papers.

47. Ruth J. Abram to Mildred Marcy, October 30, 1975, p. 2, attached to Catherine Samuels to agenda participant, November 4, 1975,box 192, file 2, WAA papers.

48. Abram to Dear Friends, July 25, 1975, box 192, file 2, WAA papers.

49. Ruckelshaus to Abrams [*sic*], August 1, 1975, box 196, file 2, WAA papers.

50. Abram to Julia Graham Lear, Federation of Organizations for Professional Women, September 2, 1975, box 194, file 4, WAA papers.

51. Public Law 94–167, December 23, 1975.

52. Catherine Samuels to Jill Ruckelshaus, May 4, 1976, box 196, file 5, WAA papers.

53. Abram to Pat Carbine, October 28, 1976, box 196, file 5; Kathryn F. Clarenbach to Ruth J. Abram, November 2, 1976, box 196, file 3, WAA papers.

54. National Meeting, NWAC, October 2, 1976, minutes, p. 2, box 193, file 1, WAA papers.

55. Betty Friedan, *It Changed My Life: Writings on the Women's Movement* (New York: Random House, 1976), 77.

56. Ruth Abram, telephone interview, July 12, 2005.

57. "The U.S. National Women's Agenda: A Background Paper" n.d. [1976], p. 2, box 192, file 15, WAA papers.

58. Ibid.

59. "Memorandum/Subject: The National Women's Agenda Organizing Problems; Draft Dictated 28 October 1976," p. 4, box 198, file 10, WAA papers.

60. Ibid.

61. Gerri Wagner (Mrs. Harry Wagner, Jr.) to Madeline Lee, February 28, 1977, box 198, file 8, WAA papers.

62. Votaw to National Women's Agenda Project, February 21, 1977, box 198, file 8, WAA papers.

63. Betsy Jaffe (director, Programs for Employers, Catalyst) to Madeline Lee, February 23, 1977, attached to Votaw to National Women's Agenda Project, February 21, 1977, box 198, file 8, WAA papers.

64. Anne Bowen to Eleanor Smeal, September 27, 1978, box 197, file 3, WAA papers.

65. Anne Bowen to Jan Kowalsky, October 27, 1977, box 196, file 4, WAA papers.

66. National Commission on the Observance of International Women's Year, *The Spirit of Houston: The First National Women's Conference* (Washington, D.C.: U.S. Department of State, March 22, 1978).

67. Bowen to Caroline Ware, April 6, 1978, box 196, file 10, WAA papers.

68. "Agenda Coalition Takes Shape" in "The National Women's Agenda Coalition Wants You," n.d., p. 26, box 198, file 5, WAA papers.

69. *The Spirit of Houston*, 15–16.

70. Women's Action Alliance, "National Women's Agenda," n.d., box 198, file 5; "A Comparative Study" prepared for the Women's Agenda Coalition Conference—December 1–2, 1978, p. 2, box 201, file 1, WAA papers [hereafter "A Comparative Study"].

71. " Comparative Study," 11.

72. Ibid., 14.

73. *The Spirit of Houston*, 83.

74. "Comparative Study," 23.

75. Executive Order 2040, April 4, 1978.

76. Carol Burris to the National Advisory Committee for Women, October 19, 1978, box 987, file "Advisory committee, Dec. 78," Abzug papers.

77. Report on the meeting with special presidential assistant Sarah Weddington, Executive Office Building, Washington, D.C., November 30, 1978, box 201, file 5, WAA papers.

78. "Statement to President Carter, January 12, 1979, Bella S. Abzug and Carmen Delgado Votaw, Co-Chairs, National Advisory Committee for Women,"box 987, file "Natl. Advisory Com. For Women," Abzug papers.

79. Executive Order 12135, May 9, 1979.

80. Ibid., 2.

81. Proposal to implement "Committee of the Conference Resolution . . . ," att. to Clearinghouse on Women's Issues, "Minutes of the Meeting of Tuesday, January 24, 1978," box 196, file 10, WAA papers.

82. "Continuing Committee of the Conference, Minutes of July 8, 1978 Meeting," box 985, file "National Advisory Committee," Abzug papers.

83. Bella Abzug and Carmen Delgado Votaw to Dear Friend, August 7, 1978, box 985, file NACW, Abzug papers.

84. "Comparative Study," 8.

85. National Women's Agenda Coalition, 1978 Conference, March 9–11, 1978, Washington, D.C., box 200, file 12, WAA papers.

86. Christine Noschese to Ruth J. Abram, July 14, 1978, WAA, box 197, file 3, WAA papers.

87. "Minutes of the Plenary Session of the National Women's Agenda Coalition Conference, December 1, 1978," Washington, D.C., p. 2–3, box 201, file 2, WAA papers.

88. Ibid., 3.

89. "Open Letter to the National Women's Agenda Coalition" n.d. [November 1978], box 201, file 6, WAA papers.

90. Ibid.

91. Anne Bowen to numerous recipients, n.d., attached to "Open Letter," ibid.

92. Ibid.

93. "Agenda Coalition Takes Shape" in "The National Women's Agenda Coalition Wants You," n.d., p. 26, WAA, box 198, file 5, WAA papers.

94. Funding for antidiscrimination programs in vocational education (90 *Stat.* 2018, October 12, 1976); tax credits for child care and IRAs for homemakers (90 *Stat.* 1480, September 30, 1976); unemployment benefits extended to domestic workers (90 *Stat.* 2667, October 20, 1976); spousal benefits for wives married only ten years to former spouse (91 *Stat.* 1509, December 20, 1977); prohibition of race and sex discrimination in the federal civil service (92 *Stat.* 1111, October 13, 1978); extension of time to ratify the ERA (92 *Stat.* 3799, October 20, 1978; affirmative action in federal training programs (92 *Stat.* 1909, October 27, 1978); a bar to discrimination based on pregnancy (92 *Stat.* 2076, October 31, 1978); and the establishment of a Women's Rights National Historic Park in Seneca Falls, N.Y. (94 *Stat.* 3539, December 28, 1980), among other measures.

95. Anne Bowen to Wilmette Brown, Wages for Housework Campaign, Anne Bowen to Karen Nussbaum, Working Women (Cleveland, Ohio), n.d. [December 1978], box 201, file 5, WAA papers.

96. "Proposal, Women's Action Network, A Project of the Women's Action Alliance, Inc." [October 1978], box 188, file 7, WAA papers.

97. http://dosfan.lib.uic.edu/ERC/intlorg/Status_of_Women/s2.html#top, accessed January 10, 2005; National Council of Women's Organizations, *Handbook of Women's Organizations and National Leaders, 2003–2004* (Washington, D.C.: National Council of Women's Organizations, 2004).

98. http://www.mith2.umd.edu/WomensStudies/GovernmentPolitics/CouncilofPresidents/, accessed January 10, 2005.

# 3. Attentive to Difference

## Ms. *Magazine, Coalition Building, and Sisterhood*

AMY FARRELL

A few weeks prior to going to press, Sian Hunter, a senior editor at University of North Carolina Press, and I went back and forth about the title of my book on the history of *Ms.*, the first feminist, commercial magazine in the United States. The point of debate focused on punctuation: should there be a question mark after *Yours in Sisterhood? Ms. Magazine and the Promise of Popular Feminism* or should there simply be a colon, as in *Yours in Sisterhood: Ms. Magazine and the Promise of Popular Feminism.* "Yours in sisterhood" was the closing phrase, always followed by Gloria Steinem's signature, the magazine used in sending out subscription renewal letters and requests for donations. For me, the question mark signaled the attention my book gave to this question of "sisterhood." In other words, was *Ms.* actually speaking to a sisterhood of women? In what ways? How was that sisterhood defined? Who was included? Who was left out? How did concepts of feminist sisterhood change over the twenty years of the magazine's commercial publication, from the early 1970s to the late 1980s? How did the commercial context of *Ms.* shape the way that sisterhood could be defined, the ways that feminism could be represented, the voices that could be and were included in the magazine, the range of readers the magazine could and did speak to?

In the end, I left out the question mark. I wanted to avoid any potential confusion with the plethora of antifeminist "feminist" books that had gained such national media attention at the time, such as Kate Roiphe's *The Morning After: Sex, Fear and Feminism on Campus* and Wendy Kaminer's *A Fearful Freedom: Women's Flight from Equality.* The emphasis of my book, however, remained the same, even if I removed the question mark. *Yours in Sisterhood* explored the extent to which this major institution of the second wave of feminism, *Ms.* magazine, was able to live up to its pledge to serve as an "open forum, a place where women of many different backgrounds can find help and information to improve their lives," as one of its first statements of purpose read, to act as a "connective tissue for all women" across the nation, as publisher Patricia Carbine promised in its early days.[1]

From its first issue in 1972 to its final commercial issue in 1989, *Ms.* worked to be a mass media umbrella for feminism, positioning itself as the space in which women could share their experiences, their various opinions and strategies, across the boundaries of race, ethnicity, class, age, and sexuality. As I argued in *Yours in Sisterhood, Ms.* promised a form of "popular feminism"—a widespread movement that drew on commercial culture and promoted an end to discrimination and the improvement of all women's lives.[2] This chapter explores the strategies that the *Ms.* editors employed to attract a diversity of readers and to allow their perspectives to be heard. It also describes and analyzes some of the difficult choices that the editors had to make, particularly when the very foundation of *Ms.*'s ability to speak to so many women—its commercial format—also ultimately limited its ability to be the "forum for all women" that the founders had originally promised. Although *Ms.* may not have ultimately been successful in creating and sustaining this all-inclusive space of "popular feminism," the magazine did provide the opportunity for women to connect with each other and to build feminist coalitions, especially within the context of a pre-Internet culture.

Considering the extent to which *Ms.* sought to encompass diversity, build connections, and use the contradictory and contested space of the mass media to accomplish this, *imagine my surprise* (to borrow a phrase from the title song of Holly Near's 1978 album) when I began teaching about third-wave feminism in my women's studies classes, and came across numerous references to the second wave of feminism as inattentive to difference; unaware of or unconcerned with the plurality of women's experiences; and, finally, unwilling to deal with contradictions, emerging out of commercial culture or from the reality of our complicated personal identities.[3] This version of feminist history is simply inaccurate: the 1970s and 1980s were filled with feminist organizations and movements that grappled with issues of diversity, worked to bridge differences, and chose a myriad of complicated tactics to accomplish their goals. For, underlying this version of second-wave feminist history—that it was inattentive to differences and complexities—is an implicit assumption that all second-wave feminist activists and organizations would have been "successful" if only they had acknowledged differences, hybrid identities, and contradictory impulses. Yet the evidence from these activists' lives and organizations suggests that issues of diversity, complexity, and bridge building were at the heart of their endeavors. The fact that they were only sometimes successful—and often failed—speaks not to their indifference but rather to the difficulty of creating and sustaining feminist, progressive movements. As Bernice Johnson Reagon, founder of the African-American women's musical group Sweet Honey in the Rock once powerfully quipped, "Coalition building is hard work."[4]

The history of *Ms.* during the 1970s and 1980s is illustrative of just these kinds of successes and challenges that second-wave feminist organizations faced in building coalitions. The preview issue (Spring 1972) of *Ms.* pictured a ten-armed Hindu goddesslike woman on its cover, holding items including an iron, a dust mop, a car's steering wheel, a typewriter—all symbols of the many roles women played. The headlines "Gloria Steinem on Sisterhood," "Women Tell the Truth about Abortions," "Letty Cottin Pogrebin on Raising Non-Sexist Children" suggested a range of perspectives and topics. Beyond those featured on the cover, articles inside the issue discussed creating fair marriage contracts, starting a racially diverse child care center, lesbian love, and the need to change the sexist foundations of the English language. Many of these first articles went on to become minor classics within the history of the second wave of feminism: "The Black Family and Feminism," an interview with Eleanor Holmes Norton by Cellestine Ware; "Welfare is a Women's Issue" by Johnnie Tillmon; "I Want a Wife," by Judy Syfer; and "The Housewife's Moment of Truth," by Jane O'Reilly. The articles often emphasized readers' connection to the women's movement, encouraging readers to take part in actions to change sexist legislation regarding abortion and job discrimination, for instance. The final section of the first issue, "Where to Get Help," listed over fifty national women's groups, from mass-based organizations such as the National Organization for Women to ones focused on women on welfare, lesbians, or academic women (recognizing, of course, that these are not necessarily mutually exclusive groups).

From its origins, then, *Ms.* worked to *connect* women to each other, to join forces across the country and among activist groups. It explicitly articulated a pluralistic feminism, one that could speak to and include the perspectives of the wide range of women who constituted their mass media audience and who were part of the women's movement of the 1970s. As their first "Personal Report from *Ms.*" read, "If you asked us our philosophy for ourselves and for the magazine, each of us would give an individual answer. But we agree on one thing. We want a world in which no one is born into a subordinate role because of visible difference whether that difference is of race or of sex. That's an assumption we make personally and editorially, with all the social changes it implies. After that, we cherish our differences. We want *Ms.* to be a forum for many views."[5] Editors simultaneously recognized both a common cause among themselves and their readers—eradicating "subordinate roles"—and the diversity of women's lives, experiences and thinking—in their words, "cherishing our differences." It was a difficult balance to maintain, but one that was very important to the growth and strength of the movement.

The genre that the founders decided to use—a commercial, glossy, women's magazine—was key to their attempt to reach out to and to connect with this broad scope of American women. The need for some type of mass media "connective tissue" among women had been recognized since the first wave of feminism in the early part of the twentieth century. One of the writers for the periodical *The Suffragist,* Freda Kirchwey, called in 1921 for a "new sort of woman's magazine," one that would "work to spread the feminist revolution." She condemned her contemporary women's magazines, such as *Ladies Home Journal,* whose purpose, she said, was to "make a domestic career endurable to all married women." Yet, she argued, this popular style of magazine was necessary to reach women, "whether they have worked for the vote or whether they have stuck steadfastly and unquestioningly to their dinner dishes." Four decades later, the 1963 publication of Betty Friedan's *The Feminine Mystique* would mark renewed attention to the role of the mainstream mass media—in particular women's magazines—in emphasizing domesticity, maternity, and female submissiveness. The 1968 Freedom Trash Can demonstration, in which activists from the New York Radical Women threw copies of magazines such as *Ladies Home Journal* and *Woman's Day,* as well as their bras, girdles, and hair rollers, highlighted once again Kirchwey's criticism of women's mass media as being part of the fundamental problem facing women.

By the late 1960s and early 1970s, feminists began to create their own periodicals, which played a crucial role in organizing women and voicing the concerns of the early women's movement. These periodicals, however, such as *No More Fun and Games,* and the still-published *off our backs,* a Washington, D.C.–based national feminist newspaper, had extremely small circulations and largely volunteer staff. Their role was key in articulating an unabashedly feminist voice and challenging the sexism in both Leftist organizations and mainstream politics, but their reach was limited. Seeing the inherent limitations of these small feminist periodicals, many early second-wave feminists continued to press for changes within mainstream women's magazines. In 1970, for instance, activists took over the office of *Ladies Home Journal* editor John Mack Carter, demanding that the magazine cover the women's movement, and that it be done in a positive fashion. Their sit-in resulted only in an eight-page insert in a subsequent issue, but it was indicative both of activists' demand for an intervention in mass media and of their desire to harness the mass media to connect the already committed activist and the woman isolated in her community—the suffragist or the dishwasher, to rephrase Kirchwey's words.[6]

Gloria Steinem, certainly the most popular of the *Ms.* founders, originally had balked at the idea of a mass media women's magazine such as the one Kirchwey had envisioned. She imagined a national newsletter for women, a space for women's organizations and activists to speak to each other and share ideas and resources. Also, according to her biographer Carolyn Heilbrun, she was uncertain if the commercial publishing world and the feminist movement would mix very well. Patricia Carbine and Elizabeth Forsling Harris ultimately convinced Steinem that what the women's movement really needed was a mass media magazine, something that could compete on the newsstands with all the other women's magazines. They pointed out that a glossy periodical, filled with advertisements, could draw from the resources of commercial industries, potentially even enriching the women's movement through a new foundation for women. They pointed out that a glossy would be available on every newsstand, from New York to San Francisco, Cleveland to Wichita, and all the small towns in between; women would not need to be in a cosmopolitan or countercultural community to be able to find it. Perhaps most importantly, it would use the language and images of popular culture that they knew readers already found pleasurable and familiar. As one of the writers for *off our backs*, Onka Dekkers, put it so aptly, *Ms.* would slip quietly into homes like "tarantulas on banana boats," transforming the lives of women and girls across the country.[7]

The immediate sellout of the preview issue in 1972 suggested that the founders of this new magazine had indeed hit a cultural nerve. Soon after the magazine hit the newsstands, editors in New York began to receive phone calls from potential readers that they could not find the magazine. Thinking that the magazine had been lost in transit or damaged, editors called the distribution centers across the country, only to find to their great pleasure that the 300,000 copies of the magazine had not failed to arrive—they had already *sold out*. The preview issue drew in almost 20,000 letters from readers, four times more than magazines with similar circulation numbers.[8] Readers wrote lengthy and personal letters to *Ms.*, about problems with their husbands and children, discrimination at work, miscarriages, doctors' visits, and political causes. *Ms.* quickly became a kind of mass media consciousness-raising forum, particularly important considering that, as historian Alice Echols pointed out, the demand for local consciousness-raising groups far outpaced the ability of newly formed women's organizations in the 1970s to provide them.[9]

For example, in 1976, a reader from Vermont recounted, "I remember vividly the rockets that went blazing into the sky when *Ms.* was announced. Wasn't it exciting! A magazine for women, and not another *Ladies Home Journal*! A serious, thoughtful magazine that would speak to us directly! I can still remember how I felt when I read it. Perhaps today, for the young women who pick it up for the first time, there is the same shock of surprise and delight. I hope so. For me, the day brightened when I found *Ms.* in our mailbox, and I remember thinking my husband must be able to tell by a subtle change in my attitude that *Ms.* had come again. I read every word in it, straight through, even the classifieds."[10] Many of the women writing to *Ms.* signed their letters "click," drawing from Jane O'Reilly's article "The Housewife's Moment of Truth," which had been published in the first issue. In her witty article, O'Reilly had outlined her "click of recognition" when she realized how subservient and unfair her role as a housewife and mother was. Readers followed O'Reilly's lead by discussing their own clicks: the places where they began to see the insidious and powerful sexism within their own daily lives, whether at their workplace, the movies, their children's school, or in other magazines and books. In 1973, for instance, a young reader from Rhode Island wrote to *Ms.* on a small piece of notebook paper: "Whenever I play baseball with my brother, and I get a hit, he says I'll never get another and it was a lot of luck. And if I strike out it is because of my sex. CLICK!"[11]

The *Ms.* letters section served as a kind of touchstone, particularly for isolated women who did not have their own feminist communities to support themselves. By the early 1970s, hotbeds of feminist activism had sprung up throughout the nation, not just in the major metropolitan areas of New York, Chicago, and San Francisco, but also in smaller Midwestern cities such as Dayton, Ohio.[12] Women in rural areas or smaller towns throughout the United States, however, often had no access to such a feminist community; for them, *Ms.* served as a lifeline, linking them to other women with similar experiences and perspectives. A woman from a tiny town in Pennsylvania wrote a lengthy note to *Ms.* in 1972, for instance, describing the difficulties of her life, her upcoming divorce, and the importance of the magazine in sustaining her: "I had grown weary of fighting everyone and anyone, I had been losing courage, and had started to believe there really was something wrong with me, until I began to receive your magazine. It has been literally a 'lifesaver,' it has been the only friend I've had, it has given me the courage to go on believing that women were not put on this earth to be the handmaidens of men. . . . A personal thank-you . . . to everyone at *Ms.* for giving me hope."[13]

Even in areas of fervent political activity, however, women often were isolated within their own homes and marriages; for them, *Ms.* served a function similar to those who were geographically isolated. In the early 1970s, for instance, a woman from a suburb of Los Angeles wrote a four-page letter to *Ms.*, which recounted in detail the ways that her husband silenced her and called her names. She concluded, "Thanks for your magazine! I've been feeling more and more depressed since I got married three years ago and hadn't known why until your magazine 'came out.' . . . Although I can't say that your magazine will definitely save me from insanity, it's nice to know that other women are in the same boat with me."[14] The isolation that women like this one from the outskirts of Los Angeles felt is indeed palpable. The era of the Internet, complete with chat rooms and the ability to search for any imaginable subject, did not exist. *Ms.* allowed people to connect easily with others of similar perspectives. In the early days of the second wave of feminism, not only were many ideas of feminism just beginning to be articulated, but the ability of women to connect with other feminists depended on the chances of geography or of finding published works on the subject.[15] In such a context, the publication of *Ms.*, found near the checkout counter at the grocery store, indeed seemed like the "lifesaver" that the Pennsylvania woman described.

The *Ms.* editors worked consciously to forge such a strong relationship with readers. They regularly wrote a "Personal Report from *Ms.*" (signed by Gloria Steinem); they solicited reader responses even when readers had decided not to resubscribe to the magazine; and, perhaps most importantly, they published many more letters than a typical women's magazine, four to five pages rather than the skimpy one page of edited letters that magazines such as *Vogue* or *Good Housekeeping* would publish. As the first "Personal Report from *Ms.*" read, "[W]e are joyfully discovering ourselves, and a world set free from old patterns, old thoughts. We hope *Ms.* will help you—and us—to explore this new world. There are few guidelines in history, or our own past. We must learn from each other. So keep writing. *Ms.* belongs to us all."[16]

When readers felt left out from the magazine's contents and perspectives, they responded with dismay and outrage. Elderly women, teenage girls, and working-class women often wrote that they found themselves invisible in the magazine. One twenty-four-year-old African American woman wrote that she wanted to hear from black women other than the famous "June Jordan and Alice Walker."[17] (Interestingly, *Ms.* had been the first magazine to publish any of Walker's work.) In 1980, a woman from California criticized the lack of coverage regarding Chicana women. "We are women, also, who are constantly struggling in this male dominated society. I think *Ms.* would be an excellent medium to educate the public on our struggles. In the future I would like to see more literature about Chicanas and Chicana feminism."[18] Steinem's promises that the magazine would speak to "all women, everywhere," that it would move beyond old divisions with its new vision of sisterhood, certainly were not always realized. Significantly, however, readers did attach themselves to the *promise* of sisterhood, and they *imagined* that the magazine could, and should, be a place where a myriad of feminist voices, including their own, were included. Readers insisted, quite passionately, that *Ms.* fulfill their expectations. As one angry reader wrote to *Ms.*, "You're not listening!" She obviously did not perceive the editorial stance of *Ms.* as an empty assurance but expected the magazine to be responsive to her needs.[19]

The *Ms.* letters section also worked as a kind of "stories from the trenches," connecting the broader policy and legislative issues to the daily lives and experiences of readers. The ongoing coverage of abortion and reproductive rights within *Ms.* makes the point most clearly. In 1969, Steinem had been assigned to report on an abortion "speak out," sponsored by the radical feminist group Redstockings, for *New York* magazine. Steinem later explained how this event "politicized" her, making her think of herself as part of the women's movement.[20] By the time *Ms.* started publication in 1972, activists from across the spectrum of the women's movement were lobbying hard for women's rights to elective abortions. The first issue of *Ms.* included an article by Barbaralee Diamonstein's "We Have Had Abortions," which listed the names of fifty-three American women who acknowledged having abortions. The article included a postcard for readers to send in adding their own names to the petition. The first editors of *Ms.* remember receiving thousands of those postcards for the first year of publication, which they then forwarded to national and state legislatures. They also sent the petitions to women in other countries who were agitating for the same rights to abortion. Throughout the 1970s and 1980s, in the "tear out" Gazette section of the magazine, *Ms.* included articles that updated readers on challenges to the 1973 *Roe v. Wade* decision, such as the 1976 Hyde Amendment, which prohibited the use of public funds for abortions, and the growth of organizations such as the National Right to Life Committee. The Gazette articles reported on the work of the National Abortion Rights Action League, Planned Parenthood, and other reproductive rights organizations. Accompanying each article was always a number or address for readers to contact and suggestions for further activism, underscoring the connection between broad national issues and individual ways to act upon them.

Because *Ms.* had established itself as a nonprofit organization by the late 1970s, it could not endorse any particular political candidate or party. That did not mean, however, that it could not investigate what particular policies or candidates' positions meant for women—it meant only that the magazine could not endorse a particular political candidate or party. Throughout its twenty-year history as a commercial feminist magazine, *Ms.* worked hard to connect women across the spectrum on issues of reproductive rights, from those first postcards to its final commercial issue in July 1989, whose cover read "It's War," referring to that year's *Webster v. Reproductive Health Services* case in which the Supreme Court declared as constitutional the state of Missouri's legislation that limited abortion in the first trimester of pregnancy.

Perhaps equally—or even more—compelling than the legislative alerts and investigative reports on reproductive rights, however, were the constant stream of letters that readers wrote to the magazine about their perspectives and experiences; *Ms.* editors often published them in their entirety. For example, in 1974, a Massachusetts woman wrote about dangerous gynecological procedures:

> I want you to call attention to this issue so women with Dalkon shields will consider trying some alternative birth control device and avert the trauma I went through. You may well wonder how a woman who had an abortion this very day, who needed 10 milligrams of Valium just to be able to relax enough to lie still, could summon the energy to write this letter. My energy comes from pain—not the physical pain of abortion, but the mental pain of knowing that women's bodies have been messed with by the drug industry for too long and it's high time we started fighting back, not as individuals, but en masse as women. In love and sisterhood . . .

The "you" in this letter is clearly something broader than the editor herself. Unlike other magazines, in which readers write to the editor, readers of *Ms.* wrote to the *Ms.* community—editors, the writers, and, most importantly, other readers. Readers wrote to the magazine about the difficult decisions they had regarding abortion, about the ways that restrictions in their own states affected themselves either as individuals or as health care providers, and about the importance of women controlling the fate of their own bodies and receiving respectful health care. In the early 1970s, a male physician from Pennsylvania wrote in explaining why he had become such an advocate for abortion rights. He explained that ten years earlier a fourteen-year-old girl had come to him for an abortion, but neither her parents nor her priest supported her; after giving birth to the child, she committed suicide. Other readers, such as the aforementioned one from California, wrote in describing their poor treatment at the hands of obstetricians. She explained that she went to the emergency room because of the extraordinary pain she felt in her pelvic region; the doctors did not believe her and would not admit her until her husband and father insisted. They later found she had an ectopic pregnancy, probably caused by an intrauterine device. Another woman, a librarian from Missouri, wrote in 1973 regarding the poor sex education children receive, asking other readers to insist that their local libraries place sex education books on the shelves directly, instead of secreting them away behind the front desk as they often were.[21]

Throughout its two-decade history as a commercial magazine, *Ms.* drew public attention to a number of issues that had previously gone unnamed and unrecognized as women's issues: violence against women, particularly within the home; sexual harassment at the job; the "pink collar" ghetto; and issues of comparable worth. Each of these cover issues cut across issues of race, and they ran side by side with Gazette articles that listed names of relevant organizations, forms of activism, numbers to call and books to read. Each of these cover issues also elicited hundreds of letters from readers, recounting their own stories of abuse or harassment and often challenging the editors to represent more accurately their own realities. Importantly, readers perceived *Ms.* as a magazine and an institution that would indeed be inclusive of their stories and their experiences, and they used that belief as their ammunition to push editors to include as wide a variety of articles and perspectives as possible.

The evidence from the first two decades of *Ms.*, then, suggests that although the magazine may not always have been successful at creating a space inclusive of "all women, everywhere," the editors, writers, and readers were hardly "inattentive" to diversity. In contrast, they sought it out and dealt with both the strengths and the challenges that such diversity created. The editors of *Ms.* wanted to speak to the plurality of women's experiences and to women at various stages of feminist consciousness; simultaneously, however, they were very aware of the ways that some perspectives explicitly contradicted each other, or, more troubling, disagreed with some of the basic tenets of a belief in women's empowerment and challenges to a patriarchal culture. They were keenly aware of the dangers of an "anything goes" perspective, which Rory Dicker and Alison Piepmeier so articulately critique in their book *Catching a Wave: Reclaiming Feminism for the 21st Century.* They write:

> We call this the "feminist free-for-all": under this rubric, feminism doesn't involve a set of core beliefs that one shares or goals that one works for, but instead involves claiming beliefs and ideas one day and discarding them the next, as they go in and out of fashion or as they become personally or intellectually difficult to sustain. This is the worst interpretation of bell hook's edict that "feminism is for everybody": it implies that anybody can be a feminist, regardless of her or his actions.[22]

One of the most telling examples of the *Ms.* editors' dilemma regarding an inclusive feminism came up with the May 1977 Jane Broderick cover story, focusing on Broderick's life as a Catholic, a stay-at-home mother of eight, and a self-proclaimed feminist. The editors chose to do a story on a homemaker due to the large number of housewife-reader complaints and "feeling left out accusations," as Letty Cottin Pogrebin described in an internal memo. The editors pondered at length the requests to do a story on traditional mothers; certainly, the magazine was filled with stories on raising children and marriage, but these all came from a point of view that challenged the conventional assumption of women's "proper" sphere. Pogrebin wrote that she thought homemaking was an "indulgence allowed to the few who can afford to choose it. So it's bullshit," she continued, "to evolve a series, column, or even one article that presents it through the eyes of the beleaguered Middle Class homemaker." She added that if they did such a piece, it needed to be "in-depth, not another 'it's okay to stay at home' try." In other words, Pogrebin argued for an honest debate and discussion about the implicit and explicit class and race issues that shape the life of a homemaker.

What the editors decided on—the Broderick story—was something quite different from what Pogrebin had initially argued for, perhaps because of the very divisiveness that she herself had recognized. In the story, Broderick was photographed in her crowded home; she recounted her endless housework, meals, laundry, and her exhaustion with her eighth pregnancy. Broderick also revealed that she thought of her husband as the "head of the household," and that she supported the Church's teachings on abortion and birth control. To the embarrassment of the editors, *Newsday* even picked up on Broderick's story and found out that she supported a constitutional ban on abortion. In subsequent issues, *Ms.* published letter after letter of readers criticizing Broderick's ideas, challenging her positions about women's proper role and reproductive duties.[23] What is so interesting about the editors' choice to include the Broderick story is that the story implicitly criticized the "stay at home Catholic mom," but the editors did not have to say this directly. Instead, they left the readers to decide if this really was feminism, while they continued to espouse a position that feminism was, as scholar bell hooks noted, "for everybody." As the internal debate among editors made clear, however, they were very cognizant of the fact that incorporating such a complex and sometimes opposing set of perspectives brought with it tremendous debate and discussion and often unsatisfactory solutions. Indeed, part of what made many of the founding editors stay with *Ms.* despite problems and the ongoing struggle to balance their own voices and perspectives on feminism, the desires of multiple readerships, and the demands of advertisers was this recognition that a mass media forum for the women's movement was a necessity.

It was the demands of advertisers that ultimately limited the ability of *Ms.* to espouse an inclusive feminism, despite the editors' best intentions. The founders of *Ms.*—Steinem, Carbine, and Harris—raised money from outside sources (Katherine Graham and Warner Corporation), sought help from already established magazines (*New York* magazine), and put together a business staff to solicit sufficient advertising both to support the magazine financially, and, hopefully, to fund a new foundation—the *Ms.* Foundation for Women. They set up guidelines about what kinds of advertising to accept— nothing that was for products harmful to women (e.g., no vaginal deodorant spray) and more ads for products that represented the full range of women's lives (e.g., more car, airline, and credit cards ads, none of which appeared in women's magazines prior to the publication of *Ms.*)

Although the original statements of purpose emphasized these guidelines, the ad staff found that advertisers were often very reluctant to advertise in a women's movement magazine, one whose goals were political rather than commercial. Advertisers like to buy space in a magazine that has a particular "niche" market; they like to "know" and to "buy" certain kinds of readers. In contrast, *Ms.* promised to speak to the full spectrum of U.S. women, from Midwestern homemakers to sophisticated urban working women; young women, old women, middle-aged women; women in high paying jobs as well as waitresses and hairdressers; even women in prison. The title of the magazine itself—*Ms.*—publicized the women's movement with a one-syllable word that refused to paint a definitive picture of the "typical reader." As the explanatory material in the first issue stated: "The use of Ms. isn't meant to protect either the married or the unmarried from social pressure—only to signify a female human being. It's symbolic, and important. There's a lot in a name."[24]

Moreover, ad staff found it very difficult to convince advertisers to buy space in a magazine that refused to shape editorial content to fit the advertising or rejected the complementary copy of recipes and makeovers that filled the pages of traditional advertising. Consequently, *Ms.* constantly had to compromise its original advertising guidelines to pull in sufficient revenue to continue reaching a mass audience. What the commercial context meant was that *Ms.* relied heavily on cigarette and alcohol advertising, despite its policy not to include products dangerous to women; it increasingly created special sections ("Beauty and Health" for instance) that served as a form of complementary copy; and it published covers designed to appeal to the kinds of moneyed and educated readers advertisers wanted. Compromising to cater to advertisers also meant that the text of *Ms.* often looked rather contradictory: ads for liquor next to articles on feminist environmentalism, and pages promoting consumer products next to articles on the feminization of poverty. From its origins, *Ms.* was an organization that made concessions to stay true to its larger mission: to provide a feminist magazine for women across the nation, one that would allow readers to feel connected to other feminists and would provide information and perspectives on the myriad of issues raised by the women's movement. The title of the internal report signed by editor Letty Cottin Pogrebin in the late 1970s summed up their approach well—"Compromises En Route to the Revolution."

Readers never easily acquiesced to these compromises, however. The commercial format both meant *Ms.* had large circulation (approximately 300,000 issues were sold each month with an estimated readership of over one million) and allowed *Ms.* to infiltrate the women's magazine genre that had been so resoundingly criticized as part of the oppression facing women. What the commercial context also meant was that the *advertising* that many readers found so offensive, as well as the editorial compromises that most readers did not like, even if they did not recognize them as such, were necessarily linked to advertisers' demands. In 1980, for instance, a reader from Massachusetts complained about the quality of the August issue, particularly what she termed the "silly" articles such as "Better Loving through Chemistry" and "The Chocolate Factor." She continued: "I'm too poor to own clothes that have to be dry cleaned, to travel alone, to be eligible for credit cards and to purchase tickets for plays, no matter if males or females are acting in the lead roles. I enjoyed as usual the book reviews and the Gazette, but the mascara, lipstick, liquor and cigarette ads obtruded on my enjoyment of even these sections. The selection of articles and ads tells me I am too poor and too serious to be a *Ms.* feminist. Perhaps I am too poor and too serious about feminist revolution to continue subscribing to the magazine. In the future, please do not trivialize our movement with such displays as the August issue. Remember, you are representing feminism to millions of people who consider *Ms.* the only feminist magazine."[25] The editorial files of *Ms.*, collected at the Sophia Smith Archives, demonstrate just how frustrating these editorial compromises were to the *Ms.* staff. They thwarted some of these advertisers' demands by publishing many critical letters about the advertising in the letters section and including a one-to-two page "No Comment" spread, in which readers sent offensive advertising. None of the offensive ads from *Ms.* itself were published until the magazine went advertising-free in the early 1990s, but the No Comment section nevertheless provided a critical edge to the published advertisements.

During the 1970s and 1980s, the *Ms.* staff dealt with constant struggles as they attempted to create a broad umbrella for feminism: Whose stories should be included? How do we represent sisterhood? From what perspectives should those stories be told? How do we create a diverse, fair, and feminist workplace? How do we reconcile the demands of advertisers, whose money was needed to fund a broad-based, mass-marketed magazine, with our mission to be a forum for all women? The history of *Ms.* suggests just how difficult—but also how promising—these issues were. *Ms.* discontinued publication as a commercial magazine in 1989. This was not at all due not to reader disinterest as the magazine maintained a subscription rate of 300,000–400,000 each issue. Advertisers, however, became increasingly unwilling to buy space in a political, "controversial" magazine whose foremost purpose was not to encourage readers to perceive themselves primarily as consumers, but to support their endeavors to be thinking, full human beings. The magazine reappeared in 1990, published as an advertising-free magazine, owned by Dale Lang Incorporated. When Lang decided to sell *Ms.* in the late 1990s, it was another major feminist organization in the United States, the Feminist Majority, that decided to buy the magazine, building on both of the institutions' reputations for coalition building.

In the twenty-first century, the magazine is published in both paper and online formats, and activists still look to the magazine to reflect accurately a full range of feminist positions and perspectives, which is probably the strongest evidence of the magazine's success in building connections among women.[26] Indeed, the history of *Ms.* is crucial to understand if we are to explore seriously how second-wave feminists dealt with diversity, hybrid identities, the complexities raised by commercial culture, and the desire to create a broad coalition of feminisms and feminists.

## Notes

1. Amy Erdman Farrell, *Yours in Sisterhood: Ms. Magazine and the Promise of Popular Feminism* (Chapel Hill: University of North Carolina Press, 1998); Wendy Kaminer, *A Fearful Freedom: Women's Flight from Equality* (Reading, Mass.: Addison-Wesley, 1990); Kate Roiphe, *The Morning After: Sex, Fear and Feminism on Campus* (Boston: Little, Brown and Co., 1993); *Ms.* magazine, Personal Report from *Ms.*, January 1973, 97.

2. Farrell, *Yours in Sisterhood,* 5.

3. For examples of such characterizations of second-wave feminism, see Rebecca Walker, *To Be Real: Telling the Truth and Changing the Face of Feminism* (New York: Anchor Books, 1995), esp. xxxii–xxxiii, and even Rory Dicker and Alison Piepmeier, *Catching a Wave: Reclaiming Feminism for the 21st Century* (Boston: Northeastern University Press, 2003), esp. 10. For a discussion of the way that second-wave feminism has become a "straw feminism," see Jennifer Purvis, "Grrrls and Women Together in the Third Wave: Embracing the Challenges of Intergenerational Feminism(s)," *NWSA Journal* 16 (2004): 93–123; Holly Near, *Imagine My Surprise,* Redwood Records, 1978.

4. Bernice Johnson Reagon, "Coalition Politics: Turning the Century," *Home Girls,* ed. Barbara Smith (Boston: Kitchen Table/Women of Color Press, 1983), 359.

5. *Ms.* magazine, "Personal Report from *Ms.,*" July 1973, p. 97.

6. Freda Kirchwey, "Woman's Magazine and Why," *The Suffragist* 9 (January/February 1921): 356; Betty Friedan, *The Feminine Mystique* (New York: W. W. Norton, 1963); Ginette Castro, *American Feminism: A Contemporary History,* Trans. Elizabeth Loverde-Bagwell (New York: New York University Press, 1990), esp. 189–91.

7. Carolyn Heilbrun, *The Education of a Woman: The Life of Gloria Steinem* (New York: The Dial Press, 1995); Onka Dekkers, "Periodicals," *off our backs*, September 1972, 19.

8. Farrell, *Yours in Sisterhood*, 45.

9. Farrell, *Yours in Sisterhood*, 160; Alice Echols in *Daring to Be Bad: Radical Feminism in America 1967–1975* (Minneapolis: University of Minnesota Press, 1989) provides an excellent historical account of how consciousness-raising groups worked within the early movement and the demands placed on the early groups to accommodate increasing numbers of women.

10. All the letters readers wrote to *Ms.*, with the exception of the letters written in response to the Spring 1972 Preview issue, are collected under the name of "*Ms.* Magazine Letters" at the Arthur and Elizabeth Schlesinger Library on the History of Women, Radcliffe College, Cambridge, Mass. Some of the letters are also available in the editorial records of the *Ms.* staff, which are collected under the name of "*Ms.* Magazine Records," Sophia Smith Collection, Smith College, Northampton, Mass.; Letter from reader, April 27, 1976, #90S-5, "L," *Ms.* Magazine Records.

11. Letter from reader, July 13, 1973, box 1, folder 3, *Ms.* Magazine Letters.

12. Anne Sisson Runyan and Mary V. Wenning, "Prospects for Renewed Feminist Activism in the Heartland: A Study of Daytonian Women's Politics," *National Women's Studies Association Journal* 16 (Fall 2004): 180–214; Judith Ezekiel, *Feminism in the Heartland* (Columbus: Ohio State University Press, 2002).

13. Letter from reader, December 16, 1972, box 1, folder 2, *Ms.* Magazine Letters.

14. Letter from reader, n.d. , box 1, folder 2, *Ms.* Magazine Letters.

15. For an excellent discussion of the role of the Internet for women's activism, see *Wired Women: Gender and New Realities in Cyberspace*, ed. Lynn Cherny and Elizabeth Reba Weise (Seattle: Seal Press, 1996).

16. Farrell, *Yours in Sisterhood*, 156–57.

17. Letter from reader, June 14, 1974, box 75, Ruth Sullivan's file, *Ms.* Magazine Records.

18. Letter from reader, April 29, 1980, box 7, folder 228, *Ms.* Magazine Letters.

19. Farrell, *Yours in Sisterhood*, 159.

20. Heilbrun, *The Education of a Woman*, 170–72; Gloria Steinem, *Outrageous Acts and Everyday Rebellions* (New York: Holt, Rinehart and Winston, 1983), 17–18.

21. Letter from reader, July 1, 1974, box 1, folder 5, *Ms.* Magazine Letters; Letter from reader, n.d., box 1, folder 5, *Ms.* Magazine Letters; Letter from reader, March 18, 1974, box 1, folder 9, *Ms.* Magazine Letters; Letter from reader, July 21, 1973, box 1, folder 2, *Ms.* Magazine Letters.

22. Dicker and Piepmeier, *Catching a Wave*, 17.

23. Farrell, *Yours in Sisterhood*, 76–77.

24. Farrell, *Yours in Sisterhood*, 32.

25. Letter from reader, July 11, 1980, box 7, folder 228, *Ms.* Magazine Letters.

26. For a discussion of how the expectations of *Ms.* to represent a diverse and inclusive feminism hold true even within an international context, please see Amy Farrell and Patrice McDermott, "Claiming Afghan Women: The Challenge of Human Rights Discourse for Transnational Feminism," in *Just Advocacy? Women's Human Rights, Transnational Feminism, and the Politics of Representation*, ed. Wendy Hesford and Wendy Kozol (New Brunswick: Rutgers University Press, 2005).

## 4. The Making of *Our Bodies, Ourselves*

### *Rethinking Women's Health and*
### *Second-Wave Feminism*

WENDY KLINE

In the spring of 2005, Simon and Schuster published *Our Bodies, Ourselves: A New Edition for a New Era.* "It's hard to believe that thirty-five years have passed since we first gathered around our kitchen tables to create *Our Bodies, Ourselves,*" the founders of the Boston Women's Health Book Collective (BWHBC) remark in the introduction. "What we couldn't have foreseen then was that our book would help create a women's health movement and radically change the way many people think about health care. Nor could we have known that the book's great success would generate a need for an ongoing women's health organization in which, over the next three decades, some of us would remain active as board or staff members."[1]

The collective authors are not alone in their belief that the book had an enormous impact on women's health and feminism. Many more women vividly recall reading the book for the first time in the 1970s. "It felt biblical," remembers Joanne Williams, when she discovered the book in a Denver bookstore in 1974 at the age of twenty-seven. "I remember just sitting down with it and almost reading it completely through the first night of the weekend I had it."[2] Historian Estelle Freedman remembers that her best friend from childhood sent it to her in 1972 or 1973, when she was twenty-five. "I immediately sat and read through the book and felt a shift in my world view," she recalls. "Some of my housemates asked what I was reading and there was clearly a sense that it was subversive in some way!"[3] By 2005, the book's message appeared more conventional than subversive, in large part because of its long-term success, measurable by the number of similar self-help texts that now line the shelves of popular bookstores. A new generation of women has been raised with new expectations and awareness of female bodies and health, as mothers and mentors passed along the book's message.

Given the complexities and fragmentation within the feminist movement in the late-twentieth-century United States, how did the BWHBC remain a vibrant source of information about health and sexuality to female readers over the past thirty-five years? The formation and development of the collective in the 1970s, as well as the group's relationship with its readers, help to explain its longevity.[4] By exploring the ways in which the group and its followers struggled to maintain a collective ethos during the first two decades, this chapter challenges us to rethink the organizational and geographic boundaries of feminism. In this particular example, the self-conscious desire of feminist writers and readers to create an accurate, accessible text on women's health allowed for widespread coalition building, far beyond the doors of the collective's Boston office.

Women's health emerged as a major social and political issue in a turbulent decade, affected by the antiestablishment sentiment of the student movement, a crisis in health care, and women's liberation. By the late 1960s, women inspired by the civil rights movement and the demand for equal citizenship created a new wave of feminist activism.[5] Though a fragmented movement (historians refer to several branches of feminism, including liberal, socialist, radical, cultural, and multiracial),[6] one unifying characteristic has been the claim that the personal is political. By challenging the divide between the two, feminists asserted that the most private aspects of their identity—relationships, sexuality, health, and family life—were indeed political issues.[7] Ideas and personal experiences, rather than goals or strategies, united a broad range of women who came to identify themselves as feminists. Women's liberation, according to Sara Evans, depended "on the ability of women to tell each other their own stories, to claim them as the basis of political action."[8] For many, these stories and their political implications emerged through consciousness raising, a process in which the sharing of personal stories led to a "click"—a sudden recognition and clarity that sexism lay at the root of their struggles.[9] Coined by early members of New York Radical Women, consciousness raising became "an intense form of collective self-education."[10]

Part of this collective self-education was women's health. The women's health movement was a grassroots campaign that used a wide range of strategies to increase women's power over their own bodies, including alternative health care organizations, advocacy, and education.[11] By 1974, there were over twelve hundred women's groups providing health services in the United States, indicating the early success of the feminist health movement. Other groups worked through legislative channels to ensure protection and services, from abortion to the Food and Drug Administration's regulation of contraception.[12] As more and more women became active consumers in the health care industry, they sought out accurate, easy-to-understand information on women's health.

Such information became available through women's health literature. The first and most comprehensive book to provide information about women's health and sexuality was *Our Bodies, Ourselves.*[13] Beginning as a 130-page newsprint manual in 1970, this comprehensive book on women's health was by 2005 an 832-page treatise (complete with a companion Web site) that had sold over four million copies and had been translated and/or culturally adapted into eighteen different languages. This success was not inevitable; internal divisions and outside conflict in the early years threatened the stability of the collective and its publications. Despite the group's "growing pains," a passion for and commitment to women's health enabled it to persevere.

In May of 1969, Emmanuel College in Boston hosted a female liberation conference. This in and of itself was not so unusual: "women's liberation" had erupted in major cities beginning in 1967, and had introduced consciousness raising as a formative process by which women could explore the political aspects of personal life. However, what made this particular weekend conference significant was a two-hour workshop on Sunday afternoon, called "women and their bodies." The twelve participants, some of whom had never before been in any kind of women's group, spent their time sharing stories of frustration and anger about experiences at the doctor. They resolved to continue meeting after the conference, calling themselves the "doctor's group," with the idea that they would create a list of "reasonable" obstetrician gynecologists in the Boston area. (By reasonable, they meant doctors who listened to the patient, respected her opinions, and explained procedures and medications.)[14]

They quickly discovered, however, that they were unable to put together such a list—and, more importantly, that the women who attended the workshop shared a desire to learn as much as possible about their bodies and their health. So they decided on a summer project. Each member would research a topic of personal importance about their bodies and bring the information back to the group. Group members would then share personal experiences related to this topic. "In this way," they later explained, "the textbook view of childbirth or miscarriage or menstruation or lovemaking, nearly always written by men, would become expanded and enriched by the truth of our actual experiences. It was an exciting process."[15]

The following winter, the "doctors group"—now calling themselves the "Women and Their Bodies group"—offered several evening courses in the Boston area, each lasting ten to twelve weeks.[16] In the first course alone, over forty women signed up to learn what this group had uncovered over the summer and fall in their quest to learn more about women's bodies. The group intended to offer a formal presentation at each meeting, followed by discussions, but the participants were so engaged and energized that the sessions quickly turned into a total-discussion format. The workshop leaders promptly updated their original research and mimeographed their findings so that others could teach similar courses. "The papers in and of themselves are not very important," they explained. "They should be viewed as a tool which stimulates discussion and action, which allows for new ideas and for change."[17]

As the number of topics and papers increased over the year, the group decided to publish them in an inexpensive newsprint volume. "They are not final. They are not static," explained the authors, who now called themselves the Boston Women's Health Course Collective. "They are meant to be used by our sisters to increase consciousness about ourselves as women, to build our movement, to begin to struggle collectively for adequate health care, and in many other ways they can be useful to you."[18] In December 1970, the small movement publisher New England Free Press published 5,000 copies of *Women and Their Bodies* at a cost of $1,500, selling it for 75 cents. In April 1971, the press published 15,000 more copies, reduced the price to 30 cents to make it affordable to a larger number of women, and changed the name to *Women and Our Bodies,* then finally *Our Bodies, Ourselves.*[19]

After eleven printings and 225,000 copies, the women decided to publish a revised expanded version with Simon and Schuster under the name of the BWHBC. This was one of the most difficult decisions the group ever made, and the first that was by vote, not consensus. Ultimately, they decided to go with a commercial press because they wanted to get the book out as quickly as possible to women in more places, women who would not have had access to the Free Press edition: "We feel a tremendous sense of urgency. . . . We want the book to reach women who don't ordinarily come in contact with movement publications," they explained. "We have a sense of the women's movement becoming larger and more unified than it is now."[20] With the aid of a lawyer, they successfully negotiated a contract that "proved to be nothing short of phenomenal," included complete editorial control, and offered bulk discounts for women's clinics.[21]

The distributors and copublishers at the New England Free Press were, not surprisingly, opposed to the collective's decision. "We at the Free Press feel strongly that 'Our Bodies, Our Selves' should continue to be distributed through the Movement where it will help build a socialist women's consciousness," they wrote at the end of the eleventh printing. "Women are now getting the book from political people and organizations they trust. This makes the book part of a personal process of political education. Selling the book through capitalist distributors in bookstores or even supermarkets will only impede that process." Both the collective and the publishers thanked those who had written letters supporting their side of the controversy. The publishers claimed that most responses "have supported our position in this matter, which is heartening." However, the authors disagreed, stressing that letters received "give us a good sense of who the book is reaching so that we're not just talking among ourselves." One college student in Oberlin, Ohio, supported their decision, explaining, "I can tell you that you are doing all of us a service by publishing so a wider audience can be reached. If any book is important to have widely read, it's yours."[22]

The commercial success of the book, which stunned its authors, brought new demands: public relations, financial matters, book distribution, international rights, and revisions. As the nature of the tasks changed by the mid-1970s, so did the group dynamics. Members began to question whether the original group structure could survive these changes. "The initial success of our wonderful book has passed," reflected Joan in the fall of 1974, "and we are personally and collectively trying to answer the question—where do we go from here?"[23] Although the group commonly disagreed on a number of issues, they shared a concern that the collective was disintegrating. "Our fear is that the group will fall apart without our agreeing to that," Nancy, Joan, and Ruth wrote later that year. "Obviously we don't want that to happen. Okay, what are we going to do (because we gotta do something)!!!?"[24]

Fear and frustration generated a dialogue among collective members over the next two years about the past, present, and future of the BWHBC. As they moved beyond their initial goal of teaching and publishing *Our Bodies, Ourselves,* they questioned their commitment to feminism, women's health activism, and each other. Factions within the collective, individual needs, outside obligations and interests, and time constraints all affected group dynamics. Given the number of women's groups that did not survive these internal divisions, it is not surprising that the BWHBC suffered its share of struggles. Yet the ways in which they characterized their particular fears about the group's future help to explain how they survived. Most felt they had too much invested in the project to give up. Nancy expressed her eagerness "for us to all come together and hug and fight and get on with another stage in our growing."[25]

Though the group was used to disagreements and conflicts, these appeared to intensify in the summer of 1974. Many lamented the lack of a clear working structure. Meetings were poorly attended and rarely started on time. "It's hard for us to say this because it scares us," wrote three members. "Therefore we hold on to our old group process—however haphazard—because it seems better than nothing. Or it has seemed that way, but it's clearer to us that it's more frustrating than effective now." These three attributed some of the problems to the growing tasks that the collective faced. "The problem is," they wrote, "how can we maintain ourselves as the casual and loving collective we are, take care of each of our individual needs, and still accomplish professional tasks which demand lots of time and energy?"[26] Determining the boundaries between emotional and professional support proved challenging at times.

Similar concerns emerged during the following summer. "I feel out of touch," wrote Jane. "Do other people feel this way?" Continuing the "where do we go from here?" questions, she asked, "What do we each want to do outside of the group and within the group? Do we all want to do one thing or several things? . . . Are we as involved in the group as we were when we were working on the book?" For Jane, the group, beyond the book, was crucial. "I want the feeling of process to continue. I want to feel I am growing as a person within the group. I want to feel the joy of really contacting all of you when we are together."[27] How could the BWHBC move forward in a way that benefited members individually and the group as a whole? Was the success of the collective based on providing emotional support or professional success, or both?

Herein lay the problem. No one could agree on which aspect was most important: individual needs, group needs, or professional goals. By 1976, the group had fractured further over what the group's professional goals should be. The drama centered on the development of the "parenting project": a goal on the part of four members to write a book on parenting on behalf of the collective. As these four began to meet separately and form their own agenda for the book (to be entitled *Ourselves and Our Children*), other members felt alienated and became wary of the breakdown in communications.

Judy articulated it first in April of 1976. In a letter to all members, she expressed concern over the group's "lack of a more 'formal' communications mechanism." She realized that for months she had been completely unaware of the parenting group's plans. "I think that three, or four, or even five of us cannot really duplicate the process that was such an important part of doing *OBOS*."[28] Others chimed in, stressing the need for accountability, given that the new book would claim the name and spirit of the original book. Could a subgroup of the collective speak for all of them? "How much control should the nonparenting people in the *OBOS* collective have over the project, which is being presented in their name?" asked Wendy. "If others in the group do not agree with some of our process and content, how can the disagreement be dealt with in the most positive way?"[29]

Those not involved in the parenting project felt concerned that they did not express their reservations earlier in the process. They had been excluded from meetings during fall, winter, and spring of 1975–76. Addressing the parenting group, Wendy wrote, "I realize that you felt that when others came sporadically to meetings, it was hard to get down to work. Also, in our collective only the four of you felt deeply committed to the project and had the time to put into it. At that point, however, I wish we had all had the wisdom to see that this might cause problems." The result was, in Wendy's words, "an unfortunate inside-outside dynamic which left several members of the larger group feeling left out."[30]

But Norma felt that the "sense of split, the we/they of which Wendy wrote so sensitively, has actually been a reality for a long time." She believed, in fact, that the parenting project was "simply a manifestation" of a larger shift in focus, as the work energy of the group drifted away from its original goals. The problem, as Norma articulated it, was that the group was *so* close that it was difficult for individual members "to realize the precise ways in which our work energies have diverged, almost irrevocably." Trying to balance individual needs, emotional needs as a group, and professional needs as a group was proving to be quite a challenge. Norma continued:

> For me personally, the business of looking at the reality (and unreality) of the splits, in both group work energy and direction and personal career direction, VERSUS the personal relationships in our group as a support group and a personal group of the most intimate kind, is our very first task. If we can do this, really look at it and see it the way it is, I think we can solve the rest of our problems; because I think re-affirming our solidarity as a group has been the source of our ability to solve other problems in the past. After all, even when we were unanimous in committing our work energies to women's health, we were far from unanimous at all times on the precise form that commitment should take. It took time to work out.[31]

An open acknowledgment of the inevitable challenges involved in collective work undoubtedly helped repair some of the damage and ultimately reaffirmed their commitments to collective politics.

However, although members attempted to encourage and support each other, they also feared that these conflicts, however lovingly expressed, signaled the decline of the collective. In the same letter that Norma expressed her love and commitment to the group, she also warned against the dangers of letting their affection blind them. She perceived the collective as a family, but believed it to be "inherently impossible for a family to be both encouraging to the growth of everyone in it and still at the same time produce work with which every member can feel deeply identified."[32] Could the collective mature in such a way that all members continued to feel fulfilled? Could the passion for parenting that some members felt be translated into an effective sequel to *Our Bodies, Ourselves*—even if not all members shared that vision? What would it mean if the product did not speak for everyone in the collective?

For those concerned with the direction of the parenting project by 1976, more than just a new book was at stake. "The process by which the book was (is) being produced is contrary to, is a denial of the collective group spirit which we have so clearly articulated, and on which our own processes and our very reputation is built," explained Norma. Three or four authors were simply not enough; the real power that the book could have had "was missed because we were not really attempting to reflect a broad reality." As pioneers of the women's health movement whose work had resonated with so many readers, they had an obligation to continue speaking to as wide an audience as possible. She warned, "if our book fails to do that it will not simply be too bad; it has the power to disillusion and disappoint literally millions of people, their faith in the women's movement, in our collective, in the power of the collective process, in the courage of people to really confront their social reality—the implications are enormous."[33]

Joan, a member of the parenting group, felt it was important to acknowledge the challenge that they faced. "We all have to agree that the *OBOS* project was a magical event and probably will never be reproduced by ourselves or anyone else. In developing our book we developed a tool for consciousness raising that has touched the hearts and minds of women all over the world," she wrote. However, it raised expectations in intimidating ways. "Clearly this is a hard act to follow and it is realistic to assume that no project that we develop will have as great an appeal and impact as *OBOS* did."[34]

Indeed, Joan was right. *Ourselves and Our Children* created some interest when it was published by Random House in 1978, but did not enjoy the broad appeal—or sales—of the first book. Their editor noted by April of 1979 that sales were "sluggish" (approximately 130,000 sold in the first five months).[35] Reviews were mixed; while the *Library Journal* declared it "the definitive book on parenting," others found it far less innovative than *Our Bodies, Ourselves*.[36] For some readers, the emphasis on the roles of fathers as well as mothers diluted the empowering feminist political ideology they came to expect with *Our Bodies, Ourselves*. Even though the parenting group continued to meet into the 1980s with the intention of revising the book, they never completed the task and the book is now out of print. Despite this letdown, the BWHBC persevered and continued to debate the role of parenting in their long-term goals. One even proposed a new book, *Our Bodies, Ourselves, Our Children,* suggesting a desire to effectively merge the two projects. Such a merger, however, proved impossible, leading Judy to comment somewhat defensively, "Given how little built-in overview and communication between the groups there has been, it's amazing that things have gone as well as they have."[37]

By creating something new and controversial within the collective, the parenting group also generated a debate about what had been so unique about the first book. "*OBOS* was not a book that we 'made' happen," Wendy reflected. "It was part of a large groundswell movement, much larger than us. We were in some sense privileged to be there at the right time, although who we are certainly played a vital role in its getting put together and shared in such an effective way."[38] Norma agreed. "We have often said with genuine pride and humility that any women could have written our book, it just happened to be us," she wrote to the group. "Terrific as we are, I have a strong need to believe that, because it implies that we are accountable to the feelings and experience of that wider world of women out there, that we are simply a filter or a reflecting pool for those other women's lives."[39]

That sense of accountability, which shaped the concerns about the parenting project, was not limited to collective authors. In their desire to reflect that "wider world of women out there" (in Norma's words), they welcomed their audience into the conversation. In the first editions of the book, writing was under the direction of the twelve-person BWHBC, but included other voices. "Many, many other women have worked with us on the book," they explained in the 1973 preface. "A group of gay women got together specifically to do the chapter on lesbianism. Other papers were done still differently. . . . Other women contributed thoughts, feelings and comments as they passed through town or passed through our kitchens or workrooms. There are still other voices from letters, phone conversations, a variety of discussions, etc., that are included in the chapters as excerpts of personal experiences."[40]

Including as many voices and stories as possible turned out to be crucial. One of the authors, Susan Bell, recalls the challenge of translating medical information to nonspecialists. The authors themselves were outsiders to the medical field; their role was to understand and interpret medical information in a way that would speak to as many women as possible. When revising the chapter on birth control in 1984, Bell had to attempt "to see from and speak to the perspectives of teenagers, single women, women of color, poor women, women with disabilities, and women without health insurance (and so forth) without falling into the trap of believing I could 'be' simultaneously in all, or wholly in any, of these subjugated positions."[41]

How, then, could she attempt to speak for such a broad spectrum of women? "One way out of this trap lies in positioning, opening up the process of knowledge construction to diverse perspectives by being attentive and responsible to other people," she acknowledged.[42] The collective could not claim to represent all women, but by including their stories, it could speak to a more diverse body of women. In her study of the impact of *Our Bodies, Ourselves* on global feminism, sociologist Kathy Davis noted that "it was the method of knowledge sharing and not a shared identity as women which appeared to have a global appeal."[43]

Indeed, letters from American readers suggest that although not all women identified with the tone or content of every chapter of the book, it still had enormous appeal. Written at a time when feminists stressed the power and importance of consciousness raising, it confirmed that women's liberation depended on such knowledge sharing. As the collective authors declared, "knowledge is power," and personal stories were a crucial aspect of that knowledge. *Our Bodies, Ourselves* offered a level of intimacy that encouraged readers to respond to its text. At the suggestion of the authors (who solicited feedback for book revisions in magazines such as *Ms.*) or of their own accord, over two hundred women wrote to the collective in the 1970s and 1980s to share stories, seek advice, chastise, or praise. They commented on what was helpful, what was vague, what made sense, and what was missing, on subjects ranging from dental care to diaphragms. These letters leave many questions unanswered; names and addresses have been blacked out and most do not reveal the writer's economic, racial, or educational background.[44] Viewed as a whole, however, they suggest both the appeal of the book and the expectations it engendered. Because readers strongly identified with the book (or at least the idea behind it), they believed their own experiences should be represented or accounted for in the text. The emotional expressiveness of the letters reveals readers' desires to be part of a virtual community of health feminists, from locations across the United States. Indeed, reader input helped shape revisions of the book and explain its longevity.

The responses from readers also tell us something more broadly about the development of feminist ideas and communities.[45] Women did not have to be actively involved in an organized group of feminists, or even in a consciousness-raising group, to participate in the movement.[46] Because many women did not have access to these groups (demand far outstripped available resources), they turned to reading *Our Bodies, Ourselves* as a consciousness-raising resource. Lisa Maria Hogeland argues that feminism can be understood as a form of literacy, a set of "reading and interpretive strategies that people who identified themselves as feminists applied to texts and to the world around them."[47] Feminist community was a "fantasy" that could be explored in complete geographic isolation.[48] "If not in a group," she argues, "then presumably one experienced the collective speaking of women's experiences in the activities of reading and writing."[49]

Certainly, that was the case with *Our Bodies, Ourselves*, where reading was often described as a revelatory experience—as a click that drew them out of isolation and into a widespread dialogue about feminism and health. "When I realize how similar my feelings are to some of the letters in your book, it is indeed reassuring," one reader confided.[50] Establishing connections by reading personal accounts enabled readers to experience consciousness raising at their own kitchen tables. They did not have to join a feminist organization or a self-help group to recognize their oppression in the stories of others. "I was overwhelmed by the support I felt in all the information you gave me," another reader wrote. "What I felt then as skepticism about the women's movement vanished and my lonely farm-housewife lifestyle became a step in a steady progression of changes."[51] One particularly enthusiastic reader declared: "Let me tell you I love your books! They make me feel great reading them—like I'm really a part of something bigger than myself!"[52]

By its very formation, then, *Our Bodies, Ourselves* encouraged readers to respond to its contents. It provoked passionate letters filled with heartfelt personal accounts of infections, miscarriages, depression, and disability. Some were humorous, and some were angry. Some readers wrote in the name of sisterhood, but others were simply scared. Together, their responses reveal that readers were active agents who identified women's health as a crucial component of feminism. From Maine to Montana, readers transcended traditional geographical and organizational boundaries of feminism, simply by reading and responding to the book.

For example, Brenda described herself as "trying desperately to find a cure for vaginitis." Not knowing where else to turn, she had contacted the collective back in March of 1979 in the hopes they could put her in touch with one of the female gynecologists quoted in the book. So far, she had had no luck with doctors; the first was "sarcastic" and "ridiculed the fact that I was concerned about the problem." So she left him. "I pity everybody who still goes and sees that particular man. (And I frankly hope he gets an itch one day!)" Her second doctor prescribed the antibacterial drug Flagyl, and although she had a bad reaction, she was told to finish taking the pills, and the nausea stayed with her for over two months.[53]

She wrote the collective again in September of 1979 with a positive update.

She had found a new doctor—"a gynecologist from the Old World, with a great bedside manner." He suggested cotton underwear, gentle detergents, and eating yogurt, and so far, it was working. "By voicing my concern to others, I was shocked to hear how many people had had (or were having) similar problems, and that they didn't know who to turn to also, or were equally irritated and depressed by their doctors' impatience." For this reason, she hoped her information might help others, speaking to a common desire for dependable, sympathetic doctors. "Perhaps the problem *is* very common, but the patient suffers enough living with it day after day, for a 'dumb' doctor not to have sympathy. As I told one of the doctors I dropped, '*I* itch; you don't.'"[54]

Many women wrote the collective to express appreciation for the encouragement the book provided or to share advice (as Brenda did), but others wrote out of anger when they did not find the support they had come to expect. Encouraged by the text itself to "demand answers and explanations from the people you come in contact with for medical care,"[55] some interpreted this to include not only doctors, but also the authors of *Our Bodies, Ourselves.* As a result, the members of BWHBC found themselves as mediators between organized medicine and female readers. They faced the difficult task of going into enemy territory—the medical establishment—and attempting to divorce medical "facts" from their assumed misogynist context. However, as these reader responses attest, the boundaries between medical facts and misogyny were never entirely clear. Nor was the exact role of BWHBC authors in bridging the gap between organized medicine and female patients.

A series of letters exchanged between Sarah and author Norma Swenson in 1979 demonstrates the collective authors' struggle to translate medical knowledge effectively to their readership. It began in February when Sarah wrote, "I have trusted you and learned much from your book in the past. But having spent the last year trying to conceive a child, and coming up with nothing, and then a Class 3 pap smear, the cause of which has not been terribly easy to find out, the last thing I need is a statement like the one I tripped over on page 147."[56] She was referring to the discussion of D&C (dilation and curettage) in a chapter on medical health problems. Sarah's abnormal pap smear suggested the possibility of cervical cancer, and her doctors recommended a D&C and possibly conization (removing a cone of tissue from the cervix during the procedure). She returned home and immediately picked up her copy of *Our Bodies, Ourselves* to learn more about it. The 1979 edition concluded the discussion of D&C by stating that conization "may lead to complications in future pregnancies."[57] Her reaction to that sentence was so powerful that she described it to the collective in not one, but two different letters. Already feeling cheated, she stated that she "got to the line that said conizations might lead to complications in pregnancy. New paragraph. You didn't tell me *what* complications. *The* book didn't tell me; it just added another layer of mystery and innuendo. I hate veiled warnings, vague threats—just tell me what the options are, or the facts. I know enough to worry, but not enough to answer my own questions. . . . Before you and your book there was nothing, but still. . . .[58] Angrily, she demanded that the collective take responsibility; she ended her letter by stating "your part in the trauma of the last few days will long be remembered."[59]

For Sarah, the one publication she thought she could rely on had failed her. This was a serious charge; her trauma stemmed not only from her bout with an irregular pap smear and the threat of cervical cancer, and not only from the medical response, but from the book's "vague threats." The book had the potential to join the enemy, to become part of the problem rather than the solution. Concern about cooptation and "selling out" was common among women's health advocates by the mid-1970s as feminist health was becoming a lucrative business.[60] Indeed, many were opposed when the collective opted to leave the New England Free Press and publish with Simon and Schuster in 1973 for the same reason. Sarah's letter suggests an attempt to shore up the boundaries between feminist women's health and what she and others believed to be a misogynist medical establishment.

Coauthor Norma Swenson responded carefully, sensitive to the charge. "We are really sorry that you found our section on conization in relating to pregnancy upsetting and unhelpful." She admitted that there was no way of knowing who had written the passage, but accepted full responsibility. Without knowledge of authorship, culpability had to be shared by all members of the collective.

Swenson made it clear that the authors faced quite a challenge when discussing and analyzing medical treatment. "One of the problems we constantly stumble over as we try to research medical practice," explained Swenson, "is that habits of treatment and prognosis get established with very little real evidence. . . . In sharing this kind of information with women, we want to be sure to include as much as we can of what is known, while at the same time leaving women some room to question and challenge the dogma about themselves and their conditions." However, according to some readers, too much room remained. "I wouldn't have sensed how unhelpful our sentence was if you hadn't shown us," Swenson acknowledged. "I'm not sure how to fix it, but you can be sure we'll make some modification next time around. We'll also try to do more research."[61] Indeed, the statement was omitted in the next edition and replaced with a more specific description of what the potential complications are and why they happen.

Sarah was clearly moved by Swenson's response, calling it a "generous" letter. In the "relative calm of early summer," she was able to reflect upon her experience. "I don't blame anyone for that open-ended response; I just wish it hadn't been written," she noted and then added, "(except that there are definitely good points to this correspondence)." The dialogue, which Sarah now cast in a positive light, had begun directly from the text (because Sarah believed it did not speak adequately to her) and had expanded into a warm exchange of ideas and explanations. "I probably wrote initially partly because it matters to me what your book says," Sarah explained. "By writing it you stuck your and our necks out, and I want us to look good, since efforts like these are still scrutinized so closely."[62] Like other readers, Sarah perceived *Our Bodies, Ourselves* as a broader collective in which the readers as well as the writers all shared responsibility for the outcome.

It may seem surprising that feminist readers would direct their hostility toward the BWHBC rather than at what they believed to be misogynist medicine. Yet Amy Farrell locates a similar trend in the relationship between the readers and editors of *Ms.* magazine during this time. As Farrell argues, readers "forged strong yet volatile ties" with the magazine, both identifying with it, but also insisting it "live up to its promise as a resource for the women's movement."[63]

In the case of women's health, an erosion of trust with the medical establishment created critical consumers. These consumers were more willing to critique those feminist texts that claimed to speak for all women; they saw it as crucial that their particular perspective or experience was included in such a text. Indeed, the most common complaint of readers who wrote to the collective had to do with their sense of exclusion. Readers expected to find themselves described within the pages and expressed confusion, disappointment, frustration, or anger if they did not. Although the women's health movement had the potential to cut across racial and class boundaries, argued feminist scholars Barbara Ehrenreich and Deirdre English in 1973, it would become only "'some women's health movement' unless the diversity of women's priorities were taken into account."[64] Over time, readers ensured that such diversity was reflected in *Our Bodies, Ourselves*.

Surprisingly, one of the most fundamental categories of exclusion—namely, race—does not emerge from the letters.[65] Yet many women have voiced their concern in other venues about the book's limited treatment of race and more generally, the ways in which white women had paid scant attention to the specific health needs and perspectives of women of color. Sheryl Ruzek noted in 1978 that the women's health movement remained "largely white and middle class—especially in leadership and in focus."[66] African American health activist Byllye Avery recalled that "white women had no idea about certain issues affecting black women."[67] For this reason, she spearheaded a national grassroots project on black women's health, with the support of the National Women's Health Network.[68] At the BWHBC, racial tensions erupted in the 1990s; in 1997, four BWHBC staff members resigned, arguing that the organization refused to "grapple honestly with racism and issues of power with respect to the women of color within the organization."[69] Sociologist Kathy Davis notes that these were "turbulent years" for BWBHC as they struggled to diversify and experienced tension similar to that of other predominantly white feminist organizations created in the 1970s.

Collective authors acknowledged this painful transition in the next edition of the book, *Our Bodies, Ourselves for the New Century* (1998):

> While it is exciting that this book stays alive, growing and changing, the process of becoming more inclusive has been difficult and painful at times. For example, like many groups initially formed by white women, we have struggled against society's, and our own, internalized presumption that middle-class white women are representative of all women and thus have the right to define women's health issues and set priorities. This assumption does a great injustice by ignoring and silencing the voices of women of color, depriving us all of hard-won wisdom and crucial, life-saving information. This time around, many more women of color have been involved in creating the book, writing some of the chapters, and editing and critically reading every chapter. During this process, tensions sometimes arose about what to include or leave out and how to frame certain issues. The resulting vigorous discussions have greatly enriched the book's content. But as in any organic process, some conflicts still remain to be resolved.[70]

The most divisive issue that the collective struggled with in reader correspondence and revisions during the early years of the book's existence was lesbianism, an issue that divided many feminists in the 1970s.[71] So many women wrote letters in response to the lesbian chapter that *The New Our Bodies, Ourselves* gave special thanks to the hundreds of women "all over the country telling about their experiences and asking for advice, news, contacts, support."[72] Although many respondents were enthusiastic, they also pushed for more material. "What I most wanted to comment on was the assumption of heterosexuality throughout the book," wrote Barbara. "There is a way that even though lesbianism is acknowledged as an option for women, it is still ghettoized in the one chapter and male-female relationships become the norm throughout."[73]

In the New England Free Press edition, the sixteen-page chapter on sexuality had just over one page on homosexuality. By the 1973 Simon and Schus-

ter edition, it was the subject of an entire eighteen-page chapter, entitled
"In Amerika They Call Us Dykes" and written by women involved in gay
liberation. Conflict between the collective and the lesbian authors of "In
Amerika" was apparent in the published introduction of the chapter. "We
had no connection with the group that was writing the rest of the book . . .
and in fact we disagreed, and still do, with many of their opinions," wrote the
lesbian authors. The collective clarified its position with a footnote linked
to the chapter's title: "Since the gay collective insisted on complete control
over the style and content of this chapter, the Health Book Collective has
not edited it. Because of length limitations, however, the gay collective has
had to leave out much material that they feel is important."[74] In meeting
minutes and memos of the mid-to-late 1970s, the collective authors made it
clear that they were not happy with some of the content and the title of the
article. Based on reader feedback "from both gay and straight women," they
recognized that the chapter "gives only part of a picture," and that it needed to
be "balanced out in some way (with input from older women, poor women,
women with a longer experience of living a gay life, etc.)." They also felt that
the title was problematic; Wendy argued, "someone who isn't a lesbian and
who is fearful might feel pushed away." She suggested alternatives, including
"Loving Women: Lesbian Life" (which eventually became part of the title
in a later edition with different authors), but the gay collective insisted on
keeping the original title.[75]

Internal meeting notes reveal that by 1978 there was a great deal of frustration about how to integrate material on lesbianism into the next edition.
When the collective attempted to revise the chapter, the gay women rejected
the changes, instead asking for more space (sixty manuscript pages instead of
thirty-five). After a divisive meeting with them, one collective member proposed stopping the writing process entirely until the disputes were resolved,
despite the upcoming revisions deadline imposed by Simon and Schuster.
Some resented the fact that although "the gay women haven't been part of our
process, we spend our precious hours talking about the gay chapter." Finally,
at midnight, the collective resolved to limit the gay paper to fifty manuscript
pages and to explain in the revised edition that "they weren't with us writing
other chapters and they feel other chapters don't reflect them."[76]

However, readers continued to complain. "I'm a Lesbian, which means that
only about 1/3 of the book applies to me," wrote Maggie in 1982. "Now I'm sure
you've had it suggested many times before that the rest of the book should
integrate lesbianism more thoroughly," she chided. "These things should be
obvious in 1982—every section except 'In Amerika' assumes the heterosexuality of the reader." Even "In Amerika" had problems. Although it was "very

influential" in her coming out, and was "probably the most well read piece of Lesbian literature in the English language," it was "completely out of date now." She was sorry to see it go (note her assumption that it would not make it into the next edition) because it exuded the excitement of the beginnings of an important movement: "It would be hard to find someone to write a new one who would seem, like these Lesbians did, to be sharing something new which they were just putting together themselves for the first time."[77]

Maggie's assumption was correct; "In Amerika" did not survive the next edition. "Loving Women: Lesbian Life and Relationships" replaced the former chapter and was authored by the "Lesbian Revisions Group." None had worked on the original piece; in fact, "it provided crucial support and inspiration for several of us when we first came out as lesbians." They had written a chapter "quite different in focus and tone from the original one, using briefer stories so as to make room for more topics." This time around, the collective authors' footnote linked to the chapter title was more conciliatory: "Although this edition of *Our Bodies, Ourselves* includes lesbian voices throughout, the collective decided also to have a separate chapter for a more careful focus on issues and information which specifically affect lesbians."[78] *The New Our Bodies, Ourselves* thus incorporated the suggestions and concerns of lesbian readers. However, it and later editions also revealed tensions within the text, underscoring the most basic challenge to the movement: there simply was no universally shared perspective on women's health.

When the BWHBC urged women to gain control of their bodies beginning in the 1970s, they were also, in the words of scholar Catharine Stimpson, assigning "extraordinary moral weight to the body."[79] Along with collective authors, women readers from all over the country contributed to that assignment by articulating very specific ways to reclaim their bodies. They became part of a widespread network of women determined to rethink the relationship between gender and medicine. Their stories challenge us to consider the role of ordinary women in shaping the development of the women's health movement. Since the first "women and their bodies" workshop in 1969, participants in the movement, broadly defined, have struggled to make knowledge about women's health accessible to all women. What they discovered early on was that even within a small group of white, Boston-based feminists, perspectives and experiences could differ radically. Attempting to make all decisions by consensus and include all women's voices proved impossible. However the commitment to try, to see themselves inextricably bound as a family where everyone's individual needs would not always be met, resulted in a more powerful and accessible book.

The book was influenced not only by the formal collective but also by readers who participated in a dialogue about women's health. By challenging the
writers of *Our Bodies, Ourselves* on a number of points, readers influenced
the way in which collective authors, in the words of one of them, "translated science to the people." Confrontational letters to the collective reveal
readers' expectations and assumptions about how women's health should
be portrayed, as well as their desire to have their perspectives included. By
demanding greater inclusion and diversity within the text, these readers
ensured that *Our Bodies, Ourselves* would continue to be read by generations
of women. These exchanges between collective authors and readers reveal a
virtual community of activists who shaped the feminist health movement.
The conflicts expressed in letters—over how to define women's health, the
inclusion of lesbians, and other issues—were experienced by many second-
wave feminist organizations. Yet these very tensions—coupled with the fact
that they made their way into revisions of the text—allowed *Our Bodies,
Ourselves* to prosper decades after the second wave.

## Notes

1. Boston Women's Health Book Collective, *Our Bodies, Ourselves: A New Edition for
a New Era* (New York: Simon and Schuster, 2005), xiii.

2. Joanne Williams, response #63 to "Reading *Our Bodies, Ourselves*," submitted January
1, 2003. http://chnm.gmu.edu/tools/surveys/467/. This is an online survey that I created
with the financial and technical assistance of the Center for History and New Media at
George Mason University. To date, 262 people have submitted responses to the survey.

3. Estelle Freedman, response #260 to "Reading *Our Bodies, Ourselves*," submitted May
20, 2006. http://chnm.gmu.edu/tools/surveys/467/.

4. For a more in-depth analysis of the changes within the BWHBC and the text over
the entire span of its history, with an emphasis on its global circulation, see Kathy Davis,
*The Making of* Our Bodies, Ourselves: *How Feminism Travels across Borders* (Durham:
Duke University Press, 2007).

5. Sara Evans, *Tidal Wave: How Women Changed America at Century's End* (New York:
The Free Press, 2003), 18.

6. Becky Thompson, "Multiracial Feminism: Recasting the Chronology of Second Wave
Feminism" *Feminist Studies* 28 (2002): 337.

7. Evans, *Tidal Wave*, pp. 3–4 n17.

8. Ibid., 29.

9. The "click" process was first described in Jane O'Reilly, "The Housewife's Moment
of Truth," *Ms.* 1, no. 1 (Spring 1972): 54–55, 57–59.

10. Evans, *Tidal Wave*, 30.

11. Carol S. Weisman, *Women's Health Care: Activist Traditions and Institutional Change*
(Baltimore: Johns Hopkins University Press, 1998), 73–74.

12. The Women's Health Forum—HealthRight conducted a nationwide survey in 1974.

See Sheryl Ruzek, *The Women's Health Movement: Feminist Alternatives to Medical Control* (New York: Praeger, 1978), 144; see also Myra Marx Ferree and Beth B. Hess, *Controversy and Coalition: The New Feminist Movement across Four Decades of Change*, 3rd ed. (New York: Routledge, 2000), 108.

13. Other groups have also produced feminist health literature, although none as successfully as BWHBC. For example, the Vancouver, B.C., Women's Health Collective published *A Woman's Place* in 1972. Newsletters included *The Monthly Extract—An Irregular Periodical* and the Women's Health Forum's *HealthRight*. In addition, feminist newspapers and journals regularly covered women's health issues, including *off our backs* and *Ms.* magazine. By the early 1970s, traditional women's magazines such as *Vogue* and *Redbook* published articles on women's health that challenged traditional medicine. See Ruzek, *The Women's Health Movement*, 147, 210, 218, app. B.

14. Ruzek argues that "selective utilization" of physicians was a strategy of health movement activists, noting that lay referral systems began as informal affairs. See Ruzek, *The Women's Health Movement*, 162.

15. Wendy Sanford and Judy Norsigian, "Ten Years in the *Our Bodies, Ourselves* Collective—Draft"; BWHBC papers (unprocessed), 99–M147, box 5, p. 2, Schlesinger Library, Cambridge, Mass. (hereafter BWHBC papers).

16. Barbara A. Brehm, "Knowledge is Power: *Our Bodies, Ourselves* and the Boston Women's Health Book Collective," in *Women on Power: Leadership Redefined*, ed. Sue Freeman, Susan Bourque, and Christine Shelton (Boston: Northeastern University Press, 2001), 156.

17. Boston Women's Health Book Collective, *Our Bodies, Our Selves* (Cambridge, Mass.: New England Free Press, 1971), 1.

18. Boston Women's Health Book Collective, *Our Bodies, Our Selves*, 1.

19. Brehm, "Knowledge is Power," 157.

20. Boston Women's Health Book Collective, *Our Bodies, Our Selves* (1971), last page (not numbered).

21. Davis, *The Making of* Our Bodies, Ourselves, 24.

22. Lynn to BWHBC, July 31, 1972, BWHBC papers (unprocessed), 99–M147, box 1, Schlesinger Library, Cambridge, Mass.

23. Joan to group, Fall 1974, BWHBC papers, box 1.

24. Nancy, Joan, and Ruth to group, July 25, 1974, BWHBC papers, box 1.

25. Nancy to group, Labor Day 1976, BWHBC papers, box 1.

26. Nancy, Joan, and Ruth to group, July 25, 1974, BWHBC papers, box 1.

27. Jane to group, Summer 1975, BWHBC papers, box 1.

28. Judy to group, April 19, 1976, BWHBC papers, box 1.

29. Wendy to the parenting group, August 24, 1976, BWHBC papers, box 1.

30. Wendy to the parenting group, August 24, 1976, BWHBC papers, box 1.

31. Norma to group, September 5, 1976, BWHBC papers, box 1.

32. Ibid.

33. Ibid.

34. Joan to group, September 4, 1976, BWHBC papers, box 1.

35. Nancy and Joan, Memo #2, April 3, 1979, p. 2, BWHBC papers, 99–M125, box 6, parenting.

36. Reviewed by Victoria K. Musmann, *Library Journal Review* 103, 17 (October 1, 1978):

1967. Negative reviews include Pat Hosking, *Broadsheet* (New Zealand), April 1979; Molly Lovelock, "Narrow Viewpoint," *Sojourner,* Feb. 1979, 13, BWHBC papers, 99–M125, box 6, parenting.

37. Meeting minutes, June 2, 1980, BWHBC papers, box 1, p. 2.

38. Wendy to group, August 24, 1976, BWHBC papers, box 1.

39. Norma to group, September 5, 1976, BWHBC papers, box 1.

40. Boston Women's Health Book Collective, *Our Bodies, Ourselves* (1973), 2.

41. Susan E. Bell, "Translating Science to the People: Updating *The New Our Bodies, Ourselves,*" *Women's Studies International Forum* 17 (1994): 10.

42. Ibid.

43. Kathy Davis, "Feminist Body/Politics as World Traveller: Translating *Our Bodies, Ourselves,*" *The European Journal of Women's Studies* 9 (2002): 241.

44. Approximately 250 letters remain in the BWBHC Collection at the Schlesinger Library. They were not systematically organized by the collective. Some were sent on to authors for future revisions while others were lost. See also Davis, *The Making of* Our Bodies, Ourselves, 150.

45. This is not the first time that women's responses to medical literature led to activism. Carol Weisman interprets recurring episodes of women's activism in America as waves in a women's health "megamovement" beginning in the early nineteenth century. From the popular health movement to late-nineteenth-century and Progressive Era movements, women have responded to health products and information and demanded that the health care system be sensitive to their needs. See Weisman, *Women's Health Care,* 29.

46. Though, as Kathy Davis points out, most readers appear to have some education and a middle-class background. See Davis, *The Making of* Our Bodies, Ourselves, 152.

47. Lisa Maria Hogeland, *Feminism and Its Fictions: The Consciousness-Raising Novel and the Women's Liberation Movement* (Philadelphia: University of Pennsylvania Press, 1998), 4.

48. Ibid., 10.

49. Ibid., 30.

50. Libby to BWHBC, November 25, 1979, BWHBC papers, 99–M147, box 2, "PID" folder.

51. Mary Elizabeth to "Jane and everyone in the collective," n.d., BWHBC papers, 99–M125, box 1, "History: 10th anniversary" folder.

52. Helen McMillan to BWHBC, July 8, 1981, BWHBC papers, 99–M147, box 2 "menstruation brochure requests" folder.

53. Name blacked out to Judy Norsigian, September 23, 1979, BWHBC papers, 99–M147, box 2, "Correspondence to File '79, '81–'82" folder.

54. Ibid.

55. Boston Women's Health Book Collective, *Our Bodies, Ourselves* (1973), 268.

56. Name blacked out "to those who wrote this book," February 17, 1979, BWHBC papers, 99–M147, box 2, "pap smears" folder.

57. Boston Women's Health Book Collective, *Our Bodies, Ourselves, Revised and Expanded* (New York: Simon and Schuster, 1979), 147.

58. Name blacked out to Norma Swenson and Jane Pincus, June 28, 1979, BWHBC papers, 99–M147, box 2, "pap smears" folder.

59. Name blacked out "to those who wrote this book."

60. See, for example, Sandra Morgen, *Into Our Own Hands,* chap. 7.

61. Ibid.

62. Name blacked out to Norma Swenson and Jane Pincus, June 28, 1979.

63. Amy Erdman Farrell, *Yours in Sisterhood: Ms. Magazine and the Promise of Popular Feminism* (Chapel Hill: The University of North Carolina Press, 1998), 151.

64. Barbara Ehrenreich and Deirdre English, *Complaints and Disorders: The Sexual Politics of Sickness* (Old Westbury, N.Y.: The Feminist Press, 1973), 86–87, quoted in Ruzek, *The Women's Health Movement,* 187.

65. In her study of *Our Bodies, Ourselves,* Davis also notes that most readers did not directly address the issue of race. She notes, "In a racialized context where whiteness is treated by many white people as being without race, a condition of invisibility not available to people of color, this would indicate that many of the letters were probably written by white, Anglo-American women." Davis, *The Making of* Our Bodies, Ourselves, 152.

66. Ruzek, *The Women's Health Movement,* 192.

67. Martha Scherzer, "Byllye Avery and the National Black Women's Health Project," *Network News* (May/June 1995): 4.

68. Morgen, *Into Our Own Hands,* 43.

69. Alba Bonilla, April Taylor, Mayra Canetti, and Jennifer Yanco, "An Open Letter to the Board of Directors, Boston Women's Health Book Collective," *Sojourner: The Women's Forum,* December 1997, 4.

70. Boston Women's Health Book Collective, *Our Bodies, Ourselves for the New Century* (New York: Simon and Schuster, 1998), 22.

71. Alice Echols, *Daring to Be Bad: Radical Feminism in America, 1967–75* (Minneapolis: University of Minnesota Press, 1990), 212. See also Karla Jay, *Tales of the Lavendar Menace: A Memoir of Liberation* (New York: Basic Books, 2000); Susan Brownmiller, *In Our Time: Memoir of a Revolution* (New York: Random House, 1999); Kimberly Springer, *Living for the Revolution: Black Feminist Organizations, 1968–1980* (Durham, N.C.: Duke University Press, 2005)

72. Boston Women's Health Book Collective, *The New Our Bodies, Ourselves,* 141.

73. Barbara Smith to Wendy Sanford and Lily, July 7, 1981, BWHBC papers, 99–M147, box 2, "Correspondence to File '79, '81–'82" folder. See also Ruzek, *The Women's Health Movement,* 190.

74. Boston Women's Health Book Collective, *Our Bodies, Ourselves,* "In Amerika" chapter, 56n1 (1973 ed.), 81 (1976 and 1979 eds.).

75. Sanford to "the women who worked on the lesbian chapter of *Our Bodies, Ourselves,*" December 15, 1974, BWHBC papers, 99–M125, box 1, "history—1976 *Our Bodies, Ourselves*" folder.

76. Meeting minutes, "Tuesday March 28" [1978?], BWHBC papers, 99–M125, box 1, "minutes/memos 1974–76" folder.

77. Name blacked out to BWHBC, March 14, 1982, BWHBC papers, 99–M147, box 2, "orgasm" folder.

78. Boston Women's Health Book Collective, *The New Our Bodies, Ourselves,* 141.

79. Catharine Stimpson, "*Our Bodies, Ourselves*" review, *Ms.,* April 1973, 35.

## 5. Taking the White Gloves Off

*Women Strike for Peace and*
*"the Movement," 1967–73*

### ANDREA ESTEPA

On September 20, 1967, about five hundred members of Women Strike for Peace (WSP) gathered in Washington, D.C., for a long-planned demonstration in support of young men who were resisting the draft. A few weeks before, the Department of the Interior had issued an edict that restricted the number of people who could picket in front of the White House to one hundred at a time. WSP organizers lobbied to have the order rescinded in time for their action, but did not succeed. Undeterred, the women arrived as planned, carrying a black coffin that read, "Not My Sons, Not Your Sons, Not Their Sons." Helmeted police officers allowed one hundred of them access to the sidewalk in front of the White House and herded the rest into a fenced-in holding area across the street. Frustrated and angry, some of the women attempted to push their way out and eventually succeeded in trampling down part of the fence. As they ran to join the demonstration, the police tried to force them back by shoving, tackling, and swinging their nightsticks at the women. The WSPers pushed back. "At the height of the noisy fracas, about ten women were seen lying on the ground," the *New York Times* reported the next day. "One had blood on her head." The demonstrators then sat down in the middle of the street and blocked traffic to protest their treatment at the hands of the police. Two women were arrested and charged with disorderly conduct.[1]

The *Times* ran its coverage of the demonstration on the front page under the headline, "Women Fight Police near White House." Anyone who had followed WSP's history to that point could not help but be shocked by the news. WSP was founded in 1961 to advocate international disarmament and to oppose nuclear testing and the arms race; since 1964, the group had been focusing its energies on opposition to the Vietnam War. However, these were not student radicals with a penchant for provoking the authorities. WSP's membership, which was overwhelmingly white, middle-class, and middle-aged, generally took great pains to project an image of ladylike dignity, dressing for protest actions in knee-length skirts, hats, pearls and, in some cases, white gloves. They claimed a particular moral authority on issues of war and peace because, they argued, as women and as mothers, they had a special responsibility for nurturing and protecting life.[2] That they could have participated in what was variously described as a "fracas," "clash," and "wild melee" threatened to undermine the image of respectability that they had carefully constructed over the previous six years.

During the days immediately following the White House demonstration, WSP's Washington office was deluged with letters, phone calls, and telegrams from supporters and critics from around the country, asking the women who had participated to account for their uncharacteristically rowdy and, it appeared, violent behavior. Did the events of September 20 signal a larger change in WSP's philosophy and tactics? WSP founder Dagmar Wilson addressed this question two days later at the group's sixth annual conference. "We didn't plan to go out and fight policemen. They fought us," she pointed out.[3] "We women have not changed—our goals are the same—it is the conditions under which we work that have changed," Wilson declared.[4]

Despite Wilson's demurrals, the September 20, 1967, demonstration did mark a turning point in WSP's development. It was true that conditions had changed. Between 1961, when WSP mounted its first action, a nationwide protest against the arms race and nuclear testing, and 1967, when WSPers found themselves involved in a direct confrontation with police, the United States had, in many ways, become a different country. Those years witnessed the assassination of President Kennedy; the escalation of the Vietnam War and expanding opposition to it; the growth of the civil rights movement and the development of black nationalism; a series of deadly riots in the nation's biggest cities; the birth of the New Left, the student movement, and the counterculture; and the first stirrings of the women's liberation movement.[5] What Wilson did not acknowledge was that, in response, WSP had begun to change as well, redefining both its mission and its activist style.[6]

During the late sixties, WSP grew increasingly concerned with questions of economic and racial justice (especially the plight of poor women and children) and began to understand peace as a domestic as well as a foreign policy issue. WSPers began to characterize poverty and racism as forms of violence against the spirit. They also came to believe that racism was fueling the war—racism against the Vietnamese and racism against blacks and Latinos that caused them to be disproportionately represented in the troops sent to fight (and die) in Vietnam. They saw the growing cost of the war undermining the government's ability to provide its citizens with the kind of social services and quality of life envisioned by Lyndon Johnson's War on Poverty and Great Society programs. Where WSPers had initially focused their attention on reaching white, middle-class, middle-aged women like themselves, by the late sixties, the group had begun to build coalitions with activists from different races, generations, and socioeconomic backgrounds. WSP's coalition work linked them to two very different activist communities—young, white New Leftists with whom they did their antiwar and draft resistance work ("We marched with hippies and yippies," recalled Cora Weiss, who served as national cochair of the New Mobilization Committee to End the War in Vietnam, as a representative of WSP[7]) and poor women of color with whom they joined forces in support of antipoverty and child welfare measures.

In both cases, it was their identity as mothers as much as their political beliefs that defined WSP's relationship with their coalition partners. They related to the women of the National Welfare Rights Organization and the Poor People's Campaign as mothers trying to make a better life and better world for their children; with younger antiwar protesters, WSPers served as mothers of the Movement[8]—supporting and attempting to protect, but also scolding and criticizing their political children. These relationships helped transform WSP's political priorities, its self-image, and the way its members were treated by the authorities. The more that WSPers allied themselves with those who could not rely on the protection of white skin and white gloves, or who rejected the trappings of middle-class respectability, the less effective those protections became for the WSPers themselves. As antiwar demonstrations grew larger, more frequent, more confrontational, and more likely to include acts of civil disobedience, both local police forces and federal officials became less accommodating and more repressive in their interactions with protesters, including WSP members. As conditions changed, projecting an image of ladylike decorum became both less effective and less practical.

Although the confrontation at the White House was the first time an action sponsored by WSP had received such a harsh response from the police, individual WSPers had already gotten the message that the climate was changing. Philadelphia WSP leader Ethel Taylor was arrested for the first time at a D.C. sit-in two years earlier, during a demonstration sponsored by the Assembly of Unrepresented People, a coalition of civil rights and antiwar activists. In a crowd where middle-class white ladies were outnumbered by black power activists and student antiwar protesters, the "hat, gloves, and heels" that the 49–year-old Taylor thought "a real protection" were no longer working. Carted to jail in a police van, Taylor waited quietly for an officer to come and help her negotiate the four-foot drop to the street. "A policeman came back to see what the hold up was. I put out my gloved hand, but he had no intention of wasting chivalry on a criminal. He looked me straight in the eye and said, 'Jump, sister!'" Taylor jumped.[9]

Taylor recalled later that at that moment she felt as if she were jumping into "an entirely new world."[10] In a way she was. This new world of increasing militance on the part of social activists and harsher reactions and reprisals from the authorities led WSPers such as Taylor to perform a delicate balancing act throughout the late 1960s and early 1970s. The women attempted to espouse militant views without alienating the mainstream; to put the privileges accorded to them as white, middle-class women to work on behalf of the disenfranchised; to march with hippies and yippies, while continuing to wear high heels.

When Women Strike for Peace was founded in 1961, it was to insert what they claimed was a nonpartisan critique of the arms race with the Soviet Union into a political debate dominated by red-baiting. McCarthy was gone, but McCarthyism lingered. Because WSP's founders wanted to win the widest possible hearing for their views at a time when publicly criticizing the arms race was still likely to result in accusations of subversion and communist-sympathizing, the women took great pains to make their critique of government policy sound like good common sense rather than an ideological position. From the first, WSP was sensitive to the importance of creating, projecting, and maintaining a sympathetic public image.[11]

In an effort to attract a broad constituency, they initially promoted themselves as a group whose members had diverse backgrounds and interests. In an early document titled, "Who Are These Women?—You Ask," WSP's founders focused primarily on their wide-ranging professional identities, introducing themselves as, "teachers, writers, social workers, artists, secretaries, executives, saleswomen." They then added, "most of us are also wives and mothers. . . . First of all we are human beings."[12] However, they soon dropped the emphasis on careers and broad humanist values, making a strategic decision that an appeal for peace from mothers, housewives, and "the woman next door" would get a more sympathetic response than one from women who presented themselves as workers, political activists, or, even, concerned citizens given the conservative gender politics of the time. A report on WSP's first lobbying day in Washington, D.C., published just a few months after "Who Are These Women?" referred to the participants exclusively as "housewives and mothers" and argued that it was their shared identity as nurturers that made them a force to be reckoned with: "Have you ever seen the mother animal protecting her young? The meekest ones become lionesses."[13] By comparing themselves to the "mother animal," the early WSPers implied that there was something inherent, biological, and inevitable about their opposition to nuclear testing and the arms race, something that existed outside of politics. (The reference to the lioness allows for a more feminist interpretation, as well—WSPers were also suggesting that they were strong, angry, fierce, and determined to achieve their goals.[14])

That the group's maternalist rhetoric was more the projection of a cultural ideal than a completely accurate description of its membership is born out by the results of a 1962 survey of WSP participants.[15] Though the overwhelming majority of the respondents were, in fact, mothers, they did not usually identify motherhood as the focal point of their political identities. Although they called themselves "housewives," they were not necessarily full-time homemakers. (Dagmar Wilson was a professional illustrator who nonetheless claimed she could legitimately call herself a housewife because she did her artwork at home.[16]) When asked what kinds of women were attracted to WSP, the majority said it was "intellectual, civic-minded humanists." Very few cited motherhood as either the inspiration or motivation for their activism. More than half said that it was reading a book, seeing a movie, or participating in a discussion in school or church—as opposed to having a child—that sparked their passion for the issues of war and peace.[17]

The essentialist ring of WSP's early rhetoric was also meant to support the idea that women of "all . . . political persuasions" could, and should, be committed to ending the arms race and atomic testing. WSP's initial commitment to being nonideological and nonpartisan stemmed from both sincere conviction and political savvy. Because of their belief that saving the planet was more important than any other single issue, WSPers felt certain that the peace movement could and should be a mass movement, uniting women in spite of differences in partisan affiliation. (They also believed that all women would share this conviction.) At the same time, WSP's claim that it stood outside the ideological debates of the time was a strategic response to the cold war context in which the organization developed, an attempt to avoid the rounds of red-baiting and purging that were undermining the unity and effectiveness of other peace organizations such as the Citizens for a SANE Nuclear Policy (SANE) and Women's International League for Peace and Freedom (WILPF).[18]

Because their main concern in the early sixties was attracting "ordinary women" to the cause, WSPers initially gravitated to activities that were controversial enough to attract media attention but not so controversial as to frighten or alienate middle-aged, middle-class Americans like themselves.[19] Picketing was acceptable, for example, as long as it was carried out in a dignified way and as long as the picketers were dressed in conservative, feminine attire. Civil disobedience, on the other hand, was something the women initially hesitated to embrace because they feared it would alienate the people whose support they most wanted to attract. In 1962, for example, a WSP delegation staged a legal demonstration at the U.S. Atomic Energy Commission test site in Mercury, Nevada. While there, they encountered a member of the Committee for Non-Violent Action (CNVA), a radical pacifist group, who was planning an act of civil disobedience. Years later, Eleanor Garst, a WSP founder, recalled:

> It was Doris Rudder who was able to persuade a CNVA girl not to commit civil disobedience until our non-violent walk at the test site had ended. WSP, she explained, wanted all women to join us; to do so, they had to identify with us; most of them dreaded nuclear testing too, but wouldn't yet speak out and certainly rejected civil disobedience. The young woman waited, but later, when she was arrested, alone, we felt wretched. Were we wrong? we asked ourselves. Should we too have broken the law to show the depth of our concern?[20]

The conflict Garst describes between taking actions that expressed "depth of concern" and the desire to win mainstream support, between "issue and image" as long-time member Bernie Steele put it, was a source of tension within WSP throughout its history.[21] During the organization's early years, as Garst's anecdote suggests, the balance tended to tip in favor of image.

There was more than one way in which the image that WSP chose to project in its early years was not always an accurate reflection of its membership. As noted above, many WSPers worked outside the home in spite of their tendency to refer to themselves as "mothers and housewives" in their literature. Although WSP's founders may have believed they represented the interests of all women, and especially mothers, their outreach campaigns tended to target highly educated white women with a preexisting interest in public affairs and commitment to political participation—the same group that comprised the majority of their membership, according to the findings of the 1962 survey.[22] Although the policy statement approved by attendees at WSP's first national conference in Ann Arbor, Michigan in June 1962 read, "We are women of all races, creeds, and political persuasions," WSP remained an overwhelmingly white organization.

Ironically, given WSP's big tent rhetoric, the most heated debates at that first conference revolved around the stand the organization would take regarding the relationship between the campaign for disarmament and the civil rights movement. For a number of attendees, what this discussion was really about was WSP's commitment to black women and their issues. When a group of black women from Detroit calling themselves the Independent Negro Committee to End Racism and Ban the Bomb arrived at the conference, a debate ensued over whether they should be seated because they were not, technically, a WSP affiliate. In fact, the Negro Committee had formed after Detroit WSP had refused to allow the black women to carry signs reading "Desegregation Not Disintegration" at a demonstration. The white Detroiters felt that it was a mistake to combine the two issues in this way because it might confuse or alienate potential supporters. The black women started their own local group, but still considered themselves part of the larger women's peace movement. When the white women of Detroit WSP did not invite representatives of the Negro Committee to attend the Ann Arbor conference as part of their delegation, the black women decided to attend anyway and demand recognition from the national body. The minutes of the conference indicate that "after some discussion and a period of silence," it was agreed that the black women from Detroit be allowed to participate. In spite of this resolution, some white WSPers felt the fact that the Negro Committee's participation in the conference had to be debated (rather than simply welcomed) put the lie to the organization's claims of inclusiveness.[23]

Over time, WSP would come to share the Negro Committee's view that racial equality and world peace were equally important, even indivisible, causes but at this early stage in its development, many WSPers were wary of complicating their basic message. As noted earlier, the group's founders believed that all women shared an interest in and responsibility for preserving life and protecting children. In the early sixties, for these middle-class white women, atomic warfare (which promised sudden death) and nuclear testing (which promised slow death through the poisoning of the environment and, more specifically, the contamination of milk) were both dire and immediate threats to their children's safety and, by extension, the safety of all children in the United States and around the world. In short, they believed not only that all women were motivated to protect children but that all women would agree on what children most needed protection from. They believed that all women, regardless of race or class or partisan affiliation, once they were made aware of these threats, could be convinced to support WSP's basic demands "that nuclear weapons tests be banned forever, that the arms race end, and that the world abolish all weapons of destruction."[24] Almost forty years later, Shirley Sapin, who attended the Ann Arbor conference as a representative of Voices of Women—New England, recalled how these assumptions were challenged during the discussion of the relationship between peace and civil rights.

One of the things that stood out that has never left my mind was when a black woman stood up and said, "A pox on all of you. What difference does it make to my child whether or not there's nuclear testing and the milk contamination when none of you has brought up the issue of racism in this country? Nowhere have any of you talked about the racist factor that's demoralizing all of us, and affecting our black children." And it was very poignant because in effect it helped many of us people there, white people, recognize that no effort had been made around the injustice and the racist society in which we were living.[25]

But not everyone at the conference was as quickly convinced as Sapin. This does not mean that WSPers opposed the civil rights movement. In fact, a number of them were actively involved in the movement as individuals. It was the question of how the two causes could or should be weighted on their activist agenda that was debated at virtually every WSP conference beginning with the very first. Because of what they perceived as the universal appeal of the disarmament issue, many white WSPers were initially hesitant to take stands on other issues, such as civil rights, as an organization for fear that it would alienate women who would otherwise support their cause. They did not seem to recognize that refusing to make an organizational commitment to the civil rights movement could also alienate women they might other-wise attract. Consciously or unconsciously, WSP seemed more concerned initially with not alienating Southern white women than with winning the support of black women. For example, in the fall of 1962, WSP chapters in the Mid-Atlantic region composed an "Open Letter to Women of Mississippi" in which they appealed "to *all* women and mothers in Mississippi to exert their wise and gentle influence in these days of crisis. . . ."[26] The letter was most likely a response to the violent repression of a voter registration drive in the Mississippi Delta during which two Student Nonviolent Coordinating Com-mittee (SNCC) workers were injured in a drive-by shooting and a number of black residents were beaten, arrested on trumped-up charges, and otherwise intimidated.[27] The bland wording, however, did not clarify the nature of the "crisis" or acknowledge who was responsible. By intimating that all women (regardless of race) were equally capable of exerting "influence" that could prevent further tragic events, it avoided making a clear statement about the racist nature of the violence.

Although many white WSPers appear to have supported keeping the issues separate during the early sixties, arguing that "civil rights without disarma-ment won't do any of us any good," the few black women who got involved in the organization tended to argue that the causes of international peace and domestic justice were naturally intertwined and that without civil rights, "we don't care whether there is peace or not."[28] The view that the causes of peace and racial justice went hand in hand, that you could not achieve one without the other, was most consistently articulated by Coretta Scott King. Already active in WILPF when WSP was formed, King attended the 1962 Conference of the Seventeen-Nation Committee on Disarmament in Geneva, Switzerland at WSP's invitation; she was one of four blacks in the fifty-woman delegation. When she returned, the *Southern Patriot* declared King's participation "the first instance of an outstanding figure in the civil rights movement taking an active and leading part in the organized movement for world peace." For King, the two issues—civil rights and world peace—were inseparable: "As Negroes we've been too long concerned with just this question of civil rights. This is rather narrow, when there is a very real possibility that man will destroy himself with the weapons he has created. Peace concerns all human beings. I believe we can strengthen our own position in regard to civil rights if we can reach out from ourselves and lend our efforts to this matter that affects all mankind."[29]

Coretta Scott King, like the members of the Negro Committee, was ahead of many black civil rights activists as well as white peace activists in her ability to see the two causes as equally important and inextricably connected. Following a major WSP demonstration in Washington in January 1962, a local black newspaper editorialized that its female readers should leave such activities to white women and focus on their own struggle for integration and economic justice.[30] Enola Maxwell, a black woman who became involved in WSP and WILPF in the mid-1960s, acknowledged that "peace and civil rights were not always connected for me; most blacks got involved in civil rights way before peace work." One reason for that was the role the military played in the economy of the black community. "In the South we didn't worry too much about peace because the Army was an employment agency for black people," Maxwell said. "It did break down a lot of barriers in discrimination, and it did provide better income and jobs."[31] Not until Martin Luther King Jr. began speaking out against the Vietnam War and drawing attention to the disproportionate number of young black men who were dying in combat, did Maxwell recognize that ending the war was, in fact, a civil rights project.

Gradually, more and more white WSPers began making the same connections. In 1963, the group's annual conference adopted a resolution stating that the goals of peace and civil rights were "inseparable," just as Coretta Scott King had argued the year before. "As a movement working for an atmosphere of peaceful cooperation among nations, we support the movement for peaceful integration in our own nation," the resolution read.[32] However, aside from occasional announcements at meetings and in *Memo* that encouraged WSPers to donate money or supplies, write letters to the president, or attend demonstrations in support of civil rights, little effort appears to have been made to integrate the two issues as a matter of policy until the late 1960s.

In the wake of the 1967 demonstration at the White House, WSP began developing a new analysis of what it would come to call "the multiple crises facing our nation."[33] The women began to see peace as a domestic as well as a foreign policy concern. Dozens of riots in American cities during the summers of 1966 and 1967, a sharp increase in the number of violent crimes, the heightened militance of the black power movement, and Martin Luther King Jr.'s call for a Poor People's Campaign inspired a new level of concern among WSPers for the poor and minority citizens of their own country. At the same time, their participation in the peace movement was exposing them to examples of police brutality and state repression. It was becoming routine for confrontations between protestors and authorities at anti-Vietnam War demonstrations to end in beatings, injuries, and arrests. This may explain why, at a time when many white Americans were losing sympathy for the civil rights movement, "black power," and the War on Poverty, WSP made support for those causes a priority on par with its antiwar work.[34] In national and local steering committee meetings during the first half of 1968, the group identified racism and economics as the factors that linked the war in Vietnam to the war at home. In their "Statement on the Crisis in American Cities," WSP members argued: "Our foreign policies are an extension of our domestic policies. As long as we allow millions of American children to suffer the indignities of prejudice, racism and neglect . . . we will only be tackling half the problem in demanding an end to war. . . . We must recognize the same source of oppression in the use of trained dogs or mace in Saigon, Mississippi, or Detroit."[35] They also made the point that the causes of urban unrest were directly linked to the war budget. WSP needed to work not only for "an end to the Vietnam war, but sharp cuts in our military appropriations, our armaments, and armed forces, so that our country can begin to give its attention to the critical problems here at home: our decaying cities, our neglected schools, the problem of police brutality and racial injustice, the grinding poverty that blights the lives of one-fifth of our affluent society."[36]

At the same time, WSP members began to directly acknowledge and discuss the fact that they were "primarily a white group" and to recognize a need to develop "close ties with the women of the black ghetto."[37] This was a departure from the earlier assumption that WSP was an already integrated organization and that black women would join because of their maternal concerns. Now the tendency to say "women" when they were referring almost exclusively to white, middle-class, middle-aged women was supplanted by an effort to be specific. They began to make distinctions between work in "our own communities" and efforts to support, involve, or build coalitions with "black women," "welfare mothers," "working-class women," "union women," "young women," "our black and Puerto Rican citizens," and "women in ghettos."[38] WSPers hoped that by supporting causes of immediate concern to poor black women, such as the burgeoning campaign for welfare rights, they would in turn win black women's active support for WSP's antiwar efforts. The WSPers came to understand that providing food, clothing, shelter, and a decent education for their children was going to be the top priority for low-income mothers, but they also hoped to get poor women to share their view that military spending was largely responsible for domestic poverty. The war, according to WSP's analysis, was diverting funds from social programs that could help poor women better provide for their families. Even more important, it was killing their sons.

Ethel Taylor and other members of Philadelphia WSP, for example, began meeting with members of the local branch of the National Welfare Rights Organization (NWRO) in 1967. The white women had never been able to understand why more black women had not gotten involved in their antidraft campaigns when "their sons were at the front of the line for being drafted." They discovered that in Philadelphia, just as in Enola Maxwell's South, joining the military was sometimes seen as an employment opportunity rather than a death sentence. Some of the mothers in the Philadelphia chapter of NWRO felt that the draft offered their sons opportunities that would otherwise be beyond their reach. "If they were drafted they would receive training for a future job, and at the same time would avoid the real dangers of street gangs at home," Taylor recalled. "It was a sad commentary on the hopes of poor mothers for their sons."[39] As in the early days of WSP's disarmament campaign, when the white middle-class mothers who protested atomic testing could not imagine a more immediate threat to their children's safety than contaminated milk and nuclear warfare, so too were they unable, during the Vietnam War, to envision any worse hazard to their sons' health than being drafted. Mothers whose children faced the perils of poverty and racism on a daily basis had to protect their children from dangers much closer to home than the war in Vietnam. This was underscored for Taylor when the son of a NWRO member was killed in a gang fight on a day when Philadelphia WSP and NWRO activists had planned to hold a flea market to fund a trip to an antiwar demonstration in Washington.[40] Although WSP and NWRO continued to cosponsor campaigns and actions that linked war expenditures to economic deprivation into the 1970s, their success at coalition building was limited. As Taylor saw it, this was because "the luxury of joining the two issues is one [the NWRO women] cannot afford—their need is too immediate—food and welfare increases."[41]

For WSPers in Washington, D.C., supporting the Poor People's Campaign provided a comparable consciousness-raising experience regarding the struggles of poor mothers. The campaign was conceived by Martin Luther King Jr. in the last year of his life. King envisioned an encampment of poor people of all races and regions in the shadow of the Capitol, pressing the federal government to recommit itself to solving the problems of hunger, inadequate housing, poor schooling, lack of health care, and high unemployment in both urban and rural areas. After King's assassination in April, his staff at the Southern Christian Leadership Conference went ahead with their plans to mount the encampment during the summer of 1968. WSP announced that it "unequivocally" supported the campaign. The women pledged to "bring our greatest commitment and zeal to organizing in our communities . . . [we will] mobilize white community support behind a Mother's Lobby for Poor People's demands."[42] Resurrection City, as the encampment was known, went up in May and was immediately plagued by heavy rains, muddy grounds, and internal dissension. In addition to raising money, lobbying, and helping to organize a solidarity day that brought 50,000 people to the Mall, WSPers spent time at the encampment, helping out in any way they could. "This really changed the picture a bit for us peace ladies," Dagmar Wilson told the group's national conference the following November. "Although we knew about poverty and we knew about racism, I don't believe any of us *really* understood it until we were that close to it . . . my God, there are children being born here [in the U.S.] who are half-starved, because their mothers haven't had a diet before they were born. . . . How can it be that a country like ours can even tolerate this kind of thing? . . . It's this basic inhumanity that was such a shock to me. . . ."[43]

Her experience at Resurrection City inspired Wilson, the group's founder, to rethink WSP's mission. Children had to be protected not just from violence and war, but also from hunger and neglect. Challenging the nation's foreign policy was no longer enough; they had to address domestic issues as well. "We've got to dig in," Wilson told the national gathering of "peace ladies," "and really work with the intention of affecting the power structure in our country, either changing it or removing it, which ever way it happens to turn out, or turning it upside-down."[44] It sounded very much like a call for revolution.

At a retreat of the Washington-area membership in October 1968, Dagmar Wilson suggested that WSP needed to broaden its agenda. The discussions that took place at that meeting—during which women argued over whether

WSP had become subsumed in the amorphous Movement, losing its own identity in the process—reflected debates that WSPers were having around the country. Over the course of the previous year, the women had spent the majority of their time working on coalition-sponsored activities rather than their own independent actions. They had become, you might say, the mothers of the Movement—supporting and attempting to protect, but also critiquing the behavior of young New Left activists who shared their opposition to the war, poverty, and racism but disdained their efforts to win the support of Middle America. Although WSP's positions on issues were generally in sync with those of their younger "comrades," their style and tactics often were not. Yet instead of disassociating themselves from hippies and yippies, they tried to influence them.[45] For example, they pressed the other organizers of the National Mobilization Committee to End the War in Vietnam (Mobe) to make the mass demonstration planned for the Pentagon in October 1967 welcoming to nonradicals. "There was a good deal of criticism of the Mobe Committee for not having done enough to develop a program that would appeal to all sections of the anti-war populace," Memo reported. "[We] concluded, however, that this weakness could most effectively be overcome by large numbers of WSPs actively working with each mobilization committee."[46] WSPers saw their role in helping to organize mass demonstrations against the war as providing "a wedge, an opening, to the broader community. . . . It was always a first demonstration for some of the women. It wasn't successful if it wasn't a first for lots of people."[47]

In New York that December, the local WSP claimed it was "the only adult group" to cosponsor and participate in all the events of Stop the Draft Week. During planning sessions, WSPs "tried to act as a moderator between groups of different philosophies." During the protest actions, "WSPs were at Whitehall [Induction Center] every day . . . trying to calm and help wherever possible." Some were arrested for civil disobedience and more than a thousand did legal picketing.[48] In 1968, the Chicago branch (along with a small contingent of WSPers from other parts of the country) participated in the protests at the Democratic National Convention. Two days before the convention opened, they mounted a demonstration of three hundred women in front of the hotel where the platform committee was meeting. They were greeted by "solid ranks of blue-helmeted policemen . . . almost shoulder-to-shoulder, their riot gear very much in evidence."[49] Arlen Wilson, one of the participants, reported to Memo that, "all went well in spite of the oppressive atmosphere." The same could not be said for the rest of the week. Chicago WSPers played their maternal role—"helping to feed Yippies in the parks, getting kids out of jail, etc."—and also joined some of the demonstrations that took place throughout the week where "many were harassed by the police, some hurt."[50] In Chicago, as at the Whitehall Induction Center, WSPers acted as both demonstrators and caretakers.

For many of the Chicago women, Arlen Wilson reported, this was their first exposure to police brutality: "The extent to which some of our police (whose motto is "We Serve and Protect") seemed to enjoy their work of clubbing every reachable head (newsmen, women, and bystanders included) came as a jolt to some of us. . . . Our black and Puerto Rican citizens generally stayed back in their ghetto neighborhoods and out of the way during all this, doubtless to let us get a sample of "law and order" as they experience it."[51] This experience, Wilson concluded, was leading Chicago's WSPers to a "re-evaluation of much of our entire system, and the reliance on armed force to perpetuate it."[52] As they became frequent witnesses to and, increasingly, victims of harassment and repression, many of the women joined Dagmar Wilson and Arlen Wilson in questioning their relationship to the entire power structure of the country.

This is not to say that all WSPers were radicalized to the same degree. Those who lived in or near large urban areas or who participated in mass demonstrations were much more likely to be exposed to the effects of poverty and the manifestations of police brutality that Dagmar Wilson and Arlen Wilson found so appalling. However, because these demonstrators were the kinds of women who tended to dominate the national steering committee, contribute to the newsletter, and plan the demonstrations, the image WSP presented to the public definitely took on a more radical cast. Where WSP had once made a deliberate choice not to practice civil disobedience, its members were now being arrested on a regular basis for "trespassing" on government property during demonstrations. Where they had once claimed to be women of "all political persuasions," they were now routinely taking positions that were identified by most of the American public with the radical Left. Where they had once been a single-issue group focused on disarmament, they now promoted a multi-issue agenda equally concerned with "poverty, racism, [and] war."[53] The media charted these developments with headlines such as "Women for Peace in Battle at White House," which suggested that maintaining matronly decorum had become the least of WSP's concerns.[54]

Internally, however, WSPers continued to debate "issue and image" and, more specifically, whether it was possible to bring their traditional white, middle-class constituency along as they articulated more overtly leftist positions. At the 1968 D.C. retreat, Dagmar Wilson floated the idea of starting a women's party that would run candidates on a platform advocating a wide array of child welfare measures. The women immediately began discussing whether, given that kind of program, they would have to identify their party as socialist in orientation. Folly Fodor, hostess of the event and one of the founding members of WSP, demurred. "I think one could say the same thing in a conservative language," she argued. "Among ourselves we can use words like radical, but when we talk to other people, I think we should try to phrase things with the phraseology people are used to."[55]

The women's party never got off the ground. The closest WSP came to becoming a force in electoral politics was its active role in Bella Abzug's successful congressional campaign in 1970. A New York civil rights attorney, Abzug was part of the first generation of WSPers and the leading strategist of the group's legislative campaigns and lobbying efforts. Running as an antiwar candidate, but equally committed to the causes of women, minorities, and the poor, Abzug was the perfect representative of WSP's late sixties fusion agenda in her ability to link domestic and foreign policy concerns. WSPers claimed Abzug as their voice in the House. On her first day in Congress, January 8, 1971, they sponsored a kind of people's inaugural to demonstrate their support for Abzug and to show that they would hold her accountable for her positions. A flyer inviting women to participate in the event read: "The angry women who banged their shoes on the door of the Pentagon send their first woman to Congress. . . . Stand with Bella on the Capitol steps as she takes her solemn oath to the people of the 19th CD and to the women of America to work for an end to the war and for the needs of the American people."[56] WSPers from around the country supported Abzug's campaign and felt that she was their representative, even if they did not live in her district.

Although the idea of the women's party did not take off, discussions of broadening WSP's agenda to include positions that could be considered socialist continued. Articles in *Memo,* along with the minutes of national conferences and meetings of the national steering committee, from the late sixties and early seventies regularly incorporated language and discussed issues associated with the Left. The minutes of the 1968 national conference, held a month after the D.C. chapter's retreat, announced that attendees had "adopted a whole new perspective on the role of WSP in the coming year . . . our emphasis should be on the larger picture." Although they would continue their work to end the war, the women would also begin "exposing to the American public the nature of the military industrial stranglehold on our foreign policy and the racist-repressive stranglehold on our domestic affairs."[57] In her keynote address, Dagmar Wilson exhorted her audience to "dig in and really work with the intention of affecting the power structure in our country, either changing it or removing it."[58] In 1970, the national steering committee adopted a resolution recommending to the WSP membership that "the indivisibility of the struggle for human rights at home and for peace abroad be understood."[59] They began to discuss the costs of war not solely in terms of lives lost as they had in the mid-sixties when "Not My Sons, Not Your Sons, Not Their Sons" was their main slogan, but in terms of the domestic economic and social costs of a war economy.

WSP's new approach still addressed middle-class women in their roles as housewives and mothers, arguing that the war was to blame for inflated prices of household goods and cuts to public education budgets. However, it also attempted to raise consciousness about poverty and the need for a redistribution of wealth. In a time of growing backlash against antipoverty programs and welfare spending, WSP argued that it was military spending, not social programs, that was devouring the tax dollars of working Americans. "The decaying cities and suicidal cuts in social services can all be directly attributed to a war economy. . . . In particular, we must challenge the concept that welfare is taking all the money away and let people see that the war . . . is siphoning off the life-blood of the community," WSP National Coordinator Rita Handman wrote to the membership in 1972.[60] In coalition with the NWRO during the early seventies, WSP organized a number of actions calling for cuts in military spending and a redirection of those funds to welfare, education, and public health.

The change in imagery and rhetorical style in WSP's literature derived not only from the women's desire to address questions of racial and economic justice. With the advent of the women's movement, WSP could no longer count on being able to reach the majority of American women with the language of maternal devotion and responsibility. "We cannot appeal to women anymore on the basis of their sons, brothers and husbands dying," Handman wrote in 1972. "We have to recognize that the appeal to most women today must be made on their own self-interest."[61] WSP had begun a conscious effort to reach out to younger women with a New Left orientation as early as 1966. An article in *Memo* that year touted their success at "involving new women" in a lobbying effort against the Vietnam War and profiled a few of the "first-timers."[62] Although in their early twenties, these women were wives and mothers for whom WSP probably offered a more comfortable fit than the student Left. WSP's first attempt to work with women's liberation activists came in 1968 when they participated in the Jeannette Rankin Brigade, a coalition of women with a wide variety of organizational commitments (peace, church, labor, New Left, and women's liberation) named for the first woman elected to Congress. Well into her eighties, Rankin, the sole member of the House to vote against U.S. entrance into both world wars, helped organize the brigade's march on Washington.[63]

Many WSPers thought women's liberation would provide them with a new constituency of women eager to join an autonomous women's organization with progressive politics and were surprised by the degree to which the traditional gender roles they embodied alienated young feminists. For instance, at the Jeannette Rankin Brigade action, WSPers were attacked by young feminist participants for basing their opposition to the war on their motherhood rather than their citizenship. In 1971, Gladys Knobel, a WSP leader from the suburbs of Chicago, sent a memo to the national steering committee arguing that "women's lib has opened millions of doors for us and our message." She wrote that it was "particularly painful" that WSP had not taken advantage of the opportunity to expand by organizing this new constituency. In the same memo, however, Knobel expressed concern at the degree to which WSP had become "submerged" in the Movement and argued, "our activities and programs must appeal to women—to their special needs and feelings." She was apparently unaware that the idea that women had "special needs and feelings" vis-à-vis issues such as the war is what alienated many young feminists from WSP.[64]

Knobel's concern about WSP's relationship to the Movement demonstrates that although the group's national leadership had begun prioritizing coalition work while making decisive moves to the left, it had not brought the entire rank and file along with it. Because of WSP's loose, bottom-up organizational structure, local affiliates were encouraged but not required to follow the national steering committee's lead.[65] Local groups had always functioned independently of the national office, which had been established more to facilitate communication among women from around the country than to provide them with specific marching orders. At the same time, WSP's early nonideological, big-tent approach had instilled members with the belief that partisan disagreements would not divide the organization as long as they all remained committed to disarmament. Local groups felt no obligation to follow the suggestions of national leaders. Neither the national steering committee nor the staff of the national office had the power (or desire) to "purge" members for noncompliance, so disagreements over agenda and strategy were debated continuously but rarely resolved.[66]

Knobel's group, for example, organized a local daylong boycott of all consumer goods called "Don't Buy War." Women were "not to shop and not to spend money on anything" for one day as "a symbol of protest against the war and the inflated economy." Knobel called this "a uniquely women's effort." Although these kinds of protests had successfully mobilized WSP members in the past, they were not especially appealing to the younger generation of feminists. Older WSP members, particularly those who did not work outside the home, did tend to be responsible for the family shopping and were happy to change their spending patterns as a form of protest. However, the younger women, whether or not they were married or mothers, tended to reject both the "homemaker" identity and the stereotype that men were producers and women consumers. Knobel's group "tried repeatedly but unsuccessfully" to convince WSP's national office to make the boycott the basis of a national campaign. Knobel's group went ahead anyway and declared the action a great success, involving thousands of women and garnering coverage in all the Chicago and suburban papers, as well as the national Huntley-Brinkley newscast.[67]

Other groups associated with the Movement splintered over disagreements about philosophy and tactics. The most militant members of Students for a Democratic Society (SDS) became the Weathermen, the most militant members of SNCC formed the Black Panthers, the most militant members of Women's Liberation formed separatist collectives such as the Furies. Despite differences, both ideological and tactical, among its members, WSP did not undergo a similar split. Even though the group's national actions and official publications became increasingly militant and leftist, some local affiliates held fast to the group's early strategy of never doing anything that might make the white, middle-class housewife uncomfortable. Even Barbara Bick, the longtime editor of *Memo* who frequently served as WSP's representative to New Left coalitions, let a hint of nostalgia for the group's early, "respectable" days enter a description of a 1969 demonstration in New York City:

> There were no screaming Yippies, far-out politics, or violent confrontations in front of the Hotel Pierre in New York on January 15. Instead close to 1,000 women, women students, mothers with babies, 30s and 40s, grandmothers, working women and women of "leisure," elegantly mink-clad and old wool-coated, bright young mini-skirts and high boots beside the serious middle-of-the-knee contingent—all were doing that traditional circular sidewalk dance to let President-elect Nixon know that he could expect them to be around until he "cut out the bloody war."[68]

What both this passage and Knobel's memo expressed was an enthusiasm for women of different ages, classes, and sartorial styles working together— apart from men. This belief in the political potential of sisterhood was something WSPers shared with the younger generation of radical feminists. As Mickey Flacks, a member of the Ann Arbor branches of WSP *and* SDS saw it, "Women Strike for Peace was an unheralded precursor of the women's movement. It was a combination of caring passionately about what we set out to do and caring passionately about each other."[69]

Although their experience with the Jeannette Rankin Brigade alienated some WSPers from women's liberation, for others it was a consciousness-raising experience that inspired a rethinking of WSP's use of traditional gender roles.[70] By 1970, many WSPers saw themselves as part of the women's movement and participated in actions such as that year's Women's Strike for Equality. They redoubled their efforts to attract students and working women as well as housewives to the organization—in 1973 an "Airline Division" of WSP was founded by a group of stewardesses and ticket agents—with the slogan "Peace is a Women's Issue."[71] However, in general, this was a less effective appeal in the seventies than it had been in the early sixties. WSP leaders such as Ethel Taylor lobbied fervently to win a place for peace and disarmament on the agendas of feminist coalitions but found that these issues were either ignored or marginalized. For most active feminists, reproductive rights, ending discrimination in employment and education, and access to daycare were women's issues; peace was no longer central to their agenda.[72]

The Vietnam peace accords went into effect in 1973, but WSP "refus[ed] to fold up its tents and go away," as the *New York Times* put it.[73] Once again, the conditions under which the group worked changed dramatically. In a way, WSP had come full circle. The women returned to their original cause of advocating disarmament and opposed the development of new weapons of mass destruction, from the Trident submarine to the neutron bomb. However, the end of the war and the disintegration of the New Left meant that the group was back to being an independent and often lonely voice. Ironically, in spite of being an autonomous women's organization, WSPers played a less central role in the women's movement than they had in the Movement. The group's passionate opposition to the war in Vietnam, its development of a strong commitment to economic and racial justice, and its willingness to play a supportive role in the struggles of draft resisters, welfare mothers, and others placed them at the hub of sixties radicalism, despite the younger activists' discomfort with what they saw as the older women's cultural conservatism. However, WSP's insistence through the seventies that peace was a feminist issue was undermined, even when they attempted to couch the argument in economic terms (e.g., cutting the military budget would free up funding for more obvious feminist concerns such as daycare, reproductive health care, and education and job training for poor women), by the longtime association of women's peace activism with the stereotypical image of women as nurturers.[74] However, for WSP to relinquish the idea that women had a special responsibility for promoting peace—the most basic of its founding principles—would have left the group with no raison d'etre.

In spite of the wide-ranging and complex role that WSP played in the social movements of the 1960s and '70s, it has largely fallen through the cracks of both New Left and second-wave feminist history. This is due, I think, to a tendency among the first generation of historians of these movements to define their terms narrowly and to write about the activists most like themselves, particularly in terms of race and age. As the historian Van Gosse has argued on more than one occasion, early scholarly works on the New Left tended to focus on the student Left and, more specifically, SDS. In fact, *New Left* was originally coined to identify a progressive third way that rejected both the doctrinaire nature and class-oriented politics of the Old Left and the fervent anticommunism of cold war liberals. During the 1960s, activists used the terms *New Left* and the *Movement,* pretty much interchangeably, to refer to participants in the peace, civil rights, antipoverty, student and, eventually, the women's liberation movements. As Gosse has written, "it is highly problematic to make age, whiteness, and student status the defining characteristics of the New Left; however unintended, the consequence is to put those white youth at the center of the narrative, with other movements at the margins." Gosse argues, "too many key activists . . . were over thirty, or even fifty, to permit us to equate the New Left solely with a 'youth revolt.' The typical local leader of the antiwar or Civil Rights movements was a middle-aged woman or a Protestant minister, not a college student."[75]

If the focus on youth had not dominated the early New Left narratives, it might have been noted that WSP was founded at the dawn of the sixties, along with SDS and SNCC and shared many of the values that set those organizations apart from older leftist and civil rights groups. WSP, like SDS and SNCC, was founded in opposition to cold war politics as usual. Like their student counterparts, WSPers developed nonhierarchical structures and favored a consensus-based approach to decision making. All three groups were committed to grassroots organizing, direct action, and what became known as "participatory democracy." One of WSP's founding documents stated, "in these days of super-organizations, we feel the individual has virtually ceased to participate directly in support of his views," a sentiment that would have fit comfortably in the Port Huron Statement, the founding document of SDS.[76]

The early narratives of the women's movement also skew young: the older generation of so-called liberal feminists receiving much less attention than the younger radicals do. This can be attributed, at least in part, to what historian Ruth Rosen calls the "female generation gap." For members of the women's liberation generation, Rosen writes, "the immediate past conjured up images of claustrophobic marriages, coercive motherhood, and constrained chastity. . . . The ghost haunting these young women wore an apron and lived vicariously through the lives of a husband and children."[77] Although this depressing description hardly applies to most WSPers, the fact that they claimed rather than critiqued the role of mother and housewife made them part of the problem, rather than part of the solution in the eyes of many younger feminists. It was largely the perspective of this younger generation—through their participation in oral history projects and their own writings—that shaped the early histories of the women's movement.[78] Those early works tend to focus on divisions: between the so-called liberal, radical, and cultural wings of feminism; between feminists and leftists; white women and black women; middle-class and working-class women; straight women and lesbians; mothers and nonmothers; separatists and women who continued to work with (and live with) men. Most WSPers, whose views on the war and issues of domestic social justice were quite radical, would probably fall into the liberal camp of feminists (both Bella Abzug and Ethel Taylor would play prominent roles in the liberal feminist establishment in the 1970s and '80s) in the late '60s. By the mid-1970s, many of their views would be taken up by cultural feminists.

It is likely that WSP's neglect at the hands of second-wave historians has less to do with their politics and more to do with the fact that mothers and motherhood in general are largely invisible in this literature. As Alice Echols has written, much of the younger generation of New Leftists and feminists was "in flight from both the nuclear family and the gender conventions of their day." Perhaps this is why historians have found it difficult to see that a group of women who publicized their adherence to those gender conventions could also play a part in those movements.[79] Although a significant number of the founding members of women's liberation were or became mothers during the movement's early years, they are rarely identified as such in histories of the second wave of feminism. Very little has been written specifically about women's struggles to integrate feminist ideas and/or activism with the practice of motherhood during those years.[80]

Recognizing that WSP was not just part of the antiwar movement, but part of the larger Movement, working in coalition with a variety of leftist, feminist, civil rights, and antipoverty groups, changes our understanding of the group's historical significance. WSP should be studied not only within the context of women's peace activism or protests against the Vietnam War, but as part of the mainstream of post–World War II social movement history. This in turn will force us to rethink whom we are referring to when we use terms such as New Left and second wave. These movements comprised a more diverse and fluid set of adherents than much of the literature to date has acknowledged, including a significant number of middle-aged women in white gloves. WSPers did not just "jump in to a whole new world" of militant protest in the mid-1960s; as mothers of the movement, they helped bring it life.

## Notes

For their helpful comments on earlier versions of this article, I would like to thank the following: Nancy Hewitt, Steven Lawson, Dee Garrison, Susan Carroll, Linda Gordon, Stephanie Gilmore, Norma Basch, Phyllis Mack, Carla MacDougall, Emily Zuckerman, and the three anonymous readers of the University of Illinois Press.

1. "Women Fight Police near White House," *New York Times,* September 21, 1967, A1. See also: "Women for Peace in Battle at White House," *Washington Post,* September 21, E1; *Memo* [WSP newsletter] 5, no. 10 (October 1967): 2, publication file, Tamiment Collection (hereafter TC), New York University; and Amy Swerdlow, *Women Strike for Peace: Traditional Motherhood and Radical Politics in the 1960s* (Chicago: University of Chicago Press, 1993), 177–80.

2. For an in-depth discussion of the group's early history, see Swerdlow, *Women Strike for Peace.*

3. "Minutes, WSP National Conference, September 22, 1967," WSP papers, series A.1, box 3, Swarthmore College Peace Collection (hereafter SCPC).

4. Quoted in *Memo* 5, no. 10 (October 1967): 11, publication file, TC.

5. For a comprehensive survey of these events, see Maurice Isserman and Michael Kazin, *America Divided: The Civil War of the 1960s* (New York: Oxford University Press, 2000).

6. This transformation has gone largely unremarked in the historiography. When WSPers are mentioned at all in histories of the 1960s, it is usually as "moderate" or "liberal" supporters of the antiwar movement or as members of a generation of activist women who were "harbingers" of second-wave feminism. Even Swerdlow, author of the one historical monograph on the group, does not really address the women's growing engagement with domestic social issues in the late 1960s and early 1970s. For WSP's place in the peace movement, see, for example, Charles DeBenedetti, *An American Ordeal: The Antiwar Movement in the Vietnam Era* (Syracuse: Syracuse University Press, 1990) and *The Peace Reform in American History* (Bloomington: Indiana University Press, 1980); Harriet Hyman Alonso, *Peace as a Women's Issue: A History of the U.S. Movement for World Peace and Women's Rights* (Syracuse: Syracuse University Press, 1993); and Nancy Zaroulis and Gerald Sullivan, *Who Spoke Up? American Protest Against the War in Vietnam* (New York: Holt, Rinehart and Winston, 1984). For WSP's relationship to second-wave feminism, see Alonso; Ruth Rosen, *The World Split Open: How the Modern Women's Movement Changed America* (New York: Penguin Books, 2000); and Sara M. Evans, *Tidal Wave: How Women Changed America at Century's End* (New York: The Free Press, 2003).

7. Judith Porter Adams, "Cora Weiss," in *Peacework: Oral Histories of Women Peace Activists* (Boston: Twayne Publishers, 1991), 42.

8. In this article, I use the term "the Movement" as it was colloquially used in the 1960s and '70s to refer to political activism that addressed a range of issues including civil rights, poverty, and the Vietnam War.

In this, I follow other scholars of the era, including Sara Evans and Terry H. Anderson. As Evans explains, "There was no way to join; you simply announced or felt yourself to be part of the movement—usually through some act like joining a protest march. Almost a mystical term, 'the movement' implied an experience, a sense of community and common purpose." Anderson describes the movement as "a kaleidescope of activity" that comprised "all activists for social change." I would clarify this characterization by adding that these activists shared a progressive or leftist perspective. The conservative Young Americans for Freedom, for example, were activists for social change, but they were not part of "the Movement." Sara Evans, *Personal Politics: The Roots of Women's Liberation in the Civil Rights Movement and the New Left* (New York: Vintage Books, 1979), 102. Terry H. Anderson, *The Movement and the Sixties: Protest in America from Greensboro to Wounded Knee* (New York: Oxford University Press, 1995), xv.

9. Ethel Barol Taylor, *We Made a Difference: My Personal Journey with Women Strike for Peace* (Philadelphia: Camino Books, 1998), 34.

10. "Ethel Taylor" in Adams, *Peacework*, 12.

11. They had good reason for concern. In 1960, the year before WSP was founded, the Committee for a SANE Nuclear Policy was devastated by a split over whether to "purge" communists from the organization after it was accused of "harboring" communists by Senator Thomas Dodd of Connecticut. For the impact of McCarthyism on peace groups, see DeBenedetti, *The Peace Reform in American History*, chap. 7; Alonso, *Peace as a Women's Issue*, chap. 6, as well as her article, "Mayhem and Moderation: Women Peace Activists During the McCarthy Era" in Joanne Meyerowitz, ed., *Not June Cleaver: Women and Gender in Postwar America* (Philadelphia: Temple University Press, 1994), 128–50. In spite of WSP's efforts to appear nonideological, fourteen members from the New York area were subpoenaed to appear before the House Committee on Un-American Activities (HUAC). The organization refused to be cowed by HUAC, standing behind the subpoenaed women. See Swerdlow, *Women Strike for Peace*, chap. 5.

12. Quoted in Swerdlow, *Women Strike for Peace*, 19.

13. Women Strike for Peace newsletter (undated), Women Strike for Peace National Organization folder, TC.

14. In their literature, WSPers referred to themselves as "angry women" on a regular basis throughout the 1960s and '70s—as did many proponents of women's liberation. The WSPers clearly did not see themselves as "passive suppliants [sic] begging for favors," although this is how they were described by members of one women's liberation group. See Radical Women's Group, "Burial of Weeping Womanhood," in *Dear Sisters: Dispatches from the Women's Liberation Movement*, ed. Rosalyn Baxandall and Linda Gordon (New York: Basic Books, 2000).

15. My interpretation of WSP's maternal rhetoric as strategically motivated by the desire to win sympathy for a controversial position and to defuse red-baiting builds on work by historians of U.S. women's activism in the 1950s including Dee Garrison, "'Our Skirts Gave Them Courage': The Civil Defense Protest Movement in New York City, 1955–61"; Deborah A. Gerson, "'Is Family Devotion Now Subversive?' Familialism Against McCarthy"; and Ruth Feldstein, "'I Wanted the Whole World to See' Race, Gender, and Constructions of Motherhood in the Death of Emmett Till," all in Meyerowitz, *Not June Cleaver*; and on the work of feminist scholars of recent Latin American women's movements, especially Las Madres de la Plaza de Mayo, including Jo Fisher, *Out of the Shadows: Women, Resistance, and Politics in South America* (London: Latin American Bureau Ltd., 1993); Marguerite Bouvard, *Revolutionizing Motherhood: The Mothers of Plaza de Mayo* (Wilmington, Del.: Scholarly Resources, Inc., 1994); and Diana Taylor, "Making a Spectacle: The Mothers of

the Plaza de Mayo" in *The Politics of Motherhood: Activist Voices from Left to Right*, ed. Alexis Jetter, Annelise Orleck, and Diana Taylor (Hanover, N.H.: University Press of New England, 1997), 182–97. The survey was sponsored by the Conflict Resolution Center at the University of Michigan at Ann Arbor. Its author, Elise Boulding was both a social scientist and long-time peace activist whose interest in the subject was motivated by a desire to understand how WSP was different from WILPF. (Boulding was active in both groups.) She identified 14,000 women who were on the mailing lists of WSP affiliates around the country and sent a questionnaire to every eighth name on the lists, ending up with 1,770. She received replies from 279. Elise Boulding, "Who Are These Women?: A Progress Report on a Study of Women Strike for Peace," 1963, WSP papers, series A.1, box 2, SCPC.

16. Swerdlow, *Women Strike for Peace*, 55. Betty Friedan criticized Wilson's decision to identify herself as "just a housewife." Friedan, *The Feminine Mystique* (New York: W. W. Norton & Co., 1963; rev. ed., 2001). Historian Ruth Rosen cites numerous examples of professional women in the 1950s and early '60s who downplayed, camouflaged, or out-and-out lied about their working lives, claiming "mother" or "housewife" as their primary identity to avoid criticism and blame at a time when working mothers were seen as undermining the American way of life and held responsible for social problems such as juvenile delinquency. Rosen, *The World Split Open*. For an in-depth analysis of the cold war's impact on the gender politics of the period, especially in regard to marriage and family life, see Elaine Tyler May, *Homeward Bound: American Families in the Cold War Era* (New York: Basic Books, 1988).

17. Boulding, "Who Are These Women?"

18. Alonso, "Mayhem and Moderation"; Alonso, *Peace as a Women's Issue*, chap. 6; DeBenedetti, *The Peace Reform in American History*, chap. 7.

19. One question in Boulding's survey asked WSPers to articulate the "fundamental purpose" of the organization. One-third of the respondents, the largest single group, said it was "educating and arousing the community." Directly working for "peace and disarmament," "changing U.S. foreign policy and/or the international machinery for solving conflicts," and "stopping atomic testing" were chosen by smaller numbers of respondents. That so many women placed "arousing the community" ahead of actually achieving their goals helps explain why maintaining a "respectable" image was so important to them during the early years.

20. Eleanor Garst, "A Reminiscence," *Memo*, April-May 1969, 13–14, publication file, TC.

21. Bernie Steele, quoted in transcript of "Washington WSP Retreat Meeting at Folly Fodor's. Saturday, October 5, 1968," 38, WSP papers, series A.1, box 2, SCPC.

22. "Lobbying Day against Vietnam War," *Memo* 4, no. 7 (February 1966): 6. publication file, TC. For example, the media outlets they most relied on to advertise their activities and positions during the early years included the *New York Times* and the liberal political magazines the *New Republic* and the *Nation*, rather than popular women's magazines.

23. "Report on The National Conference, June 8–10, 1962," WSP papers, series A.1, box 3, SCPC. Swerdlow, *Women Strike for Peace*, 90–93 and Grace Lee Boggs, *Living for Change* (Minneapolis: University of Minnesota Press, 1998), 107.

24. "Report on The National Conference, June 8–10, 1962," WSP papers, series A.1, box 3, SCPC.

25. Oral history interview with Shirley Sapin, conducted by Rohna Shoul, October 2000 (audiotape), T-278, VOW-NE Records, Schlesinger Library (hereafter SL), Radcliffe Institute.

26. "Open Letter to Women of Mississippi from New York, New Jersey, Connecticut, Philadelphia, Baltimore, and Washington D.C. Women Strike for Peace," October 2, 1962, WSP papers, series A.3, box 4, SCPC.

27. For a detailed discussion of these events, see Charles M. Payne, *I've Got the Light of Freedom: The Organizing Tradition and the Mississippi Freedom Struggle* (Berkeley: University of California Press, 1995), 153–57.

28. Swedlow, *Women Strike for Peace,* 91–92.

29. "Mrs. Coretta King Leads Peace Effort," *Southern Patriot,* May 1962, 4.

30. "Minutes, Washington, [D.C.] WSP, January 17, 1962," WSP papers, series A.1, box 1, SCPC.

31. "Enola Maxwell" in Adams, *Peacework,* 110.

32. Quoted in Marjorie Collins, "WSP Links Fights for Peace and Negro Rights," *National Guardian,* June 20, 1963, 7.

33. Ibid.

34. For more about the changing political climate, see Isserman and Kazin, *America Divided,* chap. 10.

35. "WSP Statement on the Crisis in American Cities," *Memo* 6, no. 3 (February 12, 1968): 14.

36. Betty Lankford and Eda Hallinen, Oakland Women for Peace, "Letter to National Convention," October 31, 1968, WSP papers, series A.1, box 3, SCPC.

37. "National Consultative Council Minutes," January 17, 1968, WSP papers, series A.1, box 1, SCPC; "Around the Nation," *Memo* 6, no. 1 (November 1967): 8, publication file, TC.

38. The transformation in WSP's rhetoric was probably influenced, at least in part, by contemporary debates over integration versus separatism in the civil rights and black power movements. Beginning in the mid-1960s, black nationalists argued that they had to achieve their own liberation; whites who wanted to help the black cause were encouraged to educate and organize other whites around issues of their own racism. The triumph of this viewpoint was symbolized by the expulsion of white staffers from SNCC at the end of 1966. Women of color would later argue that the tendency of some middle-class white women to act as if they were speaking for all women when they were really speaking for themselves was one of the major flaws of second-wave feminism. Scholarly works that problematize the category "woman" with an emphasis on racial differences include Elizabeth V. Spelman, *Inessential Woman: Problems of Exclusion in Feminist Thought* (Boston: Beacon Press, 1988); Deborah K. King, "Multiple Jeopardy, Multiple Consciousness: The Context of a Black Feminist Ideology, *Signs* 14 (Autumn 1988): 42–72; Patricia Hill Collins, "The Social Construction of Black Feminist Thought," *Signs* 14 (Summer 1989): 745–73; Evelyn Brooks Higginbotham, "African-American Women's History and the Metalanguage of Race," *Signs* 17 (Winter 1992): 251–74; and Patricia Hill Collins, "Shifting the Center: Race, Class, and Feminist Theorizing about Motherhood," in *Mothering: Ideology, Experience, and Agency,* ed. Evelyn Nakano Glenn, Grace Chang, and Linda Rennie Forcey (New York: Routledge, 1994), 45–66.

39. Historian Gerald Gill's findings demonstrate that Taylor's perceptions did not apply to all black women: he notes that contemporary public opinion polls regarding U.S. involvement in Vietnam found "more opposition than support" among black women and, "from early 1966 until the end of the war, what most galvanized black women to oppose the war was the escalating number of black troops killed in Vietnam." Gerald Gill, "From Maternal Pacificism to Revolutionary Solidarity: African-American Women's Opposition to the Vietnam War" in *Sights on the Sixties,* ed. Barbara L. Tischler (New Brunswick, N.J.: Rutgers University Press, 1992), 177–95.

40. Ethel Taylor, *We Made a Difference,* 27–28.

41. Ethel Taylor, "Keynote Address, WSP National Convention, October 1973, " WSP papers, series A.1, box 3, SCPC.

42. "Proxy and Lobby," 2; and "Second WSP National Consultative Conference—St. Louis," 4. publication file, TC.

43. Dagmar Wilson, "Keynote Address, November 9, 1968," *Report of the Seventh Annual WSP Convention, November 8–11, 1968,* WSP papers, series A.1, box 3, SCPC.

44. Ibid.

45. "Cora Weiss" in Adams, *Peacework,* 42.

46. "October 21 Demonstration," *Memo* 5, no. 10 (October 1967):13, publication file, TC. According to the *Washington Post,* the demonstration "started out as a peaceful, youthful rally but erupted into violence at the Pentagon late in the day" when "a surging band of about 30 demonstrators rushed into the Pentagon." Approximately 55,000 people participated; 179 were arrested, including Dagmar Wilson who "sat down in a group of about 50 persons gathering in an off-limits area of the Pentagon grounds." "GI's Repel Rush on Pentagon," *Washington Post,* October 22, 1967, A1, A11.

47. "Cora Weiss" in Adams, *Peacework,* 42.

48. "New York City Demo to End Draft," *Memo* 6, no. 3 (February 12, 1968): 9. publication File, TC. Stop the Draft Week was December 4–9, 1967. There is evidence that other "adult" peace activists from groups such as the War Resisters League and WILPF also participated in some of the week's actions. Zaroulis and Sullivan, *Who Spoke Up?,* 145–46.

49. *Memo* 6, no. 6 (September 1968): 3.

50. Ibid.

51. Ibid.

52. Ibid.

53. Sylvia Lichtenstein, quoted in transcript of "Washington WSP Retreat Meeting at Folly Fodor's. Saturday, October 5, 1968," 13, WSP papers, series A.1, box 2, SCPC.

54. *Washington Post,* September 21, 1967, E1.

55. Folly Fodor, quoted in transcript of "Washington WSP Retreat Meeting at Folly Fodor's. Saturday, October 5, 1968," 40, WSP papers, series A.1, box 2, SCPC.

56. Undated invitation, "Demonstrate with Bella Abzug," WSP New York Office organization file, TC. On WSP's involvement in Abzug's congressional campaign, see Swerdlow, *Women Strike for Peace,* 153–55. "Women who banged their shoes on the door of the Pentagon" refers to a 1967 WSP action when 2,500 demonstrators protested the military's use of napalm in Vietnam under the slogan, "Children are not for burning." The women marched to the Pentagon's entrance to demand a meeting and were locked out of the

building. They responded by taking off their shoes and banging them against the doors. Swerdlow, *Women Strike for Peace*, 134–35. Like the September demonstration at the White House, this action shows the women's new comfort with "rowdy" behavior and their increased willingness to risk negative publicity and possible arrest.

57. "Report of 7th Annual WSP National Conference Held in Winnetka, Ill., Nov. 8–11, 1968," 1, WSP papers, series A.1, box 3, SCPC.

58. Dagmar Wilson, "Keynote Address to the National Conference, November 9, 1968," 5, WSP papers, series A.1, box 3, SCPC.

59. Evelyn Alloy, "To NCC July 11, 1970," WSP papers, series A.1, box 1, SCPC.

60. Rita Handman, undated letter, 3, WSP papers, series A.3, box 13, SCPC.

61. Ibid.

62. "Lobbying Day against Vietnam War," *Memo* 4, no. 7 (February 1966): 6, *Memo* publication folder, TC.

63. For a discussion of the Jeannette Rankin Brigade from the WSP perspective, see Swerdlow, *Women Strike for Peace*, 135–41; for the perspective of women's liberation activists, see Shulamith Firestone, "The Jeannette Rankin Brigade: Woman Power? A Summary of Our Involvement" in *Notes from the First Year* (New York: The New York Radical Women, 1968.) Found online in Duke University's On-Line Archival Collection of Documents from the Women's Liberation Movement (http://scriptorium.lib.duke.edu/wlm/notes); Alice Echols, *Daring to Be Bad: Radical Feminism in America, 1967–1975* (Minneapolis: University of Minnesota Press, 1989), 54–59; and Rosen, *The World Split Open*, 201–3. The generational divide was not absolute: a number of young women identified with the civil rights, New Left, and women's liberation movements also participated in WSP. See Alonso, *Peace as a Women's Issue,* chap. 7; Swerdlow, *Women Strike for Peace,* 52; Casey Hayden, "Fields of Blue" in Constance Curry et al., *Deep in Our Hearts: Nine White Women in the Freedom Movement* (Athens: The University of Georgia Press, 2000), 348; and Mickey Flacks, interviewed Bret Eynon, transcript, September 25, 1978, Contemporary History Project, Bentley Historical Library, University of Michigan, Ann Arbor.

64. Gladys Knobel, "Report from North Shore Women for Peace, June 7, 1971," WSP papers, series A.1, box 1, SCPC.

65. The national steering committee was officially known as the National Consultative Council and included regional representatives selected by local groups. There were no officers or elections.

66. WSP's decentralized, bottom-up approach to organization (or "unorganization" as they liked to call it) also makes it difficult to determine how many women can be identified as WSPers. Partly out of a philosophical opposition to hierarchical and bureaucratic structures (which, as far as the founding members were concerned, served primarily to hamper individual initiative and make it difficult to respond quickly to critical events) and partly out of a desire to deflect potential red-baiting and government investigations, the group did not charge dues or keep official membership records. To be a WSPer was primarily a matter of self-identification; participation could range from going to an occasional protest action to regular attendance at the meetings of a local affiliate to devoting forty hours a week of unpaid labor to peace work. The group's estimate that 50,000 women in sixty cities participated in the initial one-day "strike" in 1961 was widely reported in the media and has been repeated in most of the scholarly works that mention WSP. In

attempting to verify this figure as part of the research for her book, WSP member and historian Amy Swerdlow came up with the much lower figure of 12,000. By its first anniversary in November 1962, the group was claiming a national membership of 500,000, according to the *New York Times*. Though this figure sounds overblown, the evidence suggests that WSP did continue to grow steadily between its founding and the mid-1960s. References in the group's newsletter and correspondence show that WSP locals formed in dozens of cities and towns beyond the original sixty and that large metropolitan areas such as New York, Los Angeles, the Bay Area in California, Chicago, Boston, and Detroit were home to so many WSPers that they were able to support neighborhood-based groups. That WSP participants numbered into the tens of thousands seems certain, but whether "membership" ever reached the hundreds of thousands remains a question for me. Swerdlow, *Women Strike for Peace*, 247n1; "Progress Hailed by Peace Women," *New York Times*, November 2, 1963, 10

67. Knobel, "Report from North Shore Women for Peace," 4.

68. "Cut Out the Bloody War!" *Memo* (January/February 1969): 14–15, publication file, TC.

69. The Mickey Flacks quote comes from an untitled, undated videotape of an Ann Arbor Women for Peace Reunion. VOW-NE Records, unprocessed materials, SL.

70. Swerdlow, *Women Strike for Peace*, 140–41.

71. Nadine Brozan, "Women's Group Began as One Day Protest 4,215 Days Ago," *New York Times*, May 16, 1973, 52.

72. Ethel Taylor, *We Made a Difference*, chap. 24; Brozan, "Women's Group Began as One Day Protest."

73. Brozan, "Women's Group Began as One Day Protest."

74. This changed in the 1980s when a new international women's peace movement challenged the old ideological divisions, bringing together cultural feminists, lesbian separatists, ecofeminists, and maternalists in various combinations.

75. Van Gosse, *Rethinking the New Left: An Interpretive History* (New York: Palgrave MacMillan, 2005), 5. See also Gosse, "A Movement of Movements: The Definition and Periodization of the New Left," in *A Companion to Post-1945 America*, ed. Roy Rosenzweig and Jean-Christophe Agnew (London: Blackwell, 2002), 277–302; and Gosse, *Where the Boys Are: Cuba, Cold War America, and the Making of a New Left* (New York: Verso, 1993).

76. Swerdlow, *Women Strike for Peace*, 18–19. Port Huron called for "the establishment of a democracy of individual participation." For an excellent discussion of the significance of the Port Huron Statement to the development of New Left ideology and political practices, see James Miller, *"Democracy Is in the Streets": From Port Huron to the Siege of Chicago* (New York: Touchstone, 1987). The text of the statement appears on pp. 329–74.

77. Rosen, *The World Split Open*, 39.

78. As Sherna Berger Gluck has suggested, regarding second-wave history, "because so many of the white, middle-class activists themselves—or their admirers—initially charted the course of feminist history, it is no surprise that their own pasts have shaped how their own history has been written." Gluck, "Whose Feminism? Whose History? Reflections on Excavating the History of (the) U.S. Women's Movement(s)" in *Community Activism and Feminist Politics: Organizing Across Race, Class, and Gender*, ed. Nancy Naples (New York:

Routledge, 1998), 33. Gluck's article challenges the view that the second wave was almost exclusively a white, middle-class movement. Other more recent scholarly works also challenge that view, including Wini Breines, *The Trouble Between Us: An Uneasy History of White and Black Women in the Feminist Movement* (New York: Oxford University Press, 2006); Dorothy Sue Cobble, *The Other Women's Movement: Workplace Justice and Social Rights in Modern America* (Princeton, N.J.: Princeton University Press, 2004); Premilla Nadasen, "Expanding the Boundaries of the Women's Movement: Black Feminism and the Struggle for Welfare Rights, " *Feminist Studies* 28 (Summer 2002): 271–301; Benita Roth, *Separate Roads to Feminism: Black, Chicana, and White Feminist Movements in America's Second Wave* (New York: Cambridge University Press, 2004); Kimberly Springer, *Living for the Revolution: Black Feminist Organizations, 1968–1980* (Durham, N.C.: Duke University Press, 2005); Becky Thompson, "Multiracial Feminism: Recasting the Chronology of Second Wave Feminism, " *Feminist Studies* 28 (Summer 2002): 337–55.

79. Alice Echols, "'We Gotta Get Out of This Place': Notes Toward a Remapping of the Sixties." *Socialist Review* 22 (April 1992): 22. In this essay, Echols also argues that women's activism in general and the women's liberation movement in particular have been marginalized in sixties' narratives. It is likely that not only their generational location and gender politics but also the fact that they were women helps explain why WSPers are so largely ignored in the historiography, given the fact that older male activists who were not particularly "countercultural" (e.g., David Dellinger, Staughton Lynd, Michael Harrington, and the Berrigan brothers) are much more frequently mentioned.

80. The most significant scholarly works on motherhood in the context of women's liberation are M. Rivka Polatnick, "Diversity in Women's Liberation Ideology: How a Black and a White Group of the 1960s Viewed Motherhood," *Signs* 21 (Spring 1996): 679–706; and Lauri Umansky, *Motherhood Reconceived: Feminism and the Legacies of the Sixties* (New York: New York University Press, 1996). For significant anecdotal evidence regarding the participation of mothers in the early years of the second wave, see Rachel Blau DuPlessis and Ann Snitow, eds., *The Feminist Memoir Project: Voices from Women's Liberation* (New York: Three Rivers Press, 1998).

# 6. Enabled by the Holy Spirit

## Church Women United and the Development of Ecumenical Christian Feminism

### CARYN E. NEUMANN

In the early 1960s, two women observed widespread dissatisfaction among their female friends and acquaintances. Political activist Betty Friedan diagnosed this malaise as "the feminine mystique" in her best-selling book of the same name, which challenged the popular notion that women could find complete fulfillment in their roles as wives and mothers. Episcopal minister's wife Hannah Ronsey Suthers identified a parallel phenomenon among Christian women, who in her view worshipped a false idol in the form of housework. She revised Friedan's term, coining the phrase "Christian mystique" to describe the belief that women should find all their happiness in the home by seeing their work as part of God's work and by seeing its spiritual implications. Like Suthers, other members of Church Women United (CWU) refused to regard the wielding of a vacuum cleaner as a religious experience. They believed that a proper Christian woman should not limit herself to the domestic sphere.[1]

CWU represents an organizational coalition of women from a variety of faiths and denominations, mostly Protestant. As such, it is the largest ecumenical association of religious women in the post–World War II years. Women worked within their churches and as part of the CWU coalition. CWU is one of the major liberal and multiracial organizations of this era—as well as the first group to combine Christianity with feminism. For the members of CWU, identity as Christian women necessitated a political agenda that was rooted in civil rights and feminism. The ecumenical traditions of the organization offered a path to coalition building and, particularly in the later years of the group, served as a stumbling block. This essay examines CWU's efforts on behalf of women and people of color.[2]

Viewing Christian principle as the only important factor motivating their politics, CWU members took a spiritual journey into feminism and civil rights. Following in the footsteps of many first-wave feminists, CWU viewed equality between the sexes as a right ordained by God. As more than one woman stated, Eve was created from Adam's rib to be a partner, not a servant. Engaged in social welfare work from the inception of the organization, CWU members adopted the promotion of racial equity as a logical extension of their activities. In doing so, CWU joined many other biracial organizations of the twentieth century that had traveled the same path to civil rights and feminism.

Despite the evident importance of the church to women, histories of the women's movement rarely consider mainstream religion.[3] Yet some second-wave feminists found religion to be a liberating force, both spiritually and in the public world. To understand how feminism and civil rights have become embedded within American society, it is necessary to reimagine the second wave to include an emphasis upon traditional religious beliefs.

CWU had a clear intent to actively spread a message of Christianity. Simply backing male leaders by filling pews and raising funds was not sufficient service to God. To be good Christians, these women had to become involved in politics. They had a God-given obligation to help the weak and to end oppression. This responsibility mandated active participation in the public world. Christian identity necessitated a political agenda rooted in liberal activism. CWU focused on civil rights and on challenging racism within the ranks of churchwomen. A growing sense of empowerment as women prompted the group to split formally from the male-dominated National Council of Churches (NCC). As an independent organization, CWU then addressed women's issues from a Christian feminist perspective, focusing on women's labors, poverty, and abortion. Throughout the postwar era, CWU carefully balanced the beliefs of the various denominations within the organization with the need to maintain an ecumenical dialogue.

Religion has long served as one of the pillars of U.S. society, and religious faith held a place of enormous importance in the hearts of mid-twentieth-century Americans. The 1950s welcomed a religious revival that swept up millions of people seeking relief from the anxieties of the cold war. The postwar baby boom created countless new families for whom attachment to church became as normal as increased personal prosperity and a move to the suburbs.[4] As the decade began, more than 95 percent of Americans professed a belief in God with 74 percent thinking about him daily.[5] Best-selling books in those years included the Reverend Norman Vincent Peale's *Power of Positive Thinking,* Bishop Fulton J. Sheen's *Peace of Soul,* and Rabbi Joshua Loth Liebman's *Peace of Mind.* A 1958 study by the U.S. Bureau of the Census found that 66.2 percent (78,952,000) of Americans regarded themselves as Protestant, 25.7 percent (30,669,000) as Roman Catholic, 3.2 percent (3,868,000) as Jewish, and 1.3 percent (1,545,000) with other faiths.[6]

Most churchgoers have historically been women, and women have played a much more significant role than men in supporting community churches. Among African American congregations, women have long been described as the "backbone of the church" but the phrase applies equally to churchgoing women of other races. In 1953, a survey on the status and service of women in the churches, sponsored by CWU and covering thirty communions, discovered that women made up about 60 percent of church members.[7] A NCC report disclosed that total church giving increased more rapidly than membership among forty-seven Protestant and Eastern Orthodox communions in the twenty-one years prior to 1953. Evidently, women were not only filling pews but also digging deeply into their purses to help maintain ministers, church buildings, and church programs.[8] The paradox lies in the fact that while women gave support, spiritually and materially, to the church, they remained in a subordinate role. They served as the spine, not the brain.

CWU traces its beginnings to the time just before Pearl Harbor. In 1941, as war spread around the globe, the Federated Church Women and the missionary associations met to further peace through ecumenism. They shared civic and religious goals and felt the need for a national umbrella organization to provide expertise and coordination.[9] CWU worked on a broad range of projects including war relief and opposition to the internment of Japanese Americans, then later reconstruction and reconciliation especially as they affected women and children; efforts for peace; and the cultivation of just racial relations. Furthering the aims of ecumenical education and fellowship across the nation and around the globe were additional objectives.[10]

The membership and leaders of CWU came from nearly every Protestant denomination. Individual women from Roman Catholic, Orthodox Christian, Southern Baptist, and other religious bodies such as the Salvation Army that were not formally related to CWU participated in the movement at all levels.[11] Jewish women's groups cooperated with CWU on common social concerns and in ecumenical dialogue. In 1948, CWU estimated the number of its affiliated churchwomen at 10 million, with 25 state councils and 1,000 local councils.[12]

Women practice religion in ways both similar to and different from men. Many of the elements closest to religious meaning—conceiving life, giving birth, nurturing, and providing care through the passages of life—have been connected more with women than with men. However, women did not engage with religion only in the confines of church and home. In 1948, *Ladies Home Journal* sponsored a nationwide survey designed to determine the intensity of religious faith in the United States and the extent to which it governed behavior. Fifty-four percent of respondents declared that their religious beliefs had no effect upon their politics or business dealings, but a not-insignificant 39 percent did indeed mix religion with politics and money matters.[13]

Like the religious women in the survey, CWU members practiced religion in public life. Dorothy Dolbey, CWU board member and a 1951 candidate for the Cincinnati City Council, ran for political office because "citizenship is our Christian concern. We must care enough for the privileges of democracy to make them work." CWU President Mossie Wyker declared, "we are banded together to do His work." In 1953, CWU named "Citizenship—Our Christian Concern" as its annual promotion. Cynthia Wedel, then a member of the executive committee and later a CWU president, explained, "if a Christian's love for his fellowman is real and urgent, it will drive him to seek the causes of slums, juvenile delinquency, poor schools, and lack of health facilities." Five years later, Wedel observed that "freedom from fear of anyone but God is one of the glorious liberties of the Christian. . . . We may be despised and rejected by men—but we need have no fear if we are sincerely trying to obey God. If He is for us, who can be against us?"[14] In 1964, CWU President Louise Wallace stated, "no one who professes belief in Christ is exempt from some kind of responsible leadership in expressing one's loyalty to him." A decade in the future, Nelle Morton, another CWU member, would combine an obligation to God with feminism. She declared, "being Christian means more than community service. It means working through our differences about what it means to be a woman, about ERA [Equal Rights Amendment], the meaning of liberation. It means overcoming theological differences and . . . convincing bishops and archbishops that being ecumenical is not dangerous."[15]

From its beginnings, CWU strongly supported a goal of racial inclusiveness. The organization declared that it intended to make the organization open to all women, whether European American, African American, Japanese American, or Mexican American. In October of 1952, CWU issued a statement that the organization had come into being through the efforts of an interracial group and that it would continue to work until "every barrier that separates people because of race or color has been removed." The organization further vowed to make race relations a priority because they were "determine[d] to take steps toward the fulfillment of our Christian purposes."[16] CWU also reiterated its emphasis on human rights by reaffirming its belief "on the inclusiveness of our Christian fellowship across denominational and racial lines." CWU called upon its members "to appraise all meetings in regard to representative attendance," "to act when another's rights are threatened," and "to strive for the integration of all Christian women in all phases of the work of local councils."[17] With these statements, the churchwomen took a clear stand in support of integration. In many areas, particularly the Deep South, CWU would stand practically alone.[18]

The puzzle is why CWU women were willing to take the risks that others were not about to assume. The South certainly had no shortage of devout Christians, but those who were willing to face harassment on behalf of blacks were rare. In Southern states, one self-proclaimed "outside agitator" observed that "local people dare not write or speak out [against segregation] unless they are prepared to be tracked down by police in their every act, lose contracts, have mortgages withdrawn, credit ended or endure some kind of harassment."[19]

Such behavior did not mesh well with CWU's defined purpose of "encouraging church women to come together in a visible fellowship to witness their faith in Jesus Christ and, enabled by the Holy Spirit, to go out together into every neighborhood and nation as instruments of reconciling love."[20] Jane Schutt, a CWU Mississippi leader, explained that she had "words to live by," an Episcopal prayer that began "Almighty God, who has made of one blood, all nations to dwell upon the face of the earth." A second prayer contained the phrase "make no peace with oppression." Schutt had grown up with these prayers and she debated exactly what they meant. Upon deciding that God created all men of one blood, Schutt decided that she should accept the wisdom of a higher power and be welcoming to African Americans.[21] CWU members, such as Schutt, offered independent Christian witness.

The privileges of gender and belief that women had little power anyway may have permitted the women to be more radical than other like-minded Christians. In many ways, it was easier for white women than white men to challenge racial norms. Although women would be hurt economically if their husbands suffered a drop in income, only about one-third of white American women were employed outside the home in the early 1950s.[22] Removed from the danger of being fired, white women who supported civil rights generally risked only social ostracism, although cross burnings in front yards and threats of violence did occur. As one example, the white supremacists of the Ku Klux Klan (KKK) burned a cross in the front yard of Jane Schutt's home one December night because of her stand on integration. Schutt gathered with her family before deciding to string garlands of pine over the burned beams in an act of both Christian witness and Christmas decorating. The

KKK never bothered her again, but Schutt's children suffered the loss of friends because she invited African Americans to come to the family home for prayer groups.[23]

In 1960, CWU went on record as opposing segregated lunch counters and in support of sit-in demonstrations as a measure of protest against segregation.[24] At the state level, the Commission on Human Rights of Kentucky asked CWU to join its Equal Service for All campaign. The Kentucky churchwomen agreed to carry in their handbags a supply of small cards to be left at public eating places that they visited for meals. The cards mentioned Kentucky's policy of equal service in places of public accommodation and asked the restaurateurs to extend their services to all, regardless of race or color.[25]

In 1965, CWU national leaders joined Coretta Scott King, herself a board member, in the rush to Selma, Alabama, after black demonstrators were attacked by cattle prod–wielding, rioting state troopers and Dallas County deputies on the Edmund Pettus Bridge. Led by Martin Luther King Jr., the group of about a thousand blacks and half as many whites included the Reverend James J. Reeb of Boston. Beaten by white hoodlums after the march, Reeb died of his injuries.[26] Civil rights activism, even by white people of the cloth, brought readily evident dangers.

CWU did more than support civil rights activism. It developed a comprehensive program and worked with determination to raise consciousness about race among its own members. In 1957, CWU began its first major program to combat racism. From 1957 to 1959, the organization conducted forty-three human relations workshops throughout the nation to help churchwomen focus on whom and what needed to be changed. Although aimed at improving race relations, these workshops also raised consciousness of gender-based discrimination among the women who participated. The participants in a typical workshop would ask each other such questions as Who are the respected citizens in this town and why? Who really is the power in the schools, the labor market, the churches, and the welfare system?[27] The participants learned not to stereotype by race, but in confronting the power of whites, they also made comparisons between the position of African Americans and the position of women.

The largest undertaking ever attempted by CWU, Assignment: Race encouraged every member to explore racism in herself, her family, and her community. Begun in 1961 and lasting until 1964, the program grew out of Methodist activism. The women of the Methodist Church had a tradition of being at the forefront of social action. They designed and introduced a program to bring about reconciliation between the black and white races.[28] Clearly aimed at whites, the race of the majority of CWU members, the program nevertheless managed to cause some soul-searching among devout black women. It forced both black and white women to define justice and to contemplate power relations within their communities.

As part of Assignment: Race, each participant wrote, on a pledge card, how she planned to carry out the CWU aim of justice for all the races. Each CWU member was expected to act in support of African Americans, and the card asked for a description of specific activities to be undertaken to better the lives of blacks. The very act of completing the card was empowering for many women. A white member of the Evanston, Illinois, chapter, Elizabeth Hazelden, saw the assignment as a way to close ranks with other Christian women. She wrote: "Memories engulfed me and I thought of the various activities in which I have engaged in the years past. I felt again the strictures of inadequacy, the frustration, the spiritual weariness on the part of both Negro and white women."[29] Black women in CWU tended to focus more on economic than racial inequality when completing the cards. A black member of another local chapter, Juanita J. Saddler, skipped over integration, named poverty as the greatest evil facing society, and vowed to take action against economic injustice. Saddler stated that prejudice in any form is "worth struggling against not only because of the growth in wholeness that comes to anyone with the courage to face such questions."[30]

In trying to awaken its membership to the problems of racism, CWU had opened the door to a discussion about all of the injustices in society. Along with examining what it meant to be black or white in America, CWU members were exploring what it meant to be without power or material resources.

Upon receiving the Assignment: Race cards, a national committee then utilized the comments to mold a CWU educational program. Assignment: Race helped women to be community leaders by assisting them with development of the skills and knowledge needed to establish a movement. The program brought together blacks and whites and encouraged these women to share strategies for making society more Christian, more livable for all people. As women, the members believed that they could act where men feared to tread because it was more difficult to punish women for activism. Edna Sinclair, a white woman who led CWU from 1964 to 1967 commented, "we were freer to integrate meetings, eating places, churches—we were not so apt to be fired from jobs."[31] CWU women integrated meetings, eating places, and churches. They learned to work together with other women in trying situations, experience that would be used later in the women's movement.[32]

Responding to demands from members for civic activism, CWU formulated a civil rights program and many of its members became activists. CWU's activism in the area of race relations indicates a shift among organized religious women from seeing the role of a Christian woman as merely supporting decisions already taken to assuming an active role in the power to make decisions about policy and practices. In the long run, as Margaret Shannon stated, the value of Assignment: Race may not have been what CWU contributed to civil rights throughout the nation. Its greatest value was what it caused to happen within the membership of CWU.

CWU, despite scattered opposition through the years from some members, expected Christian women to put their faith into practice by supporting the downtrodden and oppressed.[33] Supportive of civil rights, CWU members found themselves pressured in the 1950s and 1960s to halt their activities to "make the Earth fair."[34] Some members did indeed leave CWU because of the group's civil rights stand, and the organization's work did become more difficult in conservative areas, but CWU continued to fight for civil rights and now began to strongly challenge the status of women.

Certainly, their commitment to civil rights helped to raise feminist consciousness among CWU members, although an awareness of women's subordination was present from the beginnings of the organization. Perhaps the best example of the gradual awakening of feminism in CWU can be seen in its dealings with NCC. In 1950, the Council of Church Women decided to join with other "movement" church groups in the formation of an umbrella organization, the NCC.[35] In doing so, CWU expressed some early feminist statements. Although the move offered the hope that the women's group would gain influence through a guarantee of representation on the various sections and committees of the NCC including the executive committee, the decision to join the NCC met with much controversy in CWU. Fears that CWU would lose its unique identity and that the interests of women would be ignored made many women hesitate to endorse the merger. In the end, Marjorie Terrell, the head of the merger committee, helped complete the union by remarking, "it is only fair to remind ourselves that in the event of a negative decision a Woman's Department will be set up within the National Council in which case the CWU will find itself outside the mainstream of the cooperative ecumenical movement."[36]

On January 1, 1951, the General Department of United Church Women officially started life with its general secretary, Dorothy MacLeod, working to ensure both the representation of women in all NCC matters and the independence of CWU.[37] As some members had feared, the merger did not proceed smoothly.[38] CWU struggled as an administrative and policy-making organization to establish its place within the council.[39] The women tried to preserve as much autonomy as possible, but as a subordinate of the larger group this was not always possible. Additionally, NCC made promises to

CWU about the distribution of power that were not honored to the satisfaction of the women.[40]

Some years later, leading churchwomen attempted to explain the changing position of women within the denominations and the NCC. As Margaret Shannon, a CWU national leader in the 1940s and 1950s explained, women knew what they were free to do in their own sphere. Women generally served as elders and lay ministers, but experienced difficulty moving out of supporting roles to a place of leadership within the church. "In the early days we had to fight every inch of the way for our voice to be heeded and our person to be involved in policy making," Dorothy Dolbey explained when describing the NCC of the fifties. Even though some men did support the efforts of women to be heard, equality proved to be elusive.

Although male leaders often blocked CWU members from church administration and decision making, the women gradually became more radical in their attempts to exert influence over church and secular matters. Tensions between CWU and NCC had been building for years. The loss of CWU autonomy, a strong desire to return to grassroots activism, and the influence of feminism all contributed mightily to a desire among the women to break with NCC.[41] In 1966, a monetary dispute centered around the amount of money designated for black women's issues finally prompted CWU to walk away from the NCC's control. Although the NCC strongly supported civil rights, it did not share CWU's interest in the special concerns of black women. CWU did not see the concerns of black women as being the same as the concerns of black men, and it refused to subordinate the interests of women to those of men.

The members of CWU had come to the realization that they could easily stand on their own, apart from the men of the church. Once frightened into joining the NCC for fear that a separate women's group would be undercut by the formation of a women's group within the NCC, the CWU members now believed that they had little to lose by going it alone. With CWU marginalized by the NCC, separation offered the promise of greater success for CWU activism.

By 1969, CWU was no longer quite as contented to be a subgroup of the NCC. In the early 1960s, CWU leaders recognized the subordinate position of women but did not organize within NCC to change it. Louise Wallace, CWU president from 1961 to 1964 recalled, "we were very aware of the lack of representation of women in the churches, as lay leaders and staff, of the denominations, frequently raised the issue and though we felt terribly underacknowledged as leaders in the churches, there was no organized movement to initiate changes."[42] By the late 1960s, a CWU member proclaimed, "[women] have courted social action from the periphery in the past; now we need to understand power!"[43] A CWU national leader stated, "we no longer see our role as merely [being] supportive of decisions already taken. We now see a shift of emphasis to an active role in sharing the power which makes basic decisions."[44] Dorothy Dolbey, CWU president from 1967 to 1971 realized that a women's movement was emerging. "Everywhere I went I tried to translate its impact and effectiveness in political terms as well as religious," she remembered, adding that "CWU related to the women's movement then by encouraging women to 'do their thing' and sending representatives to national conferences on women's goals and projects who then reported back to us."[45]

The women's movement was just beginning to emerge and a growing sense of feminist consciousness began to bloom. In learning to analyze power relations between the races, the members of CWU also taught themselves to examine power relations between men and women. Dorothy Dolbey, who had lamented in 1951 that women did most of the volunteer work yet remain shut out of political life, sent a letter to male church leaders in 1969 in which she complained, "all people, not just Black, are weary and literally 'fed up' with being left out of representation in decision making."[46] The women of the church were directly challenging the men of the church over matters of policy, an area traditionally out of purview of women.

As Margaret Shannon declared in a 1970 letter to the NCC, "Women are not something that can be 'administered.' They are participants in the ecumenical movement and are increasingly reluctant to participate without a role in the decision making process."[47] Edna Sinclair, the national president in the mid-1960s, explained, "it was a gradual realization that if we went to a movement of Church women outside of the [male-dominated] National Council of Churches we would be more adequate to assist women of the church and others."[48] In June of 1970, the NCC voted to recognize CWU as a related movement and to work with it as the council's primary link to church and secular women's organization.[49]

CWU became an independent movement with its own bylaws. All financial ties between the two groups were cut in 1971, following a reorganization of the NCC.[50] "It was a fight over how much money the women could have and how much everybody else could have," Margaret Shannon explained. Along with a lack of representation of black women on NCC committees, the NCC was not taking the needs of African American women into consideration and the CWU was refused money to assist these women. The NCC offered the women $10,000 to finance the entire CWU race program. CWU leaders wanted money specifically designated to assist black women, particularly because the NCC was in the midst of devoting money to the concerns of black men.[51] As Bessie Marsh added about the progressiveness of the NCC, "it was clear to see that we were so far ahead of them. . . ."[52]

To address the pressing concerns of 1950s women, CWU began to explore the problems faced by women in the labor force. The paid labor force participation of CWU members is unknown. Anecdotal evidence indicates that many were identified as housewives or minister's wives. The members were apparently well aware, however, of prejudice toward women who worked outside of the home. Cynthia Wedel noted, "in discussing the Church's attitude toward women who work, we need to remind ourselves again and again of the Christian doctrine of man . . . every person is an individual endowed by the Creator with certain talents and abilities and given freedom to exercise those talents."[53] In short and in sharp contrast to societal teachings in the 1950s, women had a God-given right to work. By focusing on female employment outside of the home, CWU addressed the concerns of women trying to balance work with traditional notions of womanhood, what Betty Friedan would term in 1963 as the "feminine mystique."

The early stirrings of feminism can be seen in CWU in the 1950s. Cynthia Wedel, CWU president from 1955 to 1958, named the increasing employment of women as the main issue effecting women during her presidency. A growing consciousness of being a woman was beginning to be evident in CWU members, Wedel recollected, spurred on by the World Council of Churches Department on Cooperation of Men and Women and CWU's participation in it, and CWU responded by becoming concerned about working women.[54] Many CWU members listed their professions as housewife, but they also set up programs to assist women working outside of the home. When 950 CWU members gathered to address "womanpower" in a St. Louis hotel in 1957, the keynote speaker, Margaret Hickey, noted that the American economy depended for one-third of its labor force upon women and that over half of these women were married. CWU had worked to set up development programs for women outside of the United States, doing so because, as Hickey stated, "the arguments concerning women's rights are outmoded. Today, it's a question of human rights."[55]

Like most other women's organizations of this era such as the American Association of University Women and the National Council of Negro Women, CWU opposed the Equal Rights Amendment (ERA). It did so under the belief that passage would invalidate existing legal protections for women and result in discrimination against women.[56] This stance met some opposition from the rank-and-file, one of whom belonged to the Connecticut Committee for the Equal Rights Amendment in 1952. Florence L. C. Kitchelt said she supported the amendment because "much as I should like to see women in policy-making positions, I do not believe that second-class citizens are going to be appointed, or elected, to important jobs."[57] Undoubtedly because of its opposition to the ERA, CWU received an invitation to participate in a new government commission formed to study the problems of women.[58]

When President John F. Kennedy established a Committee on the Status of Women (PCSW) in 1961, several CWU members, including Hickey, offered recommendations to achieve greater freedom for women in the United States. The PCSW assessed the position of women and the functions that they performed in the home, the economy, and society. The commission established subcommittees to explore in depth the following areas: education; home and community services; private employment, in particular that under federal contracts; employment in the federal government; labor standards; federal social insurance and taxes as they affect women; and the legal treatment of women in respect to civil and political rights. Hickey, the public affairs editor for *Ladies' Home Journal,* served as a Kennedy appointee to the commission. Cynthia Wedel had served as CWU president from 1955 to 1958 and worked as the assistant general secretary for program in the NCC when appointed to the commission. Pauli Murray, an active African American Episcopalian member of CWU chosen by the commission to assist it because of her legal expertise as a senior fellow of Yale University Law School, served on the Committee on Civil and Political Rights. CWU took part in the PCSW as a cooperating organization.[59] The PCSW completed its work in October 1963 and issued a report with proposals for reducing sex discrimination against women while also emphasizing women's maternal role. It recommended significant changes in government policies and employment and educational practices. Ultimately, along with increasing awareness of the penalties experienced by women by virtue of their sex, the PCSW brought visibility and legitimacy to women's concerns.[60]

Following the report, CWU set up its own committee on the role of women. The need for the committee was explained when a member wrote in 1965: "From Genesis to Paul there needs to be some clearer understanding of what is being said to our time on the being and the role of women. Some pressures are for equality, others for women to maintain a subordinate role in the home. In the midst of all this the church seems to be saying practically nothing to help women understand who they are and to deal with these often conflicting pressures."[61]

CWU attempted in a variety of ways to assist women in adjusting to societal changes. The organization's largest effort became an ecumenical one, involving cooperation with the Young Women's Christian Association, the National Council of Jewish Women, the National Council of Catholic Women, and the

National Council of Negro Women. President Kennedy had challenged these women in 1963 to find a way to end domestic inequality, racism, and poverty.[62] They responded by forming Women in Community Service (WICS), part of the War on Poverty, in 1965.

The organizations coordinated their efforts to focus on combating poverty among young women. To fulfill this aim, WICS served as the primary recruiter of women for the Job Corps. Part of the 1964 Economic Opportunity Act, the Job Corps aimed to end poverty within a generation by providing young men and women with the skills necessary to succeed in the workplace. The program accepted individuals from poor families who required additional education, training, or other intensive assistance in order to secure meaningful employment, continue schooling, qualify for other training programs, or, in the case of men, meet military entrance requirements. The legislation approving the program mandated that corps members had to be drawn from living environments characterized by cultural deprivation, a disruptive home life, or other disorienting conditions that would substantially impair their prospects for successful participation in any other program. The enrollees also had to be permanent U.S. citizens between the ages of fourteen and twenty-one. (In practice, only people over sixteen were chosen.) Lastly, they had to be capable and motivated individuals free of any medical or behavioral problems that would impair judgment. Job Corps planners had focused only on male unemployment in the assumption that workforce participation of women would be interrupted by marriage and pregnancy. Women, less than 25 percent of participants, would be underrepresented.[63]

WICS solicited and screened women for the Job Corps, referred to other programs those girls who did not qualify for the Job Corps, and provided pre–Job Corps support to selected applicants. The volunteers also provided special services, such as transportation, to corpswomen in some centers.[64]

WICS strove to bring new opportunities for women of the working class. In Arizona, CWU member Barbranell Stake recalled trying to recruit girls by discussing the program with their families. "Many of these girls came from homes where their parents didn't want them ever to leave home. The Indian girls would be out on the reservation, but even in town in the barrios for the Hispanics, their fathers would not want them to leave the barrio," she remembered.[65] Stake, a Baptist and strong ecumenist, became involved with CWU after watching some of the women bring food to the migrant worker camps around Phoenix in the 1950s.

The Job Corps came under attack because of high costs per trainee and because of poor discipline prevalent in some of the centers, including much-publicized criminal incidents involving enrollees. Many rural white enrollees and many predominantly white communities were disconcerted and resentful to find some centers almost entirely black. Following the election of President Richard Nixon in 1968, the program moved from the Office of Economic Opportunity to the Department of Labor. This transfer, ostensibly designed to coordinate labor programs to provide better service, resulted in Job Corps cutbacks and the closings of several sites including a West Coast Women's Center in Southern California tied to the churchwomen. WICS stopped being the sole recruiter for the Women's Job Corps. CWU believed that the changes would be disastrous because children from slum and ghetto areas needed a complete change of environment to become responsible and useful citizens.[66] WICS lamented that rural girls were not even considered in the Nixon administration proposals. The group undertook a new program of supportive services in the 1970s to continue its support of poor women.[67]

CWU supported both birth control and abortion because it had an imperative to mobilize churchwomen to "bring an end to the pauperization and marginalization of women."[68] The NCC had a policy of long-standing support for birth control. As a department of the larger group, CWU also adopted this policy.[69] After separation, CWU maintained a belief in the benefits of birth control.

However, the presence of women from different denominations, including Roman Catholics, in the movement complicated the question of choice for CWU at the national level. Local chapters, often less ecumenical in composition, had the opportunity to be more activistic. The Oxford, Mississippi, chapter considered supporting a Planned Parenthood program for its community in 1969. The idea was abandoned because organizing a Planned Parenthood clinic required five thousand dollars, a sum outside the unit's financial reach. Instead, Oxford CWU encouraged its members to use word-of-mouth to alert the women of the town to the availability of the pill at the Public Health Office. At least half of the Oxford members were African American so, even though Southern whites often supported birth control as means of eugenics for blacks, this does not appear to be the case with these women.[70]

Christian concern prompted CWU to support the right of women to make the final decision about the termination of a pregnancy but, again, ecumenicalism made the decision a difficult one. On March 19, 1970, CWU called for the repeal of the current abortion laws that denied this right to women. "New medical techniques make abortions safe, but current laws force women into dangerous situations and discriminate particularly against the poor woman," the churchwomen declared. They adopted a resolution asking the upcoming CWU Commission on Women in Today's World to consider the ethical and theological aspects of abortion so that "women find adequate understanding and support." Five board members, including Catholic nun Sister Mary Luke Tobin, refused to take a public stand on abortion but agreed with "the objective of reforming inequitable laws which do not recognize the rights of women."[71]

In March 1970, abortion rights advocates were setting up abortion counseling clinics throughout the country; legislatures in places such as New York (home of CWU) were debating repeal of their criminal abortion statutes; the American Civil Liberties Union was preparing a test case in New York to argue that abortion laws were unconstitutional; and pro-choice forces were putting referenda on the ballot in states such as Washington. By the time the Commission on Women met in June of 1970, oral arguments in *Roe v. Wade*, the case that would result in the legalization of abortion, had already opened in Texas.[72] Pauli Murray, an Episcopalian minister on the commission as well as an African American feminist of considerable note, pointed out that the question of abortion needed to be related to that of reproductive control. She argued that it had to be reconciled with the principle of "a woman's right to control her own body and the right of a man to become a father." The commission made no decision.[73] Apparently, deeming the subject too controversial, CWU at the national level never again voiced unqualified support for abortion.

Yet local leaders enjoyed the freedom to be advocates for abortion and did not hesitate to use religion to bolster their positions. Rosa Trigg of Indiana CWU wrote about the split within the CWU of Clark County over the matter of control over a woman's body. The antiabortion Clark County CWU members had passed around a petition in 1973 after the *Roe v. Wade* decision stating, "we as Christian women . . . feel the responsibility of safeguarding the moral philosophy of our nation." The pro-choice Clark County churchwomen took great offense at this wording. Trigg explained, "we do not agree that abortion is an unmitigated evil; sometimes it is the lesser of two evils. We are therefore glad that the Supreme Court has found the anti-abortion legislation to be unconstitutional . . . we regretfully accept abortion as one means to prevent the bringing to existence of unwanted, unloved, pitiful, and neglected babies." Trigg closed with the coup de grâce, "Jesus once said: 'It would be better . . . if he had not been born.' (Mark 14:21)"[74]

The women's movement by the early 1970s formed two distinct branches, although many a woman had a foot on each branch. The long-established groups, CWU among them, focused on women's rights and moderate change. The younger organizations defined themselves as radical and sought women's liberation. Cynthia Wedel recognized the value in the two sides working together. She stated, "[CWU] should be deeply involved [in the women's movement] as I believe we are. We can be a 'bridge' between militant feminists and more conservative women."[75]

The national leadership, as evident in the questions it posed, viewed CWU as being a part of the feminist movement. A good number of rank-and-file members, although not surprisingly admitting that a desire for fellowship prompted most of them to join CWU, showed awareness of and concern for feminist goals. In 1974, 68 percent of the women agreed that there was some consciousness among the women of being part of a national women's movement with 14 percent believing that a "great deal" of consciousness about sex-based discrimination existed. Sixty-four percent of respondents expressed concern about the ability of women to "fulfill aspirations," and 77 percent of those surveyed expected CWU members to "relate to women in transition (welfare, divorced, etc.)."[76] In most organizations, a small percentage of the membership constitutes the most active group with many of the participants seeking nothing more than camaraderie while expressing passive support for the organization's goals. CWU is not an exception to this rule, but most of its members did recognize the feminist direction of the organization and approved of feminist activism.

By 1969, a feminist consciousness among organized religious women had clearly emerged. In this year, Peggy Billings, an executive of the United Methodist Church and CWU, stood before the General Assembly of the National Council of Churches and declared that the Women's Caucus of the NCC supported the movement to liberate women.[77] Three years later, Billings stated that it would be easier to leave churchmen alone to go about their business, "if it were your business, but it's *our Lord's business* [Billings's emphasis] . . . and we must participate."[78] She added, "among women, many of us are experiencing a new sense of sisterhood, a new understanding of community, revealed in a supportive, non-competitive style and an actualization of non-hierarchical process. For all of this we are grateful to God."[79]

By 1975, CWU's liberalism and efforts to reform society were made apparent in a public relations statement approved by the leadership. This brochure, distributed widely in the churches, is worth quoting heavily because it is explicitly feminist in its words. Along with a line advocating activism to reduce racial and economic injustices, the pamphlet includes the statement that the CWU movement functioned to "enable women to make more fully their full contribution to society; to develop among women a sense of their own identity, confidence in their ability to be full participants in society and in today's liberating movement; to develop a lifestyle appropriate to the faith alive in them; and to venture in new forms of witness and service."[80]

Working in male-focused arenas, CWU helped advance liberal reforms in an effort to provide women from every racial and class background with the opportunity to direct the course of their own lives. The organization took an early and clear stand in support of civil rights and equality of opportunity for women.[81] It is a radical organization and yet it is also clearly part of the mainstream.

CWU attracted a broad nationwide base of typical Americans—the Presbyterian or Methodist or Episcopalian ladies next door. Photos of CWU gatherings reveal middle-aged women, predominantly white, with gloves, hats, and conservative dresses. Many of them look like the minister's wives that they, in fact, are. However, contrary to appearances, the women of CWU were rabble-rousers, passionately motivated by their faith. As one of them stated, "it is profoundly un-Christian to put people in pigeon holes according to sex or race or class. . . ."[82] The organization defined its purpose as "encouraging church women to come together in a visible fellowship to witness their faith in Jesus Christ and, enabled by the Holy Spirit, to go out together into every neighborhood and nation as instruments of reconciling love."[83] By constructing a Christianity-based justification for women's involvement in the public world, CWU also created a justification for activism on behalf of the oppressed. It advanced the status of women because that was what Jesus would do.

## Notes

1. Church Women United (CWU) has been known as the United Council of Church Women and United Church Women. To reduce confusion, I will refer to the organization by its final name, CWU. Hannah Ronsey Suthers, "Religion and the Feminine Mystique," *Christian Century* 82 (July 21, 1965): 911–14.

2. Several other scholars have also addressed antiracism activism among multiracial groups and on the part of white Southern women. See Becky W. Thompson, *A Promise and A Way of Life: White Antiracist Activism* (Minneapolis: University of Minnesota Press, 2001) and Gail S. Murray, ed., *Throwing Off the Cloak of Privilege: White Southern Women Activists in the Civil Rights Era* (Gainesville: University Press of Florida, 2004) as well as Sara Mitchell Parson, *From Southern Wrongs to Civil Rights: The Memoir of a White Civil Rights Activist* and Catherine Fosl, *Subversive Southerner: Anne Braden and the Struggle for Racial Justice in the Cold War South* (New York: Palgrave Macmillan, 2002).

3. Notable works that do address women include Susan M. Hartmann's *The Other Feminists: Activists in the Liberal Establishment* (New Haven, Conn.: Yale University Press, 1998); Sara Evans, *Personal Politics: The Roots of Women's Liberation in the Civil Rights Movement and the New Left* (New York: Vintage, 1979); Lois A. Boyd and R. Douglas Brackenridge, *Presbyterian Women in America: Two Centuries of a Quest for Status* (Westport, Conn.: Greenwood, 1996); Cheryl Townsend "The Politics of 'Silence': Dual-Sex Political Systems and Women's Traditions of Conflict in African-American Religion," in

*African-American Christianity: Essays in History,* ed. Paul E. Johnson (Berkeley: University of California, 1994); Mary A. Kassian, *The Feminist Gospel: The Movement to Unite Feminism with the Church* (Wheaton, Ill.: Crossway Books, 1992).

4. Mark A. Noll, *A History of Christianity in the United States and Canada* (Grand Rapids, Mich.: William B. Eerdmans, 1992), 437.

5. Lincoln Barnett, "God and the American People," *Ladies Home Journal* 65 (November 1948): 36.

6. John Corrigan and Winthrop S. Hudson, *Religion in America* (Upper Saddle River, N.J.: Pearson Prentice Hall, 2004), 366.

7. "Women in the Churches," *National Council Outlook* (June 1953): 8.

8. "Stewardship is More than a Word To Churchmen," *National Council Outlook* (February 1953): 5.

9. Virginia Lieson Brereton, "United and Slighted: Women as Subordinated Insiders," in *Between the Times: The Travail of the Protestant Establishment in America, 1900–1960,* ed. William R. Hutchinson (Cambridge: Cambridge University Press, 1989), 149.

10. Geraldine Sartain, "Those Women!" *National Council Outlook* (September 1955): 12–13; "United Church Women," [1963?], box 59, folder 19, CWU papers; Susan Hill Lindley, *"You Have Stept Out of Your Place": A History of Women and Religion in America* (Louisville, Ky.: Westminster John Knox Press, 1996), 390.

11. CWU's inclusion of Unitarians on their boards led to tension with the NCC.

12. Edith Groner in Dorothy MacLeod oral history, December 15, 1965, box 78, folder 17, CWU papers.

13. The survey did not separate male respondents from female ones because there was no appreciable difference in the answers given by both groups. Barnett, "God and the American People," 36, 239.

14. Beata Mueller, "Christians Should Practice What They Preach," *National Council Outlook* (April 1953): 15; "Church Women," *National Council Outlook* (January 1953): 11; "Citizenship: Our Christian Concern," *National Council Outlook* (March 1953): 7; Golda Bader, "Christian Freedom: Its Dimensions and Responsibilities," *National Council Outlook* (June 1958): 15; Helen McAllister, "Church Women United History," [mid 1970s?], box 54, folder 40, CWU papers.

15. "Church Women," *National Council Outlook* (January 1953): 11; Bader, "Christian Freedom," 15; Louise Wallace, "Not Master but Servant," *Church Woman* (April 1964): 11; McAllister, "Church Women United History."

16. "Report of the General Department of United Church Women, 1950–1952," p. 2, box 15, no folder number, CWU papers.

17. "Next Steps in Race Relations," 1952, box 62, folder 1, CWU papers.

18. Clarice T. Campbell, *Civil Rights Chronicle: Letters from the South* (Jackson: University Press of Mississippi, 1997), 17.

19. Clarice Campbell lived and worked in Mississippi and South Carolina. Her comments, however, also apply to the rest of the Deep South. Campbell, *Civil Rights Chronicle,* 183.

20. Marjorie M. Armstrong, "Church Women Celebrate," *Christian Century* 79 (December 5, 1962): 1498.

21. Jane M. Schutt oral history by Leesa Faulkner, 3 October and 10 October 1994, University of Southern Mississippi Oral History Program, transcript, 4–5.

22. According to the U.S. Census, the labor force participation rate by women was 31.4 percent in 1950 and 33.5 percent in 1955. See "U.S. Bureau of the Census 1983b, 383" in Leila J. Rupp and Verta Taylor, *Survival in the Doldrums: The American Women's Rights Movement, 1945 to the 1960s* (New York: Oxford University Press, 1987), 12–13.

23. McAllister, "Church Women United History"; Jane M. Schutt oral history, 5.

24. Ruth Van Winkle, *United Church Women of Kentucky* (Danville, Ky.: n.p., [1965]), 17.

25. Van Winkle, *United Church Women of Kentucky,* 21.

26. Lindley, "*You Have Stept Out of Your Place,*" 391; Harvard Sitkoff, *The Struggle for Black Equality, 1954–1980* (New York: Hill and Wang, 1981), 191–93.

27. Margaret Shannon, *Just Because: The Story of the National Movement of Church Women in the U.S.A., 1941–1975.* (Corte Madera, Calif.: Omega Books, 1977), 112.

28. Jane M. Schutt oral history, 7; Mark A. Noll, *A History of Christianity in the United States and Canada* (Grand Rapids, Mich.: William B. Eerdmans, 1992).

29. Shannon, *Just Because,* 114.

30. Ibid., 115.

31. Martha Edens and Edna Sinclair, "Women and Ecumenism questionnaire," August 11, 1978, box 56, folder 48, CWU papers.

32. Edna Sinclair to Martha Edens, August 11, 1978, box 56, folder 48, CWU papers.

33. It is difficult to measure opposition because women who left CWU or never joined the organization did not typically leave written records explaining their decision.

34. "Recommendations and Resolutions of the Sixth National Assembly," October 5–8, 1953, box 2, folder 14, CWU papers.

35. In an interview in 1974, past leaders of CWU described four groups that joined the NCC as "movements." These movements became the theological, student, women's, and Christian youth wings of the NCC. United Church Men also entered NCC as a self-described movement, but faded into oblivion. The UCW leaders did not regard UCM as a movement because, as Margaret Shannon stated, "They weren't anything but a bunch of board secretaries that were in men's work." Interview with Helen Baker, Margaret Shannon, Ruth Weber, and Bessie Marsh, May 13, 1974, box 78, folder 21, CWU papers.

36. Brereton, 159.

37. Dorothy MacLeod oral history, box 78, folder 17, CWU papers.

38. In her study of male-dominated liberal organizations of the 1960s and 1970s, Susan Hartmann charts the steps taken by CWU to increase the role of women, specifically including African American women, within the NCC. She also notes the frustrations that many CWU members experienced when working with the NCC. See Hartmann, *The Other Feminists,* 94–100.

39. Mossie Allman Wyker, *Church Women in the Scheme of Things* (St. Louis: The Bethany Press, 1953), 36.

40. Brereton discusses the dispute over membership in more detail. CWU proposed a governing body that included four Unitarians. Much to the surprise of the CWU, the NCC General Board then set strict standards regarding the appointment of members to the boards of NCC departments. The Unitarians did not meet the new qualifications and were not permitted to take office. See Brereton, 159.

41. Brereton, 160–63; Dorothy Dolbey to R. H. Edwin Espy, March 25, 1970, record

group 4, box 37, National Council of Churches of Christ in the U.S.A. records, Presbyterian Historical Society.

42. Martha Edens and Louise Wallace, "Women and Ecumenism questionnaire," July 28, 1978, box 56, folder 48, CWU papers.

43. "Some Queries," [1969?], box 62, folder 6, CWU papers.

44. The national leader is not clearly identified. "Some Queries."

45. Edens and Dolbey, "Women and Ecumenism questionnaire."

46. Mueller, "Christians Should Practice What They Preach," 15; Dorothy M. Dolbey to Arthur Flemming and R. H. Edwin Espy, June 13, 1969, box 3, folder 21, CWU papers.

47. Margaret Shannon to DCU Cabinet, January 2, 1970, record group 10, box 7, National Council of Churches of Christ in the U.S.A. records, Presbyterian Historical Society.

48. Edna Sinclair, untitled typescript, [1967?], box 78, folder 22, CWU papers.

49. "Minutes of the General Board of the National Council of Churches, 20–21 May 1970," record group 3, box 4, National Council of Churches of Christ in the U.S.A. records, Presbyterian Historical Society.

50. Margaret Shannon to Cynthia Wedel, January 29, 1970, record group 4, box 37, National Council of Churches in Christ in the U.S.A. records, Presbyterian Historical Society.

51. Margaret Shannon, "Interview with Baker, Shannon, Weber, and Marsh," May 13, 1974, box 78, folder 21, CWU papers.

52. An additional cause of anger resulted from the large financial contributions made by UCW to the NCC, contributions that did not receive acknowledgment by the NCC. Shannon, "Interview with Baker, Shannon, Weber, and Marsh"; Margaret Shannon to DCU Cabinet.

53. Cynthia Wedel, Employed Women and the Church (New York: National Council of the Churches of Christ in the USA), 42.

54. Wedel noticed a slight concern for equality of civil, social, and political rights for men and women though "this was growing." See Edens and Wedel, "Women and Ecumenism questionnaire."

55. "Church Women Get Insights on Womanpower," National Council Outlook 8 (January 1958): 14.

56. Mrs. Leon W. Ellis and Esther C. Stamats, "Christian Social Relations: The Equal Rights Amendment," Church Woman (February 1954): 30.

57. Florence L. C. Kitchelt, "Personal Convictions," Church Woman (January 1953), 3.

58. The CWU National Board voted to support the ERA in 1970. Citizen Action, "Memo to Whom It May Concern," 1975, box 55, folder 9, CWU papers.

59. Margaret Mead and Frances Balgley Kaplan, eds., American Women: The Report of the President's Commission on the Status of Women and Other Publications of the Commission (New York: Charles Scribner's Sons, 1965), 9, 255–65.

60. Mead and Kaplan, American Women, 210–13; Susan M. Hartmann, From Margin to Mainstream: Women in American Politics since 1960 (Boston,: Twayne, 1986), 52.

61. "Outline for Discussion UCW Committee on the Role of Women," April 26, 1965, box 54, folder 6, CWU papers.

62. Josephine Weiner, The Story of WICS (Alexandria, Va.: Women in Community Service, 1986), 1.

63. Sar A. Levitan and Benjamin H. Johnson, *The Job Corps: A Social Experiment That Works* (Baltimore: Johns Hopkins University Press, 1975).

64. Women in Community Service brochure, box 5, folder 3, CWU papers.

65. Doris Anne Younger, interview with Barbranell Stake, March 19, 1992, p. 12, box 78, folder 24, CWU papers.

66. Policymakers in the 1960s spoke often of a "culture of poverty." They argued that the hard-core poor possessed a distinctive cultural profile, a way of life passed on from generation to generation, characterized by unstable families, high rates of illegitimacy, low levels of voting and political participation, and poor self-esteem. Some activists, including CWU members, wanted to pluck young women out of poor neighborhoods to get them away from negative influences. The legislation that created the Job Corps reflected the notion of a culture of poverty.

67. Weiner, *The Story of WICS*, 33; Edith Chase, "Women's Job Corps Imperiled," [California] *State Church Women United News, CWU of Southern California—Southern Nevada* 24, no. 5 (May 1, 1969); Christopher Weeks, *Job Corps: Dollars and Dropouts* (Boston: Little, Brown, 1967); Patricia G. Zelman, *Women, Work, and National Policy: The Kennedy-Johnson Years* (Ann Arbor, Mich.: UMI Research Press, 1982).

68. "Separating Fact From Fiction," April 1988, box 17, folder 6, CWU papers.

69. George Dugan, "Church Unit Hits Death Penalty," *New York Times,* September 14, 1968, 37.

70. Lisa K. Speer, "Struggling for Justice: Church Women United, Oxford, Mississippi 1962–1991," unpublished manuscript, p. 19, Special Collections, J. D. Williams Library, University of Mississippi. For eugenics, see Dorothy Roberts, *Killing the Black Body: Race, Reproduction, and the Meaning of Liberty* (New York: Pantheon, 1997) and Andrea Tone, *Devices and Desires: A History of Contraceptives in America* (New York: Hill and Wang, 2001).

71. "Resolution on Abortion Adopted by the Board of Managers, Church Women United, St. Louis, Missouri," March 19, 1970, box 54, folder 20, CWU papers; "Commission on Women in Today's World," June 5–6, 1970, box 54, folder 20, CWU papers.

72. N. E. H. Hull and Peter Charles Hoffer, Roe v. Wade: *The Abortion Rights Controversy in American History* (Lawrence: University Press of Kansas), 121.

73. Commission on Women in Today's World.

74. Rosa Trigg to Margaret Shannon, March 4, 1973, box 69, folder 21, CWU papers.

75. Edens and Wedel, "Women and Ecumenism questionnaire."

76. CWU employed the term "community reconciling agent" instead of "healer" but the goal remained that of reducing tensions in American society. The summary is based upon forty-nine questionnaires although it is impossible to know how many women participated because contacts were made in different ways using different approaches. One state president, for example, sent questionnaires to one hundred women representing different denomination, racial, economic, social, and educational backgrounds as well as a wide age span. See Miriam Phillips, comp., "Committee of 74—Statistical Summary of Survey," 1974, box 5, folder 2, CWU papers.

77. CWU is not part of the women's caucus. CWU did not serve as a division of the NCC but existed as a sister organization and many women, Cynthia Wedel among them, held positions of power in both groups.

78. Peggy Billings, "Report of Women's Caucus to the Assembly of the National Council of Churches of Christ," December 6, 1972, box 54, folder 34, CWU papers.

79. Billings, "Report of Women's Caucus."

80. Public Relations Department, "CWU in the USA," 1975, box 5, folder 9, CWU papers.

81. Hartmann also notes the early and consistent stance that CWU took against racism. See Hartmann, *The Other Feminists*, 96–100.

82. Wedel, *Employed Women and the Church,* 42.

83. Armstrong, "Church Women Celebrate," 1498.

# 7. Fighting for Abortion as a "Health Right" in Washington, D.C.

## ANNE VALK

On Monday, September 8, 1969, radical feminists and welfare rights activists stunned administrators, staff, and patients at the D.C. General Hospital when they threw up a picket line at the hospital's entrance. For several hours, more than two dozen women marched in front of the hospital. Waving placards calling for "abortion on demand" and "free medical care for all," the activists expressed their fury at the inadequate care the hospital provided to poor Washington, D.C., residents. Long waits, crowded wards, and overburdened doctors led to fearful and frustrating experiences for all patients. However, to the picketers, the ways the facility implemented local abortion laws most clearly demonstrated the maltreatment poor Washington, D.C., women experienced.

In the view of radical feminists and welfare rights activists, D.C. General's implementation of abortion laws caused needless suffering and perpetuated egregious inequalities. In 1969, city statutes—on the books since 1901—permitted licensed medical practitioners to perform abortions when necessary to preserve the life or health of women. Across the District, local hospitals and physicians established varying criteria to determine when a woman's situation met the legal requirements. The city's numerous private hospitals and physician's offices imposed relatively lenient guidelines, granting women with financial means a range of services. In contrast, D.C. General, the only public facility in the city that provided therapeutic abortions at no cost to low-income patients, mandated that applicants obtain documentation from three hospital-affiliated physicians verifying that pregnancy or childbirth would threaten their life or health. This policy unduly disadvantaged poor women who lacked the time and money to undergo multiple examinations

and forfeited their choice over the doctors who examined them. In addition
to being cumbersome, D.C. General's policy was arbitrarily applied, leaving
some women who met the hospital's criteria still inexplicably denied abortions. When the rejection occurred too late in a woman's pregnancy, she had
little choice but to give birth or arrange for an illegal abortion.[1]

Not surprisingly, this disparate access yielded significant consequences for
women. During all of 1967, D.C. General Hospital doctors had conducted only
8 therapeutic abortions, whereas staff at two of Washington, D.C.'s private
hospitals had completed on average 170 each month. Still, D.C. General Hospital's rigorous policy did not stop poor women from circumventing the law
to seek abortions and many women who underwent illegal or self-induced
abortions consequently rushed to the facility for emergency care. In 1969
alone, the hospital staff performed twenty-one therapeutic abortions (up
from the eight performed in 1967), but admitted more than nine hundred
women who suffered grave—and sometimes fatal—complications caused by
botched abortions.[2] Given the city's demographic composition, poor black
women represented the majority of those denied abortions at D.C. General
and endangered by illegal procedures.[3]

The coalition that formed in September 1969 pressed for changes that would
end these disparities. Denoting new directions for the abortion rights movement, the pickets at the General Hospital represented the first mass protests for
abortion rights held in the city. Over several months, women from the Citywide Welfare Alliance (CWA) and the D.C. Women's Liberation Movement
(WLM) came together, bringing skills and resources developed through their
separate initiatives, to fight for change in the streets, the courts, and the halls
of government. Working as allies, but retaining their affiliations to separate
organizations, the coalition allowed each group to draw on their individual
priorities even as they reached in new directions. Members of the coalition
were inspired by the era's liberation and antiwar movements, which presented
an arsenal of protest tactics and ideas about women's status they found useful
in trying to transform local policies. The decision to act in coalition represented one such tactic, chosen for its potential to mobilize Washington, D.C.,
women to demand improved health and reproductive care.

This essay examines the collaborations that women activists formed in
Washington, D.C., in the late 1960s and early 1970s to secure broader access
to safe abortions and win a series of related demands. Beginning with the alliance between welfare rights activists and radical feminists to reform policies
at the public hospital, the campaigns expanded as participants in the city's
WLM and members of the CWA coordinated an array of initiatives meant to
improve health care by eliminating restrictions that blocked access to abor-

tion, securing distribution of safe birth control, and ending the practice of forced sterilization. After the WLM and CWA alliance ended, Washington, D.C., activists continued to fight for abortion access through coalitions that linked separate women's organizations. Given activists' reliance on them, these cooperative activities are critical for understanding how women in the nation's capital fought to increase the availability of abortion and improve reproductive care in the years leading up to the Supreme Court's 1973 *Roe v. Wade* ruling affirming a woman's right to abortion. Specifically, activists devised multiple ways to raise public consciousness about the shortcomings in laws, to define women's health rights, and to claim their authority to shape new policies: they organized mass demonstrations, set up counseling and public education programs, clamored to join regulatory boards, mounted lawsuits, lobbied officials, and testified at public hearings. Collaborative activity, whether through the formation of formal alliances or in short-lived projects that connected activists across organizations and movements, was a key strategy in these campaigns.

Significantly, coalitions played a critical role in establishing a political platform that expressed activists' demand for available abortions as a central component of Americans' "health rights." Through the cooperative activity of the CWA and WLM, activists articulated quality health care and safe, legal abortion as rights that should extend to all women. Furthermore, as welfare rights and radical feminist activists bridged organizational and political boundaries to fight for expanded abortion access and better health care, they articulated a health rights agenda that asserted the importance of women's control of their bodies and affirmed women's expertise over public policy matters. This campaign for health rights served as a precursor to the reproductive rights campaign that emerged in the early 1970s.

The coalitions that developed to support D.C.'s abortion rights campaigns illuminate the benefits that activists perceived from working across race, class, and organizational lines and the considerable impact that such alliances exerted at the local level. The short-lived coalition between the CWA and the WLM was especially important in generating changes that extended beyond its brief existence, ushering in a new phase in Washington, D.C.'s abortion rights movement that used direct action tactics and insisted on women's right to participate in setting public regulations. In addition, welfare activists and radical feminists redefined the abortion movement's goals to demand women's bodily self-determination and to call attention to the array of legal, cultural, medical, and economic forces that restricted women's control of their health and bodies. By so doing, they conceptualized a health rights agenda that asserted women's authority to make decisions and linked a constellation of demands they defined as central to women's control of their fertility. Through their cooperative activities, feminists and welfare activists influenced public policy and reproductive health services in the city. Moreover, even after this coalition collapsed in early 1970, the local abortion movement retained aspects of the earlier mobilization, particularly the use of mass protests and arguments that stressed reproductive control as a key component of women's liberation. Like women's liberationists and welfare rights proponents, later activists connected demands for abortion to women's right to resist other threats to their physical safety and reproductive and sexual autonomy. However, as the movement grew in the 1970s, advocates of reproductive control framed their battle differently, adopting slogans and goals that prioritized legal rights and stressed women's "right to choose," but downplayed the economic and social obstacles that continued to prevent many women from controlling their health and reproductive lives.

The coalition that formed between the white, middle-class activists in Washington, D.C.'s women's liberation group and black, low-income members of the city's welfare rights groups represented an important and unusual moment in the history of the modern women's movement.[4] In 1969, few participants expected that women activists could find common ground across racial and class differences. As numerous historians have shown, the late 1960s was characterized by a racial rift regarding the relative importance of feminism to participants in the era's many radical social change efforts. Largely sympathetic to the principle of women's liberation, many black women nonetheless elected to remain separate from organized feminism. This separatism reflected the black freedom movement's predominant view that feminism constituted a threat to racial liberation, an understanding backed up by the biases that seemingly blinded white feminists to their racial privilege and to differences in women's experiences and opportunities. Because of the collision between the limitations of organized feminism and the imperatives of racial unity expressed by the black liberation movement, many African American women activists rejected membership in predominantly white feminist organizations but nonetheless fought male chauvinism within the black freedom movement and welfare rights campaigns. Many white feminists, in turn, struggled to expand their movement but failed to effectively confront the political and personal dynamics that made their groups inhospitable and their demands often irrelevant or secondary to women of color and poor women.[5]

   This rift extended to the area of abortion, where, in the words of one historian, campaigns for reproductive rights were "in many ways racially defined."[6] Most historians have argued that although African American and white women shared the struggle to control their fertility, racial differences played a determinative role in shaping the nature of that struggle and whether, and how, women organized for reproductive control. Since the early 1900s, birth control advocates had attacked laws and cultural prohibitions that restricted contraception, arguing that the ability to seize power over reproduction would represent an essential step toward freeing women from men's domination. Other advocates of contraception stressed health and economic concerns, viewing women's ability to control births as vital to the physical health of women and the well-being of their families. Yet early twentieth-century family planning initiatives, such as those affiliated with the Planned Parenthood Federation of America, often advocated birth control without arguing in favor of the liberation of *all* women. Contraception and sterilization could improve society, some asserted, by limiting the size of poor, immigrant, and African American families whose members were considered incapable of responsible citizenship and a threat to the well-being of American society. According to historian Linda Gordon, these family planning initiatives had concentrated on developing programs for black and poor Americans: "coercively, singling them out as a problem, rather than a people with a problem, and using [contraception] as an alternative to and buffer against structural social change and economic redistribution."[7] Although Washington, D.C., did not enact the eugenic sterilization laws that other states imposed to take reproductive choices away from those deemed "unfit," politicians nonetheless encouraged publicly funded birth control programs concentrated in the capital city's poor African American neighborhoods. Backers of these programs implied that by shrinking the numbers of poor black children, welfare spending would drop and the community's morality and safety would improve.[8]

Through most of the twentieth century, top federal officials had insisted that birth control fell outside the purview of appropriate government activity, but in the decades following World War II, government agencies became increasingly involved in funding and oversight of contraceptive programs, a shift in priorities that many activists saw as more than coincidental. In the 1960s, the federal government's support for birth control initiatives in Third World countries and in impoverished minority communities provided evidence that seemed to back the claims of activists who accused the United States of engaging in a systematic attempt to diminish the world's black population and squelch liberation movements. Within the United States, some federally funded programs used coercion and deception to sterilize welfare recipients and poor women, violations that occurred disproportionately among African

American, Hispanic, and Native American women. Activists' suspicions about the assault on black communities that such programs represented magnified within the context of continued resistance to civil rights efforts and as news broke of research projects that endangered African American bodies for the sake of medical research—as in the case of the infamous Tuskegee syphilis experiments that became public news in 1972. To counter this genocidal mission, some activists urged black women to throw away birth control and instead produce large families that would form the frontlines of a new battle for black liberation. As Angela Davis, Jennifer Nelson, Loretta Ross, and other historians have shown, this complicated history of coercion and exploitation dampened the support and heightened the suspicion many black activists expressed for abortion or birth control. Even African American proponents of contraception contended that women needed authority to make decisions about fertility and that organizations rooted in black communities should exercise control of family planning initiatives.[9]

The coercive uses of birth control within poor and African American communities starkly contrasted with the common experiences of middle-class white women. After World War II, images idealizing the domestic life of white families predominated in popular culture, supported by federal programs such as low-interest home mortgages and loans for college tuition that encouraged the growth of the suburban middle class. Married white, middle-class women who sought abortions, birth control, or sterilization, even when legal, often were turned away by physicians who assumed they would be good mothers. Thus, at the same time that women of color struggled to resist sterilization and to assert their ability to choose motherhood, many white American women were forced to lie about their marital status to legally obtain birth control and to seek illicit means to control or terminate pregnancies.[10]

These vastly different histories limited the likelihood of interracial organizing on behalf of abortion rights or other reproductive issues. At least until the *Roe v. Wade* decision secured the legality of abortion, historians have argued, white feminists put abortion at the center of their demands for reproductive choice, while black activists prioritized the fight against other forms of bodily abuse that took away their choice to have children.[11] The coalition between black welfare activists and white radical feminists in Washington, D.C., however, presents new perspectives on the history of women activists' demands for abortion, reminds historians of the changing definitions of reproductive freedom that women have employed, highlights the role of poor women in shaping feminist agendas, and points to the importance of understanding the local context that shaped both women's activism and their demands.[12]

When the CWA and WLM joined forces in 1969, residents of the District of Columbia enjoyed one of the most permissive abortion laws in the country: at a time when most states sanctioned abortion only to save a mother's life, the D.C. statute also considered preservation of a pregnant woman's health.[13] From a legal standpoint, however, the allowance for abortions to preserve the mother's health created ambiguity for medical practitioners, lawyers, and the police. D.C. General interpreted the statute narrowly, seldom approving abortions, but physicians affiliated with other facilities employed more expansive eligibility standards. One practitioner, Dr. Milan Vuitch, challenged the law in court, arguing that preventing risks to mental health, as well as physical health, constituted legal grounds for approving abortions. Vuitch's position was affirmed by a November 1969 decision in the District Court of the District of Columbia. *United States of America v. Milan Vuitch* declared the city's law unconstitutional, lacking the clarity required to guide doctors and law enforcement personnel. Invoking the Fourteenth Amendment, the ruling raised the issue of economic discrimination in the District: "it is legally proper and indeed imperative," the judge decreed, "that uniform medical abortion services be provided all segments of the population, the poor as well as the rich. Principles of equal protection under our Constitution require that policies in our public hospitals be liberalized immediately." The following month, the mayor's health care task force weighed in, calling for an end to economic discrimination in women's reproductive care. The U.S. Attorney's Office quickly appealed the *Vuitch* decision to the Supreme Court. In the interim, Washington, D.C., medical practitioners continued to apply the law unevenly and city officials scrambled to standardize guidelines governing abortion decisions.[14]

The 1960s feminist movement and the welfare rights movement, as well as the era's black liberation and New Left movements, energized and transformed the abortion rights movement by introducing new strategies, arguments, and activists. As historian Rosalind Petchesky has acknowledged, across the country organized feminists acted as "shock troops," leading the battle to topple legal barriers to abortion and pushing to expose and overturn troublesome restrictions followed by medical practitioners.[15] Previously, physicians, clergy, and representatives of family planning organizations such as Planned Parenthood had formed the front lines of the birth control and abortion movement, pressing for reform through professional associations and publicizing research that exposed the dangers resulting from illegal abortions. In the late 1960s, U.S. feminists started to push for abortion rights as a way to save women's lives and increase their autonomy. At the heart of this challenge lay feminists' insistence that abortions be more widely available,

whether for matters of physical health or personal choice.[16] The same week
that D.C. welfare rights and women's liberation activists organized their protests, women and lawyers in New York filed a class action suit contesting that
state's abortion laws. That same month in Texas, lawyer Sarah Weddington
began research that would culminate three years later in the *Roe v. Wade*
decision. State-level campaigns were complemented by an emerging national
movement spearheaded by the National Association for the Repeal of Abortion Laws. NARAL (now the National Abortion and Reproductive Rights
Action League) formed in February 1969 to coordinate feminists, lawyers, and
health care practitioners in a national campaign to repeal abortion laws.[17]

Simultaneous with these developments, legal challenges brought by Vuitch
and other reformers created a shifting statutory landscape in the District that
activists exploited through mass protest, civil disobedience, and other forms
of collective action. The CWA and the WLM formed their coalition during
this period of flux, beginning their protests in the months leading up to the
judge's ruling in Vuitch's case. They began working together after each group
learned that D.C. General had turned away two women who seemingly met
the hospital's strict criteria to qualify for abortions. Enraged at the danger
and desperation that poor women endured, members of CWA and WLM,
with the support of doctors from the Medical Committee for Human Rights,
took action. They first requested conferences with the director of public
health and D.C. General obstetricians. After administrators and physicians
refused to meet them, they launched their picket line. The demonstration
in front of the hospital was timed to coincide with a protest by D.C. General
medical staff, concerned about the conditions at the facility. The next day,
about thirty women and children barged into the office of the director of
public health, not moving until he agreed to include coalition members and
health professionals on a new committee to recommend revisions to D.C.
General's abortion policy.

Over the course of several weeks, WLM and CWA representatives also
repeatedly tried to attend closed meetings of a task force convened by the
mayor to investigate complaints about the public hospital.[18] Accusing the task
force of operating with inappropriate secrecy, they demanded to participate
in the hearings. They also objected that male doctors made up the majority
of the task force members. Without input from residents who used the public
health facilities, and especially without participation by women, the activists
feared that the task force would trivialize the dire health crisis facing the
city. After withstanding several weeks of pressure, the mayor consented to
open the task force's meetings to the public and to seat CWA members on
the committee. Although snubbed by the mayor, women's liberation activists

nonetheless received, and accepted, invitations to informally assist the task force subcommittees. By the end of the year, the coalition's efforts yielded tangible results in the form of a statement, issued by the mayor's task force, pronouncing abortion a "health right which must be available to everyone regardless of ability to pay or social class." D.C. General Hospital must "immediately make available services to perform abortions on those women who request such service," the task force ordered.[19]

Shortly after the task force produced its recommendations, the coalition disbanded. The task force's statement represented a largely symbolic victory, however, and D.C. General resisted attempts to alter its regulations. Consequently, CWA and WLM members, working within their separate organizations, continued their fight to expand access to abortion and to improve women's health care, choosing new targets and strategies. Over the next several years, welfare rights and women's liberation representatives spoke at rallies supporting abortion rights and attempted to influence public policy through their testimony at hearings of the D.C. City Council and the U.S. Senate. For the most part, future activities to expand reproductive freedom were organized by women's liberation activists, with welfare rights activists joining as participants but not partners. Still, their influence remained significant.

Welfare rights and women's liberation activists both considered quality health care and abortion access worthy issues that warranted the expenditure of time and energy. Neither the CWA nor the WLM, however, intended to make the fight for improved health care and abortion access their primary focus; instead, they viewed the health care campaigns as part of their broader struggles to win welfare rights and women's liberation, respectively. Retaining their larger—and separate—goals even when uniting to protest the hospital and the city's medical facilities, welfare rights activists and women's liberationists based their collaboration around their shared desire for improved health care. As one member of the WLM put it, "the reality (is) that all of us are health poor. The blackest and the poorest are the most victimized, but we all suffer—particularly if we are women—all of the time."[20] Yet despite their cooperation, the coalition neither obscured nor eliminated the divergent membership, history, analyses, and approaches of each group.

The CWA had formed in 1966 as an affiliate of the National Welfare Rights Organization (NWRO). The local and national organizations shared the goal of gaining "more money, more dignity, and more justice" for welfare recipients.[21] Between 1967 and 1971, the CWA served as an umbrella organization, connecting Washington, D.C.'s many NWRO chapters and representing the city's chapters at meetings of the national organization.[22] Open to all welfare recipients and others who lived in poverty, most members were African

American women raising children without the support of a husband or male breadwinner.

CWA participants fought to reform the municipal and federal welfare systems, pressing to increase monetary benefits and to formulate bureaucratic procedures that treated welfare recipients respectfully and realistically, given the struggles that poor women and their families faced. They conducted headline grabbing protests against the "heartbreaking" practices of the welfare department, criticizing subsidies that kept incomes well below the federal poverty level and failed to cover many household necessities. Moreover, mandatory work programs that forced welfare recipients into paid labor—typically at low wages—without support for child care exacerbated the problems of poor families.

Through the activities, images, and language they used to convey their grievances, welfare activists confronted prevalent beliefs about black women's sexuality and their domestic role. Stereotypes that highlighted black women's alleged immorality dated back to slavery and segregation when they helped justify black women's sexual exploitation. At the same time, images of black women as bad mothers pervaded popular thought, rationalizing black women's place at the bottom of the labor market, where they were paradoxically confined to low-paying jobs taking care of other people's homes and families. In addition, the notion that receipt of welfare correlated with undesirable personal characteristics—laziness, slovenliness, and promiscuity—was communicated through the priorities of the bureaucrats and politicians who devised welfare programs that forced poor mothers to work and to stay single in order to retain their eligibility for relief. Inspectors hired by welfare departments conducted unannounced home visits, reputedly to ascertain whether any men lived in the home whose income would disqualify families for aid. Welfare recipients resented these surprise inspections as incursions on their privacy and chafed at the assumption of their dishonesty and the prohibition on intimate relationships with men. Welfare rights activists sought to dispel these judgments—and change the policies based on them—by stressing their overriding commitment to their children and their desire to create stable families.[23]

Acting collectively, Washington, D.C., welfare activists asserted their right to have a say in formulating better procedures. Two months before the protests at D.C. General Hospital, more than fifty welfare recipients marched to the mayor's office calling for the cessation of home inspections, increased Aid to Families with Dependent Children payments, and dispensation of grants to purchase furniture and children's clothing, items the women considered essential but that were not covered under the food stamps program. When the welfare department ignored their demands, CWA members resumed pickets, requesting money for back-to-school clothing just four days before the hospital protests.[24] They also consistently targeted the inferior health care available to impoverished Washingtonians. In 1968, members of the alliance had mobilized to protest one hospital's disregard for low-income patients. Located in a part of the city containing a high concentration of public housing, the hospital nonetheless refused to accept Medicaid. The following year, group members testified before Congress, lambasting the quality of medical care available to low-income city residents and pointing out how poor women and their families suffered when private hospitals refused to allow Medicaid payments.[25]

The high level of publicity and activity the CWA had sustained for several years contrasted with the more recent emergence of the WLM. Formed in 1968, the WLM consisted of loosely connected feminist discussion circles and protest-oriented groups. Unlike NWRO affiliates that restricted membership to poor people, any woman could join WLM groups and activities, although most participants were white and young. Many had attended college and held professional jobs; others devoted their time to political activism, living off welfare or depending on income earned by a spouse or pooled within a commune.[26] Few WLM participants were mothers, but those who were pushed the radical feminist movement to pay attention to the impact of child rearing on women's personal and professional lives.[27]

WLM activists concentrated on increasing awareness about women's oppression and taking direct action to end male supremacy. Using consciousness raising and forming nonhierarchical, democratically run groups, radical feminists hoped to gain insight into women's oppression and to free themselves from constraints derived from their socialization as women. They identified capitalism as the root cause of sexism, racism, and economic disparities. America's race- and sex-segregated economy severely constricted women's opportunities, according to an essay written by Marilyn Webb, one of the local movement's founders. "Secretary, sexpot, spender, sow, civic actor, sickie" described the typical roles to which American women were confined and from which feminism sought to free them. The path to women's liberation lay in making women cognizant of their oppression and then attacking the social institutions that enforced these limited roles. Through acting together, women would reshape their own lives and create an egalitarian society.[28]

By the fall of 1969, eight groups, addressing child care, ecology, women's health, abortion, and other concerns, affiliated with WLM. Members of these groups made public presentations around the city, taught noncredit courses at a local free university, and wrote and distributed pamphlets and essays. Through public education, radical feminists intended to spread their analysis of the roots of women's oppression and to raise political consciousness among women who did not yet identify as feminists. WLM participants especially hoped to inspire teenagers and African American women, thereby making the movement better reflect the city's demographic composition.[29]

Within the WLM's health and abortion groups, women sought to understand how they experienced oppression because of their sex and to devise strategies for improving their lives and transforming society. Gathering in discussion, WLM participants divulged ailments they suffered after using oral contraception, the difficulties they endured when undergoing abortions, and the pressures they felt to become mothers. A few members were health care practitioners whose professional expertise added to the personal insights shared in meetings. Their common experiences alerted members that because of intense pressures on women to become mothers, reproductive control would form a central element of women's liberation. Whereas welfare rights activists targeted the welfare bureaucracy, WLM members focused on changing social relationships and creating resources to enhance women's autonomy. In a WLM pamphlet, member Alice Wolfson argued that American women lived in a "sexist society where a woman is defined by her marital status and her childbearing abilities. Freedom for women means the freedom for other forms of life work and identity than just the family."[30] Similarly, Judith Coburn asserted, "women's liberation must fight to change society to allow women to make their own reproductive choices and whether or not to choose other careers than housewife and mother. For married women, this means round-the-clock day care centers at the place of work. For men, it means sharing equally the responsibilities of children, household, and conception."[31] Coburn and Wolfson's statements revealed the WLM's biases: they assumed that employment offered a path to women's liberation, and that men would be available to take on domestic responsibilities as women shrugged them off when they found meaningful work.

WLM participants also recalled the vulnerability, humiliation, and anger they felt at doctors' indifference to, or exploitation of, their plight. The male-dominated medical system represented a "microcosm of the capitalist system under which we live, based on the exploitation of the many for the profits of the few," they concluded. Women suffered the most, oppressed as a result of men's control of medicine.[32] Responding to the need to help women obtain safe abortions, the WLM initiated a counseling service to provide information about available resources and contemplated setting up free abortion clinics.[33] The reality of women's desperation compelled them to take these actions, but members demurred that providing referrals and pushing for legal reform would not bring about women's liberation. Individual women could get help via these avenues, but neither approach would mobilize large numbers of women to fight oppression, nor topple the country's existing legal, medical, and political systems so they could be replaced by more egalitarian structures. By fall of 1969, WLM members settled with an uneasy balance between their long-term goals and short-term realities; they offered counseling and dreamed of starting a clinic, but also searched for activities that would energize a mass movement and create a society free from oppression.[34]

The hospital protests emerged against the background of these distinct organizational histories and priorities. The alliance built on strategies and ideas about women's liberation in particular, and social change more broadly, which welfare activists and women's liberationists shared. Anger at the inadequacies of the country's health care system rose to the fore and they began to jointly conceptualize quality health care as a right that Americans should possess. Better abortion treatment, as a health care issue, could be achieved by making the medical system and its practitioners more humane and just. In articulating such points of agreement, coalition participants did not take identical positions but rather they adopted overlapping and complementary approaches and arguments that facilitated cooperation and allowed each organization to maintain flexibility and autonomy when pursuing separate directions.

First, members of both groups identified an interlocking array of legal, cultural, and economic factors that blocked women's access to quality medical care. They argued that ensuring access to safe and affordable medical treatment, including abortion, required transforming the country's economic, welfare, and medical structures. Welfare activists emphasized the city and federal governments' responsibility to women, insisting that Medicaid should cover abortions but that federally funded programs not become mechanisms jeopardizing women's health or promoting genocide. They also urged that government agencies not treat birth control, sterilization, or other forms of family planning as a substitute for sustained efforts to end poverty through jobs programs and vocational training. In a flier addressed to the D.C. City Council, the welfare activists urged the city's politicians to "protect women" by creating new public services to provide abortion "information and advocates (not expediters). Referral and counseling on abortions. Jobs."[35] Linking jobs and abortion, they insisted on women's right to informed control over fertility without economic restraints or other coercive forces. Such reforms would require "getting some heads out of the sand," proclaimed Etta Horn, head of the CWA, who vented her frustration at "hearing about women dying and still have those congressmen afraid to talk about it." Despite bureaucratic and official obstruction, Horn proposed that the matter was quite simple. "It comes down to whether you want to support the racketeers or the women who have the right to decide when and whether they want a baby. It's a matter of changing attitudes as much as a legal question," she alleged.[36]

Taking another tack, WLM activists explained that women's restricted access to abortion resulted from a variety of factors—high costs typically exempted by insurers, a shortage of doctors and hospital beds, and racist and sexist physicians.[37] The demand for women's control of reproduction, WLM members pronounced in one essay, "implies much more than just abortion law repeal. It implies upheavals in economic and social organization so that people will gain control over technology and resources and not have their lives determined for them." Moreover, they argued that all Americans, even those with economic means, lacked adequate health care. Quality medical treatment "requires a system that is not based on profit for hospitals, doctors, drug industries and private insurance companies. Health care must be seen as a national responsibility and it must be approached with a system of preventive as well as curative medicine."[38]

In identifying medical and economic forces that curtailed women's reproductive freedom, members of the CWA and WLM articulated clearly distinct, but corresponding, views of the chief obstacles preventing women's autonomy. The groups overlapped in accepting that abortions would continue to take place within a medical structure, performed by trained professionals and within hospitals and clinics. In addition, both groups rejected abortion law repeal, an approach favored by many abortion activists, as inadequate to solve the many problems women experienced when seeking to control their health and fertility. Indeed, this view was verified by the situation at D.C. General, where rigid policies continued even after the *Vuitch* ruling and the mayor's health task force confirmed that the facility needed to expand its abortion services.[39]

In addition to their analysis of the obstacles that prevented women's ability to exercise their "health rights," coalition participants held similar views about political strategy. Welfare activists had masterfully used pickets, sit-ins, and mass demonstrations to register their grievances. Similarly, women's liberationists embraced direct action tactics as essential weapons in the arsenal of otherwise disempowered people. Inspired by the civil rights and antiwar movements, these strategies reflected the angry tenor of the times. By putting up picket lines at the hospital's entrance and disrupting hearings of the mayoral task force, women registered impatience at their exclusion from regulatory bodies and confronted policy makers with the full force of their outrage. Airing grievances so directly not only made it more difficult for policy makers to evade women's needs, but also seemed an appropriate way to convey the life-or-death matters at stake. Finally, through direct action, women could upset the business of hospitals and the public health department until they were heard. They showed this effectively when they disrupted meetings of the public health task force and when they sat-in at the office of the director of public health.

Direct action tactics also helped build public sympathy for the movement. Mass protests combated the secrecy typically surrounding abortion. This goal coincided with both the welfare rights and the women's liberation activists' analysis that shame—at poverty, welfare dependency, sexual abuse, or pregnancy outside of marriage—kept women passive and silent, thereby contributing to their own oppression. In contrast, coalition members hoped their audacity would embolden other women to support the abortion cause. Taking the courageous step of publicly associating with this controversial issue, activists reinforced their commitment to the abortion rights movement and generated a community bound by their mutual interests. Speaking forthrightly about the dangers and obstacles women encountered when seeking to control their fertility, abortion rights activists grounded the movement in human experiences rather than abstract legal or moral principles.[40]

Third, welfare rights activists and radical feminists framed the abortion campaign around women's voices and experiences, especially those of poor African American women who encountered the worst frustrations and dangers occasioned by existing laws and practices.[41] Hearing about the ordeals and dilemmas surmounted by welfare-recipient activists and women who consulted with the WLM counseling service forced women's liberationists to stretch beyond their own experiences to comprehend obstacles that prevented reproductive autonomy. Moreover, stressing the fears and risks endured by women served to remind administrators and public officials that abortion and health care were not abstract medical issues but urgent personal matters. CWA leader Etta Horn reminded policy makers about this: "We know the lousy condition of D.C. General because we are the people you take care of," she exclaimed during one protest at the hospital. By asserting poor women's personal knowledge, Horn attempted to establish their authority and generate compassion for their plight, while subtly challenging the so-called experts who had the legal authority to make decisions on behalf of women patients.[42] In addition, arguments emphasizing women's experientially based expertise connected to the conviction that women needed to control their fertility. Because women's lives were at stake, they should make their own decisions. WLM members were especially moved by the stories they heard when staffing the hotline or working in health care professions. These stories made them realize, one member commented, "if it is hard for us (to get information about abortion), how much harder must it be for the poor and black who need it most."[43] Working with the CWA reinforced WLM participants' view that African American women's perspectives should be central to any movement for health care and abortion rights in Washington, D.C. The coalition made it "immediately clear," WLM activist Alice Wolfson recalled, "that if we wanted to be politically effective in a 76 percent black city, we could not see abortion as a single issue but were going to have to make the connections to other women's health issues."[44] As Wolfson implied, by formulating their campaign around the perspectives of the District's poor African American women, the WLM might make their movement more inclusive and, thus, politically effective.

The push to make women's expertise primary—whether gained through first-hand experiences or in a second-hand fashion as an abortion counselor—underlay WLM and CWA's efforts to contribute to policy making. The activists had scorned hearings and task forces that featured medical professionals but omitted women and other D.C. General Hospital patients.[45] However, they tempered their push for inclusion with distrust of policy makers. After all, if policy makers could be trusted, women would not need to fight to be heard. Not only did politicians and bureaucrats ignore the wisdom that women gained through their personal experiences, they seemed unduly influenced by corporations or medical practitioners whose motives generally encapsulated little concern for women's health. WLM members disparaged the mayor's health task force for being "lethargic and apathetic," and they roundly objected to an explanation given by the head of obstetrics and gynecology at the D.C. General Hospital that his staff performed few abortions because they considered them "too boring."[46]

Balancing their suspicion about policy makers and politicians with optimism that they could contribute to discussion and decisions, coalition members still searched for ways to shape laws and regulations. In the spring of 1970, WLM activists tried to influence the federal government's policies regarding the distribution of birth control pills. As they had done with the mayor's health task force, women disrupted congressional hearings investigating health risks associated with birth control pills. After learning that Congress planned to hear from only medical professionals and representatives of pharmaceutical companies, with no women presenting research data or describing their personal ordeals, WLM members called out questions from the floor and prevented further testimony until the senators consented to additional witnesses.[47]

Not content with letting Congress run the show, the WLM organized their own hearings on the safety of oral contraceptives and the risks related to women's circumscribed reproductive control. Gathering in one of the city's churches, speakers sounded off about the medical and social impact of the pill. More than one hundred men and women listened to the CWA's Etta Horn describe the dangers and dilemmas experienced by women on welfare. Without money to pay for legal abortions and without access to safe birth control, poor women either had to carry their pregnancies to term or go to "butcher shops"—underground abortionists. Charlotte Bunch-Weeks of the WLM charged that when drug companies and doctors withheld information about side effects, they prevented women from making informed contraceptive choices. Other speakers urged men to take responsibility for birth control and questioned the lack of research to develop male contraceptives.[48] As with pickets, these hearings gave women a way to raise public awareness about an important aspect of women's lives and to conquer silences surrounding a topic previously shrouded with shame. Although denied the right to testify in front of Congress, women's testimony collected at this event later became part of Congress's official publication of its proceedings.

However, the points of strategic and philosophical agreement that underlay the alliance's activities did not preclude the distinctive and sometimes oppositional views adopted by welfare rights activists and radical feminists. Even as CWA and WLM participants articulated overlapping concerns and analyses, they dissented over the role of reform, the definition of reproductive rights and women's liberation, and the purpose and desired outcome of their coalition. Although it is impossible to know all of the reasons that the coalition ended, clearly political differences played a role in splintering the alliance and foreshadowed conflicts that would arise in the broader women's and reproductive rights movements.

Specifically, welfare rights activists and radical feminists differed in their reasons for acting collaboratively and the perceived benefits of the coalition. Here, each movement's particular goals, and the place of health care and reproductive control within those demands, played a determinative role. Consistently skeptical about the possibility of making lasting changes through municipal committees, the WLM nonetheless saw longer-term benefits to working with the CWA. In tactical terms, an alliance with welfare rights activists could yield some short-term improvements and could broaden radical feminism by raising the consciousness of their coalition partners regarding sex-based oppression. WLM members expressed dismay at the outcomes generated by the mayor's task force and the department of public health. When CWA members were seated on the mayor's public health task force but WLM representatives were not, radical feminists accused city officials of trying to use "divide and conquer" tactics to break apart their alliance. Once the task force issued its recommendations, declaring abortion a "health right" and urging the public hospital to amend its policies, the WLM considered this outcome ineffectual and typical of the shortcomings of a reformist approach. WLM members watched with resignation as the task force recommendations failed to translate into action and as the coalition with welfare activists slowly broke up. Yet they concluded that health care represented a powerful issue for mobilizing masses of women, a revelation that propelled some WLM participants deeper into activism developing initiatives to inform women about health care resources in Washington, D.C., and to press for changes in medical treatment.[49]

The CWA's ideas about the role of the coalition and the issue of reproductive control contrasted markedly with those of the women's liberationists. Since its inception, the CWA had solicited and received support from local women's, African American, religious, and labor groups who provided legal assistance and political training and publicly backed welfare reform measures. However, in keeping with their fight for self-determination in all aspects of their lives, participants in Washington's welfare groups insisted on setting priorities and fostering leadership from within their own ranks. The coalition with WLM threatened the independence that welfare rights activists so highly valued. Etta Horn criticized the kinds of interaction that occurred; the groups had supported each other, but they had not "really gotten together to work on abortion reform" in an effective way. Although CWA never intended to build a permanent alliance with the WLM, Horn's statement hinted at regret over a missed opportunity to do more to fight for abortion access. This regret was not shared by a NWRO employee who observed that WLM members "co-opted the whole thing" by controlling the agenda and presuming to speak for the welfare activists. She characterized this as "old patterns of black and white trying to work together" with the white WLM participants insensitive to the potential discomfort welfare activists might feel in the presence of more affluent and educated radical feminists.[50]

The difference in the membership and strategy of the two groups determined the CWA's and WLM's views about the obstacles that prevented women from exercising control over reproduction. Both groups were adamant that abortion constituted a health right that all women deserved. They also agreed that quality health care would guarantee safe, free (or affordable) treatment that allowed women to decide whether or when to have children. They contrasted, however, in framing abortion as a path to liberation or as a tool of oppression. Welfare rights activists tied their health concerns to the threat of genocide and the struggle for survival poor women faced. Welfare recipients who supported regulatory and legal changes to increase women's access to safe abortions also stressed poor women's vulnerability to governmental pressures that limited their reproductive control. Etta Horn dramatized the powerlessness that women felt when welfare department employees made continued eligibility for public funds contingent on women's consent to abortions, sterilization, or birth control use. "You don't want to make anyone mad," Horn explained, "you're really on your knees."[51] Such coercion not only circumscribed women's ability to control their own bodies but the poor health that had caused many welfare recipients to stop working threatened to exacerbate the damage posed by oral contraceptives. The city government's public health and welfare bureaucracies also instigated genocide by offering women no alternatives to risky illegal abortions. Thus, abortion formed one part of a larger structure that endangered poor women's lives and constricted their ability to control their fertility.[52]

But although CWA called attention to abortion as a procedure that perpetuated genocide, its members declared women's right to control their fertility by any means, even if doing so entailed using publicly funded birth control programs that might have been created with more nefarious designs. As Washington, D.C., welfare activist Bobby McMahan put it when registering her support for government family planning programs, "we believe in the dignity of women and motherhood and the right of every woman to know that she can and is able to decide for herself if and when she wants to have children." Aware that politicians who advocated family planning might not intend to increase women's autonomy, McMahan nonetheless asserted that poor women could discern the potential benefits of contraceptive programs. Eager to control their fertility, poor women were "not going to cut off a nose to spite a face whatever the real motives of you legislators may be."[53]

WLM members concurred that lack of access to birth control represented only one symptom of their "lack of control over our bodies and lives. . . . Until we can provide adequate health care for all, repeal of abortion laws will mean little to those without money."[54] Despite their professed commitment to tackling abortion within the context of a broader range of health care issues and as part of a push for women's liberation, however, WLM members could not reconcile their insistence that "free abortions on demand" would increase women's liberation with the reality that abortions could be used for coercive or destructive ends.[55] Searching for concerns that all women shared in common, the WLM sought universal terms to describe why safe legal abortions could expand women's power. The inability to merge these two demands may have revealed WLM members' distance from the realities of poor women's lives or their overriding belief that putting power in women's hands represented the key to eliminating other forms of oppression. Whatever the reason, after the coalition dissolved, WLM members continued to fight for abortion and birth control but without sustained attention toward eradicating the economic constraints that limited women's choices. Instead, subsequent activities by the WLM tied reproductive issues to a variety of health and family concerns, including natural childbirth techniques, adoption and divorce, and sexuality. Without ongoing collaboration with welfare activists, radical feminists' earlier concerns about race, class, and women's disparate access to abortion and health care seemed to take a back seat to more universal calls for women's liberation.[56]

The battle for abortion and health rights in D.C. did not end, however, when the CWA-WLM coalition dissolved in 1970. During the next three years, and thanks to the pressure that activists continued to exert, city officials loosened criteria to determine women's eligibility for abortion and allowed abortions performed in clinics not attached to hospitals. As a result of these policy shifts and subsequent rulings in *United States of America v. Milan Vuitch,* the number of places where women could get legal abortions increased and restrictions slowly, albeit unevenly, relaxed. Members of the WLM and welfare rights groups continued to champion women's right to reproductive self-determination, asserting the importance of women's control as new clinics opened and keeping the issue of forced sterilization in the public eye.[57]

However, new alliances spearheaded the city's reproductive rights movement after 1970. In 1971, three new groups—the Metropolitan Abortion Alliance (MAA), the Citizens Committee for Safe Abortion, and a chapter of the Women's National Abortion Action Coalition—formed to stir up activity in D.C. in support of abortion rights. Working through these umbrella associations, activists united across differences in political ideologies, protest strategies, and organizational affiliations to refine the abortion rights agenda and coordinate their battles. The new coalitions served a strategic function within the city, uniting numerous feminist organizations sprang up, many of them multi-issue oriented. By working cooperatively to address abortion, such multi-issue organizations could channel resources and energy toward this important cause without narrowing or redirecting their primary goals. Within a city where women's political groups continued to be differentiated along race and class lines, collaborations also offered opportunities to bridge these distinctions.[58]

Some actions coordinated by these new organizations resembled the undertakings previously instigated by the WLM-CWA coalition. This continuity both suggested that the earlier arguments and tactics still resonated in Washington, D.C., and indicated how much unfinished work remained, despite the gradually changing laws and regulations. The MAA's approach particularly harkened back to the earlier radical feminist–welfare rights coalition by similarly communicating the abortion issue as a fight to expand access in the face of racism, poverty, and a profit-driven health care structure. In the spring of 1971, MAA representatives proposed pickets at D.C. General and another hospital that primarily served Washington, D.C.'s poor, to publicize how the stiff criteria the public facilities still employed when evaluating abortion requests represented discriminatory application of the law. The MAA also echoed WLM by asserting that women's reproductive autonomy should extend to their control of facilities that provided abortion services, and they called for a "reorganized publicly-supported health plan" and further research on the health effects of the birth control pill. In this instance, the alliance chose tactics, arguments, and a location that showed its indebtedness to the 1969 welfare rights–women's liberation protests.[59]

However, increasingly after 1971, the abortion rights movement shifted away from framing abortion as a health right and from fighting to expand access. Instead, local activists generated mass participation by articulating abortion at the center of a national reproductive rights campaign focused on changing laws. The growing calls to preserve women's lives by legalizing abortion resonated with activists from across the political spectrum, and socialist feminists, members of the National Organization for Women, students, federal employees, and black liberationists joined proabortion groups in the District. The national repeal movement also glossed over local particularities, focusing on a largely moot issue in Washington, D.C., and in several of the country's most populous states, where the most pressing problem was not passage of more permissive laws but discriminatory application of already liberal statutes.[60]

Moreover, as the legal impediments to abortion slowly toppled, before and after the 1973 *Roe v. Wade* ruling, the issue of "choice" assumed paramount importance in the arguments made by abortion rights proponents, replacing earlier calls for "free abortion on demand" and "free health care for all." The pro-choice movement shared the earlier CWA-WLM coalition's adherence to the principle of women's control of their bodies, favoring the elimination of impediments to women's right to determine when and whether to give birth or raise children. The antiabortion movement that took off in the early 1970s also played a role in defining reproductive rights in moral terms and solidifying the oppositional nature of two campaigns that pitted women's choices against the rights of the unborn. However, the emphasis on choice neglected earlier activists' assessment that abortion restrictions symbolized one way that America's health care system prioritized profits over people and downplayed their insistence that the elimination of restrictions on abortion must occur as part of an overall transformation in the medical system. Instead, the *Roe* ruling specified that women's decisions about abortion must be made in consultation with their physicians, thereby strengthening doctors' power, rather than questioning biases within the health care system.[61]

At the same time, the shifting demands revealed a transition in activists' recognition of the obstacles that curtailed reproductive control. Implying that legal changes would enable all women to exercise their voluntary right of choice, the pro-choice movement obscured the systemic social and economic inequalities that obstructed women's ability to control their fertility. By making poverty an implicit, rather than an explicit barrier to reproductive control, the movement suggested that middle-class women's experiences were normative.[62] Welfare rights activists challenged this assumption, continually balking at the coercive use of birth control measures, particularly attacking government-supported compulsory sterilization of poor women.[63] Even these efforts, however, unwittingly highlighted the notion of choice by focusing on the importance of informed consent, in addition to the array of economic and social inequalities that cut off poor women's options and compromised their health. When Congress passed the Hyde Amendment in 1976, which barred the use of Medicaid funds to pay for abortions, the act crystallized the disjunction between economic and legal access.[64]

Looking back at the CWA-WLM coalition illustrates alternative ways that activists conceptualized the abortion struggle and shows the important consequences of an alliance of feminists and welfare rights activists. The cooperation and interaction between these two groups played a pivotal—if temporary—role in expanding activists' understanding of the nature of women's oppression. As a result of coming together to devise strategies and craft arguments, welfare rights proponents and women's liberation activists transmitted their distinct perspectives into a broader effort to improve health care, secure abortion access, and end coercive and dangerous practices that limited women's reproductive control. Linking abortion, sterilization, and birth control, Washington, D.C.'s radical feminists and welfare-recipient activists helped articulate a health rights agenda and introduced faces, voices, and tactics that propelled the abortion rights movement in new directions.

## Notes

1. Marilyn Salzman Webb, "Abortion Practices Assailed," *Guardian* 27 (September 1969): 6; Myra McPherson, "Abortion Protest Stymied," *Washington Post*, September 9, 1969, B1–B2. The D.C. General Hospital's policy is outlined in D.C. Department of Public Health, "Statement by Washington Women's Liberation to the Mayor's Task Force on Public Health Goals," September 1969, folder 42, carton 2, Charlotte Bunch papers, Schlesinger Library, Radcliffe Institute for Advanced Study, Harvard University, Cambridge, Mass. (hereafter Bunch papers).

2. In 1967, five hundred to eight hundred women received treatment at D.C. General for complications after illegal abortions. The D.C. Department of Public Health recorded forty-two deaths from abortions between 1960 and 1967 and a sharp increase in the number of therapeutic abortions performed at four D.C. hospitals from 1959 to 1969, totaling more than two hundred in 1967. However, health department data did not identify which hospitals provided the figures. "Statement by Washington Women's Liberation," and "Committee on Abortions Meeting," folder 42, carton 2, Bunch papers. Figures in other reports differ, but reveal the same disparities between abortions at D.C. General Hospital relative to other facilities and compared to the numbers of women who sought treatment after illegal abortions. *Report of the City Council's Health and Welfare Committee on Abortions in the District of Columbia, October 1970* (Washington, DC: Government of the District of Columbia City Council, 1970); Richard D. Lyons, "Study in Capital Urges Abortion Aid," *New York Times*, December 13, 1969, 37; Donald Hirzel, "Court Turns Down Plea for Abortion," *Washington Evening Star*, March 7, 1970, Abortion article file, Washingtoniana division, Martin Luther King, Jr. Memorial Library (hereafter MLK Library), Washington, D.C.; "The Abortion Racket—What Should Be Done?," *Newsweek*, August 15, 1960, 50–52.

3. Historian Leslie Reagan has argued that in the 1950s and 1960s, nearly four times as many women of color as white women died as a result of illegal abortions. Leslie J. Reagan, *When Abortion Was a Crime: Women, Medicine, and Law in the United States, 1867–1973* (Berkeley: University of California Press, 1997), 211–13.

4. For discussions of the connection between feminism and welfare rights see Premilla Nadasen, *Welfare Warriors: The Welfare Rights Movement in the United States* (New York: Routledge, 2004); Guida West, *The National Welfare Rights Movement: The Social Protest of Poor Women* (New York: Praeger, 1981); Martha F. Davis, "Welfare Rights and Women's Rights in the 1960s," *Journal of Policy History* 8, no. 1 (1996): 144–65.

5. This broad generalization ignores the important presence of African American women who participated in predominantly white feminist groups and white antiracist activists who struggled to broaden the membership and perspectives of feminist organizations. See Sara Evans, *Tidal Wave: How Women Changed America at Century's End* (New York: Free Press, 2003); Alice Echols, *Daring to be Bad: Radical Feminism in America, 1967–1975* (Minneapolis: University of Minnesota Press, 1989); Sara Evans, *Personal Politics* (New York: Vintage Books, 1979); Ula Taylor, "The Historical Evolution of Black Feminist Theory and Praxis," *Journal of Black Studies* 29 (November 1998): 234–53; Deborah Gray White, *Too Heavy a Load: Black Women in Defense of Themselves, 1894–1994* (New York: W. W. Norton, 1999); Becky Thompson, "Multiracial Feminism: Recasting the Chronology of Second Wave Feminism," *Feminist Studies* 28 (Summer 2002): 337–60.

6. Rickie Solinger, *Pregnancy and Power: A Short History of Reproductive Politics in America* (New York: New York University Press, 2005), 182.

7. Linda Gordon, *Woman's Body, Woman's Right: Birth Control in America*, rev. ed. (New York: Penguin Books, 1990), 398–99.

8. "Byrd Urges Birth Control for Slum-Area Negroes," *Washington Post*, August 17, 1967; Cornelia Ball, "Byrd Backs Birth Control," *Washington Daily News*, October 15, 1963; William Grigg, "Birth Control Study Started by District," *Washington Star*, October 16, 1963, all from Birth Control article file, MLK Library. On eugenic sterilization laws, see Johanna Schoen, *Choice and Coercion: Birth Control, Sterilization, and Abortion in*

*Public Health and Welfare* (Chapel Hill: University of North Carolina Press, 2005) and Pippa Holloway, *Sexuality, Politics, and Social Control in Virginia, 1920–1945* (Chapel Hill: University of North Carolina Press, 2006).

9. Angela Y. Davis, *Women, Race & Class* (New York: Random House, 1981); Loretta J. Ross, "African American Women and Abortion," in *Abortion Wars: A Half Century of Struggle, 1950–2000,* ed. Rickie Solinger (Berkeley: University of California Press, 1998); Jennifer Nelson, *Women of Color and the Reproductive Rights Movement* (New York: New York University Press, 2003); Jane Lawrence, "The Indian Health Service and the Sterilization of Native American Women," *American Indian Quarterly* 24 (June 2000): 400–419.

10. Stephanie Coontz, *The Way We Never Were: American Families and the Nostalgia Trap* (New York: Basic Books, 2000); Elaine Tyler May, *Homeward Bound: American Families in the Cold War Era* (New York: Basic Books, 1988).

11. Nelson, *Women of Color and the Reproductive Rights Movement,* 3–7.

12. On the changing definitions of reproductive freedom, see Rosalind Petchesky, *Abortion and Woman's Choice: The State, Sexuality, and Reproductive Freedom* (New York: Longman, Inc., 1984); Gordon, *Woman's Body, Woman's Right.*

13. State abortion laws as of January 1971 are listed in Nanette Davis, *From Crime to Choice: The Transformation of Abortion in America* (Westport, CT: Greenwood Press, 1985), app. A.

14. Because Congress must change the laws that govern the District of Columbia, Gesell's ruling did not overturn the 1901 law but drew attention to the law's application and motivated the D.C. City Council's deliberations regarding whether to recommend that Congress amend the laws. Lawrence Lader, *Abortion II: Making the Revolution* (Boston: Beacon Press, 1973), 1–17; *United States of America v. Milan Vuitch* and *United States of America v. Shirley A. Boyd,* 305 F. Supp. 1032 (1969), U.S. District Court for the District of Columbia. On appeal to the U.S. Supreme Court, Vuitch's case was overturned in April 1971. The justices declared the 1901 law constitutional but ruled that the definition of *health* must include a woman's mental health. John P. MacKenzie and Stuart Auerbach, "D.C. Abortion Law Upheld by Supreme Court, 5 to 2," *Washington Post,* April 22, 1971, A1, A9. See *United States v. Vuitch* 402 U.S. 62, 91 S. Ct. 1294, 28 L. Ed. 2d 601 (1971).

15. Petchesky, *Abortion and Woman's Choice,* 127.

16. Petchesky, *Abortion and Woman's Choice,* 125.

17. District Court Judge Gerhard Gesell, who ruled in the Vuitch case, may have had a personal interest in abortion. In 1964 and 1965, his wife sat on the board of the Planned Parenthood Association of Metropolitan Washington, D.C. The spotty records of the chapter do not reveal whether she still served on the organization's board in 1969. Board of Trustees, Planned Parenthood Association of Metropolitan Washington, D.C., minutes, box 134, Planned Parenthood Federation of America records II, Sophia Smith Collection, Smith College, Northampton, Mass. For more on the movement to repeal abortion laws, see Reagan, *When Abortion Was a Crime;* David Garrow, *Liberty and Sexuality: The Right to Privacy and the Making of Roe v. Wade* (New York: MacMillan Publishing Company, 1994); Lader, *Abortion II;* Gordon, *Woman's Body, Woman's Right;* Diane Schulder and Florynce Kennedy, *Abortion Rap* (New York: McGraw-Hill Book Company, 1971); Amy Kesselman, "Women Versus Connecticut: Conducting a Statewide Hearing on Abortion," in Solinger, ed., *Abortion Wars,* 42–67.

18. Marilyn Salzman Webb, "Women Fight for Health Care," *Guardian,* October 11, 1969, 6; Irna Moore, "Hearings Set on State of D.C. General," *Washington Post,* September 11, 1969, A26; Stuart Auerbach, "Hospital Employees Join Doctors' Protest," *Washington Post,* September 17, 1969, C3; Carl Bernstein, "Hospital Needs Told at Probe," *Washington Post,* September 18, 1969, B2.

19. "Statement by Washington Women's Liberation"; Lyons, "Study in Capital"; MacPherson, "Abortion Protest Stymied"; Webb, "Abortion Practices Assailed"; Webb, "Women Fight for Health Care"; "Women's Liberation Fights Washington, D.C. Health Crisis," *Women: a Journal of Liberation* (Winter 1970), reprinted in Leslie B. Tanner, ed., *Voices from Women's Liberation* (New York: Signet, 1970), 136–37.

20. Alice Wolfson, "Women vs. Health Industry," unpublished pamphlet, Health Care Position papers, Women's Ephemera files, Northwestern University Library.

21. Carol Honsa, "Welfare Mothers Fighting for Dignity," *Washington Post,* May 5, 1967, M4.

22. Chapters needed at least twenty-five members, each paying annual dues of one dollar, to affiliate with the NWRO. A majority of chapter members had to be welfare recipients but others could join if their incomes fell below the poverty line. In July 1970, approximately 1,300 people belonged to the twelve Washington, D.C.-area chapters; in October 1971, thirteen local chapters were active. Membership and chapter information comes from "1968 Membership Report, November 9, 1968," and "National Welfare Rights Organization—Membership Reports for 1969," both in box 2018, National Welfare Rights Organization collection, Moorland-Spingarn Research Center, Howard University, Washington, D.C. (hereafter NWRO papers); Carol Honsa, "District to Ask Federal Welfare Aid," *Washington Post,* June 26, 1970, C8; J. Y. Smith, "Welfare Rights Protestors Fail to 'Evict' System's Chief," *Washington Post,* October 28, 1971, B2.

23. White, *Too Heavy a Load;* Anne M. Valk, "'Mother Power': The Movement for Welfare Rights in Washington, D.C., 1966–1972," *Journal of Women's History* 11 (Winter 2000): 34–58. For discussion relating these stereotypes to public policy, see Rickie Solinger, *Beggars and Choosers: How the Politics of Choice Shapes Adoption, Abortion, and Welfare in the United States* (New York: Hill and Wang, 2001); Dorothy Roberts, *Killing the Black Body: Race, Reproduction, and the Meaning of Liberty* (New York: Vintage Books, 1997).

24. "Mothers Meet with Mayor," *Washington Post,* July 1, 1969, E2; "School Clothing for Welfare Children," *WRO Welfare Fighter,* September 1969, 7.

25. Press release issued by D.C. Citywide Alliance, November 5, 1968, box 2083, NWRO papers; "Testimony of the Citywide Welfare Alliance of the District of Columbia," May 20, 1969, folder 11, box 24, George Wiley papers, State Historical Society of Wisconsin, Madison, Wisconsin. NWRO chapters in other cities also organized around birth control and reproductive issues, including women in Pittsburgh who rallied in support of family planning clinics. See Thomas B. Littlewood, *The Politics of Population Control* (Notre Dame, Ind.: University of Notre Dame Press, 1977), 69–87.

26. The WLM structure makes it difficult to reconstruct the number of people involved. A May 1969 newspaper article claimed that approximately 100 women were involved in the movement; a March 1970 article described 250 women as "hard core" participants plus another 250 on the group's mailing list. The names of 289 women appear on an undated membership list (circa 1970–71). Barbara Stubbs, "The Angry Young Women," *Washington Star,* May 25, 1969, Women 1968–69 article file, MLK Library; Mary Wiegers, "Women's

Lib: 'Only Active Radicals in Town,'" *Washington Post*, March 11, 1970, B1, B3; "Washington Women's Liberation—Mailing List," folder 1970–71, box 1, Joan E. Biren papers, Lesbian Herstory Archives, Brooklyn, New York. More information on the WLM can be found in "Ourstory Herstory: A Working Paper on the DC Women's Liberation Movement," May 1971, in author's possession; Anne M. Valk, *Radical Sisters: Second-Wave Feminism and Black Liberation in Washington, D.C. (Urbana: University of Illinois Press, 2008);* Evans, *Tidal Wave*, 99–102; Echols, *Daring to be Bad*, 69–72. Alice Wolfson, a WLM member, described living in a commune where the only steady income came from her husband, in Barbara Seaman, *The Greatest Experiment Ever Performed on Women: Exploding the Estrogen Myth* (New York: Hyperion, 2003), 129–30; Linda Grant, *Sexing the Millennium: Women and the Sexual Revolution* (New York: Grove Press, 1994), 178.

27. "Ourstory Herstory," 3.

28. The ideas contained in this essay were generated through WLM discussion groups and appeared in earlier writings by participants. Marilyn Salzman Webb, "Woman as Secretary, Sexpot, Spender, Sow, Civic Actor, Sickie," *Motive* 29 (March-April 1969), 48–59.

29. "Washington Women's Liberation Project Groups," Fall 1969, folder 21, carton 1, Bunch papers.

30. Washington, D.C., Women's Liberation, "It's Alright Ma (I'm Only Bleeding)," folder 41, carton 2, Bunch papers.

31. Judith Coburn, "Off the Pill?," *Ramparts* 8 (June 1970): 46–49.

32. "It's Alright Ma (I'm Only Bleeding)"; D.C. Women's Liberation Health Group, "How the Health System Oppresses Women as Women," November 1969, Women's Ephemera file, Health Care, D.C. Women's Liberation Health Group, Deering Special Collections Library, Northwestern University.

33. In Chicago, radical feminists established their own abortion service to make available safe and affordable abortions. See Laura Kaplan, *The Story of Jane: The Legendary Underground Feminist Abortion Service* (New York: Pantheon Books, 1995).

34. "Ourstory Herstory," 3–4; Webb, "Woman as Secretary," 59.

35. D.C. Family Welfare Rights Flier, February 1972, Abortion subject files, box 10, D.C. City Council papers, Special Collections, Gelman Library, George Washington University, Washington, D.C.

36. "Horning In," *off our backs*, December 14, 1970, 6.

37. One study of physicians' attitudes toward sterilization seemed to validate the claim that racism and sexism factored into doctors' decisions about birth control. See Bernard Rosenfeld, Sidney M. Wolfe, and Robert E. McGarrah Jr., *A Health Research Group Study on Surgical Sterilization: Present Abuses and Proposed Regulations* (Washington, D.C.: Health Research Group, 1973).

38. Marilyn Salzman Webb, "Facts about Abortion in America," *Guardian*, July 19, 1969, 8; "It's Alright Ma (I'm Only Bleeding)."

39. In early 1970, after D.C. General rejected two women who seemed to meet the criteria for receiving abortions, the American Civil Liberties Union, NARAL, and WLM sought a court order to force the facility to comply with the *Vuitch* ruling. The lawsuit charged that the hospital continued to reject most abortion requests, failed to consider women's mental health as grounds for abortion, and adhered to more restrictive eligibility requirements than other District medical facilities. Caroline Nickerson, a member of the WLM, was one of the lawyers involved in the suit. See front page stories in the *Wash-*

*ington Post,* March 10–14, 1970; Gordon Pettey, "'Mary Doe' Finally Gets an Abortion," *Washington Post,* March 15, 1970, D1–D2; "Contempt of Women," *off our backs,* March 19, 1970, 4; Hirzel, "Court Turns Down Plea for Abortion;" Peter Osnos, "D.C. General is Sued Again Over Abortion," *Washington Post,* April 30, 1970, A1–A2; Mary Ann Kuhn, "Mother at 14 Decries Hospital," *Washington Daily News,* April 30, 1970, Abortion file, MLK Library; Lader, *Abortion II,* 113.

40. "Another Reaction," *off our backs,* June 26, 1971, 20.

41. The vulnerability of African American women was not specific to Washington, D.C. According to one physician, in 1967, nationwide women of color were seven times more likely to die from infection after an unsafe abortion than were white women. Warren M. Hern, "The Politics of Abortion," *The Progressive* 36 (November 1972): 26–30. See also Reagan, *When Abortion Was a Crime,* 211–13.

42. Auerbach, "Hospital Employees Join Doctors' Protest."

43. Weigers, "Women's Lib;" Webb, "Abortion Practices Assailed;" Marilyn Salzman Webb, "A Hard Rain's Gonna Fall," *WIN Magazine* 6 (January 1970): 4.

44. Alice J. Wolfson, "Clenched Fist, Open Heart," in *The Feminist Memoir Project: Voices from Women's Liberation,* ed. Rachel Blau DuPlessis and Ann Snitow (New York: Three Rivers Press, 1998), 270.

45. Bernstein, "Hospital Needs Told at Probe"; Webb, "Abortion Practices Assailed."

46. "Health Crisis Breaks in D.C."; Alice Wolfson, "Women and Health," folder 42, carton 2, Bunch papers.

47. Judith Coburn, "Off the Pill?," *The Village Voice,* February 5, 1970, 14–15; Wolfson, "Clenched Fist, Open Heart," 270–73. Statements collected at the WLM hearings were published in Subcommittee on Monopoly, Select Committee on Small Business, U.S. Senate, *Competitive Problems in the Drug Industry* (Washington, D.C.: Government Printing Office, 1970), app. X.

48. Alex Ward, "Women Hold Own Hearing on Pill," *Washington Post,* March 8, 1970, L7; Malcolm Kovacs, "The Pill Hearings," *D.C. Gazette,* March 23, 1970, 6–7; Nancy Beezley, "How Safe the Pill?," *Quicksilver Times,* April 3–13, 1970, 8–9; Seaman, *The Greatest Experiment Ever,* 122–42. Women's liberation groups in other locations also organized public hearings, or "speak-outs," to promote public education and consciousness raising and to challenge women's exclusion when Congress, courts, or other administrative bodies refused to allow their participation. The first abortion hearings were staged by the New York group, Redstockings, in March 1969. Susan Brownmiller, *In Our Time: Memoir of a Revolution* (New York: Dial Press, 1999), 107–9; Echols, *Daring to be Bad,* 141–42; Nelson, *Women of Color and the Reproductive Rights Movement,* 30–38.

49. "Ourstory Herstory," 4–5; Webb, "Women Fight for Health Care."

50. "Horning In"; "A Black Woman Responds to Women's Liberation," *off our backs,* April 15, 1971, 18.

51. Etta Horn testimony in *Competitive Problems in the Drug Industry,* 7285–86.

52. Calvin Zon, "In Memory of Sisters Murdered by Abortion," *Washington Star,* May 8, 1972, Abortion file, MLK Library.

53. "Statement of Mrs. Bobbie McMahan," February 19, 1970, Subcommittee on Health, Committee on Labor and Human Resources, U.S. Senate, *Family Planning and Population Research* (Washington, D.C.: Government Printing Office, 1970), 277.

54. "It's Alright Ma (I'm Only Bleeding)."

55. "Ourstory Herstory," 4.

56. In 1971, the Abortion Counseling Collective of WLM outlined the ten projects the group contemplated starting. They included creating courses on natural childbirth and health and sexuality; providing counseling on adoption, divorce, and drugs; collecting and distributing information about the services offered by area doctors; and starting four groups—one for men, one on health and diet, one on art, and one to research the medical and bureaucratic procedures at D.C. General. Of the proposed projects, arguably only the last directly addressed economic discrimination and the particular problems encountered by poor women. Women from Abortion Counseling, "Health Projects for Women," *off our backs*, May 27, 1971, 21. See also the critiques made by Alice Wolfson and Linda Carcionne in Alice Wolfson et al., "On Graduating from the Women's Movement," *off our backs*, August 31, 1973, 12.

57. "Ourstory, Herstory," 4; Zon, "In Memory of Sisters Murdered."

58. These alliances took differing approaches to the fight for abortion rights, with some working for repeal and others continuing to fight for "free abortion on demand." Jean Powell, "Women Don't Agree," *Washington Star*, July 28, 1971, Abortion file, MLK Library; Fran Pollner, "Bringing Abortion Home," *off our backs*, October 1971, 20; Bev Fisher et al., "A House Divided," *off our backs*, October 1971, 11.

59. "D.C. Women Campaign for Free Abortions," *Washington Daily News*, April 16, 1971, 4; "Abortion Alliance Plans Action," *off our backs*, May 27, 1971, 21; "Bringing It Home."

60. Davis, *From Crime to Choice*, app. A.

61. Adele Clark and Alice Wolfson, "Class, Race, and Reproductive Rights," *Socialist Review* 78 (November-December 1984), 110–20, reprinted in *Women, Class, and the Feminist Imagination: A Socialist-Feminist Reader*, ed. Karen V. Hansen and Ilene J. Philipson (Philadelphia: Temple University Press, 1990), 258–67. See also the WLM critique of the expanding number of abortion clinics, operated without women's input, in "Ourstory, Herstory," 4.

62. Gordon, *Woman's Body, Woman's Right*, 411.

63. Members of the NWRO sued the Department of Health, Education, and Welfare on behalf of Minnie Lee Relf, a twelve-year-old from Alabama, who was sterilized without consent. In 1974, Judge Gerhard Gesell ruled that HEW funds could no longer be used to sterilize minors and others unable to give consent. *Relf v. Weinberger*, 372 F. Supp. 1196 (1974) and *Relf v. Weinberger*, 565 F. 2d 722 (D.C. Cir. 1977), U.S. District Court for the District of Columbia. See Nadasen, *Welfare Warriors*, 216–20.

64. The Hyde Amendment authorized the use of federal funds for abortions in cases where the mother's life was endangered, her health would be severely compromised, or the pregnancy resulted from rape or incest.

## 8. Reconsidering Violence against Women

*Coalition Politics in the Antirape Movement*

MARIA BEVACQUA

Coalition building has historically been one of the most challenging and often painful aspects of women's movement organizing. By looking to the past for successful models, activists in the present might better understand how to go about forging alliances across apparent boundaries. The emergence and growth of the second wave of feminism in the 1960s and 1970s provides an intriguing opportunity to investigate social movement actors' efforts to create and sustain coalitions that transcend ideological and racial boundaries. The first two decades of social scientific and historical accounts of the early, heady years of second-wave feminism have played up the sharp distinctions between the radical and liberal branches of the movement.[1] Such accounts likewise contend that the branches had substantially merged or that the radical feminist branch had ceased to exist by 1975.[2] Much of the same scholarship of the women's movement notes the failure of majority-white feminist groups to attract the participation of women of color in large numbers. This first wave of analysis of the second wave paints a picture of an emerging movement sharply divided along political and racial lines.[3] Even though such accounts highlight the differences among feminist camps, they fail to attest to feminist cooperation on the major women's issues being articulated at the time.

More recent analyses of the second wave provide greater accounting for coalition and cooperation among feminist groups, as well as a blurring of the ideological lines dividing the movement. For example, historian Estelle Freedman notes that attempts to categorize different trends in feminism—

liberal, radical, socialist, and so on—must acknowledge that these trends "have never been entirely distinct, and over time they have interacted with each other to blur some of their differences."[4] Furthermore, in a study of second-wave feminism in Dayton, Ohio, Judith Ezekiel finds that "in contrast to the two-branch pattern so often described, a single strand of feminism emerged in Dayton, . . . most closely resembling what various scholars have called the women's liberation, radical, or collectivist branch."[5] Similarly, more recent scholarship has located historical and contemporary moments of unity among activists of varied racial and cultural backgrounds.[6]

This interdisciplinary essay investigates the rise of the U.S. antirape movement as a social movement within the wider women's movement, or a submovement, in Freeman's terms.[7] Combining interviews with archival research, I locate the ways in which rape served as a bridge issue that united radical, liberal, white, and black feminists (the two former do not necessarily exclude the two latter) in the common cause to develop an antirape ideology, attenuate the trauma experienced by the rape victim, and elaborate strategies to eradicate rape. I hope to demonstrate that radical, liberal, African American, and white feminists traveled "separate roads to feminism,"[8] or, in this case, to antirape activism. Their own experiences and those of the members of their communities informed these roads, and in their journeys, they forged significant coalitions around the rape issue.

This account, while elucidating themes specific to a particular historical context, has contemporary implications for social movement actors: it points to the possibility and reality of meaningful cooperation even where political differences exist. I do not ignore the deep division between radical and liberal feminist politics at the dawn of the second wave. Nor do I downplay the very real reasons for women of color to distrust the majority-white women's movement and antirape campaign or the failure of the movement to sufficiently address white racism and privilege. But this account does attempt to correct a historical record that in some cases overstates these differences and erases the presence of women of color in feminist activism: it challenges scholars of feminism to rethink what we know about the second wave and its controversies. In keeping with the newer scholarship on second-wave feminism, this account can point toward the possibilities for present and future social movement actors looking for ways to cross boundaries and forge new alliances in influencing public policy and pursuing social justice.

The antirape campaign grew out of second-wave organizing and developed its own social movement organizations and strategies, but it was never divorced from second-wave analysis and networks. Elsewhere I have conceptualized the antirape movement as a submovement or a spin-off of the wave of feminist activism that surged in the late 1960s and 1970s.[9] At the time of the second wave's emergence, the radical and liberal branches were rather polarized. While radical feminists saw the reform of a sexist, racist, capitalist patriarchy as counterrevolutionary, the liberal branch pursued legal and economic equality for women, employing different strategies and different analysis. To a far greater extent than liberals, radicals sought to use the details of women's personal lives to forge feminist politics. It was in the context of the activism and theorizing of the radical branch that the articulation of rape as a serious political problem in women's lives took shape. But within a few years of this breakthrough, antirape organizing crossed over the ideological and racial boundaries and served as a bridge issue to unite feminists.

It is not surprising that radicals and not liberals were first to place rape on the feminist agenda. Radical feminists were far less concerned with maintaining a reputation of respectability, were likely to flout convention in the conduct of their often flamboyant actions, and were thus far better suited to breaking the taboo surrounding rape than were liberal feminists. Rape was first articulated as a central concern for women's liberation by way of the consciousness-raising sessions of 1970. Consciousness raising was the strategy by which women developed a political analysis of their personal lives, which would lead to the creation of a plan of action for change. New York Radical Feminists (NYRF) were at the vanguard of the politicization of rape. According to NYRF members, "rape became an issue when women began to compare their experiences as children, teen-agers, students, workers, and wives and to realize that sexual assault, in one form or another, was common."[10] Encouraged by an individualist, misogynist society, victims typically internalized their guilt and anxiety over rape, thereby privatizing the problem. Radical feminists politicized it instead by linking the issue to systemic male dominance. The radical feminist approach to rape was built on the experiences of brave women who described their rape experiences in consciousness-raising sessions and public speak-outs and translated their experiences into action.

In addition to the first raising of consciousness within feminist circles and, later, in the general public, radical feminists initiated the self-defense movement[11] and the establishment of rape crisis centers and hotlines, two centerpieces of the antirape campaign. Although self-defense efforts among Boston-area feminists predated the arrival of rape on the feminist agenda, the explicit connection between self-defense training and sexual assault prevention was not made until about 1970. In 1971, martial artist Py Bateman of Seattle founded the Feminist Karate Union, which combined inexpensive martial arts classes by women instructors with consciousness raising for its members.[12] These classes sought to reverse women's socialized passivity and instill a sense of confidence and empowerment. Radical feminists in Washington, D.C., established the first rape crisis center in 1972. Most of the founders were themselves rape survivors, and they created a center to provide the kinds of services they would have wanted in the aftermath of their traumas. The center provided comprehensive services to rape victims as well as outreach and educational programming. The center's goal was nothing less than to "abolish rape in our own lifetimes," as stated in D.C. Rape Crisis Center (RCC) meeting minutes of September 15, 1972.[13]

Liberal feminists joined the antirape cause in the years following radical feminists' initial politicizing effort. First, National Organization for Women (NOW) quietly passed a general resolution favoring more serious treatment of rape and rape victims by law enforcement at its 1971 national conference. But few or no national NOW resources were dedicated to the issue at that time. Within two years, though, antirape radicals would cause such a stir in the media that liberals could no longer stay away from the issue. In 1973, the national conference body passed by acclamation a resolution to form the NOW Rape Task Force (NOWRTF), appointing Mary Ann Largen from Virginia as chair.[14] Other liberal groups, such as the Women's Legal Defense Fund, issued statements in support of rape law reform at the same time. NOWRTF worked actively for several years to enact reform laws and effect policies that would improve the treatment of rape victims by medical personnel, police, and prosecutors, and, it was hoped, result in increased arrest and conviction rates for rape.[15] By the early to mid-1970s, antirape activism took a variety of forms, focusing on state-by-state law reform, the modification of federal rape legislation, and the improvement of the institutional response to sexual assault victims, all the while challenging attitudes and beliefs that supported rape culture.[16]

This essay argues that rape served as a bridge issue that brought together radical, liberal, African American, and white feminists in a shared struggle to address sexual violence. The bridging of the liberal-radical divide helps to illuminate the tensions and the possibilities within feminist organizing. Once the rape issue was on both the radical and liberal feminist agendas, strategies, such as crisis centers and law reform, became less closely associated with their respective camps because of activists' willingness to cross ideological boundaries. Alliances that may have been unimaginable in 1970 became possible when radical antirape activists brought the rape issue to liberal feminists to forge a common cause, and when rape crisis center staff came to understand the need for improved criminal laws. In a number of cities, antirape activists of various political stripes joined forces to engage in public events and actions to call attention to the issue, to pressure policy makers to respond to the needs of victims, and to hammer out strategies for rape prevention and eradication. This also took place at a time, the early to mid-1970s, when liberal feminist groups had adopted some of the language, style, and irreverence of women's liberation and when radical feminism was becoming more focused on either single-issue organizing or giving way to cultural feminism.[17] As a complex issue, rape required a response that marshaled the strength and strategies of feminists of every stripe and created opportunities for crossover politics in the name of feminist change.[18]

One way to raise rape consciousness among various feminist groups was for movement organizations, such as crisis centers, to use their public education talents to address diverse women's groups that might prove sympathetic to their cause. In doing so, they also tapped into existing activist networks that proved co-optable to the incipient movement.[19] In October 1972, for example, "Karen" and "Emily" of the D.C. RCC, a radical feminist collective, met with members of NOW—Northern Virginia to discuss sexual assault, the center, and self-defense, a meeting that received coverage in the *Washington Post*.[20] The D.C. RCC women introduced liberal NOW members to the issue in hopes of building alliances between the two groups. Later, the February/March 1974 issue of the D.C. RCC newsletter included a short article by Mary Ann Largen, chair of the NOWRTF. Further, D.C. RCC meeting minutes make repeated reference to the activities of Largen and NOW—Northern Virginia, suggesting that an alliance between these ideologically distinct groups had formed.[21] Instead of pursuing an ideologically pure radical feminist line, rape crisis center activists reached out to liberal feminist networks in the interest of advancing the antirape cause. Liberal feminists, also alarmed about the problem, saw the need for a dynamic response, joining forces in spite of differences.

Rape crisis advocates were uniquely positioned to recognize the need for improved rape laws. This was in spite of radical feminists' disdain for law reform (or reformist) strategies.[22] Their firsthand experience with rape victims, who reported feeling victimized a second time by the criminal justice system for numerous reasons, made clear to them the serious flaws in rape law and its enforcement. Center staff and volunteers had a vested interest in the passage of fair, victim-friendly sexual assault statutes that would directly benefit their clients, even though this interest marked a departure from radical feminist aversion to participation in "the system." The ideology of putting the survivor's concrete needs first presented the need for compromise and coalition building.

In Michigan, disgruntled crisis center advocates were responsible for initiating the state's major law reform effort. Activists with the Women's Crisis

Center of Ann Arbor (WCC), founded by radical feminists, had often been frustrated in their efforts to attain any type of justice for rape victims under existing legislation. Several WCC activists started the Michigan Women's Task Force on Rape, the coalition group that initiated Michigan's landmark law reform. The decision to pursue law reform—to some, a strategy associated with liberal ideology—was not uncontested. Commentators have noted: "Not all of those present at the initial meeting were convinced that law reform would be the appropriate avenue for change. Several radical feminists dissociated themselves from this effort, questioning the efficacy of a social change strategy to be implemented by a male-dominated institution."[23] Thus, alliances between radical and liberal activists were possible, but not free from strain and dissent. WCC members allied with law professor Virginia Nordby, who was experienced with legislative writing and had a team of women law students eager to participate in the effort.[24] From this example, it is evident that liberal and radical antirape strategies overlapped, making coalition work possible in the interest of improved laws and improved treatment for sexual assault victims.

Around the country, alliances among women's groups were being forged to call greater attention to the rape issue and press for an institutional response to the problem. In 1973, the Women's Anti-Rape Coalition (WARC) was formed in New York with the purpose of raising public awareness and pushing for the repeal of the restrictive corroboration requirement of the state's rape statute. The corroboration provision required that every aspect of a rape charge (use of force, penetration, and identity of the perpetrator) be supported with evidence other than the complainant's word. The law was notorious, even to movement activists in other states. Few rape cases ever went to trial. Because the repeal of this law was widely embraced among New York feminists, antirape activists of every ideological bent supported the effort to eliminate it.

New York Women Against Rape (NYWAR), a radical feminist rape crisis center project, played a visible role in WARC. This group was well-connected in the New York City activist community, and it used those connections for coalition building. NYWAR records demonstrate the group's eagerness to make contact with liberal feminist groups to raise awareness and join forces. For example, meeting minutes of March 21, 1973, indicate that NYWAR members had done a speaking engagement at a meeting of NOW—Riverside.[25] NYWAR and numerous other organizations also participated in a panel discussion on rape hosted by NOW, where momentum to create the antirape coalition began to mount. WARC meetings appeared on all subsequent NYWAR meeting agendas.[26]

Five groups formed WARC at its inception: NYWAR; Manhattan Women's Political Caucus, a chapter of the liberal feminist National Women's Political Caucus; NOW—New York; and New York Radical Feminists. At least two additional feminist groups joined within a year: the National Black Feminist Organization (NBFO) and the Coalition of 100 Black Women (the coalition's main goals were largely accomplished by that time).[27] WARC achieved both its goals—publicizing rape and reforming the law. It engaged in a massive awareness-raising campaign that took advantage of both existing feminist communications networks and the willingness of the popular press to cover their activities. By tirelessly lobbying state legislators, it accomplished the repeal of the corroboration requirement in 1974.

The D.C., Michigan, and New York examples illustrate the point that, even though radical and liberal rape projects often carried out divergent tasks and approached the issue from divergent feminist standpoints, they did not view their strategies and goals as mutually exclusive. Cooperative groups also took advantage of the public consciousness-raising impact of coalition work. Most importantly, participants in liberal and radical strategies shared in their concern for rape victims and for women. The ideological divisions between them were often pronounced: some radical crisis center activists, in Michigan and elsewhere, dismissed the criminal justice system as hopelessly oppressive. However, together many group members pursued the antirape goals of dispelling rape myths, redefining rape as an issue of violence and control, not sexual passion, and making the postrape experience as untraumatic as possible for the victim. These groups created strategic alliances in the interest of attenuating the trauma visited upon victims and met with significant success.[28]

In addition to drawing together liberal and radical feminists, the rape issue also served as a bridge between black and white activists. Recovering this information for the historical record provides a more comprehensive understanding of black feminist activism. The relative absence of black women in predominantly women's movement groups is well-known.[29] Those groups that made some attempt to include women of color throughout the 1970s failed to draw them in large numbers, even though polls have indicated that black women have tended to be as supportive of feminist goals as white women or even more so.[30] Feminists of color have criticized the mostly white movement for its inability to expand its agenda to include the most pressing issues facing women of color and poor women. More recently, however, scholars have traced important issues in cross-race organizing, noting that women's health and reproductive rights organizing brought together women of color and mainstream pro-choice groups to push for a more inclusive agenda.[31]

Further, African American women's resistance to rape and sexual abuse had deep roots in the antiracist struggles of the nineteenth and twentieth centuries.[32] A closer look at the antirape movement reveals sexual assault to be a bridge issue of second-wave feminism.[33]

As organizers of the Feminist Alliance Against Rape and authors of the popular booklet "How to Start a Rape Crisis Center," the pioneering D.C. RCC served as a focal point of antirape activism and enjoyed considerable national influence throughout the 1970s and 1980s. When it was established in 1972, the D.C. RCC collective was made up entirely of white women in their twenties and thirties.[34] Initially, the overwhelming whiteness of the center staff was matched demographically by the women who used the center's services, despite Washington's African American majority. In their meeting minutes, the collective expressed the desire to draw black and working class women into the group.[35] Likewise, in 1974, the NOWRTF newsletter sought advice from members on how to reach out to minority women.[36]

The apparent lack of interest in antirape organizing among black women had more to do with the framing of the rape issue by many white feminists than with a lack of concern about rape on the part of women of color, according to Angela Davis. Instead, black women have issued critiques of 1970s antirape politics that express their concerns: "The failure of the antirape movement of the early 1970's to develop an analysis of rape that acknowledged the social conditions that foster sexual violence as well as the centrality of racism in determining those social conditions, resulted in the reluctance of Black, Latina, and Native American women to involve themselves in that movement."[37] African American women, Davis goes on, distrusted majority-white antirape organizing on two grounds: first, for the movement's failure to address black women's issues; and second, because they feared that the increased regulation of rape would be borne disproportionately by black men. In Davis's view, the myopia of antirape activists and writers prevented them from understanding the deep interconnections between rape and racism in U.S. history.

The evidence indicates that many black feminists take a different view. D.C. activist Loretta Ross rejects the assertion that black women did not become involved in the antirape movement. According to Ross, the antirape movement in Washington, D.C., was a space where activist women of color flourished in their feminist initiatives. Ross describes the D.C. RCC, of which she was director for several years, as a hub of organizing activity for women of color in the 1970s. The center attracted the involvement of black and Latina women by expanding its focus from exclusively dealing with rape to the politicization of related issues, such as poverty and racism. The center's majority-white feminist board, according to Ross, was genuinely interested in developing black feminist leadership for D.C. RCC, making sure to hire women of color for staff positions and giving them a significant measure of power over the center. In an essay on the subject, Ross states, "[the] highly visible militancy on the part of white women struck a chord of interest in Third World women who became involved in the movement early on."[38] One landmark event of the movement, the first National Conference on Third World Women and Violence, was organized by Ross and other D.C. RCC activists and attracted the participation of 125 diverse women of color.[39]

Most importantly, in Ross's view, black women were active in the feminist antirape struggle nearly from the beginning of the movement. The problem is not a lack of black women's participation, says Ross, but a lack of documentation of that participation. She explains that black women did not sit idly by and wait for white women to invite them into the movement but took the initiative and organized around the rape issue on their own and in alliance with other groups. Black women used strategies that addressed the needs of their community. For example, one D.C. RCC program was a feminist reading group with male prisoners. For Ross, the existing historical record, nearly silent on this matter, functions to erase black women's experience and presents a distorted view of the movement.[40]

Nkenge Toure, an African American woman involved with D.C. RCC from 1975 to 1988, indicates that black women created in the center a safe space for women of color to come together and to organize. Like Ross, Toure had been a community organizer on other issues before joining D.C. RCC. She became involved after appearing on a radio program focusing on rapes that had taken place in her community; center activists proposed that Toure join D.C. RCC based on the ideas she expressed on the program.[41] The growing availability of federal funding in the mid-1970s enabled rape crisis centers to diversify their staffs by offering full-time paid (as opposed to part-time or strictly volunteer) positions to African American women, who better represented the community served.[42] Significantly, it was Toure who introduced her friend and political comrade Loretta Ross to the center.

D.C. RCC founders, says Toure, were "politically-minded" white women who understood that the participation of women of color was crucial for the life of the center, and Toure and others took a leadership role in shaping an organization that was responsible to—and inclusive of—the African American community. This process occurred over time and was not enacted simply by the appointment of black women to staff positions. It occurred because of the ability of activist women of color to take information about rape and about the center to the grassroots level and make the issue relevant to women in the community. Around the D.C. area, Toure notes, women of color bonded with each other and formed a network of activists working on numerous feminist issues. Toure further points out that the woman of color focus of the center began to diminish by the late 1980s.[43]

Other evidence supports and amplifies Ross's and Toure's contentions that black feminists engaged in antirape activism in the 1970s. According to Essie Green Williams of the NBFO, the first NBFO conference in 1973 held a rape workshop to explore political perspectives and women's experiences of sexual assault. Williams notes that, instead of rushing into the antirape campaign, black women needed to explore and define the rape issue for themselves before coalition with mostly white groups was possible.[44] These activists recognized that a movement addressing the needs of a community from within that community gains greater legitimacy than one that approaches the community from the outside, an observation that Ross and Toure also make. Alliances between NBFO, NYRF, and NYWAR within WARC in New York resulted in coalition work on the sexual assault issue, such as the (NYC) Mayor's Task Force on Rape, which, in addition to NOW, NBFO, and Coalition of 100 Black Women, included representatives from law enforcement and health agencies.[45] It is clear, then, that in the 1970s, rape was an item on the black feminist agenda, and white and black feminists were creating new alliances in the interest of responding to rape.

Black women within the antirape campaign brought a new perspective to the movement and helped to advance the existing antirape analysis beyond one that reflected only white, middle-class women's concerns. African American feminists and their allies understood rape to be the result of the combined oppressions of racism, sexism, poverty, and imperialism. Loretta Ross explains: "In ... America, Third World women must struggle against brutal acts of racial and sexual violence, while facing the systematic denial of society's benefits. . . . We lack access to employment, education, housing, and healthcare, and we are the targets of rape and sexual abuse by all men, not only men of our races. . . . We are the poorest of the poor, and are considered defenseless, which is why we get attacked so often. We have little or no redress through a criminal *in*justice system that at all times continues the oppression of our peoples."[46] Ross and her allies warned against antirape strategies that capitalized on the law-and-order atmosphere of 1970s public policy making, which would perpetuate law enforcement agencies' oppressiveness toward people of color and the poor. Radical black women brought this perspective to their antirape organizing, which enabled them to ally with politically minded white women who knew that a feminist analysis of rape must necessarily consider racism, poverty, and imperialism in addition to male dominance. African American women in the antirape movement were indeed forging an antirape politics that was accountable to their communities, and they worked with white allies to shape the movement to address their needs.

The impact of the antirape movement is difficult to dispute: it has wrought changes in public policy, created programs to deliver services to rape victims, and, indeed, transformed public consciousness. What emerges from this study is the importance of coalition building to the vitality of the antirape campaign: these successes would not have been possible in the absence of such boundary crossing. These coalitions not only enriched the movement but were also necessary for its growth and spread. Radical feminists, who birthed this movement, could not afford to sit quietly in their "splendid ideological purity," their politics untainted by complicity with "the system" or with liberal feminists.[47] The antirape movement's effects would have been minimal had it failed to reach across political boundaries. In the early years of the movement, the rape issue functioned to bridge the gap separating radicals and liberals—ideologically distant branches of feminism. By building coalitions, antirape campaigners raised public awareness, established crisis centers, and reformed the law in all fifty states.

Similarly, rape was also a bridge issue that united African American and white women in joint efforts to combat violence against women. By challenging barriers to their involvement, black women in the antirape hub of Washington, D.C., created a movement that took race, gender, and poverty into account and added to the movement's strength and momentum. The black women who participated in the campaign not only energized and diversified the movement, but also formed a necessary, vital component of it. Some of the white, middle-class women who founded the movement were unable or unwilling to build a campaign that could respond to the needs of women located outside this group and failed to expand their ideology of rape as a problem based exclusively on gender. But other movement founders, especially in Washington, D.C., saw the need to hand much of its leadership over to the African American women whose communities it would serve. Again, this account does not attempt to gloss over the very real differences that inform women's lives; as Freedman states, "because of historical, social, national, and personal differences, women cannot assume sisterhood, even though we can find common ground on particular issues."[48] Rape was one such issue. The women's movement generally, and the antirape campaign specifically, benefited mightily from the coalition work of these activists in the 1970s and 1980s. Scholars of the women's movement would do well to take cues from important research on coalition building—its disappointments and successes—and to reconsider the historical focus on division over cooperation. Failure to do so as Loretta Ross stated, amounts to inaccuracy in the historical record.

The cooperative strategies employed by white and black, radical and liberal feminists strengthened the antirape movement in its nascent years and created the possibility of far-reaching social change in the face of competing needs and priorities. Evidence of such alliances across ideological and racial boundaries in the past can provide a model for feminists working to challenge oppression in the present and future. The feminist alarm over rape in the 1970s created an ideal context in which radical alliances could be formed, perhaps because it is one that stirs up passion, affects large numbers of women, and requires a complex response. Other feminist issues have the potential to pull together activists of various backgrounds in common cause: women's health, reproductive rights, workplace discrimination—those issues that can motivate and energize a critical mass of people to organize. Coalition building of the kind engaged in by antirape campaigners is crucial if the women's movement—and other movements that challenge the multiple forms of oppression—is to continue to flourish in the twenty-first century.

## Notes

This essay is drawn, in revised form, from my book *Rape on the Public Agenda: Feminism and the Politics of Sexual Assault* (Boston: Northeastern University Press, 2000) and is used here by permission. An earlier version was published in Jill Bystydzienski and Steven Schacht, eds., *Forging Radical Alliances across Difference: Coalition Politics for the New Millenium* (London: Rowman & Littlefield, 2001) and is used here by permission. I would like to thank the Schlesinger Library on the History of Women in America and the Emory University Department of Women's Studies for providing research grants to support this study. I owe a considerable debt of gratitude to my many research participants—particularly Elizabethann O'Sullivan, Nkenge Toure, Loretta Ross, and Susan Brownmiller—without whom this project would not have been possible.

1. See, for example, Alice Echols, *Daring to Be Bad: Radical Feminism in America 1967–1975* (Minneapolis: University of Minnesota Press, 1989); Jo Freeman, *The Politics of Women's Liberation* (New York: David McKay, 1975); and Nancy E. McGlen and Karen O'Connor, *Women's Rights: The Struggle for Equality in the 19th and 20th Centuries* (New York: Praeger, 1983). Also see Sara M. Evans, *Personal Politics: The Roots of Women's Liberation in the Civil Rights Movement and the New Left* (New York: Random House, 1979); and Judith Hole and Ellen Levine, *Rebirth of Feminism* (New York: Quadrangle/New York Times, 1971).

2. Maren Lockwood Carden, *Feminism in the Mid-1970s: The Non-Establishment, the Establishment, and the Future: A Report to the Ford Foundation* (New York: Ford Foundation, 1977); Flora Davis, *Moving the Mountain: The Women's Movement in America since 1960* (New York: Simon and Schuster, 1991); Echols, *Daring to Be Bad*.

3. See also Rosalyn Baxandall and Linda Gordon, eds., *Dear Sisters: Dispatches from the Women's Liberation Movement* (New York: Basic, Perseus, 2000).

4. Estelle Freedman, *No Turning Back: The History of Feminism and the Future of Women* (New York: Ballantine, 2002), 72.

5. Judith Ezekiel, *Feminism in the Heartland* (Columbus: The Ohio State University Press, 2002), 242; see also Sara M. Evans, *Tidal Wave: How Women Changed America at Century's End* (New York: Free Press, 2003).

6. See, for example, Jael Silliman et al., *Undivided Rights: Women of Color Organize for Reproductive Justice* (Cambridge, Mass.: South End Press, 2004).

7. Jo Freeman, "From Suffrage to Women's Liberation: Feminism in Twentieth-Century America," in *Women: A Feminist Perspective,* 5th ed. (Mountain View, Calif.: Mayfield, 1995), 509–28.

8. Benita Roth, *Separate Roads to Feminism: Black, Chicana, and White Feminist Movements in America's Second Wave* (Cambridge, UK: Cambridge University Press, 2004).

9. Maria Bevacqua, *Rape on the Public Agenda: Feminism and the Politics of Sexual Assault* (Boston: Northeastern University Press, 2000).

10. Noreen Connell and Cassandra Wilson, *Rape: The First Sourcebook for Women* (New York: New American Library, 1974), 3.

11. See Martha McCaughey, *Real Knockouts: The Physical Feminism of Women's Self-Defense* (New York: New York University Press, 1997) on the role of self-defense in feminist theory.

12. Kirsten Grimstad and Susan Rennie, *The New Woman's Survival Catalog* (New York: Coward, McCann and Geoghegan/Berkley Publishing, 1973), 157.

13. Elizabethann O'Sullivan, papers, D.C. Rape Crisis Center documents, Raleigh, N.C. Private collection.

14. It is interesting to note that NOW did not take up the rape issue until the group's two primary focus issues were resolved: the Equal Rights Amendment passed Congress in 1972 and ratification seemed imminent; and the Supreme Court handed down *Roe v. Wade* in early 1973, securing, it appeared, women's unquestioned right to abortion. Working on the ERA and abortion issues provided activists with the political savvy necessary to pursue other issues; their apparent resolution freed up movement resources to expand the liberal agenda.

15. The effectiveness of the rape law reform effort is assessed in Jeanne C. Marsh, Alison Geist, and Nathan Caplan, *Rape and the Limits of Law Reform* (Boston: Auburn House, 1982) and Cassia Spohn and Julie Horney, *Rape Law Reform: A Grassroots Revolution and Its Impact* (New York: Plenum, 1992).

16. Emilie Buchwald, Pamela R. Fletcher, and Martha Roth, eds., *Transforming a Rape Culture* (Minneapolis: Milkweed Editions, 1993).

17. Echols, *Daring to Be Bad.*

18. Zillah R. Eisenstein, *The Radical Future of Liberal Feminism* (Boston: Northeastern University Press, 1981) examines the deep theoretical connections between liberal and radical feminist theory.

19. Freeman, *The Politics.*

20. Laura A. Kiernan, "Rape Crisis Center Described," *Washington Post,* October 12, 1972, C4.

21. O'Sullivan, papers.

22. Charlotte Bunch, "The Reform Tool Kit," in *Passionate Politics: Feminist Theory in Action* (New York: St. Martin's, 1987), 103–17.

23. Marsh, Geist, and Caplan, *Rape and the Limits*, 14.

24. Jan BenDor, "Justice after Rape: Legal Reform in Michigan," in *Sexual Assault: The Victim and the Rapist*, ed. Marcia J. Walker and Stanley L Brodsky (Lexington, Mass.: Lexington Books, 1976), 149–60.

25. New York Women Against Rape, records, Arthur and Elizabeth Schlesinger Library on the History of Women in America, Radcliffe Institute for Advanced Study, Harvard University, Cambridge, Mass.

26. Ibid.

27. Ibid.

28. Also see Stephanie Gilmore, "The Dynamics of Second-Wave Feminist Activism in Memphis, 1971–1982: Rethinking the Liberal/Radical Divide," *NWSA Journal* 15, no. 1 (2003): 94–117 on the fusion of liberal and radical feminist activist strategies in Memphis NOW in the early 1970s.

29. See, among others, bell hooks, *Ain't I a Woman: Black Women and Feminism* (Boston: South End Press, 1981); Angela Y. Davis, *Women, Race and Class* (New York: Random House, 1983). For a study of black feminist organizations of the late 1960s and early 1970s, see Kimberly Springer, *Living for the Revolution: Black Feminist Organizations, 1968–1980* (Durham, N.C.: Duke University Press, 2005).

30. Paula Giddings, *When and Where I Enter: The Impact of Black Women on Race and Sex in America* (New York: Bantam, 1984), 345.

31. Ruth Rosen, *The World Split Open: How the Modern Women's Movement Changed America* (New York: Viking, 2000), 180; Silliman et al., *Undivided Rights*.

32. Bevacqua, *Rape on the Public Agenda*; Danielle McGuire, "'It Was Like All of Us Had Been Raped': Sexual Violence, Community Mobilization, and the African American Freedom Struggle," *Journal of American History* 91, no. 3 (December 2004): 906–31; Dawn Rae Flood, "'They Didn't Treat Me Good': African American Rape Victims and Chicago Courtroom Strategies During the 1950s," *Journal of Women's History* 17, no. 1 (2005): 38–61.

33. See Nancy A Matthews, *Confronting Rape: The Feminist Anti-Rape Movement and the State* (New York: Routledge, 1994) for a study of Latina women's activism in the antirape movement in California.

34. Elizabethann O'Sullivan, interview by author, tape recording, Raleigh, N.C., June 8, 1995.

35. O'Sullivan, papers.

36. National Organization for Women (NOW), records, Arthur and Elizabeth Schlesinger Library on the History of Women in America, Radcliffe Institute for Advanced Study, Harvard University, Cambridge, Mass.

37. Angela Y. Davis, *Women, Culture, and Politics* (New York: Random House, 1990), 45.

38. Loretta J. Ross, "Rape and Third World Women," *Aegis* (Summer 1982): 43, emphasis in original.

39. Loretta Ross, interview by author, tape recording, Atlanta, Ga., October 16, 1995.

40. Ross, interview.

41. Nkenge Toure, interview by author, telephone tape recording, Atlanta, Ga., January 9, 1997.

42. I am indebted to personal communication with Elizabethann O'Sullivan for this insight.

43. Toure, interview.

44. Connell and Wilson, *Rape,* 243–46.

45. Glenn Fowler, "Reports of Rape Rise 16%; Changing Attitude is Cited," *New York Times,* June 14, 1974, 37.

46. Ross, "Rape and Third World Women," 40.

47. Freeman, *The Politics,* 6.

48. Freedman, *No Turning Back,* 8.

# 9. "Welfare's a Green Problem"

## Cross-Race Coalitions in Welfare Rights Organizing

### PREMILLA NADASEN

In 1971, Johnnie Tillmon, a poor black woman, mother of six, welfare recipient, and the most prominent spokesperson of the welfare rights movement explained: "NWRO is not a black organization, not a white organization. . . . We are all here together and we are fighting the people who are responsible for our predicament. . . . We can't afford racial separateness. I'm told by the poor white girls on welfare how they feel when they're hungry, and I feel the same way when I'm hungry."[1] Tillmon grew up in a sharecropper family in Scott, Arkansas. She spent most of her childhood picking cotton and washing clothes for white families. As an adult, she was employed as a domestic worker and in a war plant before entering another arduous occupation: commercial laundry worker. After moving to California in 1960 she juggled work and family as a single mother, eventually turning to welfare as a last resort. Tillmon's experiences with poverty, deprivation, and welfare undoubtedly shaped her political views. She and many other leaders of the welfare rights movement were firmly committed to interracial organizing. This commitment led to one of the rare instances in U.S. history where poor people of different racial backgrounds were able to work together in coalition.

This essay will analyze the cross-race alliances that were forged on the battleground of welfare rights in the 1960s and 1970s. The emphasis here is on the alliances formed among women receiving welfare, rather than the alliances between middle-class whites and the predominantly black constituency of the welfare rights movement. For a period, poor black, along with some white, Latina, and Native American, women established a national coalition to reform the system of welfare. This coalition was not problem-free. It was fraught with tensions, resentments, distrust, political accusations, and differing viewpoints. Moreover, the arena of welfare rights activity was not neutral ground. African American women, who articulated a distinctive brand of black feminism that integrated a politics of race, class, gender, and a critique of the welfare system, led the movement.[2] Because of the welfare rights movement's ties to the civil rights movement, as well as popular associations of race and welfare, disproportionately fewer white women and other women of color joined the welfare rights movement. Thus, the welfare rights movement does not provide the ideal model for interracial organizing. However, it illustrates how poor women, under certain circumstances, can come together and alerts us to some of the problems they faced.

The initial interracial encounters were eye-opening and transformative for most recipients. Both white and black women brought with them stereotypes of the "other"—what they had been told or had assumed about women of other races. The campaigns around welfare reform and day-to-day organizing enabled them to rethink these stereotypical views. They often crafted a new understanding about race and observed a similarity of experience across racial lines. Many of these women found common ground in their work as mothers and their efforts to clothe, feed, and adequately house their children. These recipients, however, never transcended race. Race was always present—a "metalanguage"—mediating their relationships, their encounters with the welfare department and their sense of self.[3] For both recipients of color and white recipients, their racial identity was inextricably interwoven with their class identity. In some cases, the recognition of how race operates in conjunction with class and gender to stigmatize poor women provided the foundation for cross-race work. In other cases, race drove a wedge between them. Welfare rights activists' political identity was not fixed or based only on race, but dynamic. It was constituted by specific social/political/economic contexts and was open to transformation. The 1960s was a particularly rich political moment when debates about poverty, racism, and sexism took center stage. Recipients adopted, challenged, and transformed the numerous discourses of liberation and oppression for their own uses and in the process created avenues for interracial organizing.

## An Interracial Movement

The welfare rights movement, from its inception, was an interracial movement of poor women. It emerged in the early 1960s when independent groups of women receiving Aid to Families with Dependent Children (AFDC), a joint federal and state program for poor single mothers and their children, came together in their local communities to discuss ongoing problems with their caseworkers and the welfare department. They developed networks in small towns and mid-sized cities, in housing projects and rural communities. Often with the help of middle-class clergy or community activists, but sometimes on their own, these women began to speak openly of their economic hardship, their feelings of isolation and shame, their sheer frustration with the welfare bureaucracy, as well as their hopes and dreams for their children. Most importantly, they realized that by speaking collectively, they were a stronger and more powerful force to counter the daily indignities of welfare and institute long-term reform.

Welfare rights groups formed in numerous cities and towns across the country, including Boston, Baltimore, New York, Chicago, Los Angeles, and Cleveland. Welfare rights organizers reached out to neighbors and other community members. The prevalence of residential segregation meant that most groups were racially homogeneous. However, groups also reflected the changing racial composition of neighborhoods. In Baltimore, Maryland, for example, Impact was a welfare rights group led by white women in the O'Donnell Heights Housing Project. Once the housing project became integrated, so did the organization. More frequently, women of color and white women formed parallel groups that worked together in city- or statewide coalitions, such as the Welfare Rights Coalition in Baltimore and the City-Wide Coordinating Committee of Welfare Rights Groups in New York.[4]

In 1966, dozens of local groups came together in a national federation under the guidance of George Wiley, head of the Poverty/Rights Action Center (P/RAC) in Washington, D.C. Wiley, an African American chemistry professor and a member of the Congress of Racial Equality (CORE), resigned his academic position at Syracuse University to devote himself full time to civil rights and antipoverty work. At its founding meeting in 1967, the National Welfare Rights Organization (NWRO) formed an Executive Committee and a National Coordinating Committee to determine policy and strategy for the organization. The committees were made up of welfare recipients elected by a national convention of NWRO members. In addition, a staff in Washington, D.C., headed by Wiley, was charged with fundraising, coordinating campaigns among local groups, and implementing the policy decisions of the welfare rights leadership. Initially, the bylaws of the organization specified that membership was open to all people on welfare, regardless of racial background. This was later expanded to include all poor people. The NWRO Executive Committee comprised mostly black women, but nearly always included one or two white women and a Latina. The national leadership consistently defended the principle of interracial organizing. Like Johnnie Tillmon, George Wiley was one of the most vociferous proponents of an integrated movement.

Despite the commitment to integration, the welfare rights movement was overwhelmingly African American, perhaps 85 percent, with some participation by white, Latina, and Native American women.[5] Yet, the welfare rolls in the mid-1960s were 48 percent African American. Black women's greater participation in the struggle for welfare rights can be explained in part by AFDC's long history of racial discrimination. The cultural, class, and racial bias of caseworkers, administrators, and local politicians affected the disbursement of welfare funds. After the passage of the Social Security Act in 1935, which created the AFDC program, Southern states routinely excluded African Americans from the welfare rolls, by relying on policies such as the suitable-home clause, man-in-the-house rule, and employable-mother laws.[6] These laws were applied selectively and gave caseworkers discretionary power to determine who was "employable," whose home was "unsuitable," and what evidence constituted the "presence" of a man who, presumably, could support the recipient and her children. Many African American welfare recipients welcomed the opportunity to mobilize to improve a system that gave them less and treated them unfairly. However, in addition, during the late 1950s and early 1960s, as larger numbers of African American women in both the North and the South claimed their right to receive welfare, race-laden political attacks on the program led to an identification of welfare as a black program. The association between race and welfare may have dissuaded white recipients from publicly identifying with a program with negative racial connotations.[7]

The numerous ties between the welfare rights and civil rights movements also partly explain the disproportionately large number of black women in the welfare rights movement. Discrimination in the welfare state attracted the attention of many organizations including the American Civil Liberties Union and the National Association for the Advancement of Colored People (NAACP). Both the NAACP and the Nation of Islam, for example, formally protested the high profile, draconian welfare cuts, framed largely in racial terms, in Louisiana in 1960 and Newburgh, New York, in 1961.[8] In addition, beginning in 1967, the NAACP Legal Defense Fund "launch[ed] a broad attack on what it called the 'widespread abuse of clients' rights in the distribution of public assistance.'"[9] Antiracist groups' challenges to the welfare system highlighted the racially discriminatory nature of the program and may have encouraged black recipients to take similar stands.

Although civil rights activists did not universally support welfare rights, many welfare recipients and organizers who became involved in welfare rights got their political training in the civil rights movement. George Wiley and his associate at P/RAC, Edwin Day, both worked with CORE before breaking away to support antipoverty campaigns. Catherine Jermany, of the Los

Angeles County Welfare Rights Organization (WRO), was involved with the Southern Christian Leadership Conference prior to her welfare rights work. Mrs. Mildred Calvert, chair of the Northside Welfare Rights Organization in Milwaukee, also rooted her welfare rights activity in the civil rights movement. She explained that a local priest, Father James Groppi, led civil rights marches in her city. Although "I was afraid of those kind of things . . . when the kids decided that they were going [on the march] . . . I had to go with them." The newspapers reported that the marchers "were doing all the bad things . . . [but] we were the ones being fired upon with rocks and bricks and sticks." She read the black newspapers and started "seeing things in a different light."[10] This was when she joined the welfare rights movement. The cross-fertilization between the civil rights movement and the welfare rights movement exemplified by Calvert's experience partly accounts for the overrepresentation of black people in the struggle for welfare rights.

Although white welfare recipients usually did not have the same close ties to the civil rights movement as black participants, the civil rights movement served as a conduit in a different way for them. Many of the Students for a Democratic Society (SDS) leaders who helped initiate welfare rights groups worked first in campaigns for black civil and voting rights. SDS's Economic and Research Action Project (ERAP), inspired by the community organizing work of the Student Nonviolent Coordinating Committee (SNCC) in the Deep South, was instrumental in the formation of early interracial welfare rights groups. Established in 1964, ERAP sent SDS members into several communities around the country to launch an interracial movement of the poor.[11] They successfully organized welfare rights groups in Cleveland, Chicago, Newark, and Boston. Similarly, Catholic and Protestant churches played a pivotal role in early welfare rights organizing. Nuns and priests became organizers, houses of worship were used as meeting sites, and money was funneled from churches to activists. In Cleveland, Reverend Paul Younger was a minister at Fidelity Baptist Church, which was part of a network called the Inner City Protestant Parish (ICPP), a group of churches committed to alleviating the hardships of the poor. Younger worked tirelessly to mobilize welfare recipients to demand their rights. In 1962, he helped form Citizens United for Adequate Welfare (CUFAW), an integrated citywide welfare rights organization. CUFAW initially drew its membership from two Cleveland churches that served different racial communities, but came together around welfare rights.

Lillian Craig's story typifies how church and civil rights contexts shaped activism. Lillian, a white woman recipient, was born in 1937 in Cleveland, Ohio. Her mother died of asthma and pneumonia when Lillian was twelve.

Lillian spent much of the rest of her childhood in foster homes and a girls' reform school. She worked after high school, married, had three children, divorced, and went on welfare. She learned of welfare rights through St. Paul's Community Church, a member of Cleveland's ICPP. She became part of a close-knit group of women, mostly welfare recipients, who provided mutual support to one another. In 1964, when SDS established the Cleveland Community Project in the near west side, Lillian became involved. SDS worked in both the predominantly black east side and the largely white west side and brought these groups together. As poor white women and poor women of color began to work together, they remarked how educational the experience of cross-race organizing was for them. Speaking of her first encounter with an interracial organization, Lillian explained in her memoir: "It was scary. I had never been around groups of black people. I didn't even know how to express my fear of blacks. But I began to get to know them through Paul [Younger] and because he was just plain folks, we soon discovered that we all were just plain folks."[12]

In New York City, Puerto Rican, African American, and white clients worked together in local welfare committees. The Committee of Welfare Families on the Lower East Side, formed in 1966 by Mobilization for Youth, a Ford Foundation and government-funded antidelinquency agency, included Puerto Ricans and African Americans. The Welfare Action Group Against Poverty was made up of a large number of older Puerto Rican, African American, and Jewish recipients.[13] In neighboring Brooklyn, a separate coalition of welfare rights groups emerged. The Welfare Recipients League grew out of grassroots storefront offices. One of these was the East New York Action Center, started in the early 1960s by Frank Espada. A Puerto Rican who had served in the U.S. Air Force and worked for an electrical contractor, Espada had a long history of political activism. In 1949 at the age of 19, Espada was arrested and spent a week in jail in Biloxi, Mississippi, for refusing to go to the back of a Trailways bus after his discharge from the Air Force. The handful of people, many of whom were women, in the East New York storefront in this predominantly black and Puerto Rican neighborhood organized rent strikes and protested inadequate garbage pickup. They soon identified welfare as a critical community problem. Espada remembered, "we had situations where an investigator would barge in to see if they could find a man in the house without notifying anyone. They would go in and look under the beds for a man's shoes or in the closet." In 1964, they started the Welfare Recipients League and named Espada chair.[14] Throughout Brooklyn, a number of other storefront action centers served as meeting grounds for welfare recipients. In 1966, three nuns and two priests from local parishes assisted in establishing several storefront action centers that formed the base for the Brooklyn Welfare Action Center. They conducted community surveys about welfare and poverty and encouraged residents to engage in collective action. By 1968, the Brooklyn Welfare Action Center had eight thousand members. Most of the membership was African American and Latino, but as Jacqueline Pope says, "whites were always welcome in the Brooklyn Welfare Rights Organization. Its members resented authority more than race or class."[15]

Pope alludes to the anger that many welfare recipients felt because of the ways in which the welfare department disempowered and mistreated them. When Aid to Dependent Children, as the program was known prior to 1962, was formed in 1935, it was a small, underfunded program serving primarily white widows and their children. The welfare program and its precursor, the mothers' pensions programs, aided only the most "worthy" needy mothers, a strategy designed to discipline and regulate the lives of poor women. Using casework investigation, welfare officials disbursing funds checked to see that each client maintained high social and moral standards, which included keeping her home spotless, refraining from intimacy with men, reporting all income, and not engaging in "immoral" behavior. Any breach of these standards (as interpreted by caseworkers) led to an immediate reduction or termination of benefits.

As the program grew during the postwar period and more women of color and unmarried mothers joined the rolls, it became controversial. Politicians and the popular press characterized welfare recipients as freeloaders intent on milking the system. The stereotypical welfare recipient was a poor black woman living in the inner city with a houseful of children, multiple sexual partners, and little inclination to work. Exploding welfare rolls and intensified political attacks on the program in the 1950s and 1960s led caseworkers to be more vigilant in their search for "welfare cheats" and welfare administrators to be more ruthless in their efforts to limit the welfare rolls and shrink the budget. The result was a welfare program that criminalized its clients, monitoring them daily for evidence that they were flouting restrictions on their personal lives imposed by the welfare system. By the time the welfare rights movement had emerged in the early 1960s, race, sex, class, and culture converged with the politics of welfare.

## Race and the Rhetoric of Welfare Organizing

There were competing views and strategies within the welfare rights movement on how to articulate the dynamics of race and welfare. Some folks stressed interracial unity of the poor, others linked welfare receipt to their racial identity and the larger black power movement. Although most welfare recipients were proponents of interracial organizing, race still played a decisive role in the welfare rights movement. The public identified welfare as a disproportionately black program populated by lazy people who were prone to "broken families." Racialized and gendered images infused conversations, academic studies, and news reports about welfare. Many people in the movement attempted to counter these stereotypes by highlighting the fact that more white people than black people received welfare and that economics, not cultural or racial traits, drove people into the AFDC program. Mrs. Rosie Hudson of Milwaukee explained, "too many people are saying welfare's a black problem, when it's really a green problem. Why don't we have decent food, clothing, or shelter? It's simple. We don't have enough money."[16] Many white welfare recipients joined the movement as well because they saw welfare as a fundamentally economic problem. Ann Warren, white public housing tenant and welfare recipient explained in a recent interview: "If you were white or black, they gave you a hard time. They made sure you felt small, going over there to ask for money."[17] The attempts to dispel the myth that welfare was a black problem sometimes led welfare rights organizers to thrust white welfare recipients into the spotlight. Lillian Craig, was quickly given a leadership role and became known in Cleveland as the "voice of the white welfare mother."[18] She explained, "I was used by a lot of groups as the token white. 'There is a white welfare mother,' you know, kind of thing because all welfare mothers are [supposed to be] black and dumb, lazy, alcoholic, pregnant, immature. . . ."[19]

For most welfare rights activists, their race or nationality was inseparable from their day-to-day experiences as welfare recipients. Women in the welfare rights movement believed that racism underpinned the welfare system. Caseworkers did not regard all poor people or welfare recipients the same. Black women welfare rights activists articulated their involvement in part because of the racism they experienced as AFDC recipients. Mothers for Adequate Welfare in Boston explained the different treatment of black and white recipients: "White recipients will almost automatically be granted special allowances at some offices, while black recipients in similar circumstances will be met with delaying tactics plus a full quota of red tape, and then will probably be turned down. Likewise, case-workers are accused of using their power to disapprove moving allowances for the purpose of keeping white recipients out of disreputable neighborhoods while black recipients are kept in."[20] The discretionary acts of racism by caseworkers and the systematic mistreatment of recipients fostered among welfare rights activists a consciousness rooted as much in their experiences as black, brown, and white people as their status as poor.

The welfare rights movement climaxed at the height of the black power movement in the late 1960s. African Americans across the political spectrum advocated self-determination and fostered black empowerment and a collective self-identity, although this took many forms. Some African American welfare rights activists, inspired by the shift to black power, espoused a language of racial pride and black power to fuel their organizing efforts. Catherine Jermany of the Los Angeles County WRO acknowledged that most welfare recipients were white, yet underscored her own black identity as an organizer.[21] Speaking before the Association of Black Social Workers, she counseled them, "to think Black is revolutionary" they should therefore "Think Black" and "Talk Black."[22] Using language that echoed black power slogans, she clearly hoped to build support for the welfare rights movement through an appeal to racial solidarity. In Ohio, welfare recipients had a training session in 1968, run with the help of black cultural nationalist Maulana Ron Karenga, "to wed the skills of massive community organization for self-determination to the black movement of self-identity."[23] Welfare recipients linked their blackness to their experiences as poor women on welfare.

The black freedom movement's articulation of racial oppression might have also resonated with poor whites who could identify with some part of the experience of marginalization, despite being relatively privileged by the welfare bureaucracy. Although evidence is minimal, it is likely that racial and class stereotypes of white poverty shaped the experiences of white welfare recipients as well. In the Midwest, for example, white migration from Appalachia accounted for much of the increase in welfare in the postwar period. Cleveland was a destination of many white Southern migrants. Over eighty thousand white Southern migrants moved to Cleveland and most settled on the west side in an area that came to be known as "Hillbilly Heaven."[24] It was an area characterized by concentrated poverty, higher rates of welfare receipt, and dilapidated housing. Jennifer Frost recounts the divisions between white student organizers and poor white residents, "revealing not only class but also ethnic and racial differences within whiteness.[25] In her memoir, Lillian Craig explains how her impoverished upbringing negatively impacted her self-esteem: "If you're white and poor, the main thing you are taught every year in school is that you are dumb."[26] However, she felt empowered as she gained respect through welfare rights activity: "At first it was important that I was in the spotlight . . . the spokesperson, with my picture in the papers and on TV. That came out of my past . . . I needed to feel that I was *somebody*. I hadn't been sure I was anybody."[27] In Chicago, Peggy Terry was also victimized by an ideology that looked down upon and marginalized poor white people. She referred to some of the white women in Chicago's Jobs or

Income Now (JOIN) who harbored racist attitudes as "hillbilly women" (a term she had once identified with).[28] Once when she was participating in a civil rights demonstration, a well-dressed white woman asked why she was picketing for civil rights. Terry replied: "Well, where else could I go and be treated with this respect that I've been treated with by Reverend King, the Nobel Prize Peace winner? No white Nobel Prize winner would pay poor white trash like me the slightest attention. Reverend King does."[29] In these cases, the shared experiences of marginalization and "outsider" status enabled whites to sympathize with the plight of African Americans, fueling the commitment to interracial organizing.

Latina and Native American recipients had their own particular experiences with the welfare system, but also identified with the broader struggle for racial equality. Mrs. Clementina Castro, vice-chair of the Union Benefica Hispaña WRO and sergeant-at-arms of the Milwaukee County WRO, explained: "When I first came on welfare, they didn't have any Spanish-speaking caseworkers at all. . . . I was so shy because I had never talked to white people, because I had been working in the fields. . . . Some whites can speak it, but they just know the language, they don't know the problems. Latins can understand better because they know, they have already passed through the same problems. They know our culture."[30] Latina welfare recipients, such as Mrs. Castro, saw race and culture mediating their interactions with caseworkers and their relationship with the welfare department.

Loretta Domencich, a Native American organizer in Milwaukee, explained: "I think Welfare Rights has also given me a clearer idea of racism. The Welfare Department has a way of lumping people together; whether you're black, white, red, or brown, you're all a bunch of niggers when you go into the Welfare Department."[31] Domencich glosses over the complex and varying ways women of different racial and cultural backgrounds encountered the welfare system. However, Domencich's statement points to a common social stigma that all women on welfare experienced—one that she equates to a kind of racialism. Receipt of welfare, she is suggesting, is a social marker leading to patterns of mistreatment akin to the pervasive racism experienced by African Americans. The widespread discussion of racism generated by the civil rights movement and the black power movement created a framework and provided a language for recipients of all colors to make sense of their marginalization. These welfare recipients articulated their problem with the welfare system as one of racial discrimination as well as poverty. From this perspective, racism is understood in broader terms than skin color, but was a larger pattern of social, political, and economic exclusion. For nonblack welfare recipients, the black experience became a trope to understand their oppression.

The deeply ingrained sense of racial identity for whites and people of color in the welfare rights movement also created a certain amount of friction. However, these differences did not always turn into divisions. The ultimate demise of the movement cannot be attributed primarily to the racial tension. The economic woes of the 1970s, the welfare backlash, personality conflicts among activists, dwindling liberal funding to NWRO, the shift from grass-roots organizing to a service-oriented strategy on the part of local groups, and harassment of activists, all account for the decline of welfare rights activity. Through all of this, recipient leaders grappled with racial conflicts, but never resolved to purge anyone. Some recipients accepted the difficulties of coalition work, keeping their eyes on the prize of welfare reform. Others became thoroughly dissatisfied and found other political outlets. Some black activists argued that white recipients—even though poor—were still favored in a society that they increasingly identified as white supremacist. This reality was compounded by the personal prejudices that many white recipients undoubtedly brought into the organization. The heightened racial consciousness of welfare recipients very likely made coalition work harder, especially for white recipients in a predominantly black formation. A white welfare recipient working in the national office resigned toward the end of 1970 because she was "so discouraged at the way in which people in this organization deal with each other." She could not continue to work for NWRO or with "the racist people I have met here, who despite the fact that poor white people are just as oppressed as poor black people and are greater in number, still feel that white people don't belong here."[32]

The situation in Chicago exemplifies many of these themes—including white racial identity, black power, the ways in which the black freedom movement shaped recipients' outlook, and the ongoing commitment to interracial organizing. Welfare Recipients Demand Action (WRDA) was a recipient-led, interracial organization that comprised primarily white Southern migrants with participation by Native Americans, Puerto Ricans, and African Americans. Two black women, Big Dovie Coleman and Little Dovie Thurman (Coleman's niece), played important leadership roles. The Chicago group formed initially as part of the SDS JOIN project, but in 1967, it established its independence. Peggy Terry, one of the white members of the organization, was born in Oklahoma, but her family periodically migrated to Kentucky, where her father was a coal miner. Both her father and her grandfather were sympathetic to the Ku Klux Klan. In contrast, Terry, who was deeply influenced by the civil rights movement, worked with CORE when she moved to Chicago in the 1950s. Shortly after that, she learned of JOIN and became involved. Terry cast a critical eye on her racist upbringing—taking firm stands for racial justice and equality: "My great discovery was that poor people, no matter what color they are, have a hard time. They should stop fighting among themselves and get together. We were having a meeting one night. Both Dovies were there. It did deteriorate into nigger this and nigger that. I finally said, 'I heard all I want to hear. You don't want to talk about welfare rights and decent housing. All you want to do is sit around and talk about niggers. I'm going home.'" Three or four women followed her out, one of them said, "Peggy, we never thought of things like that. You come back and we'll talk about something else."[33]

Terry's close ally, African American activist and recipient Dovie Coleman, moved in 1948 from St. Louis to Chicago, where she worked as a hairdresser until 1952 when a near-fatal auto accident left her paralyzed for several months. Unable to return to work, she applied for public assistance. She started working with JOIN in Chicago in 1964 and subsequently with WRDA.[34] She and other recipients broke away from JOIN and formed WRDA in 1967. Run out of Coleman's apartment, WRDA was a resource-poor organization that refused "outside" staff.[35] In 1966, Coleman represented Illinois on the National Coordinating Committee and served as NWRO's financial secretary. Reputedly an effective citywide organizer since 1968, according to the local Friends of Welfare Rights group, she knew "welfare regulations better than most caseworkers."[36] One of the people Coleman recruited to welfare rights activity was her niece, Dovie Thurman. Little Dovie Thurman was raised in a housing project in St. Louis and moved to Chicago at the age of eighteen with her three children. Thurman's involvement with JOIN in 1965 broadened her perspective on race and poverty. She explained in an interview: "I had never seen poor white people in my life. I thought all white people were rich because the only ones I had seen were doctors, lawyers, nurses, people like that."[37] At the second meeting she attended, Thurman was elected chairperson. Thurman was initially won over to interracialism, but after the murder of Martin Luther King Jr. in 1968, she was filled with rage about the state of racial politics and went—in her words—"all the way into a black nationalist thing."[38] However, her early experiences of interracial organizing, as well as her first-hand knowledge of poverty led her to question a nationalist approach devoid of an analysis of class: "I began to see things. If white people hate black people so much, how come there are poor whites like this? . . . Somebody needs to get the word over, that there is somebody else going through the same thing, that ain't even black. It's the *system*. There is somebody doing it to all of us, and you just don't see them."[39]

Racial tension also played out in California. Moiece Palladino worked with the Sunnydale Projects Mothers Group, joined the San Francisco City

Wide WRO and became the first vice president of the statewide California WRO. She believed that "economic freedom is the only real freedom in this society." From a white working class family in San Francisco, Palladino married young, divorced her husband because of physical abuse, and went on welfare to support herself and her three children. She went to her first welfare rights meeting "looking for . . . sociability." She worked for many years on welfare rights activity in her racially mixed neighborhood. Palladino remembers intense conflicts around race in the San Francisco City Wide group. "Whites" she said, "didn't want to be identified with the movement or with them blacks." Many African American activists discussed "white privilege," sometimes targeting Palladino, one of the few white people in the movement: "I understand why people would attack me because . . . they perceive me to be the representative of a majority class, culture for which they perceive got benefits they didn't get." She believed ultimately, however, that race was just an "excuse" and that the conflicts were, at the core, about economics.[40] Catherine Jermany, an African American member of the Los Angeles County WRO, reflected on the racial conflict plaguing the northern California group: "I don't think that the black women within the movement understood the relevance of having Moiece's participation. . . . People got involved in personalities and didn't necessarily look at what the contribution of a person could be."[41] Jermany believed this worked two ways. She suggested that "the contributions" of white welfare recipients "wasn't recognized. . . . It was viewed by many black welfare recipients that there was no reason for a person who was white to have to be on welfare because all the opportunities were for them." On the other hand, Jermany explained, white welfare recipients didn't "necessarily recognize their own racism."[42] Despite these conflicts, women such as Lillian Craig, Catherine Jermany, Peggy Terry, and Dovie Thurman maintained their commitment to welfare rights. Importantly, the rising tide of black nationalism in the late 1960s did not obviously derail these interracial efforts.

Welfare rights activists maintained a commitment to coalition work because of concrete, immediate issues and common concerns about motherhood. Recipients, who were relatively powerless, united to increase their leverage with the welfare department. In many cases, women used collective power to fight for basic necessities and fair hearings when they believed caseworkers made unfair decisions. They used mutual support tactics, mass protest and education, as well as lobbying and publicity to win support for their cause. Greater recognition and support for their work as mothers was an important thread running through welfare rights organizing. They referred to themselves as "mothers" and "mother-recipients," planned demonstrations on Mother's Day, and waged campaigns for school clothing for their children. They justified welfare receipt because of the work they performed as mothers. So, care work became one way that women built alliances across the color line. Mrs. Clementina Castro explained: "The mother has got a job all the time, taking care of her children. It's a big job. She has to wash and cook and do everything because she has got to manage the house. If a woman can, she wants to have an outside job to help her husband, but she already has a job with the house and the children."[43] Similarly, Cleveland organizer Lillian Craig decided to go on welfare after her divorce so she could better care for her children. In 1968, the predominantly black Mothers for Adequate Welfare in Boston claimed that "motherhood—whether the mother is married or not—is a role which should be fully supported, as fully rewarded, as fully honored, as any other."[44] For women of different racial backgrounds struggling to raise their children on a meager welfare budget, the shared value of mothering was a bridge that connected them.

Throughout the life of the movement, recipients reiterated and continued to pledge their commitment to organizing across the color line. Peggy Terry, who engaged in interracial politics throughout the black power phase, had an extremely sympathetic understanding of how racism affected black people: "Sure, there's an antiwhite feeling among blacks. Not in everyone, but in a lot. To me, that's understandable. It's unspeakable what black people have gone through since they were first brought to this country. . . . Whites [have] always been given better treatment."[45] Roxanne Jones, an African American welfare recipient, wrote in the Philadelphia WRO newsletter in 1969: "I am proud that our poor white brothers and sisters in other parts of Pennsylvania are requesting and getting their money and other benefits under welfare. . . . We must never forget that until all poor people begin working together rather than fighting each other and hating each other we will never fully achieve our basic goals."[46] Similarly, the Baltimore Welfare Rights Organization (BWRO) actively recruited white recipients. According to black BRWO activist Rudell Martin, "I don't care what color you are. Everybody gets treated the same way—nasty."[47]

For welfare activists, a racial consciousness did not preclude the possibility of working in an interracial setting, and organizing in a multiracial setting did not mean a movement devoid of an analysis of race. They situated racism as integral to the disbursement of welfare while launching an interracial movement and inviting people of any color to join them. Beverly Edmon, the founder of the Welfare Recipients Union in Los Angeles said: "There's as many white people, probably a lot more, who have the very same kind of problems we get here from welfare. Poor people have the same problems, black or white. What we have to offer is good for anybody who comes in."[48] Yet, welfare recipients framed their politics of liberation within a racial/cultural framework. Loretta Domencich of Milwaukee placed her welfare rights activity squarely within her Native American heritage: "The dignity of the welfare recipient caught me as an Indian idea. The dignity of the individual says that no matter what a person's capabilities are, whether he is the leader or whether he is a person who is crippled or elderly or can't do anything, he still has a place in the tribe. Welfare Rights is an Indian organization to me because I think a lot of things that Welfare Rights is going after are Indian ideas—Guaranteed Adequate Income is really an Indian concept. It is the way the Indians themselves ran their early communities."[49] These welfare recipients tried simultaneously to dispel the myth of welfare as a black problem and recognize the role of racism in their own experiences on welfare. Welfare leaders formulated a welfare rights agenda that attempted to toe a line, on the one hand, of addressing the racism of the welfare system and wanting to empower black women and, on the other hand, recognizing the class-based nature of their oppression, welcoming all women on welfare, and suggesting that racist attitudes were not inherent. In the context of the emerging black power movement, it was a fine line to walk and one that was not always done successfully or with circumspection on the local or national level. Thus, race was central to both understanding the welfare system and in building a movement to change it.

## Conclusion

Multiracial work within the welfare rights movement was not easy. The strains and fissures that engulfed some social movement organizations in the 1960s plagued the struggle for welfare rights as well, but proved not to be debilitating. Unlike organizations such as SNCC and CORE, NWRO never became a racially exclusive organization. Black, white, Native American, and Latina welfare recipients found common ground in their work of mothering. As poor mothers, they all battled with the welfare department to provide a safe and comfortable life for their children. In addition, the social stigma attached to welfare receipt prompted some recipients to draw parallels to the situation of racial minorities. In some cases, the experience of marginalization for white recipients and recipients of color fostered greater understanding among them.

Cross-race alliances were possible among women in the welfare rights movement because this was an issue-oriented movement, rather than an abstract and artificial alliance based on gender.[50] Women of different cultural and racial backgrounds who had experienced the deprivations of poverty and stresses of being on welfare were able to come together. Through this emphasis on the day-to-day indignities of welfare, poor women of color and white women had come to understand their common enemy in the welfare system and welfare administrators. They realized they had much more to gain than to lose by building an interracial movement for welfare reform.

## Notes

Many thanks to Eileen Boris, Stephanie Gilmore, Barbara Ransby, and Robyn Spencer for insightful feedback on this essay.

1. Hobart A. Burch, "Insights of a Welfare Mother: A Conversation with Johnnie Tillmon," *The Journal* (January-February 1971): 13–24, George Wiley papers, State Historical Society of Wisconsin, Madison, Wis. (hereafter Wiley papers), box 27. Tillmon actively recruited white recipients and wanted to dispel the myth that most recipients were black. When some members dressed up in African garb for a press conference, she urged them to change. John L. Mitchell, "A Dremer and Her Dream Lose Ground," *Los Angeles Times,* July 9, 1995.

2. Premilla Nadasen, "Expanding the Boundaries of the Women's Movement: Black Feminism and the Struggle for Welfare Rights," *Feminist Studies* 28: 271–301.

3. Evelyn Brooks Higginbotham, "African-American Women and the Metalanguage of Race," *Signs* (Winter 1992): 251–74. Higginbotham suggests, "the apparent overdeterminacy of race in Western culture . . . precludes unity within the same gender group" (255). Though this is generally true, I am interested in exploring some of the exceptions.

4. See Rhonda Williams, *The Politics of Public Housing* (New York: Oxford University Press, 2004), chap. 6

5. David Street, George T. Martin Jr., and Laura Kramer Gordon, *The Welfare Industry: Functionaries and Recipients of Public Aid* (Beverly Hills, Calif.: Sage, 1979), 124. Quoted in Guida West, *The National Welfare Rights Organization: The Social Protest of Poor Women* (New York: Praeger, 1981), 45.

6. See Frances Fox Piven and Richard Cloward, *Regulating the Poor: The Functions of Public Welfare* (New York: Pantheon Books, 1971) and Winifred Bell, *Aid to Dependent Children* (New York: Columbia University Press, 1965).

7. Carol Glassman suggests that for white women there was much more shame associated with welfare receipt and that many white recipients did not even tell family members that they were on welfare. This inhibited their involvement in welfare rights activity. See Carol Glassman, "Women and the Welfare System" in *Sisterhood is Powerful: An Anthology of Writings from the Women's Liberation Movement,* ed. Robin Morgan (New York: Vintage, 1970), 102–15.

8. See Lisa Levenstein, "From Innocent Children to Unwanted Migrants and Unwed Moms: Two Chapters in the Public Discourse on Welfare in the United States, 1960–1961," *Journal of Women's History* 11 (2000): 10–33. Joseph P. Ritz, *The Despised Poor: Newburgh's War on Welfare* (Boston: Beacon Press, 1966).

9. Charles Sutton, *Independent Press Telegram,* May 26, 1968, Wiley papers, box 24, folder 13.

10. Mildred Calvert, "Welfare Rights and the Welfare System," in Milwaukee County

Welfare Rights Organization, *Welfare Mothers Speak Out: We Ain't Gonna Shuffle Anymore* (New York: Norton, 1972), 25–26.

11. See Jennifer Frost, *An Interracial Movement of the Poor: Community Organizing and the New Left in the 1960s* (New York: New York University Press, 2001).

12. Lillian Craig, *Just a Woman: Memoirs of Lillian Craig,* with Marge Gravett (Cleveland, Ohio: Orange Blossom Press, 1981), 17.

13. Mary Rabagliati and Ezra Birnbaum, "Organization of Welfare Clients," in *Community Development in the Mobilization for Youth Experience,* ed. Harold Weissman (New York: Association Press, 1969), 102–36.

14. Frank Espada, telephone interview with author, 2003.

15. Jacqueline Pope, *Biting the Hand that Feeds Them: Organizing Women on Welfare at the Grass Roots Level* (New York: Praeger, 1989), 124–25.

16. Rosie Hudson, quoted in Milwaukee County WRO, *Welfare Mothers Speak Out,* 81.

17. Rhonda Williams interviews with Anna Warren, quoted in Williams, *The Politics of Public Housing,* 215

18. Craig, *Just a Woman,* 20

19. Craig, *Just a Woman,* 43

20. Gordon Brumm, "Mothers for Adequate Welfare—AFDC from the Underside," *Dialogues Boston 1* (January 1968), 9, William Howard Whitaker papers, box 3, folder 3, Ohio Historical Society, Columbus (hereafter Whitaker papers).

21. Robert Huldschiner, "Fighting Catherine Gets Welfare Mothers Together," *Lutheran Women,* October 1968, Wiley papers, box 27, folder 7.

22. Los Angeles County WRO, newsletter, November 1, 1968, Wiley papers, box 24, folder 13.

23. Meeting minutes of the Ohio Training Steering Committee, April 3, 1968, Whitaker papers, box 2, folder 17.

24. Frost, *An Interracial Movement of the Poor,* 62.

25. Ibid., 76.

26. Craig, *Just a Woman,* 54.

27. Ibid., 19.

28. Studs Terkel, *Race: How Black and Whites Think and Feel about the American Obsession* (New York: New Press, 1992), 55. Many of the studies of "whiteness" focus on poor white people in the South. For some examples of whites in the North, see Matt Wray and Annalee Newitz, eds., *White Trash: Race and Class in America* (New York: Routledge, 1996) and Jacqueline Jones, *The Dispossessed: America's Underclass from the Civil War to the Present* (New York: Basic Books, 1992).

29. Terkel, *Race,* 54.

30. Mrs. Clementina Castro, "Spanish Speaking People and the Welfare System," in Milwaukee County WRO, *Welfare Mothers Speak Out,* 68.

31. Loretta Domencich, "The Welfare System Is an Indian-Giver," in Milwaukee County WRO, *Welfare Mothers Speak Out,* 59.

32. Marie Ratagick to George Wiley, possibly November 1970, Wiley papers, box 8, folder 8.

33. Terkel, *Race,* 54–55.

34. The Chicago Friends of Welfare Rights Organization, "To the 'Concerned' an Invitation to Help Welfare Clients Help Themselves," May 25, 1968, National Welfare Rights Organization papers, Moorland-Spingarn Research Center, Washington, D.C. (hereafter NWRO papers).

35. Anonymous [probably Dovie Coleman], "Resignation Letter to Executive Committee," possibly February 1969, Wiley papers, box 25, folder 1. Author unknown, "Some Facts on Chicago Welfare Unions," 1967?, NWRO papers.

36. The Chicago Friends of Welfare Rights Organization, "To the 'Concerned' an Invitation to Help Welfare Clients Help Themselves," May 25, 1968, NWRO papers.

37. Terkel, *Race,* 57.

38. Ibid., 59.

39. Ibid., 59–61.

40. Moice Palladino, interview with author, 1997.

41. Catherine Jermany, interview with author, 2003.

42. Jermany, interview with author, 2003.

43. Castro, "Spanish Speaking People and the Welfare System," 68–69.

44. Quoted in Brumm, "Mothers for Adequate Welfare," 11, Whitaker papers, box 3, folder 3.

45. Terkel, *Race,* 55.

46. Roxanne Jones, PWRO, "Report of the Chairman," in *Straight Talk Newsletter,* June 11, 1969, NWRO papers.

47. Rudell Martin, quoted in Williams, *The Politics of Public Housing,* 283.

48. H. Lawrence Lack, "People on Welfare Form Union," *Los Angeles Free Press,* April 28, 1967, Whitaker papers, box 1, file 19.

49. Domenich, "The Welfare System Is an Indian-Giver," 59.

50. Wini Breines discusses the "abstract antiracism" embraced by white feminists in the 1960s. She argues that despite this rhetorical commitment to antiracism, many white feminists focused on "gender as the sole explanatory factor in the subordination of women." They ascribed to a gender universality, which minimized the importance of race, class, and culture. See Wini Breines, "What's Love Got to Do With It? White Women, Black Women, and Feminism in the Movement Years," *Signs* 27, no. 4 (2002): 1095–1133.

# 10.  Unlikely Allies

## *Forging a Multiracial, Class-Based Women's Movement in 1970s Brooklyn*

### TAMAR CARROLL

> My motivation to do community work stems from my upbringing.
> I grew up in East Harlem hearing that the "American Dream" was
> to go to school, get a good education, and move out of the ghetto.
> I always wondered who would be left to lead, if we moved "up and
> out." There seemed to be a big vacuum left in the neighborhood
> and I felt that it had to be filled. My mother and other family
> members had a strong influence on me. They were active in the
> community and fraternal organizations. As a small child, I saw
> my mother organizing in the church. Without thinking about it,
> I began to see a contradiction between "moving out of the ghetto"
> and "investing your life" in the community.
> —Ethel Velez, "Why Do You Do Community Work?"

Ethel Velez is a life-long community activist in East Harlem and former president of the James Weldon Johnson Houses Resident Council. Beginning in the mid-1970s, public housing leaders in Brooklyn and East Harlem formed a coalition with the Williamsburg-Greenpoint, Brooklyn-based National Congress of Neighborhood Women (NCNW), a working-class feminist organization. This coalition is remarkable for its ability to cross racial, ethnic, and class lines, in a historical context of racial strife and segregation and increasing economic stratification. In this chapter, I chronicle the early history of the coalition and argue that its method of consciousness raising led to an understanding of how identities can intersect, which enabled members to work across their many differences.[1]

This process represents what scholars have theorized as intersectionality, by which social relations of class, gender, and race, among others, shape each other, and are therefore best understood when analyzed together. Paraphrasing Robin Kelley, I want to argue that for these women, gender was lived through race and class.[2] By recognizing and acknowledging the important differences between women, NCNW members were able to move beyond parochial identities to construct a new, broadened community and a social movement based in mutual needs. Building trust across barriers of race and class took time; it was an ongoing process that transformed members' self-identities and generated innovative politics. Through personal interactions, guided consciousness raising, and group education and by working together for common goals, NCNW members generated a feminist philosophy that took into account "the understanding that gender always intersects with other social hierarchies."[3]

As has often been the case with women's activism, notably among labor feminists and social justice feminists, gendered understandings of women's roles as caretakers of family and community proved especially important in motivating the coalition members' political activity.[4] However, their programs also led them to challenge traditional gender roles, including those that had been encoded into social policies that assumed women's economic and social dependence on men and devalued women's labor.[5] Because state programs and policies impinged on their lives so intensely, the NCNW coalition offered a unique critique of the state. They also demanded that second-wave feminists broaden their agenda to oppose the ongoing destruction of low-income neighborhoods and the reduction of social services that denied the realization of social citizenship to poor and working-class Americans.[6] Though working-class in origin, the NCNW attracted middle-class professionals interested in engaging with a diverse women's organization. Although professional women played a played a key role in its success, the coalition eventually experienced tensions between its egalitarian goals and its actual decision-making processes. These tensions emerged particularly in the mid-1980s as NCNW founder, Jan Peterson, sought to maintain funding for the organization under the increasingly restrictive social policies enacted by the federal, state, and local governments as part of the global realignment of capital known as neoliberalism.[7] The conflict the organization experienced over its transition to an international network reveals the difficulties facing progressive social organizations challenged with adapting to changing political realities and limited resources.[8] Ultimately, however, differences of class and race were both a challenge and an asset for NCNW members, who learned from each other and benefited from members' varying strengths.

In the mid-1970s, poor and working-class neighborhoods in New York, including East Harlem in upper Manhattan and Williamsburg-Greenpoint in Northern Brooklyn, were in crisis.[9] Faced with eroding tax revenue and increasing pressure from financial institutions to cut its municipal budget, New York City clamped down on fiscal spending, hitting these neighborhoods hardest. Many basic social services, including ambulance, fire, and police service, that had once been taken for granted, disappeared. On the brink of bankruptcy in 1975–76, the city fired thousands of municipal employees, raised transit fares, cut welfare benefits, closed library branches and health facilities, and imposed tuition at the city colleges for the first time in 129 years. Head of city housing and development, Roger Starr, announced a policy of "planned shrinkage," which referred to the withdrawal of police and fire stations and the closure of schools, hospitals, bus routes, and subway stations, all in poor and nonwhite areas of the city, which, he suggested, should "lie fallow until a change in economic and demographic assumptions makes the land useful again."[10]

Responding to this state-based attack on their neighborhoods, residents organized resistance strategies. African American women took the lead in public housing tenants' associations, continuing a long tradition of "other-mothering" for their extended community by creating educational and social programs and pressuring city officials for decent housing conditions.[11] As the opening quotation from Velez indicates, these women felt a responsibility to stay in their neighborhoods and make them better. Working-class white ethnic women in Williamsburg-Greenpoint also took on leadership roles in their neighborhood, forming block associations and joining protests such as the successful sixteen-month occupation of a firehouse slated for closure by the city.[12]

This empowering sense of responsibility for improving the lives of family members and fellow community residents has been termed "activist mothering" by sociologist Nancy Naples. In her study of community workers involved in the War on Poverty, Naples found that many women from low-income backgrounds choose to stay in their communities and try to improve them, even when they had acquired education and the means to move out. She attributes this to the women's identities as activist mothers, often formed in relation to strong female role models, who practiced "political activism as a central component of mothering and community caretaking of those who are not part of one's defined household or family."[13] Members of the NCNW coalition shared this identity of community caretakers, whether or not they had children themselves. As Bronx public housing leader and NCNW member Linda Duke explained in an interview, her activism evolved from initial concern over her children's education to taking part in city and national politics:

First of all, I am a mother of five children, grandmother of four. And I've been in public housing for, I don't know, 39 years. And by being a parent, and having children, the first thing you get active and involved in is the nursery school that your kids go. And things kind of grow from there because you want to make sure that your kids and other kids in the community have better service. So now I think that was my first introduction into being a community activist. And from there it just grew, not only from the nursery being involved with my kids' daycare, but also being involved in my kids in their school system. And in the school system where I lived there was this community and it just grew to being active.[14]

As Duke emphasized in recounting her own trajectory, a sense of community was often a key motivation for activism. Rooted in this gendered sense of social responsibility, a communal activism united disparate members of the NCNW coalition. Yet, even though women of color and white women shared similar motives when forming neighborhood groups, the long and intense history of racial segregation and violence in New York initially prevented them from joining together.[15] Fortunately, Naples notes, the process of constructing community itself "offers the possibility for redefinition of boundaries, for broadened constituencies, and for seemingly unlikely alliances."[16] NCNW founder Jan Peterson played a crucial role in bringing the groups together, facilitating the creation of a new, diverse community.

A tireless organizer and astute politician, Peterson participated in the civil rights movement, second-wave feminist consciousness raising groups in Manhattan, and the white ethnic movement of the 1970s.[17] She came to Williamsburg-Greenpoint in 1969 with a War on Poverty grant to start a community center aimed at local Italian American residents. Quickly recognizing that women were doing the majority of community work in the neighborhood, Peterson became interested in creating a new, specifically women-oriented organization in Williamsburg.[18] Concerned that "the mainstream women's movement did not reach and touch a majority of women who were poor, working class or involved in neighborhoods," and also that male-led white ethnic neighborhood groups were lacking (and sometimes hostile to) "a women's analysis," Peterson sought to establish "a new movement" in which "the fight for equal rights" would be "integrated with . . . efforts to improve the quality of life for . . . families and communities."[19]

With the help of Monsignor Geno Baroni, author Nancy Seifer, and then-Baltimore Councilwoman Barbara Mikulski, all prominent members of the white ethnic movement, Peterson organized a conference of 150 "neighborhood women"—defined as "welfare poor, working poor, and working-class women who live side-by-side."[20] Held in 1975 in D.C. and funded by Baroni's

National Center for Urban Ethnic Affairs, the meeting brought together women from all over the country, including fifty from Brooklyn.[21] During an emotional consciousness-raising session, recorded on film, women described their family backgrounds and life histories, and discussed their involvement in politics and their feelings about feminism and class. Many, including Mikulski, traced their political involvement to concerns over urban renewal schemes, pollution, and public policies, all of which were affecting their communities in significant ways.[22]

Congresswoman Bella Abzug (D-N.Y.) captured the spirit of the conference when she proclaimed her own working-class background and explained, "What people don't understand is that a women's movement is a movement of all women. And fundamental to that is the participation of all women to come together. It's not some upper-middle class intellectual thing that people try to make it. It's our problems."[23] For those gathered in D.C., confronting government bureaucracies in order to preserve their families and communities in the face of mounting adversity were primary objectives, and their feminism emerged in the context of working together toward such common goals.

The women gathered at the meeting voted to form an organization of their own—the National Congress of Neighborhood Women—to "affirm their values and roles, help them improve their lives and neighborhoods, and represent neighborhood women accurately to the world at large."[24] Following the conference, Peterson worked hard to secure funding for the group, utilizing her War on Poverty ties. In 1975, she succeeded in obtaining government grants to employ twenty-five Williamsburg women to comprise the first NCNW staff, as well as to create positions in local community organizations, including the Cooper Park Housing Tenants' Association.[25] The Brooklyn office Peterson established served not only as the headquarters of the national organization, but also as the site of most early NCNW initiatives. One of the groups' most important achievements was the creation of a community-based two-year college program, founded in 1975, offering tuition-free courses taught in Williamsburg with a curriculum designed by the students and focused on urban sociology and neighborhood organizing.[26]

At first, the Italian American women Peterson had begun working with were reluctant to share the NCNW's newfound resources with African American and Hispanic neighbors, especially the Comprehensive Employment Training Association (CETA)–funded jobs and slots in the college program.[27] As Ida Susser noted in her study of Williamsburg-Greenpoint from 1975 to 1978, good jobs were scarce and many families were desperate for income, making the CETA-funded positions extremely desirable.[28] However, Peterson and Christine Noschese, who was then directing the college program, sought to involve women of color from nearby public housing complexes, especially Cooper Park, in NCNW programs.

African American public housing leaders, including Margaret Carnegie, Mildred Tudy, and Mildred Johnson, had formed the Cooper Park Tenants' Association with the goal of improving "living conditions in the project community, and uniting the tenants of the community for the betterment of the community."[29] Courted by Peterson and Noschese, leaders from the Cooper Park Tenants' Housing Association, became involved with the NCNW through the CETA jobs and college program and shared with them their considerable knowledge and experience in neighborhood-based activism.[30] Many local women reported becoming involved in the organization as mothers, utilizing the day care program or joining the college program to be able to better provide for their families.

Initially, it was difficult for both white women and women of color to work together because of suspicion and fear. As Italian American Sally Martino Fisher put it, "I was 10 when Cooper Projects were built. And it was forbidden [for me to go there] because it was . . . all minorities in there. . . . I was raised in a very white neighborhood . . . I had to change my feelings and thinking in the support groups and everything else because [before joining the NCNW] I never saw black people."[31] Martino Fisher explains that although there were people of color living in her neighborhood, she had no personal relationships with black women before joining the NCNW, and her sense of crossing racial boundaries by collaborating with women in public housing is significant. Most of the white ethnic women involved in the NCNW lived in private housing, but many of the African American and Hispanic women lived in public housing. Housing segregation was maintained, in part, by private property owners who refused to rent to people of color. Also, white ethnic families took pride in doubling or tripling up—placing several nuclear families in one house—to avoid residing in public housing, which they perceived as stigmatizing, because of its associations with people of color. The unexamined racism, fear, and hesitancy of the group's white ethnic members did not make it easy for the women of color to trust them. According to Velez, her early experiences with consciousness raising within the group were frustrating because of the racial divisions: "I hated it. I did not like it at all. . . . I used to think a lot of the women in the group were real racist. . . . There wasn't a lot of integrating going on."[32]

Women from both groups faced being disparaged for their participation. As one NCNW member reported: "The majority of women do not understand . . . if you talk to them about women being independent, they start thinking gay. . . . My husband said 'You'll never go back to the [National]

Congress [of Neighborhood Women]; after he saw some gay women there."
Similarly, she said, "when I went to the Congress, they'd say she's selling out
to the white group."[33] In a poor and working-class community where survival
depended upon family and kin networks, the threat of social ostracism and
the withdrawal of male support worked against collaboration across racial
boundaries.[34] However, as Bernice Johnson Reagon once said, "You don't go
into coalition because you just *like* it. The only reason you would consider
trying to team up with somebody who could possibly kill you, is because
that's the only way you can figure you can stay alive."[35] The NCNW coalition offered its members opportunity, an alternative support network, and
a shared vision of a better future.

Over time, both groups stuck it out because, as Velez put it, in the end,
"the good outweighed the bad."[36] The NCNW and public housing tenants' associations shared mutual needs, ranging from the immediate, such as getting
traffic lights installed at intersections where children were being hit by cars
and providing shelter for those needing to escape from domestic violence,
to the long range, such as obtaining college degrees and taking part in public
policy decision making. According to Duke, the hallmark of the NCNW was
bringing diverse groups of women together and allowing them to recognize
common goals:

> And that is one thing that I can say for National Congress of Neighborhood
> Women, they bring people together. They bring people together. And from all
> walks of life, cross cultures, definitely different religions, definitely nationality,
> they bring people together. And the way they bring people together, that we
> all have the same needs, the same problems, but we're just in different parts of
> the puzzle. But as one puzzle. We all have the same problems and we all can
> relate to one another.[37]

Professional women within the group played an important role in helping
the grassroots women recognize these mutual needs.

In June 1978, Christine Noschese explained the benefits of NCNW's college
program:

> In the "Labor and Immigration" course, women saw there was a difference
> of what it means to come to New York City as a black person, or to come as
> an Italian or Irish working-class person. The college program helped them
> to explore these similarities from a different perspective . . . [it] provides a
> forum to get together to see what their problems are without white-washing
> their differences.[38]

NCNW's college program brought white ethnic, Hispanic, and African American women together in a shared social space, highlighting, in its multiplicity,

the highly segregated residential patterns of New York City. It proved to be crucial in allowing the NCNW and public housing leaders to bridge their differences. The curriculum's emphasis on family, community, and labor history provided a guided forum for students to explore the intersections and implications of their multiple identities. For example, students explored the structural racism embedded in the local labor market that led white ethnic families, who generally were able to secure at least one regular job per household, to be identified as working-class, but some African American families were unable to secure any regular employment, and were identified as poor.[39] Discussions of immigration history and the sociology of poor and working-class families not only helped students break down the categories of "black," "Hispanic," and "white," but also to understand a variety of ethnic backgrounds and differing experiences of oppression.

African-American public housing leader and NCNW graduate Diane Jackson remembered the college program as the most important site of interracial dialogue:

> We had to get over a lot of obstacles. . . . There was some racial tension. In working with these other women from outside the community, we were able to identify what those racial issues were and talk about it. I remember when the film *Roots* came out and it was part of our assignment to watch it for class. Just to hear some of the responses from other people opened up the door to start talking about race and racism and misunderstandings. We began to find out more about each other, found out that we had a lot in common. . . . Some of the women that I met in the college program, we helped each other, we worked things out.[40]

The college program's feminist analysis of institutions including the family also led members to recognize mutual needs, such as gaining the right to be protected from domestic violence. Many of the women in the college program were victims of abuse, and, for some, participation in the NCNW increased their vulnerability, as husbands and boyfriends grew to resent their growing independence. Sociologist Terry Haywoode, who at one time taught in and directed the NCNW college program, recalled white women and women of color coming together to protect each other from abusive husbands and boyfriends: "One woman whose husband didn't want her to go to class would be escorted by four very large women."[41]

In another case, when an angry husband came to the NCNW office and began attacking his wife, the other women in the office fought him off and invited her to move in with them until she could find her own housing.[42] Offering physical protection promoted trust between members and led to future collaboration around a number of women's issues. For example, in

1976, the NCNW's college program sponsored a "speak-out on wife battering," which led to the establishment of the first battered women's shelter in New York City, the Women's Survival Space, a joint effort between the NCNW and Young Women's Christian Association.[43]

Drawing on Peterson's experiences in the civil rights and second-wave feminist movements, the NCNW used consciousness raising, followed by leadership support training, as its primary organizing methodology. Their program, which was also adopted by affiliates of the Brooklyn-based group, first recruited a diverse group of neighborhood women, who worked to develop "personal supportive relationships between themselves," using "a dialogue format." For example, questions included "What is great about being female? What are some great memories you have about growing up female? What has been hard about being female? What couldn't you stand about growing up female? What can't you stand about other women? What do you require of another woman in order for her to be your ally?"[44] Women sat in a circle, refrained from talking over each other or judging one another, and, ideally, gave each other equal talking time. Other sessions focused on additional aspects of identity, including race, class, religion, and sexuality. As they listened to each other, members came to recognize commonalities as well as differences and were encouraged to reflect upon the ways in which institutions such as the family, the mass media, and the workforce had shaped their lives and worldview.

Additional structured conversations encouraged them "to identify their particular concerns, analyze the impact of their concerns on their lives; and work with others to map out strategies that neighborhood women can act upon within their community."[45] Through this process, women were encouraged to connect their personal history with societal institutions and structures of power and to generate their own theories of identity and social change. According to Velez, this was a powerful experience, motivating and sustaining her activism, because, "for me, social change organizing needs to come out of personal experience, consciousness, and a vision of what should be."[46]

Rosalyn Baxandall and Linda Gordon describe consciousness raising, the primary mode of organization for the women's liberation movement, as "a form of structured discussion in which women connected their personal experiences to larger structures of gender" and "came to understand that many of their 'personal' problems . . . were not individual failings but a result of discrimination."[47] Because the NCNW membership was more diverse than many radical women's liberation groups,[48] the NCNW discussed race and class as well as gender and developed an understanding of the intersection of these categories of identity. Analyzing their own experiences and connecting them to social structures allowed NCNW members to overcome class and race shame and to build upon the positive aspects of their identities as poor and working-class women. For example, their resilience and commitment to furthering social justice and improving conditions for their communities are positive aspects. Hence, societal relations of power, including race, class, and sexuality, shaped but did not determine member's identities.[49]

The NCNW first developed its leadership training program for use in support groups within the college program in the late 1970s. In 1979, Lisel Burns, who was trained in peer counseling techniques, joined the NCNW and worked to formalize the group's guided consciousness-raising methodology into a leadership training program that could be used by other women's groups across the United States and internationally.[50] Outlining this leadership training program for poor and working-class women, NCNW founder Jan Peterson demonstrated a holistic conception of identity when she wrote in 1982: "Since low and moderate [income] women experience not only sex oppression but other oppressions based on their age, race, class and ethnicity, it is essential to combine this understanding in our work. . . . In understanding sexism we will have to understand all other oppressions."[51] Over time, this multidimensional understanding of power relations allowed the NCNW to see interconnections between institutions such as the family, the welfare state, and corporations and to draft a broad and inclusive agenda for social change. NCNW members were well aware of the state's regulation of their lives through punitive welfare policies targeting single mothers; urban renewal programs that uprooted their communities; and the exportation of jobs, education, and health care from their neighborhoods. Identifying the federally mandated shift of resources from urban and mixed-race areas to suburban and white areas, and linking this shift to women's ability to survive within their communities, the NCNW offered an analysis of structural inequalities embedded in state policies and practices. Challenging feminists to broaden their agendas, NCNW member Terry Haywoode argued in 1978 that the "destruction of neighborhoods through bureaucratic callousness" and budget cuts should be prioritized along with reproductive rights and the establishment of women's studies programs.[52]

Influenced by their coalition work with public housing leaders, NCNW members identified adequate housing for all families as their top priority in the 1980s and fought to secure their own, women-friendly housing development in a city-owned, abandoned hospital in Greenpoint. Peterson and NCNW member Ronnie Feit explained, "it was clear to us that the design and operation of poor and low-income neighborhoods and communities . . .

worked against the efforts of poor women to attain self sufficiency and decent lives for themselves and their families."[53] Approaching feminism from their social location as poor and working-class women, and like many others, as single mothers, they argued that to achieve equality as women, their basic needs for housing must first be met.

Class-based differences between the NCNW members and their professional allies and middle-class–oriented feminist groups sometimes led to conflict over the prioritization of issues and resources within the feminist movement. In the long term, NCNW member Caroline Pezzullo argued, poor and working-class women in the United States often had more in common with grassroots women's organizations abroad than with feminists at home: "We found that more poor women had similar problems all over the world than women in general, even though theirs may be more intensive in other countries, and it was a unifier."[54] At times these differences turned bitter as NCNW members chided white, middle-class feminists for neglecting their "bread and butter" issues of daily survival, and for "leaving behind" their families and communities in a search for self-improvement. Peterson described the NCNW's working-class feminism as distinct:

> A new women's voice is developing in the United States. This voice comes from poor and working-class women who can not fight for equity as women without trying to improve things for their families and communities. They can not or will not separate themselves from their families and communities to stand up as women, yet no longer will they step back in their community organizations when the monies come in so the men or "outside" professionals can have the jobs. At home they want partnerships with their husbands. They know that their men are also discriminated against in the areas of ethnicity, race, and class; they need each other to make it in today's world.[55]

The NCNW certainly did focus on community building, and some of its members did achieve lasting partnerships with men. However, many of the coalition members were single or divorced, and others were lesbian, suggesting that Peterson's rhetoric of "a brand new kind of feminism—pro-family, pro-church, and pro-neighborhood," with its emphasis on tradition, was designed in part to appeal to the press. Mainstream journalists endlessly attacked "selfish" middle-class women's liberation groups, who openly critiqued the domestic division of labor along gender lines and promoted more flexible family arrangements. In contrast, the *New York Times* applauded NCNW member Sally Martino Fisher for cooking her family's dinner "without complaining" before heading to Washington, D.C., to testify before a committee on urban and ethnic affairs, while another *Times* reporter noted: "The women of the

Northside sound remarkably free of recriminations about men and the past. They identify more than ever with their neighborhood, and their particular self-discovery seems less selfish than that of other revolutionaries."[56]

Even though the popular press exaggeratedly—and unfairly—charged women's liberation groups with being radical man-haters because of their call for men to take on a fair share of household duties, there were in fact important class-based differences in women's attitudes toward housework. During the NCNW's "Speak out on Housework," and in subsequent conversations in their college courses, members talked about their positive feelings toward caretaking for their families. For example, Marie Casella stated:

> I don't appreciate some middle-class woman telling me to get out of the kitchen who didn't know if there was a kitchen there, and didn't know if the struggles of her home related to the struggles of my home. . . . I happen to like my kitchen. I like being a mother and happen to like being a wife. I don't think you have to give those things up to be a liberated person. . . . I come from a very proud heritage. I know I'm Italian. It was drummed into me what Italian people are: they keep their home; they keep their husband; they keep everything. It was just a proud thing for me.[57]

For women such as Casella, pride in their cooking and household maintenance skills was tied to ethnic identity. It also reflected class-consciousness, especially for women who did not have the privilege of choosing whether to enter the workforce or not, and whose paid employment often was not fulfilling. The NCNW's dismissals of "middle-class feminists" revealed both genuine differences in perspectives as well as a desire to divert the backlash of criticism surrounding the women's movement from engulfing the organization.

Yet, despite Peterson's protraditional family and church rhetoric, it is clear that she and other members were aware of and sought to challenge traditions of male domination and female subordination within those institutions, as well as within local, state, and national governments. Notes from their consciousness-raising sessions include under "Obstacles": "Christianity is also male dominated." However, the NCNW's original goals included helping "women identify, perceive and assume power without feeling that it was a threat to family and feeling o.k. about it," making "women more aware of abilities and their rights, that they are not necessarily the weaker sex," enabling "women who didn't get out of the home to meet other women besides family members," to raise "consciousness on many levels," and to create "a new sense of identity."[58]

This tension between preserving or transforming male-dominated institutions such as the patriarchal family and the Roman Catholic Church was played out not only within the group's ideological publications, but also within member's personal lives. As one member put it in a 1976 interview, "I don't think of myself as a feminist, but I think of myself as equal to my husband. But he doesn't think of me as equal."[59] According to many members, the coalition was able to withstand the pressures generated by such tensions by allowing members to focus on working together on programs they all supported, but not taking an organizational stance on controversial issues: "It's very much of a family model, I think, and agreement was not the aim. We have these wonderful 13 principles but not like on reproductive rights. You didn't have to get agreement on issues, just agreement on wanting a better world for children and families with women taking responsible leadership."[60]

Focusing on processes-consciousness raising and support groups—and areas of mutual goals allowed the NCNW to avoid fracturing along lines of contention.[61] Despite their differences, the coalition bound together socialist feminists and devoutly religious women who opposed abortion. Many of the grassroots members were initially hostile to what they termed "middle-class feminism," which they perceived as antifamily, threatening or irrelevant to their lives. However, like Jean Kowalsky, who participated in the NCNW's CETA jobs program, many women testified to broadly supporting feminist goals. As Kowlaksy explained, at first, "the women's movement never meant a thing to me. It was the PTA, the church, that's all." In a 1979 interview with *Ms.* magazine, she reflected on her changed view: "I feel more worthwhile. I feel good about myself. And I think the women's movement is wonderful. Because I have daughters, and I want their life to be easier than mine was. I want them to get paid what they're worth, and to get money when they're promoted. I want them to feel good about themselves."[62]

Over time, NCNW members developed a feminist stance, then, both through consciousness raising in the college program and in support groups and through challenging power structures, including the patriarchal family and state bureaucracies.[63] Professional women, who generally functioned as leaders, brought important knowledge and organizing strategies to the group and worked to empower the grassroots members to participate in local, state, and national politics. As Jackson explained: "So many women in our community, through Jan [Peterson], got involved in a whole lot of other things. We got involved in school board elections, in registering to vote, getting young people involved, improving the streets in our communities, getting street lights, stop lights. . . . Learning how to work the system, how to make elected officials work for us."[64]

Defeat, as much as success, helped mold members' understandings of interlocking systems of oppression. For example, when the NCNW tried to form a multiracial women's political party to put women in local political offices in Williamsburg, Peterson recalled that, "the whole political machine came out against [the NCNW's] candidates because they saw the threat of diverse women from different racial backgrounds coming together." Male party politicians worked to divide them along racial lines, inflaming long-standing tensions to get their candidates in office. The traditional parties' candidates won the election and the Williamsburg's women's political party never got off the ground.[65] As Celene Krauss observed in her study of white working-class women's environmental justice campaigns, female activists, especially those that are poor, working-class or nonwhite, often find themselves excluded "from direct participation in political life," experiencing "a contradiction between the state's democratic promise" and its actual workings. This recognition of their exclusion allowed NCNW members, like the women in Krauss' study, to develop an oppositional consciousness[66] and to push for the realization of their citizenship rights.[67]

In addition to playing an important role in leading consciousness-raising groups and teaching in the college program, professional women within the NCNW also enabled the coalition to obtain federal grants from the Department of Housing and Urban Development (HUD) for improving public housing. Velez explained how the NCNW's initial cooperation with public housing leaders in Brooklyn deepened in the 1980s through her participation in the group:

> "In 1982, I joined the National Congress of Neighborhood Women. At first, I couldn't see how the women's issues applied to my community focus until I thought about it and realized that the leaders in James Weldon Johnson Houses were all women. Since then I have challenged the National Congress of Neighborhood Women to adapt its leadership and organizing processes to the development of the James Weldon Johnson complex. I also expanded the network of public housing tenant groups within the NCNW to help end the isolation of public housing leaders from the broader development movement."[68]

Building on the strength of Cooper Park leaders and Velez, in the early and mid-1980s, the NCNW helped organize other public housing tenant's unions through out New York City, including the largely Hispanic Borinquen Plaza Union in Williamsburg. With funds from the Community Service Society, the NCNW facilitated the formation of the Federations of Greenpoint-Williamsburg and of East Harlem Public Housing Developments, in the hopes that coalition building would allow tenants' associations greater leverage in combating the hazardous living situations they faced.[69] Many residents endured conditions similarly dismal to those described by Borinquen Plaza Tenants Union President Jesus Lorenzo in a 1986 letter to Senator Daniel Moynihan (D-N.Y.):

> We the tenants of Borinquen Plaza in Williamsburg, Brooklyn, have seen the deterioration of our housing complex since it opened in 1976. We have suffered the consequences of inadequate management by the housing authority. Crime, vandalism, lack of communication between the tenants and the New York City Housing [Authority] is rampant. The tenants have also been charged fees without justified reason. Flies, rats, overcrowding, and unsanitary conditions make living here unbearable.[70]

With the federal government pursuing a policy of privatization of public housing and cuts in social welfare, help was not forthcoming.[71] The NCNW coalition believed community action was the only recourse to ensure the survival of their communities.

Through their national network, the NCNW put New York public housing leaders in touch with St. Louis activist Bertha Gilkey, who gained recognition when Jack Kemp, director of HUD during the first Bush administration, praised her for transforming the once-dilapidated Cochran Gardens public housing development into a successful tenant-managed complex. Gilkey worked with the coalition members to develop long-range plans for improving public housing in New York City and provided both practical advice and networking ties for obtaining federal funding. In October 1994, with Gilkey's help, the NCNW and the East Harlem Public Housing Coalition successfully applied for a $400,000 grant from HUD, which went to five different public housing complexes in New York City, allowing the coalition to organize tenants into more politically effective unions through leadership training and the assignment of block captains, as well as funding physical improvements, including fencing, better lighting, and the construction of community centers within the developments.[72]

Without the specialized knowledge, formal credentials, and political affiliations of the professional members of the NCNW, the public housing tenants' associations would have been unable to obtain these federal grants. Coalition members were aware of this need for professional legitimacy. Velez noted, "what I appreciate about the [National] Congress [of Neighborhood Women] is that they allowed us the opportunity to gain resources and to broaden our perspective on things we want to do."[73] However, the professional leadership of the group also led to a patronage system, where women with graduate degrees—mostly white from working-class backgrounds—were administering the federal grant programs and, therefore, hiring and supervising the less formally educated women working at the NCNW through the CETA program or through public housing grants. As Ida Susser emphasizes in her study of community action programs in Williamsburg-Greenpoint, low-income workers' need for jobs in a climate of 12 percent unemployment made them unlikely to challenge the leadership of program administrators.[74] This funding-mandated patronage system, combined with Peterson's dominant tendencies, at times created conflict between the group's rhetoric of group empowerment and its less inclusive decision-making practices.

Peterson was an astute political actor, recognizing shifts in government and foundation funding dictates and adjusting the NCNW's programs to meet new requirements. Trained as a psychotherapist, she was also a highly charismatic leader, befriending neighborhood women and cultivating their own leadership capabilities. Christine Noschese recalled Peterson's talent for encouraging and inspiring the women around her: "When she was in your corner and she was pushing you, you could climb mountains. She was just fantastic that way."[75] Though many NCNW members testified to Peterson's ability to empower them personally, she proved unwilling to cede overall leadership to others, and NCNW members who challenged her governance, or supported women who did, eventually left the group. In 1979–80, and again in 1985–86, fractures between Peterson and the NCNW's other strong leaders over questions of the group's direction and priorities created an environment of distrust that led to the breakup of important friendships and the loss of momentum for social justice organizing.[76]

Although the organization did regroup and continue to function following both splits, these losses were extremely painful to other members such as Rosemary Jackson, who likened their fissures to "ripping out your guts." Jackson recalled the contentiousness of the organization in the mid-1980s, when grants from previous sources of funding, including CETA, the Rockefeller Foundation, and the New York City Department of Labor, had dried up, causing Peterson to increasingly seek new sources of revenue through the organization's national and international network. While some members welcomed the new opportunities afforded by the NCNW's growing network, others feared the loss of the local women's programs they had fought so hard to establish in Brooklyn in the 1970s.[77] The strong emotional connections between members were both an asset and a liability for the group; they bound members together and encouraged risk taking for social change, yet they also led to personalization of conflicts and intense feelings of pain and loss over perceived disloyalty. As one member wrote, "NCNW really is like a family—in all its aspects; it tears you apart, it puts you back together again."[78]

Like other charismatic, strong-willed leaders, Peterson's actions revealed tensions between her belief in democratic participation, and her need to direct the development of the organization she founded and devoted her life to. A pragmatist as well as an idealist, Peterson followed the funding, often acting out of necessity. These programmatic realignments frustrated some members who wanted the NCNW to continue focusing on serving the needs of low-income women in New York and not to give greater emphasis to national and international work. Interestingly, most of the public housing leaders remained in the coalition. Although they expressed feeling frustrated at times with Peterson's control, unlike some of the white ethnic members of the NCNW, they had other outlets to express their leadership capacity and needed the resources that Peterson could provide, especially access to federal funds and politicians.

The coalition of the NCNW and public housing leaders has survived into the present, a testimony to the dedication of these activists and the strength of their dream for a better collective future. NCNW's longevity and success may be best explained by Velez: "Social change is about persistence, stubbornness, and the willingness to follow a wiggly road."[79] Remarkably adept at responding to changing political tides, Peterson has refocused the NCNW from a local to a global network, forming in 1985 a new nonprofit, Grassroots Organizations Operating Together in Sisterhood (GROOTS International). Through GROOTS, Peterson has been able to secure U.N. funding and to introduce the New Yorkers to women from all over the world in an effort to share organizing strategies and to build a global grassroots women's movement.[80] This international development has been a fruitful area of growth for the NCNW in the past two decades, partially because it has allowed women's groups to work around and beyond the limitations set by national governments.[81]

As Peterson worked to expand her global network, Velez and other public housing leaders in New York built upon the coalition forged through their work with the NCNW to form a new citywide organization of public housing tenants in 1996. The New York City Public Housing Resident Alliance charged themselves with the mission of informing and connecting residents "so that they can have a strong and effective voice, and secure greater accountability" in government decisions affecting public housing. The alliance has successfully lobbied city, state, and national legislators in an effort to preserve rent ceilings and to prevent enactment of time limits on tenancy. As a result of the alliance's outreach efforts, over 1,500 public housing residents have attended the housing authority's planning meetings for city compliance with the 1998 Quality Housing Act. The alliance currently is fighting for federal repeal of mandatory community service required of public housing residents under the 1998 Act as well as working to preserve residents' role in decision making in the shaping of public housing policy in New York.[82]

The coalition between the NCNW and public housing leaders continues, and one-half of the ten-person board of the alliance is composed of women who have participated in NCNW programs. The alliance uses the NCNW's Brooklyn office to house its records and for meeting space, and the two groups continue to collaborate on grant requests and training programs. However, in interviews, many former and current members of the coalition expressed a desire to return to the closer emotional ties between members that were created in the context of daily or weekly contact in the 1970s, when the coalition provided CETA jobs, the college program, and frequent consciousness-raising sessions.[83] Although she has remained active in community organizing, Fisher recalled those years as the best of her life, saying that she felt an unequaled sense of accomplishment and belonging as a result of her participation in the NCNW:

> I mean, we're telling poor, working class women that National Congress is a vehicle for a voice for them in the women's movement. Not the traditional women's movement and we're going to bring your issues, your bread and butter issues to that movement for support. So that you could move. And you know, that's what we did, exactly what we promised. We came up with job training, we came up with women, you know, getting jobs. All of what we said, getting their high school diplomas, learning how to speak English. I mean, all of the things that we said that we would do. And that's why I feel so good about organizing around that because I saw the outcome and that made me feel that I really, you know, had a place. I really helped them and I guess that's another reason I feel so great about those years.[84]

Fisher's strong connection to the NCNW, twenty years after she left the organization, highlights the importance of creating nurturing, inclusive activist communities to achieve social change. Histories of the second wave are only recently beginning to explore the activism of working-class white women and women of color,[85] but the NCNW offers an important model for studying the ways in which a concept of intersectionality can help us understand the nature of coalition work across differences, offering insights for broader social justice movements.

Drawing upon their identities as poor and working-class white women and women of color, NCNW members formed a new, broadened community. NCNW's specific focus on recognizing and analyzing the differences between members facilitated the construction of successful cross-race and cross-class partnerships. Rather than allowing differences among them to fracture their coalition, the NCNW implemented intersectionality through its practice of guided consciousness raising, to engage in a principled coalitional form of identity-based politics. Once understanding and trust was established, NCNW members were able to identify areas of mutual needs and even to work on issues that did not directly benefit their own group because they valued the coalition and enacted their belief in working to advance the position of all low-income women and communities.

As Bernice Johnson Reagon wrote in 1981, "we've pretty much come to the end of the time when you can have a space that is 'yours only.'" Identity politics, she noted, are indeed powerful and necessary, but ultimately must be combined with coalition building in order to achieve lasting social change. Reagon reminded feminists to broaden their communities, stating that, "the 'our' must include everybody you have to include in order for you to survive."[86] Against powerful odds, NCNW coalition members recognized that they needed each other to survive and were willing to work out their differences—which has become their lasting strength. Today, U.S.-based feminists face significant challenges in forming inclusive organizations for social change. Greater residential segregation along racial and class lines is one functional barrier to the formation of neighborhood-based integrated women's groups.[87] The elimination of federal funds for organizing and service provision in poor communities makes it much more difficult for innovative grassroots groups such as the NCNW to obtain the resources they need to succeed. As the cost of higher education rises and affirmative action programs are abandoned, opportunities for meaningful exchanges across class and racial differences in educational settings are diminished. We should not give up in despair, however. Rather, we can draw on the legacy of the courageous women of the NCNW and others like them who continue to fight for progressive change and continue to challenge themselves to work through and across the differences that separate them.

In spite of the internal and external challenges they faced, the legacy of the NCNW coalition reveals the rewards of grassroots organizing. Through consciousness raising and collaborative education as long-term strategies for group empowerment and understanding, the NCNW transformed its members' lives. NCNW members achieved an oppositional consciousness and made demands for recognition of their citizenship rights and for redistribution of economic power and social decision-making responsibility.[88] Although their efforts did not always bring the results NCNW members hoped for, they did result in concrete improvements in their communities as well as greater opportunities for participants in the college and training programs. Ultimately, the NCNW's consciousness-raising and leadership support groups have been crucial in supporting and sustaining women's activism, resulting in diverse and lasting networks for social change.

This type of slow, process-oriented organizing for social change is similar to that successfully employed by the great civil rights leaders Fannie Lou Hammer and Ella Baker, as well as by members of the Young Lords Party in New York City, and the female members of Students for a Democratic Society in its Economic Research and Action Project.[89] Significantly, even though these groups did not begin as specifically feminist oriented, through consciousness raising and struggling against discrimination, like the NCNW, they came to adopt a feminist perspective. Through their activism, they enacted the second-wave feminist principle that the personal is political.[90] Activists today can learn much from the NCNW's use of consciousness raising and group education and its building of diverse coalitions, as primary social change strategies. Broad-based progressive movements must begin with individual transformation and face-to-face relationship building across lines of difference. Although this type of organizing is time-consuming and intensive, it yields long-term commitments to change—and coalitions to facilitate it—which are necessary to combat entrenched bureaucracies and other barriers to the empowerment of low-income Americans and the realization of democratic participation for all residents.

## Notes

Financial support from the University of Michigan Rackham Graduate School, History Department, Institute for Research on Women and Gender, and the Nonprofit and Public Management Center, and from the Sophia Smith Collection made research for this project possible. Sherrill Redmon, Margaret Jessup, and the rest of the staff at the Sophia Smith Collection went out of their way to make doing research an enjoyable and productive experience. Paul and Marge Barnett, Madeline Blais, and Norman Sims graciously opened their homes to me and provided intellectual companionship and wise counsel on my extended trips to Northampton. Martha Ackelsberg conducted many of the oral history interviews with me, kindly shared her own research notes, and prompted me to think more deeply about social change and democracy through our many discussions on the NCNW. J. Abigail Woodroffe painstakingly transcribed the oral history interviews. Members of the University of Michigan Community of Scholars and the American History Workshop read drafts of this chapter and provided helpful feedback. For reading multiple drafts and offering unstinting encouragement as well as insightful criticism, I would especially like to thank Rob Maclean, Jennifer Palmer, Lara Rusch, and my advisors, Gina Morantz-Sanchez and Matthew Lassiter. Stephanie Gilmore and the contributors to this volume contributed greatly to shaping my understandings of second-wave feminism and made this a better chapter. My family, especially my parents, Ted and Susan, and my brother, David, have brightened my spirits and encouraged me to keep at it. Finally, I would like to thank the many NCNW members who shared with me their experiences in oral history interviews, telephone conversations, and e-mails and continue to inspire me with their courage, commitment, and understanding.

1. The NCNW also formed coalitions with other grassroots women's groups across the United States and internationally, which I explore in Tamar Carroll, "How Did Working-Class Feminists Meet the Challenges of Working across Differences? The National Congress of Neighborhood Women, 1974–2006," *Women and Social Movements in the United States, 1600–2000* 10, no. 4 (December 2006).

Drawing upon the organizational records of the NCNW and oral history interviews, this chapter will focus in particular on the coalition between the NCNW and public housing tenants' associations in New York City. Velez joined the NCNW in 1982, but other public housing leaders including Mildred Tudy, Mildred Johnson, Margaret Carnegie, and Diane Jackson began working with the NCNW shortly after its founding in 1975.

2. Kelly writes, "Class is lived through race and gender." Robin D. G. Kelley, *Yo' Mama's Disfunktional!* (Boston: Beacon Press, 1997), 11.

3. Here, I draw on Estelle Freedman's definition of feminism: "Feminism is a belief that women and men are inherently of equal worth. Because most societies privilege men as a group, social movements are necessary to achieve equality between women and men, with the understanding that gender always intersects with other social hierarchies." Following Freedman, I consider the NCNW to be feminist although not all its members self-identified as such, because the group did articulate these beliefs in equal worth, social movements, and intersectionality. Estelle B. Freedman, *No Turning Back: The History of Feminism and the Future of Women* (New York: Ballantine Books, 2002), 7.

4. Dorothy Sue Cobble, *The Other Women's Movement: Workplace Justice and Social Rights in Modern America* (Princeton, N.J.: Princeton University Press, 2004); Nancy F. Cott, *The Bonds of Womanhood: "Women's Sphere" in New England, 1780–1835* (New Haven, Conn.: Yale University Press, 1977); Nancy F. Cott, *The Grounding of Modern Feminism* (New Haven, Conn.: Yale University Press, 1987); Nancy A. Naples, *Grassroots Warriors: Activist Mothering, Community Work, and the War on Poverty* (New York: Routledge, 1998); Nancy A. Naples, ed., *Community Activism and Feminist Politics: Organizing across Race, Class, and Gender* (New York: Routledge, 1998); Kathryn Kish Sklar, *Florence Kelley and the Nation's Work: The Rise of Women's Political Culture, 1830–1900* (New Haven, Conn.: Yale University Press, 1995); Kathryn Kish Sklar, Anja Schuler, and Susan Strasser, eds., *Social Justice Feminists in the United States and Germany: A Dialogue in Documents, 1885–1933* (Ithaca, N.Y.: Cornell University Press, 1998).

5. Nancy F. Cott, *Public Vows: A History of Marriage and the Nation* (Cambridge, Mass.: Harvard University Press, 2000); Alice Kessler-Harris, *In Pursuit of Equity: Women, Men and the Quest for Economic Citizenship in Twentieth Century America* (New York: Oxford University Press, 2001); Nancy MacLean, *Freedom is Not Enough: The Opening of the American Workplace* (Cambridge, Mass.: Harvard University Press, 2006).

6. For an overview of social citizenship, see Gordon's introduction in Linda Gordon, ed., *The New Feminist Scholarship on the Welfare State* (Madison: University of Wisconsin, 1989).

7. David Harvey defines neoliberalism as "a theory of political economic practices that proposes that human well-being can best be advanced by liberating individual entrepreneurial freedoms and skills within an institutional framework characterized by strong private property rights, free markets and free trade." The ascendancy of neoliberalism across the globe since 1970 has led to "deregulation, privatization, and the withdrawal of the state from many areas of social provision." David Harvey, *A Brief History of Neoliberalism* (New York: Oxford University Press, 2005), 2–3. The Reagan administration's embrace of neoliberalism led to severe cuts in discretionary domestic spending on social programs in the United States.

8. On this point, see also Steven Rathgeb Smith and Michael Lipsky, *Nonprofits for Hire: The Welfare State in the Age of Contracting* (Cambridge, Mass.: Harvard University Press, 1993); MacLean, *Freedom Is Not Enough*, 287–98; and Sandra Morgen, *Into Our Own Hands: The Women's Health Movement in the United States, 1969–1990* (New Brunswick, N.J.: Rutgers University Press, 2002), 181–205.

9. East Harlem is a predominantly African American and Hispanic neighborhood dominated by large public housing complexes. Williamsburg-Greenpoint was, earlier in the twentieth century, largely white ethnic, with a working-class population of Irish, Italian, and Polish residents, and a smaller group of Hasidic Jews. Construction of public housing in the 1950s introduced African American residents to the neighborhood; however, it remained heavily segregated, with many private homeowners refusing to rent to nonwhites, and a high level of white-on-black racial violence. Throughout the 1970s, Williamsburg-Greenpoint experienced tremendous population change, with the exodus of many middle-class whites and the influx of Puerto Rican and Dominican immigrants. As the Latino population of Williamsburg-Greenpoint grew, so too did the participation of Latinas—primarily Puerto Rican, but also Mexican and Dominican—in the NCNW. Over time, some men also became involved in the organization, attending its college program or working for the NCNW, although it remained a women-focused and directed group. Ida Susser, *Norman Street: Poverty and Politics in an Urban Neighborhood* (New York: Oxford University Press, 1982). Carol Brightman, "The Women of Williamsburg," *Working Papers,* January/February 1978, NCNW records, box 28, folder 12.

10. Glenn Fowler, "Starr's 'Shrinkage' Plan for City Slums Is Denounced," *New York Times,* February 11, 1976; Joshua Freeman, *Working Class New York: Life and Labor since World War Two* (New York: The New Press, 2000), 277.

11. Patricia Hill Collins, *Black Feminist Thought: Knowledge, Consciousness, and the Politics of Empowerment,* 2nd ed. (New York: Routledge, 2000), 189–92. Collins describes *othermothering* as stemming from an "ethic of caring and personal accountability among African-American women" that often leads them to care for all children in their community and to become social activists.

12. People's Firehouse Housing and Community Development Co., tenth anniversary brochure, November 23, 1985, NCNW records, box 135, folder 19; Susser, *Norman Street,* chap. 10.

13. Nancy A. Naples, *Grassroots Warriors: Activist Mothering, Community Work, and the War on Poverty* (New York: Routledge, 1998), 11. For another important analysis of the leadership role of grassroots women in antipoverty community-based programs, see

Annelise Orleck, *Storming Caesar's Palace: How Black Mothers Fought Their Own War on Poverty* (Boston: Beacon Press, 2005).

14. Linda Duke, interview by author, digital recording, Smith College, February 21, 2004. This interview and all other interviews with NCNW members by author are collected in the Tamar Carroll Oral History Project, Sophia Smith Collection, Smith College.

15. Susser, *Norman Street*. See also Jonathan Rieder, *Canarsie: The Jews and Italians of Brooklyn against Liberalism* (Cambridge, Mass.: Harvard University Press, 1985); Craig Wilder, *A Covenant with Color: Race and Social Power in Brooklyn* (New York: Columbia University Press, 2000).

16. Nancy A. Naples, "Women's Community Activism: Exploring the Dynamics of Politicization and Diversity," in *Community Activism and Feminist Politics: Organizing across Race, Class, and Gender,* ed. Nancy A. Naples (New York: Routledge, 1998), 337.

17. While the white ethnic movement is often regarded as a white racist reaction to the civil rights movement, some of its leaders advocated cooperation between poor and working-class whites and people of color, especially in urban areas. Especially influential in calling for interracial cooperation was Monsignor Geno Baroni, Assistant Secretary of Housing and Urban Development in the Carter Administration, and founder of the National Center for Urban Ethnic Affairs. Philip Shabecoff, "Msgr. Geno Baroni, a Leader in Community Organizing," *New York Times,* August 29, 1984. For Peterson's biography and an account of the NCNW's founding and early years, see Mary Field Belenky, Lynne A. Bond, and Jacqueline S. Weinstock, *A Tradition That Has No Name: Nurturing the Development of People, Families, and Communities* (New York: Basic Books, 1997), chap. 8. The civil rights, second-wave feminist, and white ethnic movements of the 1960s and 1970s provided an important context for the NCNW's organizing by politicizing gender, racial and ethnic, and class identities in a new way, allowing NCNW members to see themselves as (more) legitimate political actors. I explore this political and cultural context further in my dissertation, Tamar Carroll, "Grassroots Feminism: Direct Action Organizing and Coalition Building in New York City, 1955–1995," (PhD diss., University of Michigan, 2007).

18. Jan Peterson, interview by author, tape recording, Brooklyn, NEW YORK, August 16, 2002. Susser attributes women's greater involvement in the community to their tendency to maintain extended kin and friendship networks while visiting on stoops in their neighborhood and taking part in childrearing activities, and men's friendship networks more often centered around work, bars, or gangs. Susser, *Norman Street*, 119.

19. Jan Peterson, "A Bridge to the Neighborhoods for the Women's Movement," n.d., NCNW records, box 1, folder 23. Barbara Mikulski served as a Democratic Congresswoman from Maryland from 1976 to 1986, when she was elected to the U.S. Senate, where she continues to represent Maryland.

20. National Congress of Neighborhood Women, "The Neighborhood Women's Training Sourcebook," 1993, 7.

21. *National Congress of Neighborhood Women Quarterly* 1, no. 1 (Spring 1976), NCNW records, box 29, folder 4.

22. See the chapters in Part II of John Bauman et al., eds., *From Tenements to the Taylor Homes: In Search of an Urban Housing Policy in Twentieth Century America* (University Park, Pa.: Pennsylvania State Press, 2000).

23. *Working Class Women Changing Their World,* videocassette, produced by Jan Peterson and Christine Noschese, 1975, NCNW records, box 145, tape 4.

24. National Congress of Neighborhood Women, "The Neighborhood Women's Training Sourcebook," 3.

25. Lindsay Van Gelder, "National Congress of Neighborhood Women: When the Edith Bunkers Unite!," *Ms.*, February 1979, NCNW records, box 28, folder 10. The funds came from the pilot for the Comprehensive Employment Act (CETA). Jan Peterson, interview by author, tape recording, Brooklyn, NEW YORK, August 16, 2002.

26. Alice Quinn to Ralph Perrotta, May 22, 1975, NCNW records, box 31, folder 1. The NCNW college program proved highly successful and was adopted by six other women's organizations nationally. Belenky, Bond, and Weinstock, *A Tradition That Has No Name*, 217.

27. Christine Noschese, interview by author and Martha Ackelsberg, digital recording, New York, April 1, 2004.

28. Susser, *Norman Street*, 52–53.

29. "The Constitution of the Cooper Park Tenants Association, Inc.," November 23, 1985, p. 1, NCNW records, box 101, folder 15. The tenants' association participated in a wide range of activities, from sponsoring meetings to discuss public policies and meeting with local officials, to planning holiday celebrations and sponsoring sports teams, to coordinating tenant monitored security. They also provided referrals for services, including alcohol and drug counseling, voter registration, emergency shelter, food stamp information, and child care. Jessie Conley to Tilly Tarrentino, March 11, 1986, NCNW records, box 101, folder 16.

30. *Metropolitan Avenue*, videocassette, produced and directed by Christine Noschese, 1985, NCNW records, box 145, tape 1.

31. Sally Martino Fisher, interview by author and Martha Ackelsberg, digital recording, Queens, New York, March 23, 2004.

32. Ethel Velez, interview by author and Martha Ackelsberg, digital recording, East Harlem, New York, March 30, 2004.

33. "Ethnic Heritage Cooper Park," audiocassette, NCNW records, box 143, tape 10.

34. Johanna Brenner, *Women and the Politics of Class* (New York: Monthly Review Press, 2000), 4.

35. Bernice Johnson Reagon, "Coalition Politics: Turning the Century," in *Home Girls: A Black Feminist Anthology*, ed. Barbara Smith (New York: Kitchen Table: Women of Color Press, 1983), 356–57.

36. Ethel Velez, interview by author and Martha Ackelsberg, digital recording, East Harlem, New York, March 30, 2004.

37. Linda Duke, interview by author, digital recording, Smith College, February 21, 2004.

38. "A Dialogue on the Organization, Goals and Needs of the National Congress of Neighborhood Women," June 1978, pp. 1–2, NCNW records, box 3, folder 8.

39. Christine Noschese, interview by author and Martha Ackelsberg, digital recording, New York, April 1, 2004. For a nuanced and informative account of the post–World War II labor market in New York City, see Roger Waldinger, *Still the Promised City?: African Americans and New Immigrants in Postindustrial New York* (Cambridge, Mass.: Harvard University Press, 1996).

40. Diane Jackson, interview by Martha Ackelsberg, tape recording, New York, April 28, 2004.

41. Terry Haywoode, interview by author and Martha Ackelsberg, Boston, April 30, 2004.

42. Diane Jackson, interview by Martha Ackelsberg, tape recording, New York, April 28, 2004.

43. Lindsay Van Gelder, "Battered Wives Hit Back at the System," *New York Post,* Thursday, December 2, 1976, NCNW records, box 28, folder 10.

44. Jan Peterson to Counseling Staff, February 29, 1988, pp. 11–14, NCNW records, box 99, folder 9.

45. "Summary," n.d., pp. 2–3, NCNW records, box 98, folder 5.

46. Ethel Battle Velez, "Why Do You Do Community Work?," n.d., NCNW records, box 101, folder 34.

47. Rosalyn Baxandall and Linda Gordon, eds., *Dear Sisters: Dispatches from the Women's Liberation Movement* (New York: Basic Books, 2000), 13.

48. Alice Echols, *Daring to Be Bad: Radical Feminism in America, 1967–1975* (Minneapolis: University of Minnesota Press, 1989); Judith Ezekiel, *Feminism in the Heartland* (Columbus: Ohio State University Press, 2002); Anne Valk, "Living a Feminist Lifestyle: The Intersection of Theory and Action in a Lesbian Feminist Collective," *Feminist Studies* 28, no. 2 (2002): 303–32; Nancy Whittier, *Feminist Generations: The Persistence of Radical Women's Activism* (Philadelphia: Temple University Press, 1994).

49. For a moving discussion of class shame and its effect on identity, see Roxanne Dunbar-Ortiz, *Red Dirt: Growing up Okie* (New York: Verso, 1997).

50. Lisel Burns, interview by author, digital recording, Northampton, Mass., February 21, 2004.

51. Jan Peterson, "Draft of Leadership Training Program," September 3, 1982, NCNW records, box 3, folder 19. I am not claiming that the NCNW was the first or only group to employ an analysis of intersectionality; rather, I am arguing that using a conception of multiple identities allowed the NCNW to treat seriously the differences between members while also identifying areas of mutual needs. For an early and eloquent statement of intersectionality, see Combahee River Collective, "The Combahee River Collective Statement," in *Home Girls: A Black Feminist Anthology,* ed. Barbara Smith (New York: Kitchen Table: Women of Color Press, 1983). Kimberly Springer writes that black feminists were the first to theorize "the intersections of race, gender and class." Black feminist organizations, she argued, employed an understanding of intersectionality to mount "interstitial" politics—"politics in the cracks"—that addressed the needs posed by black women's multiple identities. Kimberly Springer, *Living for the Revolution: Black Feminist Organizations, 1968–1980* (Durham, N.C.: Duke University Press, 2005), 1–2.

52. Terry Haywoode, "Women against Women: Middle-Class Bias in Feminist Literature," September 2, 1978, NCNW records, box 118, folder 4.

53. Ronnie Feit and Jan Peterson, "Neighborhood Women Look at Housing," in *The Unsheltered Woman: Women and Housing in the 80s,* ed. Eugenie Ladner Birch (Camden, N.J.: Rutgers University Center for Urban Policy Research, 1985), 178.

54. Caroline Pezzullo, interview by author, audiocassette, New York City, August 19, 2002.

55. Jan Peterson to Counseling Staff, February 29, 1988, p. 7, NCNW records, box 99, folder 9.

56. Jan Peterson, "The NCNW," n.d., NCNW records, box 4, folder 22. Barbara Grizzuti

Harrison, "Hers," *New York Times,* May 22, 1980, p. C2, NCNW records, box 28, folder 12. Francis X. Clines, "About New York: A Quiet Revolution in Northside," *New York Times,* January 21, 1978, NCNW records, box 28, folder 12.

57. Untitled term paper, n.d., p. 2, NCNW records, box 118, folder 5.

58. "Obstacles," n.d., NCNW records, box 1, folder 11; "NCNW: Original Goals and Objectives," n.d., NCNW records, box 1, folder 7; "Goals/Objectives Staff," November 20, 1979, NCNW records, box 1, folder 11.

59. Enid Nemy, "For Working-Class Women, Own Organization and Goals," *New York Times,* January 24, 1976, p. L20, NCNW records, box 28, folder 12.

60. Lisel Burns, interview by author, digital recording, Smith College, February 12, 2004.

61. Kimberly Springer describes a similar emphasis on process and consciousness raising within black feminist groups. Springer, *Living for the Revolution.*

62. Lindsay Van Gelder, "National Congress of Neighborhood Women."

63. Many NCNW members came to embrace reproductive rights. However, some members remained opposed to abortion, which likely posed a threat to their primary identities as mothers. See Kristin Luker, *Abortion and the Politics of Motherhood* (Berkeley: University of California, 1984).

64. Diane Jackson, interview by Martha Ackelsberg, tape recording, New York, April 28, 2004.

65. Jan Peterson, interview by author, tape recording, Brooklyn, New York, August 16, 2002.

66. Jane Mansbridge writes that "members of a group that others have traditionally treated as subordinate or deviant have an oppositional consciousness when they claim their previously subordinate identity as a positive identification, identify injustices done to their group, demand changes in the polity, economy, or society to rectify those injustices, and see other members of their group as sharing an interest in rectifying those injustices." Jane Mansbridge, "The Making of Oppositional Consciousness," in Jane Mansbridge and Aldon Morris, eds., *Oppositional Consciousness: The Subjective Roots of Social Protest* (Chicago: University of Chicago Press, 2001), 1–19, quote on p. 1.

67. Celene Krauss, "Challenging Power: Toxic Waste Protests and the Politicization of White, Working-Class Women," in *Community Activism and Feminist Politics: Organizing across Race, Class and Gender,* ed. Nancy A. Naples (New York: Routledge, 1998). This process of developing a race- and class-inflected feminist consciousness through challenging existing power hierarchies is also similar to sociologist Nancy Naples's findings in her study of women community workers involved in the War on Poverty in New York and Philadelphia. Naples, *Grassroots Warriors.* Sociologist Terry Haywoode argues that the NCNW developed a working-class feminism rooted in women's sense of belonging to familial and kin-based networks, which utilized communal survival strategies. Haywoode notes, "this approach centered on the importance of community, both as an organizing tactic and as a goal. Through this approach they asserted the importance of community life and neighborhood culture in opposition to the growing emphasis on administrative rationality in government and corporate life." Terry Haywoode, "Working Class Feminism: Creating a Politics of Community, Connection, and Concern" (PhD diss., City University of New York, 1991).

68. Velez, "Why Do You Do Community Work?"

69. See, for example, "Williamsburg/Greenpoint Federation," n.d, NCNW records, box 98, folder 10; and Zan White, "Pre-Application Form—For 1986 Funding Cycle," p. 4, NCNW records, box 98, folder 12.

70. Jesus Lorenzo to Daniel Moynihan, July 10, 1986, NCNW records, box 101, folder 1. Richard Plunz, *A History of Housing in New York City: Dwelling Type and Social Change in the American Metropolis* (New York: Columbia University Press, 1990).

71. Roger Biles, "Federal Housing Policy in Postwar America," in *From Tenements to the Taylor Homes: In Search of an Urban Housing Policy in Twentieth Century America,* ed. John Bauman (University Park, Pa.: Pennsylvania State Press, 2000). Thomas Byren Edsall, "The Changing Shape of Power: A Realignment in Public Policy," in *The Rise and Fall of the New Deal Order, 1930–1980, ed.* Steve Fraser and Gary Gerstle (Princeton, N.J.: Princeton University Press, 1989), 269–93; R. Allen Hays, *The Federal Government and Urban Housing: Ideology and Change in Public Policy* (Albany: State University of New York Press, 1985); Paul Pierson, *Dismantling the Welfare State?: Reagan, Thatcher and the Politics of Retrenchment* (Cambridge: Cambridge University Press, 1994); Rhonda Y. Williams, *The Politics of Public Housing: Black Women's Struggles against Urban Inequality* (New York: Oxford University Press, 2004).

72. "Partnership in East Harlem: James Weldon Johnson Houses and the NCNW," videocassette, directed by Lynn Pyle, NCNW records, box 145, tape 2. Jason DeParle, "Cultivating Their Own Gardens," *New York Times Sunday Magazine,* January 5, 1992, NCNW records, box 15, folder 20. For more on Bertha Gilkey, see Sara Evans and Harry C. Boyte, *Free Spaces: The Sources of Democratic Change in America,* rev. ed. (Chicago: University of Chicago Press, 1992), 106–7, 96–97. James Weldon Johnson Resident Association, Needmor Fund Application Form, p. 3, NCNW records, box 101, folder 35. The NCNW and James Weldon Johnson Houses Resident Association had previously received a $40,000 grant from HUD's Tenant Opportunity Program to expand resident participation in the tenants' association.

73. Ethel Velez, interview by author and Martha Ackelsberg, digital recording, East Harlem, New York, March 30, 2004.

74. Susser, *Norman Street, 27,* 53.

75. Christine Noschese, interview by author and Martha Ackelsberg, digital recording, New York, April 1, 2004.

76. "Update on the National Congress of Neighborhood Women," March 12, 1985, NCNW records, box 71, folder 6. The conflict in 1979–80 was over who should head the NCNW: when Jan Peterson took a position in Washington, D.C., in the Carter administration as aid to Midge Constanza, presidential assistant for public liaison, from October 1977 to 1980, Christine Noschese took over as executive director of the NCNW. When Peterson returned from D.C. to Brooklyn, she fought with Noschese for control of the organization and won, and Noschese left the organization to focus full-time on her film, *Metropolitan Avenue.* Additional information for this section comes from oral history interviews conducted with more than fifteen former and current NCNW members, as well as my own observations of the group's leadership at its reunion at Smith College in February 2004.

77. Rosemary Jackson, interview by author and Martha Ackelsberg, digital recording, Northampton, Mass., February 20, 2004.

78. Rebecca Staton to Chris (sister and brother staff members and members of the board), July 22, 1979, NCNW records, box 31, folder 5.

79. Velez, "Why Do You Do Community Work?"

80. Sandy Schilen, "Presentation at the Global Coalitions for Voices for the Poor," World Bank Consultation, July 31–August 1, 2000, NCNW office, Brooklyn, New York. The international groups that the NCNW partnered with were composed of both grassroots women and professionals and were devoted to addressing the needs and values of local, grassroots women, like the NCNW itself.

81. Janet Peterson, interview by author, tape recording, Brooklyn, New York, August 16, 2002.

82. New York City Public Housing Resident Alliance, "About the Resident Alliance," June 2003, and "New York Public Housing Residents Read This," in author's possession. David Chen, "In Public Housing, It's Work, Volunteer, or Leave," *New York Times,* April 15, 2004, Juan Gonzales, "Fitting Day to Protest Housing Law," *Daily News,* January 16, 2001; J. A. Lobbia, "Home Breaker: Doing Community Disservice," *Village Voice,* June 13, 2000.

83. The job and college program were closed due to a lack of funding, stemming from federal and state cuts in social service spending, and a shift in private foundation's grant allocating priorities.

84. Sally Martino Fisher, interview by author and Martha Ackelsberg, digital recording, Queens, New York, March 23, 2004.

85. Nancy MacLean, "The Hidden History of Affirmative Action: Working Women's Struggles in the 1970s and the Gender of Class," *Feminist Studies* 25, no. 1 (Spring 1999): 42–78; Nancy MacLean, *Freedom is Not Enough: The Opening of the American Workplace* (Cambridge, Mass.: Harvard University Press, 2006); Premilla Nadasen, *Welfare Warriors: The Welfare Rights Movement in the United States* (New York: Routledge, 2005); Nancy Naples, ed., *Community Activism and Feminist Politics*;, Jennifer Nelson, *Women of Color and the Reproductive Rights Movement* (New York University Press: New York, 2003); Benita Roth, *Separate Roads to Feminism: Black, Chicana and White Feminist Movements in America's Second Wave* (Cambridge: Cambridge University Press, 2004); Kimberly Springer, *Living for the Revolution.*

86. Reagon, "Coalition Politics: Turning the Century," 357, 65.

87. See the essays in John H. Mollenkopf and Manuel Castells, eds., *Dual City: Restructuring New York* (New York: Russell Sage Foundation, 1991) for analysis of the increased racial and economic polarization in New York City since the 1970s.

88. For an explanation of recognition and redistribution and an appraisal of the role of difference in democratic politics, see Iris Marion Young, *Justice and the Politics of Difference* (Princeton, N.J.: Princeton University Press, 1990).

89. Johanna Fernandez, "Radicals in the Late 1960s: A History of the Young Lords Party in New York City, 1969–1974" (PhD diss., Columbia University, 2004); Jennifer Frost, *"An Interracial Movement of the Poor": Community Organizing and the New Left in the 1960s* (New York: New York University, 2001); Chana Kai Lee, "Anger, Memory and Personal Power: Fannie Lou Hammer and Civil Rights Leadership," in *Sisters in the Struggle: African American Women in the Civil Rights-Black Power Movement,* ed. Bettye Collier-Thomas and V. P. Franklin (New York City: New York University Press, 2001);

Charles Payne, *I've Got the Light of Freedom: The Organizing Tradition and the Mississippi Freedom* (Berkeley: University of California Press, 1995); Barbara Ransby, *Ella Baker and the Black Freedom Movement: A Radical Democratic Vision* (Chapel Hill: University of North Carolina, 2003).

90. Carol Hanisch, "The Personal is Political," in Shulamith Firestone, ed., *Notes from the Second Year: Women's Liberation* (New York: Radical Feminist, 1970).

## 11. The Cooperative Origins of *EEOC v. Sears*

EMILY ZUCKERMAN

In 1973, the U.S. Equal Employment Opportunity Commission (EEOC) began investigating Sears, Roebuck & Co., alleging that it discriminated against women because its commissioned sales force, selling big-ticket items such as home appliances and auto parts, was predominantly male. At the trial in 1985, Sears argued that female employees simply "were not interested" in these jobs because they were too stressful and competitive; they did not like the hours or could not work nights; and the jobs conflicted with their family responsibilities. Rosalind Rosenberg, an intellectual historian from Barnard, testified on behalf of Sears that women wanted jobs that complemented their family responsibilities, and that differences in hiring and promotions could be due to social construction rather than discrimination. Labor historian Alice Kessler-Harris testified for the EEOC that throughout history working women have always taken the opportunity to earn more money when it was offered to them. The court found Sears not liable for discrimination, and a debate ensued in academic circles and the media.

Although the investigation and case against Sears had been going on for almost twelve years by the time Rosenberg and Kessler-Harris testified in 1985, the media had paid relatively little attention until then. The coverage then expanded and became increasingly mainstream, pitting Kessler-Harris against Rosenberg as two distinctly opposite sides of the issue.[1] Historians engaged in the media debate to an uncharacteristic degree, through interviews, letters to the editor, conference discussions, and journal articles, and many middle-class feminists appeared to accept the polarized terms of the debate and choose sides, rather than redefine it in their own way.[2] The overall focus on the details of the debate distracted attention away from the problems faced by working women at Sears that the case was meant to address. In trying to understand Rosenberg's argument for taking cultural factors—or "differences" between men and women—into account, academics on both sides spent a lot of energy trying to resolve what eventually came to be seen as a fundamentally unworkable dichotomy, the sameness/difference dilemma.[3]

Although much was written about the expert witness testimony around the time of the trial, no one has looked at *Sears* from a broad historical perspective. Several works on second-wave feminism and the women's liberation movement in the early 1970s mention early efforts to force Sears to change its policies, usually in the context of women's groups' organizing or cases against other employers such as AT&T.[4] It is important, however, to examine the origins of the case and recover the grassroots activism from which it grew. Although the *Sears* case is remembered for its divisiveness in the feminist community, it was actually born of cooperation among women's groups trying to force corporate employers to change their discriminatory practices.

The purpose of this essay is not to examine the EEOC litigation or even to trace the women's groups' campaign against Sears during the 1970s, but rather to explore the formation of grassroots coalitions surrounding working women's issues from which the *Sears* case arose.[5] In the early 1970s, several women's groups in Chicago formed with a focus on working-class women and employment issues, trying to extend the protections of Title VII of the Civil Rights Act of 1964 in a practical way. Their members came from backgrounds in civil rights, housing, women's liberation, and the labor movement, and were generally experienced in social protest. These groups formed bonds with other groups across the country, helping each other's causes by staging nationwide protests or applying pressure to a company from several directions in an attempt to improve the workplace for women. One by one, they targeted specific industries that employed large numbers of women, such as banking, insurance, and retail, and forced employers to change their practices. They also used litigation, reaching out to working women through leafleting and community meetings and helping them file charges of discrimination with the EEOC.

Sears, headquartered in Chicago, was just one of the many targets of this coalition of working women's groups. *Sears* did not begin simply as a case where an individual woman complained to the EEOC because she was denied a promotion. Although many Sears women did file charges of discrimination, the *Sears* case was a by-product of long-term cooperation among women's groups in Chicago trying to bring about widespread changes in the workplace. Their goals were broad, encompassing direct action against many different corporations and industries. The women's groups that pursued Sears were a part of, and grew out of, the coalition atmosphere in Chicago at the time. They never intended to pursue a thirteen-year lawsuit against the Sears corporate giant, however, but only to shame and scare it into changing its employment practices as women's groups had done with companies such as AT&T.

## Women's Groups in Chicago

As the home of the Brotherhood of Sleeping Car Porters, the Packinghouse Workers, and other important labor unions, Chicago was indisputably a center of industrial unionism throughout the twentieth century. For the same reasons, it also became a center of women's labor activism, reaching its apex with the founding of the Coalition of Labor Union Women (CLUW) there in 1974. However, years before the founding of CLUW, working women's groups formed in Chicago and drew members from labor unions and civil rights organizations. Several of the founding members of the National Organization for Women (NOW) came from the Midwest labor movement, such as Catherine Conroy of the Communications Workers of America (CWA) and Dorothy Haener of the United Auto Workers (UAW). In particular, many feminist activists in the 1960s came from Wisconsin, including Kay Clarenbach, a professor and chair of the Office of Women's Education Resources at the University of Wisconsin (UW) and the first chair of NOW's board of directors.[6] When NOW first formed, Clarenbach ran its operations out of her office at UW, but it soon moved to the UAW in Detroit, which provided office space and administrative support. Then, a dispute developed between members who wanted the organization to support the Equal Rights Amendment (ERA) and labor union women who asked that the issue be put off while they tried to get their male union leaders to support it, which resulted in the national office moving from Detroit to Washington, D.C.[7] In the early 1970s, three separate headquarters were set up, in New York, Washington, D.C., and Chicago. Each office handled a different aspect of the operations, with Chicago handling membership and administration.[8] Aside from the prominent role Chicago played on the national level, a local NOW chapter also formed there in 1967, just a year after the organization began. From the beginning, it was more diverse by race and class than many other chapters and drew heavily from labor unions for its members and leaders, such as Conroy.

It was not surprising then, that Chicago NOW focused particularly on women's work and employment issues from its inception. It played an instrumental role in challenging sex-segregated job advertising, one of the first issues the young NOW organization fought in order to enforce Title VII on behalf of women.[9] In September 1973, NOW publicized a Supreme Court decision declaring sex-segregated help-wanted ads illegal. It said the victory came after three-and-a-half years of litigation based on a NOW complaint and a "5 year campaign by NOW and other women's groups across the country."[10]

Mary Jean Collins, an early member of Chicago NOW, became a leader in the effort to force employers to change discriminatory practices and later spearheaded the Sears action for NOW. Collins grew up in Milwaukee, Wisconsin, with a mother who worked outside the home. After graduating from high school in 1957, she did clerical work for two years, and then attended Alverno College, a small Catholic all-women's college in Milwaukee run by nuns Sister Austin Doherty and Sister Joel Read. Sister Austin, Collins' history teacher at Alverno, "first challenged [her] to think about woman's role in society," awakened her to "women's potential," and "got her thinking" by asking the class why half the population makes so little contribution to society. In 1966, Sister Austin became a founder of NOW and later asked Collins to join the organization.[11] After graduating from college in 1963, Collins applied for jobs at an employment agency. She told them she did not want a typing job, and when they made her take a typing test anyway, she never returned.[12] She became interested in women's rights issues when she was unable to get the jobs she was interested in and for which she was qualified. "It didn't occur to me until after I had finished college," Collins later recalled, "that I was not in the Constitution at all."[13] Collins used her secretarial skills to get a job with an electronics firm, where the sales manager gave her a chance to do some buying.[14]

Collins's activism was evident early on. She married Jim Robson and, in the late 1960s, both participated in open housing marches in Milwaukee led by Father James Groppi and the National Association for the Advancement of Colored People (NAACP) Youth Council. In 1967, she helped found the Milwaukee chapter of NOW and became its treasurer.[15] Collins and her husband combined their surnames and both used the last name Collins-Robson until their divorce in the mid-1970s. She noted with irony that it was "easy for a woman to change her name. . . . Her husband just has to change his name and hers changes automatically."[16] In 1968, Jim's job was transferred to Chicago, and he and Collins moved to Hyde Park, where she worked for Allied Radio Corporation in a management position as its first female electronics rebuyer. Around the time of their move, Collins applied for a credit card at a department store and became angry when the store would not consider her credit information, but only her husband's.[17]

Collins' origins in the women's movement were rooted in a labor and activist sentiment. When asked who influenced her and who were her "own heroes in the women's movement," she pointed to Kay Clarenbach for "helping hold the organization together when it was 'a very fragile flower,'" and to Catherine Conroy, a member of the trade union movement, for "bringing a strong element of reality to the movement because of her experience with dealing with women in the work force."[18] After Collins moved to Chicago, she met Conroy, who worked for the Bell System and oriented her toward the employment issue, which was very important to the Chicago NOW chapter.[19] Collins quickly worked her way up in the local and national NOW organization. From 1969 to 1970, she served as president of the Chicago chapter and then became NOW's Midwest regional director, organizing chapters around the Midwest. Also in 1970, she was elected to NOW's board of directors and left her job to form C-R Office programs with Jim, a printing company to distribute NOW's growing number of publications to its burgeoning membership ("25,000 members in 600 chapters").[20] Collins later became cochair of the national Sears Action Task Force, and after leaving NOW's board in the mid-1970s, she returned in the 1980s as national action vice president.

Like many of the Chicago NOW women, Collins had a strong background in organizing. She was a product of the Midwest Academy, an organization formed in 1973 by Heather Tobis Booth, which was dedicated to training "leaders and organizers working in social change projects across the country."[21] Booth had a long history of activism, including being involved in the civil rights movement and participating in Freedom Summer.[22] She was also part of the New Left and married to a founding member of Students for a Democratic Society (SDS).[23] Like many women in the New Left, she felt disenchanted with its failure to adequately address gender issues and became an early member of the women's liberation movement.[24] She helped found both the West Side Group, an early women's liberation group in Chicago, with many women from SDS and the New Left, and later the Chicago Women's Liberation Union (CWLU).[25] In the mid-1970s, Booth formed the Midwest Academy to train organizers, billing the organization as "indispensable in winning structural social change in America because it provides a decisive component—the systemic approach to political and social action." In a time of "recession and political crisis" in the early 1970s, Booth saw the skills they taught as especially important. "When people are disorganized," she wrote, "their alienation, anger and fear is exploited and turned against themselves . . . we must create strong organizations that enable people to identify and move against their real enemies—the monopolies, the corrupt officials, the arrogant corporations."[26] By 1975, the Midwest Academy claimed to have taught organizing skills to more than 120 students and consulted "with thousands of people in over 150 additional organizations."[27] As evidence of its success, the academy cited graduates of its two-week training sessions and their contributions to social change in their own organizations: "The national respect the Academy has gained is a testimony to the organizations you are building, the changes you are winning."[28]

Like Collins, the members of Chicago NOW as a whole had significant experience in activism. Other members attended the Midwest Academy, including Judith Lightfoot, Anne Ladky, and Day Piercy Creamer.[29] Both Collins and Piercy worked as consultants for the academy, Collins on the women's movement and Piercy on working women.[30] The Chicago NOW women were well-organized and experienced, even running focused election campaigns within their own organization. Upon her election to the national board of directors at NOW's 1974 convention in Houston, one Rochester NOW member thanked the "'Chicago Machine' who supported me before and during the election, and who encouraged me to put my philosophy in position statements so that those attending the conference would know where I stood on the issues."[31]

More than many other chapters, Chicago NOW oriented itself toward issues related to work. In an August 26, 1974, article about a protest and meeting with Sears Bank officials as part of Women's Equality Day activities, Chicago NOW's secretary noted, "We're after 'bread and butter' issues. . . . These are the things that affect women's daily lives."[32] NOW's national office regularly reported on such efforts by Chicago NOW, for example, noting in April 1974 its attempts to pressure steel companies and unions to improve conditions for women.[33] At NOW's 1974 national convention in Houston during the height of the nation's economic recession, Chicago NOW submitted a resolution calling "for action to maintain our rights in the affirmative action area and prevent the discriminatory use of layoffs."[34] After the 1974 Houston convention, which had been full of internal organizational battles, national NOW leader Wilma Scott Heide sent a letter of appreciation and reflection to Chicago NOW. In what appeared to be a "pep talk" in response to Chicago NOW being pushed aside at the convention, Heide praised its crucial role: "Chicago NOW's roles especially but not only in Sears actions, ERA, Steelworkers NOW, Bicentennial, etc. etc. is significant in Chicago, Illinois and nationally. . . . No other city in NOW has had and has such reality and potential for local and national leadership and membership development."[35]

Despite its intentions, however, questions remained about whether Chicago NOW really represented working-class women and their needs. An Associated Press (AP) article about the August 26, 1974, Equality Day action at Sears Bank quoted a Mrs. Kennedy, "a cashier and the 39–year-old mother of five," as saying, "'Equality day may be all right for people who have nothing else to do, but when you get up at daybreak, get breakfast, take three kids to the baby sitter, then get yourself to work, you don't have much time to think about equality'" Another woman, a housewife from Mount Vernon, New York, who returned to work when her children were grown, "said she wasn't even aware that yesterday was a special day. What did it mean to her? 'Not a thing . . . I doubt that anybody pays the slightest attention.'" Although the AP article may have been framed to include contradictory feminist and antifeminist views, it certainly challenged Chicago NOW to demonstrate that working women believed the organization's interests and concerns represented their needs.[36]

In part to address more specifically the needs of working-class women, several working women's activists formed Women Employed (WE) in 1973. Day Piercy was the moving force behind the new organization, an attempt to focus more exclusively on work issues for women, including clerical workers in Chicago's downtown Loop area. Like Booth, Piercy had a long history of activism and came out of the women's liberation movement. As a student, she was involved in community organizing and women's liberation groups. In 1969, she moved to Chicago and became the first staff member of CWLU, working out of an office at the Young Women's Christian Association (YWCA). There she became involved in day care issues after holding "rap groups with working class women," and along with Booth created an action committee for decent child care through CWLU. Modeling themselves on César Chávez's farmworkers' union, Piercy worked with Booth and the Midwest Academy to organize women workers.[37] Through her work with women at the Southwest YWCA, Piercy saw they had limited opportunity for economic independence and felt there was a need for an organization specifically to support economic rights. She asked the YWCA to transfer her to its center in the Loop, where she interviewed a lot of people and decided on community organizing goals.[38] Like the farmworkers' union, WE sought to win some legal civil rights victories and then perhaps move on to traditional union organizing.[39] WE hoped to appeal to women previously considered unorganizable, as well as those who might not join a group like NOW, identify as feminists, or organize around more controversial issues such as reproductive rights.[40] WE represented one example of different strands of the women's movement coming together on working women's issues.[41]

Piercy worked closely with Chicago NOW in founding WE. During its early years, NOW leaders volunteered at WE, holding leadership positions and using their organizing experience to help it get started.[42] One such member, Anne Ladky, served as president of Chicago NOW from 1973 to 1975.[43] Ladky grew up in the Midwest and was active in community organizing for housing and civil rights. After graduating from college she worked in publishing in Chicago, and in 1971 helped found a citywide group called Women in Publishing, which urged publishers to use nonsexist language. Like Collins, she was influenced by Conroy to join NOW and later became cochair of its Sears Action Task Force. After several years away from NOW, in 1977, Ladky moved to WE.[44]

Despite its intentions, the question of whether WE's membership was working-class is a complicated one. Many of the secretaries who joined WE were well-educated and underemployed women who wanted but could not get the same professional jobs as men. Ladky noted that some of the "angriest" women were college-educated. In fact, she argued that WE had limited success with its secretaries' network in the 1980s because it found that most women wanted to get out of secretarial work rather than improve the pay or conditions within the occupation. Ladky blamed employers for the decline of the profession because they refused to make secretarial work a viable career path with corresponding salary raises and benefits. Regardless of their aspirations or education, however, virtually all women were low-wage workers when WE began.[45] With limited opportunities for promotion, a history of exploitation by bosses, and confinement to sexualized and stereotyped jobs, they could be considered working class, regardless of whether gender or class barriers kept them there.

In its early years, WE organized around certain industries, for example, pressuring insurance companies to post job openings and speaking to women steel workers in Gary, Indiana, about their working lives. After 1976, WE became less industry-oriented and constantly adjusted its strategies as its membership and the status of women in the workplace changed. By the late 1970s, as women began moving into better jobs, there was more demand for programs such as how to write resumes and negotiate for a higher salary. In an attempt to build its membership, WE shifted its focus somewhat from working-class to middle-class women, becoming partly a self-help organization that helped individual women "help themselves." Finally, in 2000, WE leaders recognized that middle-class and professional women had more opportunities and were likely to call a lawyer if they felt discriminated against. WE decided to return to its roots, committing itself to advocacy for low-wage women, who had less power in the workplace and would benefit from its assistance the most.[46]

## Other Strategies and Actions against Employers

During the early 1970s, both NOW and WE engaged in a variety of actions directed toward forcing employers to change their practices. NOW's national organization established a compliance task force to enforce discrimination laws through direct action, lobbying, litigation, and other pressure on corporations and government agencies responsible for implementing the laws. Individual task force members coordinated action in areas such as state and local governments, compliance agencies, and newspaper employment advertising.[47]

The task force published a lengthy newsletter updating members on recent developments and court cases. One regular section, "NOT NOW CORPORATIONS," listed companies and unions targeted for action by particular NOW chapters. In September 1973, for example, the newsletter listed Allstate Insurance in San Diego, Boeing in Seattle, and General Dynamics and the International Association of Machinists and Aerospace Workers in San Diego. The task force relied on NOW's extensive chapter network to coordinate these actions, requesting that members forward any sex discrimination complaints against these companies to the local contact person: "Combining our efforts is what it's all about!"[48] NOW also used the newsletter to stir interest in possible new campaigns and recruit members to coordinate them. In September 1973, the employment areas considered "ripe" for action included primary and secondary school teaching, library work, and clerical work, all of which employed large numbers of women "massed at the bottom of the employment pyramid."[49] By April 1974, NOW also targeted "Women in Office Work" among its priorities for "Special Compliance Projects."[50]

Wherever possible, the task force tried to expand successful local actions to other regions. In 1973, a statewide coalition founded by New Jersey NOW members issued a report on the status of women in New Jersey's state government and filed a class action discrimination complaint with the state civil rights division and the EEOC. NOW's national organization took an optimistic view of what this could mean for future actions: "NOW members in at least one other state are beginning an action against sexism in their Government. We hope NOW will soon have related projects going *in all 50 states*. If you are a state government employee, you too can be a complainant. If not, you can help blow the whistle on behalf of those who are" (emphasis added).[51]

WE, which focused exclusively on employment issues, also engaged in a broad range of activities. It carefully chose corporate targets, going after the biggest and most visible companies, such as AT&T, or entire industries that employed large numbers of women and had a history of discrimination, such as insurance, communications, retail, and banking. It went after them one by one, using direct action tactics such as protests and publicity to get them to change practices such as refusing to post job openings so that women could apply and, where necessary, initiated litigation. Members handed out questionnaires and used the information they received to file discrimination lawsuits against major corporations such as Kraft.[52] New WE members checked off whether they were interested in the Insurance Project, Banking Project, Public Employees Project, Secretaries' Project, Fundraising Committee, or member-at-large, and contributors were notified that these individual committees met once a week.[53] After its first year, Chairwoman Darlene Stille listed some of WE's accomplishments, such as getting the federal government to investigate sex discrimination at Kraft; convincing the state insurance commissioner "to set up a task force of Women Employed members and representatives from various insurance companies . . . to investigate sex discrimination"; and filing discrimination suits against Carson's department store with the EEOC and the Department of Labor's Wage and Hour Division.[54]

One early target for NOW and WE was the banking industry, which employed large numbers of women in low-wage jobs. NOW's December 1973 *Compliance Newsletter* reported on a victory against the California banking industry by a coalition that included California NOW, NAACP, League of United Latin-American Citizens (LULAC), Mexican-American Legal Defense and Education Fund (MALDEF), Chicano Law Students Association, and Employment Law Center of San Francisco. They won a settlement from the Bank of California that included goals and timetables for hiring women and minorities. The coalition then asked officials of other banks to voluntarily issue affirmative action plans "to bring hiring and promotions into line with population breakdowns." This strategy succeeded, as all the major banks provided information and meetings with officials, and at least one bank agreed to the coalition's goals and timetables and set up a training program. One Los Angeles NOW member attributed this victory to the coalition maintaining its cohesiveness and power by being "united on goals which relate to the interests of all," and to relying on the Bank of California settlement precedent. NOW immediately noted that this settlement "could be used as an example nationwide, [with] the same strategy repeated by local coalitions," and the various coalition actions could then be coordinated "to put together a nationwide action."[55] By April 1974, NOW's compliance task force advertised "A Strategy Kit for Achieving Equal Employment Opportunity in the Banking Industry" to help chapters or state compliance task forces plan actions to move their area banks toward equal employment opportunity, "while also building firm coalitions with other civil rights groups and public interest law firms." The kit included a history of the California bank action, basic strategy guide, goals for banks, press clippings, and the consent decree from the *Bank of California* lawsuit.[56]

Another main target was AT&T. In 1970, AT&T applied to the Federal Communications Commission (FCC) for a rate increase. The EEOC, which lacked the power to sue companies directly for discrimination, had received many charges of discrimination from female workers of AT&T. Several EEOC attorneys creatively decided to "piggyback" on the power of the FCC by "intervening" in its case. Pointing to statistical evidence of its imbalanced workforce, the EEOC argued the FCC should deny AT&T's rate increase because it discriminated against minorities and women. NOW LDEF, NAACP, and MALDEF joined the EEOC as copetitioners in the FCC case against AT&T.[57] NOW planned grassroots actions to coincide with and support the EEOC investigation and negotiations with AT&T in Washington, D.C. For example, the compliance task force organized an AT&T Happy New Year action at the beginning of 1972, which participating chapters in Chicago, Wichita, and Delaware deemed "worthwhile, even fun." The task force also considered doing a follow-up AT&T action when the FCC hearings ended.[58]

Individual NOW chapters also coordinated actions to get the most out of the government investigation. In March 1971, New York NOW filed a sex and race discrimination complaint with the state attorney general, which eventually led to a separate consent decree with New York Telephone Company, providing "minimum percentages for filling vacancies; . . . annual targets for each job classification; . . . abolishing military service as job qualifications; [and] goals for hiring males as operators and clericals," with compliance to be reviewed by the Division of Human Rights and a committee of employees.[59] In Atlanta, "NOW chapters filed charges, picketed, leafleted and worked with the women of Southern Bell to achieve success."[60]

In January 1973, AT&T signed a major settlement agreement with the EEOC, Department of Justice, and Department of Labor providing back pay for affected workers. Although not completely satisfied with the final settlement, NOW "still believe[d] it was, by far, the most significant step ever taken by a Federal agency in combating employment discrimination."[61] In June 1974, AT&T signed another court order concerning wage discrimination in management jobs and agreed to provide $7 million in back pay and $23 million in wage adjustments. The CWA tried to set aside the January 1973 agreement, according to NOW, because it felt it constituted reverse discrimination against white males. The court rejected CWA's claim, saying it "had been given every opportunity to participate in the negotiations and had declined," and allegedly criticized CWA "for failing to represent its female members."[62]

Women's groups also tried to learn from the AT&T victory and quickly made plans to use it as a model for future actions against other corporations.

At the national NOW convention in Washington, D.C. in February 1973, EEOC attorney and NOW member David Copus presented "How Women Can Take Advantage of the AT&T Settlement." He laid out the EEOC's three-pronged strategy against AT&T: (1) attacking race and sex discrimination simultaneously and treating them as inextricably linked; (2) treating sex discrimination in pervasive, institutional terms, relying on inferences drawn from statistics; and (3) selecting "a target which was large, highly visible (both in jobs and corporate presence), and conscious of its image, and which employed a significant number of females in traditionally female jobs." After listing its gains, such as goals and timetables, changes to the transfer and promotion system, and $15 million in back pay, Copus confidently predicted that "[w]omen nation-wide should be able to demand, with considerably [sic] forcefulness, these same remedies from other employers. The fact that the EEOC and the Department of Labor . . . insisted on and received these remedies from the nation's largest employer can be a powerful precedent." Copus also offered the use of AT&T's Affirmative Action Plan, which "contains local goals, hiring shares, etc. (useful to whipsaw other local employers.)"[63]

It would be hard to overestimate the impact of the win against AT&T on the decision of working women's groups to pursue Sears. NOW saw its role in the *AT&T* case as crucial and took credit for much of its success: "NOW's pressure was responsible for the landmark case of this type in which women and minorities at At and T [sic] were awarded $50 million. NOW seeks to bring similar pressure on Sears."[64] It looked for comparisons to AT&T everywhere. NOW's June 1973 *Compliance Newsletter* noted that the Department of Justice had charged Delta and United airlines and five airline labor unions with sex and race discrimination and that it resulted in a settlement similar to AT&T's. It failed to mention one major difference, however: that no one had sued the union in the *AT&T* case, and thus the union was able to act as a powerful check on the corporation and a source of protection for complaining workers.[65]

In dealing with Sears, NOW and WE focused only on the similarities with AT&T: both were prime targets for direct action, were large national corporations, employed significant numbers of women, and had public images to protect. They failed to appreciate key differences, however, such as the fact that Sears was virulently antiunion. Most of the AT&T workforce, on the other hand, was unionized, and the significant number of complaints they filed with the EEOC motivated the agency to investigate AT&T.

Another crucial difference was the racial diversity of the workforce. AT&T had a large percentage of African American workers, and their complaints of race, rather than gender, discrimination motivated the EEOC to investigate AT&T. These complaints drew Copus to investigate AT&T in the first place, as race discrimination was still his main concern, although other staff members also tried to focus on gender. In building its case, the EEOC team relied on a book detailing how the company's discriminatory policies left blacks in low-level and low-paying jobs.[66] It also relied on the statistical work of its top researcher, Phyllis Wallace, herself a victim of race discrimination and Jim Crow education, who documented how company policies channeled African Americans into the worst jobs.[67] The EEOC issued a report based on AT&T's own documents and statistics setting forth a strong case of race discrimination. Although the company did relatively well in hiring black women, policies favoring workers with high school diplomas and requiring employment tests for craft jobs kept black women concentrated in the lowest-paid, most demeaning jobs, and rarely in management jobs.[68] By comparison, Sears had a smaller percentage of African American employees, and many of the EEOC's complaints were drafted by women's groups such as Chicago NOW and WE, with the help of individual Sears women. Although the EEOC's case against Sears was originally based on race and gender, the race cases were settled early on and only the sex discrimination claims went to trial. In general, African Americans, including black women, were in the forefront of challenging employment discrimination and their efforts spread to other groups, including white women.[69]

## Making Feminist Coalitions

In working to change employment practices, the women's groups in Chicago made significant efforts to establish coalitions to build their actions and support others. Chicago NOW, and especially Mary Jean Collins, focused particularly on class issues. They worked closely with WE, whose mission was even more specifically to help working-class women. Together, activists in these groups organized across class lines in an attempt to build coalitions around the issues faced by working women. Chicago NOW and WE had a particularly close relationship, with officers and members moving back and forth between the two organizations during the early years. Collins and Ladky had a strong personal relationship and later served as cocoordinators of NOW's Sears Action Task Force (or "Sears Subcommittee"). On Sears specifically, the two organizations worked closely and divided up the work; Chicago NOW members leafleted at the Sears Tower and WE members focused on Sears retail stores. They also maintained ties to other organizations focused on working women's issues and discrimination; for example, throughout the early 1970s, Chicago NOW held its board meetings at the Loop YWCA.[70]

More than many of her colleagues, Collins' brand of feminism focused on women's employment and issues of class, and she worked hard to make NOW's membership reflect this objective. In a 1974 interview, she noted, "we have attracted and begun to meet the needs of many new groups of women, including nurses, older women, secretaries and clerical workers, and blue collar workers" and pledged that "next year's membership rolls . . . [will] carry hundreds more names of blue collar workers." She viewed most feminist issues through the lens of economic concerns. For example, she pointed to "the new minimum wage bill cover[ing] household workers for the first time" as a success.[71] Collins argued that pay issues were "crucial . . . for women, because seven million women in this country are the sole support-ers of their families, either children, dependent parents, or another person besides themselves." She also echoed the concerns of labor feminists, such as maternity leave and child care: "Men and women should not be burdened or punished because they choose to have children, so you can expect to hear more about paid maternity and paternity leave." She further asserted, "the community must also develop good child care centers to help take the burden off individual parents, and . . . provide an enriched educational system for the children."[72]

When asked to state NOW's top priorities, however, Collins wavered be-tween employment and other issues. In a 1973 newspaper interview, she cited passage of the ERA and abortion as NOW's top priorities.[73] In a 1974 position article discussing her run for NOW's presidency, she argued, "our major pri-ority at the [Houston] convention will be passage of the Equal Rights Amend-ment (ERA)," probably in large part because her home state of Illinois still needed to ratify it. However, another "overriding concern" was economics: "We need to move faster on those jobs which have typically been considered 'women's work,' . . . such as clerical workers, secretaries, bank tellers, nurses, and social workers. Why aren't these women being paid the salaries they're entitled to? Why is it that a male nurse or a male secretary receives more than his female counterpart?" She wanted to address the needs of "new constitu-encies" such as older women, blue-collar workers, and minority women by working on employment, child care, education, and credit issues.[74]

One main project was to work with female steelworkers in Gary, Indiana, "so they could make their charges of unequal treatment stick against U.S. Steel." The EEOC and other federal agencies negotiated with the steel industry and the United Steelworkers of America (American Federation of Labor and Congress of Industrial Organizations) on an industrywide settlement in the style of *AT&T.* Chicago NOW worked on a grassroots counterpart to the fed-eral investigation and negotiations. It held a public hearing with government compliance agencies in Gary in December 1973, "at which women members of the Steelworkers Union testified on problems of sex discrimination . . . in the U.S. Steel Mills." The April 1974 *Compliance Newsletter* reported that the meeting was very successful and resulted in formation of a women's group within the union and that Chicago NOW had filed a charge with the EEOC on behalf of women steelworkers in Gary. Although the Justice Department and EEOC assured NOW that women would be included in the industrywide settlement, NOW was taking "appropriate steps to see that women's rights are protected should the agreement prove inadequate in any way."[75] Despite spending "hundreds of hours [in 1973] providing know-how to women in the mills of Gary," Collins acknowledged in 1974 that efforts to form a Steelworkers NOW faced significant obstacles.[76] One colleague wrote, "the future of Steelworkers NOW, . . . does not look promising—for both interpersonal and union/political reasons." However,

> You may be interested to know that you, Dorothy [Haener?], and some of the other members of Chicago NOW made a significant impact on [one woman, who] . . . seems to be determined to move ahead to a larger framework. By chance, last week, she met some women who had been involved in a small NOW chapter in Highland . . . , Indiana. She plans to work with them on a broad range of issues—both work-related and community, and to help broaden the base of that chapter. So, even if there is no Steelworkers NOW, all has by no means been lost.[77]

In May 1974, the EEOC, Department of Justice, and Department of Labor signed an industrywide agreement with the major steel companies and union. NOW asked the court to "modify the agreement to provide adequate protection of the rights of women" by awarding back pay and affirmative action promotions. The court refused, and NOW appealed to the Fifth Circuit Court of Appeals, arguing the agreement failed "to address the historic and pervasive discrimination which has deprived women of opportunities in the steel industry."[78]

With varying levels of success then, NOW and WE also tried to maintain a connection to union women and the labor movement. NOW had a mixed relationship with the labor movement. On the one hand, it created some enemies with its willingness to attack unions as well as corporations that discriminated against women. However, difficult economic times and resulting hardships for working women led to an awareness that union women and their organizations played a crucial role in preventing employers from laying off large numbers of women and in negotiating for better working conditions. On one memo discussing an August 1970 FCC order requiring common carriers to develop affirmative action hiring programs, a member of NOW's federal compliance committee wrote in by hand, "*Important:* Also attempt to get the support of the union, if there is one involved!"[79] NOW had a labor union task force that held well-attended workshops at its national conferences.[80] In early 1974, Dorothy Haener, who had rejoined NOW, wrote to Collins about setting up a national task force on women in poverty. She could not handle all of the requests for information and said, "it seems to me that under the crisis and serious unemployment that now exists, we are almost compelled to do something."[81] The two corresponded about related issues, with Collins noting, "it looks like we'll get the minimum wage through Congress again, if we can only pressure Nixon into signing it."[82]

Moreover, just as union women had been instrumental in founding NOW, NOW members encouraged the growth of CLUW. Because labor women often did not know what women in other unions were doing, organizations such as NOW provided one way for women from different unions to get to know each other, which aided organizing across union lines that was necessary for CLUW to emerge.[83] Collins herself maintained close ties with union allies, including encouraging the growth of CLUW in 1974. She wrote to Haener in March of that year: "It really looks like the coalition of Labor Union Women is going to draw a tremendous crowd. It is like a dream come true. I hope good things come from it."[84] After the CLUW convention, Marjorie Stern, the leader of the American Federation of Teachers caucus, credited NOW with helping to create a favorable atmosphere for CLUW: "We certainly did have over 1,000 women at the CLUW meeting! *No* one expected 3,300! What a fantastic success. . . . We may take some of the program prerogatives from NOW, but without the atmosphere in American society that NOW has created we surely wouldn't be an organization at all."[85] Collins responded, "CLUW was a wonderful success—I look forward to working on common goals. See you in Houston."[86] Collins also maintained union ties through the Midwest Academy. In 1975, she served on its board with Day Piercy, staff director of WE; Henry Scheff, research director for Citizens Action Program; and labor activists Paul Booth, international representative for American Federation of State, County, and Municipal Employees (AFSCME), and Liz McPike, coordinator for AFSCME Illinois.[87]

As for WE, some of its members were union women, and the organization saw unions as potential allies and interacted with them frequently early on. However, WE wanted to maintain its independent agenda and not become simply a feeder organization that organized women and turned them over to unions as members. Some working women's groups did affiliate with unions, most notably 9 to 5 in Boston, which formed Local 925 of the Service Employees International Union in 1981.[88]

The interest of working women's groups in developing coalitions around class issues extended to their campaign against Sears, which, they argued, was the largest general retailer in the United States and thus responsible for the poverty-level wages earned by the average female salesclerk. In August 1974, Chicago NOW pressed the U.S. Commission on Civil Rights to hold public hearings on women in poverty, focusing specifically on Sears "as the largest employer of clerical workers in the city of Chicago." Ladky testified on "the overall employment practices of Sears and the implications of Sears' strategies to avoid compliance with EEOC laws," and female workers testified about "low pay, lack of promotional opportunities and discriminatory hiring practices"—all countering Sears' claims that it was a model of equal employment opportunity. The hearings "received national media attention," helping to "make Sears' practices known to women throughout the country as well as to interested organizations," and the Sears Subcommittee subsequently made contact with other organizations with complaints against Sears with whom it hoped "to be working . . . over the coming months."[89]

Chicago NOW also worked to merge race with class and gender issues. The Sears Subcommittee planned to work with the Indiana Black Caucus, which voted to boycott Sears for moving its fifty-year-old store in central Gary, Indiana, to a suburban shopping center inaccessible by public transportation, which affected black women most. Sears ignored an August 1974 petition with 10,000 signatures and a September march led by Gary mayor Richard G. Hatcher protesting the anticipated loss in city revenue and made plans to close other inner-city stores such as its Mission District store in San Francisco. One Gary councilman declared, "we, the black community, built you up and now it's time for the black community to break you down." Ladky arranged to meet with a group from Gary and plans were made to bring the protest to the National Black Caucus, which "expressed interest in working with NOW to expose this policy."[90] In a lengthy memo to NOW leaders, Collins and Ladky noted that a nonprofit retail industry study found that minorities "continue to hold the dirtiest, lowest-paid, least-skilled jobs" and that the retail industry, particularly major chains, lag "behind all employers in hiring minorities," in part because of their location in suburban shopping centers away from large urban minority populations.[91]

Another potential coalition partner in the fight against Sears was the Asian League for Equality. In August 1974, leaders of the Asian League, the Japanese American Citizens League, and the Filipino American Council met with Sears executives such as Ray Graham, who directed Sears's equal employment opportunity efforts, about "problems of recruitment and promotion of Asian personnel at Sears." Between 1969 and 1973, the percentage of Asians employed by Sears dropped from .6 percent to .5 percent, despite increases for all other minority groups. Graham argued that the total number of Asians employed increased from 836 to 2,027 during that period, and then he alienated the Asian American leaders by claiming that Sears did not need a specific affirmative action plan for Asians because they comprised less than 2 percent of the U.S. population. The groups were eager to take action by increasing recruitment, sending a press release to Asian newspapers, and contacting legislative representatives about the meeting.[92] In September, Ladky wrote to a task force leader about "lots of coalition possibilities opening up" and mentioned that the Asian League was setting up a meeting for them with Asian women employed at Sears.[93] In return, the Sears Subcommittee helped the Asian League collect information for filing charges of discrimination.[94]

In a November 1974 memo, Collins and Ladky updated NOW chapter presidents, national and Sears Subcommittee leaders, and board members about groups they were "working with . . . on the possibility of coalition action" against Sears. A senior citizens' group, the Senior Skills Foundation, was angry about Sears' mandatory retirement policy and its refusal to hire people over sixty-five for part-time work needed to "supplement inadequate Social Security benefits." The National Consumers League focused on "product safety, widespread 'bait and switch' tactics practiced by Sears, and Sears' intensive lobbying against legislation to create a national Consumer Protection Agency."[95] While gathering evidence about Sears' employment practices, Atlanta NOW's Special Sears Committee used the YWCA, which worked on race and sex discrimination issues, as the drop-off point for their "spy" to bring data.[96]

Aside from coalitions across class, race, and ethnic lines, the women's groups in Chicago formed bonds with activists on other causes and working women's organizations across the country. One source of these coalitions was the Midwest Academy's training programs, which brought together a diverse group of students in each "class," enabling them to make connections across class, racial, and regional lines that might endure beyond the two-week training period. The academy published an alumni newsletter with updates on its students and asked them to contact former classmates to help in fundraising.[97]

Chicago NOW members were a regular fixture in Midwest Academy training sessions, including Sears committee chair, Agnes Kelley; legislative committee chair, Ryan Leary, who worked on a new ERA strategy; and Libby Tessner and Portia Morrison, who coordinated a Women's Equality Day advertising book campaign to raise money for the Women for Jobs and Justice program. Collins and Ladky attended the summer 1973 class, and by summer 1975, reported back on coordinating NOW's national campaign against Sears.

WE students included Day Piercy and Jackie Ruff, who left WE in September 1975 after a year and a half of organizing "to join the staff of 9 to 5 [in Boston] to work on its organizing drive."[98] Ann London Scott, NOW's legal vice-president from 1971 to 1975 and a Midwest Academy alumna, left a career in academia to become a lobbyist and consultant to the secretary of labor on prohibiting race discrimination by federal contractors, organized many NOW chapters, led ERA ratification efforts, and monitored EEOC enforcement until her untimely death from cancer in 1975.[99] Other Midwest Academy graduates contributed to the women's movement. Morag Fullilove proposed sending a woman's lobbyist to the Illinois legislature. Kit Duffy, who joined the Loop YWCA board as chair of Chicago Women Against Rape Task Force, worked for state legislation to ensure better reporting and treatment of rape victims. In 1975, Mary Ann Lupa, NOW's Illinois state legislative coordinator, worked on mobilization efforts for states needed to ratify the ERA.[100]

These women's activists made connections at the Midwest Academy that likely continued beyond their two-week training period. Male and female alumni from the 1973–75 classes went on to a broad range of community organizing, from the environment—a canvassing director for Citizens for a Better Environment—to civil rights—working in Claiborne County, Mississippi, to elect more black county officials. Academy alumni ran community programs in Boston; Illinois; North Carolina; and Madison, Wisconsin, to protest excessive utility rate increases. Joe Moskal campaigned for a Chicago City Council zoning ordinance in May 1975 to restrict building of high-rises on Chicago's lakefront and then moved on to organize for housing compliance and form tenants organizations in the existing high-rises. Peter Wood promoted a lifeline program for every family to get a fixed amount of electricity at a rate they could afford and pushed for broad rate restructuring.[101] In the area of labor organizing and workers' rights, one alumnus directed the Springfield office of AFSCME Illinois, whose "next step" was to organize 10,000–16,000 clerical workers throughout the state, and another organized cotton mill workers in Columbia, South Carolina, in the Brown Lung Association and targeted the state legislature for workers' compensation and the Occupational Safety and Health Administration for better health standards and enforcement in the textile mills.[102] Buddy Robinson worked with Wisconsin Welfare Rights Organization in Madison, Wisconsin, "targeting state welfare bureaucracies for proposing welfare cuts when the cost of basic needs has sharply risen." The group used "a mass rally and concerted pressure" to prevent a welfare cutback "that was otherwise assured." He also lobbied the legislature for a tenant's bill of rights and against utility companies that shut off service to welfare families unable to meet rising fuel costs. Joan White and Amy Parks, who were charged with welfare fraud by the West Virginia Welfare Department for allegedly political reasons, were long-time activists in the Welfare Rights Organization. Parks was found not guilty and the charges against White were dropped after "300 black and white supporters rallied in Fairmont, West Virginia" the night before the trials began.[103] Thus, the connections students made, though often focused on labor organizing, crossed racial, class, regional, and community lines.

By 1975, the Midwest Academy appeared to be focused on the women's movement and labor organizing. Among its key fights, the academy listed "the birth and growth" of CLUW and "the experimentation with the Women Employed model of mass work for women's rights."[104] Heather Booth explained, "we have worked with several rank and file labor efforts, and plan to expand activity supporting organizing and program to meet the current economic crisis."[105]

Collins and Ladky also attended the summer 1973 class with Ellen Cassedy, staff director of 9 to 5 in Boston, which advocated on behalf of working women in clerical jobs, and Cassedy spent two months working with WE in Chicago.[106] Back in Boston, 9 to 5 supported NOW's case against Sears when, several years into the investigation, Sears filed its own lawsuit against the federal government in an attempt to preempt the EEOC's lawsuit against it. Boston's 9 to 5 organized a protest in front of the Sears store in Cambridge, Massachusetts, where members distributed flyers and collected signatures for a petition urging Sears to drop its suit against the government agencies, "cooperate with the [EEOC] and settle the outstanding complaint," pay $20 million in back wages, and "adopt an affirmative action program."[107] Different organizations cooperated with and discussed strategies with each other, and local branches coordinated with the national organizations. Cassedy even wrote to NOW's Action Center in Washington, D.C., for guidance, proposing simultaneous demonstrations at Sears stores in several cities. Although they hoped to draw attention to Sears' opposition to affirmative action, thereby increasing the cost of its lawsuit and discouraging other employers from bringing similar ones, Cassedy was concerned that doing so might give the company "a platform they otherwise wouldn't have."[108]

Also in Boston, the YWCA, though not directly involved in the campaign against Sears, made its own pragmatic efforts to change the company's workplace policies by organizing job training programs for low-income women in nontraditional jobs such as auto repair. Sears donated the equipment and an instructor, with the intent that graduates would be qualified for higher-paying jobs in traditionally male occupations, at Sears or elsewhere.[109] Although planned through local Sears facilities, YWCA Executive Director Juliet Brudney clearly looked to national issues, even maintaining contact with former Sears CEO and philanthropist Julius Rosenwald's son and daughter-in-law, with whom she discussed the workshops when she "ran into" them on Martha's Vineyard during the summer of 1977.[110]

Despite the current historical narrative that says NOW was divided ideologically between East Coast and other chapters, Chicago NOW and WE worked closely with other working women's groups from around the country. NOW leaders also recognized that in pursuing a company such as Sears, the strength of their national action depended on the participation of chapters around the country. Only with grassroots support and local action could they apply the kind of public attention that had helped force AT&T to settle with the EEOC. The compliance task force took the lead by updating chapters and making suggestions for future actions, but acknowledged candidly in its June 1973 newsletter, "NOW's strength is all of your local actions."[111]

## Conclusion

The media attention surrounding the *Sears* case around the time of the trial in the mid-1980s gives the mistaken impression that the case developed on its own, the result of a few individual women suing the company for discrimination. By reconnecting the case to historical events, we see that it was actually the end of broader efforts by a grassroots coalition to campaign for economic rights for women, including direct action to force numerous industries to change their practices, and major successes against some of the largest employers of the day, such as AT&T. Having established a model and networks across class and regional lines, working women's groups eventually turned to Sears, though ultimately with less success.

The cross-class coalitions and NOW's and WE's efforts to build connections with African American and Asian American groups focused on economic equity challenge the notion that NOW was out of touch with the needs of working women and the larger grassroots women's liberation movement. To be sure, NOW's attitude at times reflected the self-centeredness, or lack of coalition mentality, that its critics attacked. A February 1973 compliance task force report suggested that in exchange for referring people to their "sisters" at Womanpower Consultants for consulting on model affirmative action plans, the organization might ask for a percentage of the fee, and questioned whether they should "only refer companies to consulting services run by NOW members."[112] Regardless, the presence of working women's groups in Chicago indicates that it is too simplistic to argue that all regions and members of NOW ignored the needs of working-class women.

It is not clear that the coalitions were strong enough to sustain a commitment to long-term litigation against Sears, and in fact, although it tried to cooperate with other organizations interested in Sears, NOW largely pursued the company on its own during the mid-1970s. Eventually even NOW dropped out of the case when other priorities and internal divisions competed for its attention and resources. This decreasing attention to cross-class coalitions over time limited the effectiveness of early campaigns to upgrade women's jobs at Sears and elsewhere, and may help explain why women's groups were ultimately less successful against Sears than other corporations. What is certain, however, is that cooperation and concerted organizing were present early on in a case that came to be known within the feminist community only for its divisiveness. Recovering the work of these women's groups in the *Sears* case highlights a widespread and varied effort to improve the workplace for women and a history we can draw upon in contemporary feminist-labor alliances.

## Notes

1. See Jon Wiener, "Women's History on Trial," *Nation,* September 7, 1985, 161, 176–80; Samuel G. Freedman, "Of History and Politics: Bitter Feminist Debate," *New York Times,* June 6, 1986, 1, 4; Jonathan Yardley, "When Scholarship and the Cause Collide," *Washington Post,* June 16, 1986, C2; John Leo, "Are Women 'Male Clones'?," *Time,* August 18, 1986, 63–64.

2. See, e.g., Alice Kessler-Harris, "Use of History Was on Trial in Sears Sex-Bias Case," *New York Times,* June 28, 1986, 26; Barbara Harris and Susan Sacks, cochairs for the Women and Society Executive Committee, Columbia University, to members, December 2, 1985, the Women's Center Library, Barnard College, New York, N.Y.; Ruth Milkman, "Women's History and the Sears Case," *Feminist Studies* 12, no. 2 (1986): 375–400; Sandi E. Cooper, "Women's Work on Trial," *New Directions for Women* 14, no. 6 (November/December 1985): 1; Carol Sternhell, "Life in the Mainstream: What Happens when Feminists Turn up on Both Sides of the Courtroom?" *Ms.,* July 1986, 48; Rosalind Rosenberg, "Scholarship vs. Politics: A Feminist Battleground, "*Barnard Alumnae* (Fall 1986): 9; and Jacquelyn Dowd Hall, preface, "Women's History Goes to Trial: *EEOC v. Sears, Roebuck and Company,*" *Signs* 11, no. 4 (Summer 1986): 751.

3. See, e.g., Joan Wallach Scott, "The Sears Case," in *Gender and the Politics of History* (New York: Columbia University Press, 1999); Joan C. Williams, "Deconstructing Gender," *Michigan Law Review* 87 (1989): 797.

4. See, e.g., Nancy MacLean, *Freedom is Not Enough: The Opening of the American Workplace* (New York: Russell Sage Foundation and Cambridge, Mass.: Harvard University Press, 2006), 138–39 (in the context of organizing by women's groups and founding of new groups such as WE; women's advocacy groups and workplace caucuses; and change in nonunion workplaces); Sara M. Evans, *Tidal Wave: How Women Changed America at Century's End* (New York: Free Press, 2003), 87; Lois Kathryn Herr, *Women, Power, and*

*AT&T: Winning Rights in the Workplace* (Boston: Northeastern University Press, 2003), 49, 88.

5. For more on specific organizing efforts and the entire thirteen-year case against Sears, see Emily Zuckerman, "Beyond Dispute: *EEOC v. Sears* and the Politics of Gender, Class, and Affirmative Action, 1968–1986" (PhD diss., Rutgers, in progress).

6. Wisconsin Women's Network and Wisconsin Women's Council, "25 Years: Looking Back, Moving Forward," tribute to Kay Clarenbach, October 20, 1985, The Schlesinger Library (hereafter Schlesinger), Radcliffe College, Cambridge, Mass., papers of Gerda Lerner, MC 498, box 3, folder 1.

7. Muriel Fox, interview with Mary Eastwood, March 7, 1992, pp. 48, 92–93, Schlesinger, Tully-Crenshaw Feminist Oral History Project, Hollis no. 008700348; see also Dorothy Sue Cobble, *The Other Women's Movement: Workplace Justice and Social Rights in Modern America* (Princeton, N.J.: Princeton University Press, 2004), 185.

8. Wilma Scott Heide to Anne Ladky, president of Chicago NOW, June 6, 1974, Schlesinger, papers of NOW, MC 493, box 52, folder 18.

9. Anne Ladky, telephone interview by author, March 20, 2002.

10. Suzanne Stocking, ed., *NOW Compliance Newsletter,* no. 10 (September 1973): 1, 3, University of Illinois-Chicago (hereafter UIC), papers of NOW Chicago, accession 78-34, box 2, folder 8.

11. Mary Jean Collins-Robson, resume, n.d., UIC, NOW Chicago, accession 81-18, box 41, folder 338; Mary J. Nowlen, "NOW Board member talks about role of women," *Herald,* August 22, 1973, UIC, NOW Chicago, accession 78–034, box 6, folder 7; Carol Kleiman, "Executive Wins in Man's World," *Chicago Tribune,* May 22, 1969, UIC, NOW Chicago, accession 78–034, box 2, folder 11; Phyllis Stevenson, "The woman from NOW: 'I was not in the constitution at all,'" *Herald,* March 21, 1973, 1, UIC, NOW Chicago, accession 78-034, box 6, folder 7.

12. Nowlen, "NOW Board member talks about role of women."

13. Stevenson, "The woman from NOW."

14. Kleiman, "Executive Wins in Man's World."

15. Nowlen, "NOW Board member talks about role of women"; Mary Jean Collins-Robson, personal biography, n.d., UIC, NOW Chicago, accession 78-034, box 7, folder 5; Collins-Robson, resume; Stevenson, "The woman from NOW."

16. Nowlen, "NOW Board member talks about role of women."

17. Nowlen, "NOW Board member talks about role of women"; Stevenson, "The woman from NOW"; Kleiman, "Executive Wins in Man's World"; Collins-Robson, resume.

18. Nowlen, "NOW Board member talks about role of women"; Mary Jean Collins, interview by author, November 14, 2003, Washington, D.C. For more background on Conroy, see Cobble, *The Other Women's Movement.*

19. Interview with Mary Jean Collins, November 14, 2003.

20. Stevenson, "The woman from NOW"; Collins-Robson, personal biography; Mary Jaspers, "Local Feminist Running for National NOW President," *Herald,* May 22, 1974, UIC, NOW Chicago, accession 78-034, box 6, folder 7; Collins-Robson, resume; Nowlen, "NOW Board member talks about role of women."

21. Heather Booth to "Friend" (sent to J. Lightfoot), Chicago, n.d. [mid-1975], p. 1, Schlesinger, papers of NOW Officers, Lightfoot, MC 485, box 7, folder 20.

22. See, e.g., Doug McAdam, *Freedom Summer* (New York: Oxford University Press, 1988), 127, 131–32; Sara Evans, *Personal Politics: The Roots of Women's Liberation in the Civil Rights Movement and the New Left,* 1st ed. (New York: Knopf, distributed by Random House, 1979), 64.

23. See, e.g., Kirkpatrick Sale, *SDS* (New York: Random House, 1973); James Miller, *"Democracy Is in The Streets": From Port Huron to the Siege of Chicago* (New York: Simon and Schuster, 1987), chap. 11.

24. Evans, *Personal Politics,* 207; McAdam, *Freedom Summer,* 180, 182.

25. Evans, *Personal Politics,* 207; Evans, *Tidal Wave,* 9, 85; Alice Echols, *Daring to Be Bad: Radical Feminism in America 1967–1975* (Minneapolis: University of Minnesota Press, 1989), 65–66, 72.

26. Booth to "Friend," 1.

27. Ibid.

28. Heather Booth to Judy Lightfoot, March 17, 1975, pp. 1–2, Schlesinger, NOW Officers, Lightfoot, MC 485, box 7, folder 20.

29. Hereafter referred to as Day Piercy.

30. See, e.g., Booth to Lightfoot, 3.

31. Barbara Kuzniar, "A Victory," *FQrum,* July 1974, National Organization for Women, Genesee Valley Chapter, UIC, NOW Chicago, accession 78-034, box 7, folder 5.

32. Karen Hasman, "Women here mark 54th year of vote, *Chicago Daily News,* August 26, 1974, 8, Schlesinger, NOW, MC 496, box 44, folder 19.

33. Suzanne Stocking, ed., "Women Begin to Test Their Strength against Steel," *NOW Compliance Newsletter,* no. 12 (April 1974), UIC, NOW Chicago, accession 78-034, box 2, folder 2.

34. Suzanne Stocking, ed., "NOW Conference Resolutions," *NOW Compliance Newsletter,* no. 12 (April 1974): 4.

35. Heide to Ladky, 1.

36. AP, "Suffrage Anniversary: Women Observe 'Equality Day,'" *Chicago Tribune,* August 27, 1974, sec. 1, p. 2, Schlesinger, NOW, MC 496, box 44, folder 19.

37. Evans, *Tidal Wave,* 85–86; McAdam, *Freedom Summer,* 204.

38. Anne Ladky, interview by author, March 12, 2003, Chicago, Ill.

39. Evans, *Tidal Wave,* 87.

40. Evans, *Tidal Wave,* 87; interview with Anne Ladky, March 12, 2003, Chicago.

41. As Sara Evans states, "The liberal desire to battle discrimination in the legal arena, the radical feminist insistence on awakening a female 'class consciousness,' and the socialist-feminist attraction to community organizing-all 'worked,' and each reshaped the other. NOW task forces on working women, for example, by the early seventies found ready allies among women in emerging socialist-feminist groups interested in organizing clerical workers." (Evans, *Tidal Wave,* 45.)

42. Interview with Ladky, March 12, 2003; Evans, *Tidal Wave,* 45n78.

43. Telephone interview with Ladky, March 20, 2002.

44. Evans, *Tidal Wave,* 91; interview with Ladky, March 12, 2003. Ladky is now executive director of WE.

45. Interview with Ladky, March 12, 2003.

46. Ibid.

47. Stocking, *NOW Compliance Newsletter,* no. 10, 2.

48. Ibid., 1.

49. Ibid., 2.

50. Suzanne Stocking, ed., "Special Compliance Projects," *NOW Compliance Newsletter,* no. 12 (April 1974): 2.

51. Stocking, *NOW Compliance Newsletter,* no. 10, 5.

52. Evans, *Tidal Wave,* 87.

53. Women Employed membership card, 1974, UIC, WE, accession 2000-16, box 16, folder: Membership—1974; Betsy Clarke, staff member, Women Employed to unknown (left blank), [undated unsigned draft letter], UIC, WE, accession 2000-16, box 16, folder: Membership—1974.

54. Darlene Stille, Women Employed chairwoman, to Friend of Women Employed, February 15, 1974, UIC, WE, accession 2000-16, box 16, folder: Membership—1974.

55. Suzanne Stocking, ed., *NOW Compliance Newsletter,* no. 11 (December 1973), UIC, NOW Chicago, accession 78-034, box 3, folder 1.

56. Stocking, "Bank Kit Available," *NOW Compliance Newsletter,* no. 12 (April 1974): 5.

57. Ann Scott, vice-president, legislation, "Statement of the National Organization for Women on the Appointment of John Powell as Chairone of the Equal Employment Opportunity Commission," NOW Legislative Office, December 12, 1973, p. 1, UIC, NOW Chicago, accession 78-034, box 3, folder 1; MacLean, *Freedom is Not Enough,* 153 (noting the coalitions surrounding the AT&T campaign: "Black and Latino groups denounced the discrimination affecting women, many of them white, as NOW denounced the discrimination affecting 'Blacks and Spanish Americans'"). On the *AT&T* case generally, see Herr, *Women, Power, and AT&T;* Marjorie A. Stockford, *The Bellwomen: The Story of the Landmark AT&T Sex Discrimination Case* (New Brunswick, N.J.: Rutgers University Press, 2004).

58. Mary Lynn Myers, "Report to the National Board of Directors of NOW," February 1972, p. 1, UIC, NOW Chicago, accession 78-34, box 2, folder 8.

59. *NOW Compliance and Enforcement Task Force Newsletter,* no. 9 (June 1973): 4, UIC, NOW Chicago, accession 78-34, box 2, folder 8.

60. Atlanta NOW[?], "What is N.O.W.?," Schlesinger, NOW, MC 496, box 209, folder 67.

61. Scott, "Statement of the National Organization for Women," 1.

62. Lynne Darcy, "AT&T (Or When Will the Phone Stop Ringing?)," *NOW Compliance Newsletter,* no. 14 (November 1974): 5, UIC, NOW Chicago[?], accession 78-034, box 3, folder 1.

63. David Copus, "How Women Can Take Advantage of the AT&T Settlement," Sixth National NOW Conference, Washington, D.C., February 17, 1973, pp. 13–14, Schlesinger, papers of Rosalind Rosenberg, box 2, folder 76.

64. "NOW Says Sears Shortchanges Women," 1974, p. 2, Schlesinger, NOW, MC 496, box 44, folder 18.

65. *NOW Compliance and Enforcement Task Force Newsletter,* no. 9 (June 1973): 2.

66. Stockford, *The Bellwomen,* 14–15, 28.

67. MacLean, *Freedom is Not Enough,* 131–32.

68. Stockford, *The Bellwomen,* 84–85.

69. MacLean, *Freedom is Not Enough,* sec. 1; Cobble, *The Other Women's Movement,* chap. 1. On black women coming to dominate operator positions in the Bell System, see Venus Green, *Race on the Line: Gender, Labor, and Technology in the Bell System, 1880–1980* (Durham, N.C.: Duke University Press, 2001).

70. NOW Chicago, board agenda, June 5, 1974, UIC, NOW Chicago, accession 81-18, box 15, folder 126; Mary Jean Collins and Anne Ladky to NOW Chapter Presidents, Sears Subcommittee, Board of Directors, and Task Force Coordinators, memorandum, November 9, 1974, p. 3, Schlesinger, NOW, MC 496, box 44, folder 18.

71. Colleen Dishon, "Largest feminist group: N.O.W. has outlived lib jokes," *Family today—Chicago today,* May 30, 1974, p. 18, UIC, NOW Chicago, accession 78-034, box 6, folder 7.

72. Stevenson, "The woman from NOW."

73. Nowlen, "NOW Board member talks about role of women."

74. Jaspers, "Local feminist running for national NOW president."

75. Stocking, "Women Begin to Test Their Strength against Steel," 1.

76. Dishon, "Largest feminist group," 18.

77. Nancy Seifer to Mary Jean Collins, New York, N.Y., September 4, 1974, UIC, NOW Chicago, accession 78-034, box 7, folder 4.

78. Darcy, "Steel [Or is it Steal]," *NOW Compliance Newsletter,* no. 14 (November 1974): 5.

79. Lucy Komisar, National Organization for Women, Federal Compliance Committee, "The N.O.W. Phone Company Anti-Discrimination Affirmative Action Kit," p. 4, UIC, NOW Chicago, accession 78-34, box 2, folder 8.

80. See, e.g., Marjorie Stern to Mary Jean Collins-Robson, April 14, 1974, UIC, NOW Chicago, accession 78-034, box 7, folder 4.

81. Dorothy Haener to Mary Jean Robson, cc: W. Heide, A. Hernandez, March 22, 1974, UIC, NOW Chicago, accession 78-034, box 15, folder 7.

82. Mary Jean Collins to Dorothy Haener, March 20, 1974, UIC, NOW Chicago, accession 78-34, box 2, folder 2.

83. Evans, *Tidal Wave,* 89.

84. Collins to Haener, March 20, 1974.

85. Stern to Collins-Robson, April 14, 1974.

86. Handwritten note from Mary Jean Collins to Marge Stern, n.d. [ca. 1974?], UIC, NOW Chicago, accession 78-034, box 7, folder 4.

87. Booth to "Friend," 3.

88. Interview with Ladky, March 12, 2003; Evans, *Tidal Wave,* 89.

89. Darcy, "Sears Subcommittee Coalition Activities," *NOW Compliance Newsletter,* no. 14 (November 1974): 9.

90. "Hatcher Leads Protest against Move by Sears," *Chicago Sun-Times,* September 8, 1974, 104, Schlesinger, NOW, MC 496, box 44, folder 19; Mary Jean Collins-Robson and Anne Ladky, *Sears Action Bulletin,* no. 4 (October 1974): 2, Schlesinger, NOW, MC 496, box 209, folder 66; Memorandum from Collins and Ladky, 2; Aileen C. Hernandez to Ray Graham, November 20, 1974, in possession of Rebecca Davison.

91. Memorandum from Collins and Ladky, 2.

92. Memorandum from Hiroshi Kanno to members, September 5, 1974, Schlesinger, NOW, MC 496, box 44, folder 19; Memorandum from Collins and Ladky, 2.

93. Memorandum from Anne Ladky to Lynne Darcy, September 12, 1974, p. 1, Schlesinger, NOW, MC 496, box 44, folder 19.

94. Memorandum from Collins and Ladky, 2.

95. Memorandum from Collins and Ladky, 2–3.

96. Memorandum from Judith Lightfoot to Sears Sub/Compliance re: "Thisa and Thata on the State of Affairs in Southeastern Territory," October 3, 1974, Schlesinger, Lightfoot, MC 485, box 3, folder 12.

97. Booth to Lightfoot, 4; Barb Jonesi, "Alumni Association Report," Midwest Academy, Summer 1975, p. 1, Schlesinger, NOW Officers, Lightfoot, MC 485, box 7, folder 20.

98. Jonesi, "Alumni Association Report," 3–5.

99. Ibid.

100. Ibid., 4, 6.

101. Ibid., 3–6.

102. Ibid., 3, 5.

103. Ibid., 3–4.

104. Booth to Lightfoot, 1.

105. Ibid., 2–3.

106. Evans, *Tidal Wave*, 86.

107. 9 to 5 Organization for Women Office Workers, "Equal Employment at Sears?: The Real Story Behind the Sears Law Suit," 1979, Schlesinger, papers of 9 to 5, Organization for Women Office Workers (hereafter papers of 9 to 5); Judith McCullough to Captain Cosack, Cambridge Police, March 28, 1979, Schlesinger, papers of 9 to 5; Conrad C. Fagone, Commissioner, City of Cambridge Public Works Department, to Judy McCullough, April 6, 1979, Schlesinger, papers of 9 to 5; 9 to 5 Organization for Women Office Workers, "9 to 5 Organization for Women Office Workers, Petition to Sears," Schlesinger, papers of 9 to 5.

108. Ellen Cassedy, staff director, 9 to 5, to Arlie Scott, NOW Action Center, March 16, 1979, Schlesinger, papers of 9 to 5.

109. See, e.g., Juliet F. Brudney, executive director, Boston YWCA to Charles Worcester, attaching first draft of the "How To Manual," December 23, 1976, Schlesinger, Boston (YWCA) Young Women's Christian Association Records, 1858–1988, 89–M3 (hereafter YWCA records).

110. Chamberlain to Worcester, September 20, 1977, Schlesinger, YWCA records; Juliet Brudney to Mrs. Julius Rosenwald (Dear Judy), September 26, 1977, Schlesinger, YWCA records; "Family Tree, 1963," Papers of Julius Rosenwald, 1905–1963, University of Chicago Library, Special Collections Research Center, Box 61, Folder 14.

111. *NOW Compliance and Enforcement Task Force Newsletter*, no. 9 (June 1973): 5.

112. Myers, "Report to the National Board of Directors of NOW," February 1972, p. 2.

## 12. Demanding a New Family Wage

*Feminist Consensus in the 1970s
Full Employment Campaign*

### MARISA CHAPPELL

> Given . . . the view that one of the reasons for the unpopularity and
> the subsequent demise of the social programs of the 1960s was the
> perception that their benefits were not universal . . . it would seem
> foolish to advocate anything short of a full employment policy
> at this time. A period of severe general unemployment is not an
> auspicious occasion to seek new initiatives in terms of special labor
> market programs for blacks—or for any particular . . . group.
>
> —Herrington J. Bryce, "Toward Full Employment: Minorities and
>    the Cities"

> Women are no small, special interest group with no claim to
> attention in this legislation. Rather we must be served, or the bill is
> a hollow farce serving the interests of a minority of white men.
>
> —Carol Burris, Women's Lobby, on the Full Employment and
>    Balanced Growth Act

As Congress debated federal full employment legislation in the mid-to-late
1970s, representatives of women's organizations repeatedly demanded attention to the special needs of women. Witnesses expressing this demand
spanned the gamut of 1970s women's progressive politics, from self-defined
feminist lobbyists to welfare rights groups to female labor union leaders
to so-called traditional women's organizations. The National Organization
for Women (NOW) insisted that "in order to achieve full employment and
equal opportunities, special measures will be necessary for . . . disadvantaged
groups," particularly women.[1] Rita Reynolds of the Young Women's Christian
Association (YWCA) warned that policies "must be designed particularly

for and around the gender-specific needs of women if they are to make a difference."[2] African American welfare recipient and Nevada community organizer Ruby Duncan reminded Congress that "so far all proposals for full employment have not included [poor single mothers].... Jobs should not be limited to unemployed men,"[3] while Women's Lobby's Carol Burris assured lawmakers, "If we do not do something special about [women's] problems in finding work, then the bill is really designed to serve a minority population: men who are unemployed for a short period of time."[4]

That women from predominantly African American welfare rights groups, liberal feminist lobbying outfits, and mainstay traditional women's organizations spoke with such unanimity is surprising, given prevailing interpretations of women's politics in the 1970s. In addition to sectarian squabbles and theoretical conflicts within the larger feminist movement, historians have focused on the racial and class differences that consistently bedeviled attempts at unity among those committed to gender equity. Historians interested in women's poverty and, in particular, in welfare rights organizing have focused even more attention on such divisions.[5] Yet here, speaking to Congress on one of the most important pieces of liberal legislation in the decade, women representing low-income workers, welfare recipients, women of color, and white middle-class feminists made virtually identical demands.

If such unanimity confounds expectations, the content of this testimony fits neatly within established accounts of 1970s politics. By demanding special attention to the needs of women, these witnesses seemingly practiced what many political commentators and historians have labeled *identity politics,* or what political theorist Nancy Fraser called the "politics of recognition." In what she admitted was a simplification, Fraser summarized the prevailing understanding of post-1960s American liberal politics:

> The "struggle for recognition" is fast becoming the paradigmatic form of political conflict in the late twentieth century. Demands for "recognition of difference" fuel struggles of groups mobilized under the banners of nationality, ethnicity, "race," gender, and sexuality. In these "post-socialist" conflicts, group identity supplants class interest as the chief medium of political mobilization. Cultural domination supplants exploitation as the fundamental injustice. And cultural recognition displaces socioeconomic redistribution as the remedy for injustice and the goal of political struggle.[6]

Fraser captured a key shift in American political struggles: the emergence in the late 1960s and early 1970s of a plethora of identity-based groups demanding recognition; the rise of multiculturalism; the creation of identity-based academic programs (women's studies, African American studies); and both voluntary and government mandated sex- and race-based affirmative action programs.

The shift toward a politics of recognition (identity politics) plays a central role in explanations of liberalism's eclipse in the last three decades of the twentieth century. Of course, historians have identified a wide range of social, economic, and political factors that caused the supposed "right turn" in American politics after the 1960s.[7] Some emphasize foreign policy, pointing to liberal Democrats' anti-Vietnam stance and subsequent attempts at détente with the Soviet Union as primary reasons that many former Democrats adopted a more conservative political stance. The politics of race is undoubtedly important, as well, as liberal civil rights commitments first alienated whites in the South and in working-class urban neighborhoods in the North and West. By the late 1960s, federal interventions aimed at overcoming deep-seated racial discrimination, from busing to achieve racially integrated schools, to fair housing laws, to affirmative action plans, threatened to violate what many middle- and working-class white Americans had come to see as their constitutional rights—a parent's right to send one's child to a neighborhood school, a homeowner's right to ensure his property's value, and a union member's right to control access to the skilled trades. The sexual revolution and loosening cultural standards also played an important part. Above all, economic transformation—America's declining global dominance, the increasing assertiveness of Arab oil-producing states, and the seeming collapse of the Keynesian bargain in which federal fiscal and monetary policies sustained high consumer demand and rising standards of living—prompted a reenergized business assault against organized labor and federal welfare state protections, left Americans less economically secure, and fueled a rejection of expansive federal programs. If anything is becoming clear from the recent spate of historical attention to the 1970s, it is that this was a profoundly complicated era, and that we are unlikely to locate a single reason for the collapse of the New Deal Democratic coalition.[8]

Despite the complexities, many critics, historians among them, continue to blame identity-based groups and claims for undermining what they insist is a more authentic, class-based politics. "Instead of moving to organize against rock-bottom class inequalities and racial discrimination," Todd Gitlin railed in a representative text, "many activists choose to fight real and imagined symbols of insult." Identity politics helped to "undermine the only basis for a politics of equality that might succeed on a national scale—a majoritarian spirit." The "squandering of energy on identity politics . . . is an American tragedy."[9] This analysis has become common wisdom; in many historical treatments of twentieth-century American politics, the late '60s and the

1970s represent the beginning of the end for a viable, broad-based political left: black nationalists and feminists get the lion's share of blame, along with politicians and policymakers who gave in to their demands.[10]

The political work of women's organizations during the full employment campaign forces a rethinking of prevailing views of both second-wave feminism and liberalism's fate. The full employment campaign—a major focus of mainstream liberals during the Ford and Carter administrations—epitomized the very politics liberals are accused of rejecting: class-based redistribution. Like class politics before it, though, from the development of workingman's parties in the antebellum period to the mass mobilizations of the Great Depression, this 1970s version rested on assumptions about work, gender, and family organization that privileged male breadwinners and promised little to women.[11] Feminists may have expected more by the late 1970s, but they were not unprepared to respond. From working-class women's union organizing; professional women's caucus building; and campaigns for affirmative action, comparable worth, and nontraditional jobs to welfare mothers' critiques of federal employment and income policies, two decades of feminist activism provided insights that progressive women applied to the full employment campaign.[12]

Of course, class and racial conflicts continued to plague this feminist coalition, as did disagreements over appropriate remedies for women's economic disadvantage. Working-class women often sought to improve the wages and conditions of traditionally female service sector jobs through comparable worth while, for example, some middle-class feminists battled a corporate glass ceiling and emphasized expanding women's opportunities to enter male-dominated professions. Class differences also prompted middle-class, professional women to press for child care, but working-class feminists often considered expanded parental leave an equally high priority. Meanwhile, welfare recipients continued to insist that, along with jobs and child care, poor women needed more generous income support to enable them to decide how best to care for their children. To poor, working-class, and nonwhite women, improving men's wages and job prospects seemed equally important, an issue middle-class, white feminists tended to ignore. These differences did not disappear in the 1970s, even as a broad feminist coalition mobilized on behalf of full employment. Nonetheless, the full-employment campaign does reveal some important points of consensus among feminists of all classes, and it highlights an important shift in the way liberals more broadly approached the problem of women's poverty.

Understanding from "extensive experience" that policymakers and administrators "tend to ignore the problems of women and minorities unless they are specifically directed to concern themselves with these problems," feminists from all classes demanded that policymakers recognize the special needs and peculiar disadvantages of woman workers.[13] Facing politics and policies that assumed women's economic dependence, they had little choice. The nature of liberal politics in the 1970s meant that, for women, recognition was the only route to redistribution—a strategy so obvious that it represented consensus among feminists across the class spectrum.

In June 1975, more than five hundred individuals representing 150 national organizations attended the nation's first annual Full Employment Conference.[14] Two years later, over one million Americans participated in a wide range of activities, from picnics and parades to teach-ins and vigils, to mark Full Employment Week and pressure Congress to pass full employment legislation.[15] Spearheading these efforts was the National Committee for Full Employment and its action arm, the Full Employment Action Council, a broad-based coalition cochaired by Murray H. Finlay, president of the Amalgamated Clothing and Textile Workers, and Coretta Scott King of the Martin Luther King Jr. Center for Social Change. The group's membership roster reads like a who's who of 1970s liberalism, including leaders of labor unions; civil rights organizations; and women's, civic, religious, and social welfare organizations.[16] The campaign for federal full employment legislation was the centerpiece of liberal activism in the 1970s.

The full employment campaign garnered such support because it represented class politics *par excellence*. To many on the left of the American political spectrum, full employment seemed, as a headline in the American Federation of Labor and Congress of Industrial Organizations' monthly magazine put it, "the key to all goals."[17] By requiring Congress and the president to orient fiscal, monetary, and social policy toward the ultimate goal of a full employment economy, defined in most proposals as a 3 percent unemployment rate, and by providing guaranteed public service jobs for any Americans who wanted paid employment but who could not find jobs in the private sector, full employment legislation would have instituted a "universal" social program without offending Americans' deeply ingrained "work ethic." Indeed, to many Democrats and liberal activists, full employment seemed the perfect solution to a host of problems—from economic and social problems such as unemployment, poverty, social disorder, and the impoverishment of inner cities to political problems such as a fracturing New Deal coalition.[18]

This political context is critical to understanding the full employment campaign, which was part of a larger strategy to adjust progressive politics to rapidly altered economic and political circumstances. For while some groups on the political Left practiced an increasingly assertive identity politics, main-stream liberals—labor unions; civil rights, religious, civic, and social welfare organizations; Democratic Party strategists; foundations; and antipoverty activists—turned to policies that promised to shore up (or rebuild) the falter-ing New Deal Democratic coalition and to unite its various constituencies. That coalition, which had provided the electoral base for the Great Society's antidiscrimination legislation and expansive federal social spending, seemed to crumble as Alabama Governor George Wallace and Republican nominee Richard Nixon routed Democrat Hubert Humphrey in the 1968 presidential election. Seeking an explanation for what seemed an intensifying conservative shift in local and national politics, political pundits and strategists focused on the discontents of the white working class, a key New Deal constituency that seemed to have abandoned the Democratic Party. The result was what one observer called "a flurry of official and journalistic concern over the average worker and his problems."[19] Liberals sought answers in a rash of books and ar-ticles, while the Ford Foundation, the National Federation of Settlements, the National Conference on Social Welfare, and the American Jewish Committee (AJC) sponsored some of the numerous conferences on the subject.[20]

They all came to virtually the same conclusion, one which still structures our understanding of the supposed "right turn" in American politics: by tar-geting minorities and the poor, Great Society programs had alienated what journalist Peter Schrag called the "forgotten man," living "between slums and suburbs."[21] In response, liberals sought to woo back the white working- and lower-middle classes—the "shock troops of anti-Negro politics," as the AJC's Irving Levine called them. A politics that appealed to these middle Americans and that emphasized the "old economic issues" seemed the key to building a "new majority."[22]

This new majority strategy is evident in the major liberal organizing ef-forts of the mid-1970s, from the Coalition for Human Needs and Budget Priorities[23] and Common Cause[24] to the Full Employment Action Council and the National Committee for Full Employment[25]—all broad liberal coali-tions emphasizing issues that "relate to the needs of middle class America as a whole, in contrast to the needs of the so-called underclass," as Levine put it in his "Strategy for White Ethnic America."[26] George Wiley is a particularly powerful example of this new emphasis. An early leader of a national welfare rights movement built around the needs and rights of poor, mostly nonwhite single mothers, Wiley in the early 1970s rejected what he called "defensive minority politics" and targeted instead tax reform and cuts in education and health care in an effort to organize the 70 percent of Americans earning less than $15,000 a year into his Movement for Economic Justice.[27]

Because in popular understanding the "blue-collar backlash" was also, fundamentally, a "white backlash," new organizing strategies had to downplay the concerns of minorities, particularly African Americans. As young African Americans increasingly demonstrated their racial pride through new cultural styles and a rhetoric of black nationalism, many mainstream civil rights leaders insisted that any chance of improving the lot of African Americans rested in coalition politics that spoke to whites as well as blacks. In 1973, Vernon Jordan of the National Urban League was not alone in declaring that "the gut issues of today—better schools, jobs and housing for all, personal safety and decent health care" would not be addressed if they were "falsely perceived as 'black issues.'" From articles in the National Association for the Advancement of Colored People's (NAACP's) *Crisis* to the pronouncements of young leaders like Jesse Jackson, much of the country's civil rights leadership downplayed racial identity in favor of a politics of coalition.[28] Perhaps the most vociferous spokesperson for this strategy was Bayard Rustin, a longtime opponent of black separatism. Rustin warned civil rights supporters, "nothing identified in the public mind as a 'black program' or 'black issue' will gain support either from politicians or voters." Instead, the goal should be "a total social package that can appeal to our traditional allies like trade union members, middle-class people, farmers, ethnic groups, and liberals."[29] Broader redistributive policies would attract white support while helping the "black silent majority."[30]

When sociologist Charles Hamilton labeled that group, the "black silent majority," he pointed to a key feature of liberals' "new majority"—family structure. In fact, Hamilton coined the term to describe the majority of African American families consisting of a married couple with children and an employed father—a contrast, in other words, to the "underclass" of female-headed households: welfare mothers.[31] Since its inception in the Social Security Act of 1935, Aid to Families with Dependent Children (AFDC) had provided federal-state cash grants to families without breadwinners, the vast majority of whom were single mothers and their children. Over time, as social insurance expanded to cover the widows of insured male workers and as civil rights and welfare rights activism broke down barriers to welfare, the AFDC rolls increasingly consisted of deserted, separated, or never-married mothers, and the proportion of nonwhite recipients increased to nearly half by the late 1960s. AFDC rolls also grew precipitously during the 1960s, particularly toward the end of the decade, as welfare rights activism emboldened poor women, intimidated caseworkers, and overturned restrictions. Politicians and journalists screamed about a "welfare crisis."[32] Of course, attention to "broken families" threatened to taint all black Americans, which is why civil rights organizations had long kept their distance from organized welfare recipients.[33] A National Urban League spokesman demonstrated this fear when a 1971 census report noted rising numbers of black, female-headed households. Why, he asked, could not the press focus instead on "the hard-working, father-dominated families" who "constitute the great majority."[34]

Liberal strategists targeted AFDC (*welfare* in common parlance) as a particular affront to "forgotten Americans," not only because it was perceived as a black program but also because it rewarded what Andrew Levison called "the disorganized families of the unemployed," thereby offending what sociologist Lee Rainwater called the "deep family orientation of the working class." These liberal strategists insisted that a more politically viable redistributive program would conform to "working class logic"—that the ticket into the social and economic mainstream was a "good and faithful [male] provider" and a "sensible, responsible, and loving housewife-mother."[35] According to Worth Bateman and Jodie Allen of the Urban Institute, the "predominantly male-headed, white, and working" blue-collar families resented social programs targeted at "female-headed, nonwhite, and non-working" families.[36] The message was clear: the best response to the backlash was to target working- and lower-middle-class Americans with programs that supported—indeed, privileged—the male breadwinner family.

Conservative opponents of full employment legislation encouraged such a strategy by dismissing the plight of unemployed women, whom they defined as "secondary earners" without breadwinning responsibilities. According to business organizations and publications as well as officials from the Federal Reserve Board, women's presumably illegitimate (or less legitimate) entry into the labor market was largely responsible for rising unemployment.[37] Even if women were not responsible for the crisis, their status as "secondary" earners made their joblessness less tragic. Unemployment was "vastly overrated," insisted Senator Edwin (Jake) Garn, because "at least half" afflicted "someone who is not a breadwinner."[38] Congress should not get "carried away" by unemployment levels, agreed Treasury Secretary John Connelly, because the "unemployment rate for males, heads of families" was only 3 percent.[39] In a subtler version of the same strategy, opponents of the bill's public service employment provisions, including the Chamber of Commerce and Alan Greenspan of the Council of Economic Advisors, implicitly dismissed the long-term unemployment crisis among women and minorities by insisting that economic recovery was right around the corner.[40] Calling full employment a "utopian concept," representatives from the chamber and the National Association of Manufacturers warned that the bill would flood the labor market with individuals who had "a loose attachment to the labor force" and a "marginal propensity to work." Those individuals—women, minorities, and youth—needed training, they insisted, not a job guarantee.[41]

In a tongue-in-cheek critique of such arguments, liberal academic Alan Gartner noted that unemployment was rising for "even that most precious group, whose unemployment seems to matter more, adult men."[42] Many supporters of the bill joined Gartner in emphasizing full employment's potential boon to the cause of gender and racial equality. The original bill, the Equal Opportunity and Full Employment Act, placed this goal at its core. "Only under conditions of genuine full employment and confidence in its continuation," the bill read, "is it easier to eliminate the bias, prejudice, discrimination, and fear that have resulted in unequal employment under unequal conditions of women, older people, younger people, [and] members of racial, ethnic, national, or religious minorities."[43] Such concerns cropped up among witnesses from religious, social welfare, and academic circles, but they were emphasized most emphatically by women and African Americans. Women from unions, feminist organizations, and welfare rights groups expressed particular concern with the bill's effects on women's economic status, while African American representatives like members of the Congressional Black Caucus and the Urban League and Federal Employment Action Council cochair Coretta Scott King called attention to disproportionate unemployment among nonwhites.

Much of the focus on African American unemployment, though, expressed a specifically gendered concern about black families and social disorder in America's inner cities. Many witnesses who testified in favor of the legislation correlated high unemployment among African American youth with what City University of New York Urban Affairs professor Stanley Moses called negative "social behavior—crime, addiction, alienation, mass rioting, [and] depression."[44] Long associated with young African American men—an association with increasing public legitimacy in the wake of several "long hot summers" of rioting in black urban neighborhoods in the 1960s—this language of social disorder implied a critique of black families, as well. From early twentieth-century sociological literature to public debates about welfare, income policy, and poverty programs in the 1960s and early 1970s, American experts blamed the "pathological behavior" of black men on their inability to become family breadwinners.[45] This analysis permeated the full employment debate. Outside of witnesses from women's organizations, Michigan Representative Charles Diggs, a member of the Congressional Black Caucus, was almost alone in mentioning the problem of unemployment among "women who are the support of their households."[46] Liberal witnesses more often cited academics whose concern lay with young black men, or what one professor quoted by the AJC called the "generation of black teenagers going from childhood to manhood without any job or any prospect of getting a job."[47] Appropriate to this emphasis, the National Council of Churches quoted Elliot Liebow, whose book *Tally's Corners* chronicled the street corner culture of jobless black men in Washington, D.C. "A man without a job or a working man who is unable to support his family," Liebow indirectly warned Congress, "is being told clearly and for all to hear that he is not needed."[48]

Other liberal witnesses similarly evoked the psychological and emotional effect of male unemployment but emphasized instead the plight of more recently unemployed workers. Drawing on the "new majority strategy," which sought to downplay minority-targeted legislation, and responding to opponents' cavalier emphasis on the lesser and presumably temporary unemployment of (implicitly white) male breadwinners, a number of full employment proponents insisted that, as Milwaukee's Sister Regina Williams put it, "the people begging for jobs today are not limited to the unskilled nor to minorities."[49] Augustus Hawkins, an African American member of Congress and the bill's cosponsor, used the testimony of labor union members to remind his fellow lawmakers that "there are a lot of skilled persons among the unemployed who are males and who are also white."[50] The *Progressive* magazine's take on unemployment exemplifies the male-breadwinner focus of many liberal full employment supporters. The author drew a portrait of a typical victim of the 1970s economy, a Flint, Michigan, man, long employed with a "decent income, a modest house," and "unemployment compensation and union benefits" to carry him over in hard times. However, long-term unemployment dries up his resources, and "something goes out of the family because he's around." He loses the respect of his children and his wife, for while "he was the boss, the breadwinner" once, now he can no longer provide.[51] Even Bayard Rustin highlighted the economic security of white, blue-collar men when he spoke to a construction worker union about "Black Rage, White Fear: The Full Employment Answer."[52]

Certainly, long-term unemployment did cause significant psychological and emotional disruption for American men, so long taught that their identity lay in being their family's economic provider. However, this emphasis also reveals a powerful 1970s trope that potentially ignored the needs of female and even nonwhite male workers, a trope that permeated congressional debate. After lobbying three congressional committees considering the full employment bill, Carol Burris of Women's Lobby reported that "much of the discussion of jobs for women is not based on fact, but on the assumption that we will leave the job market if times are good and our husbands earn enough to keep us."[53] Indeed, though explicitly egalitarian in language, the legislation contained what one economist called "ambiguities, loopholes, and special measures which pose a real threat to the employment of women."[54] Women from a variety of arenas would challenge policymakers and legislators to jettison anachronistic assumptions about male breadwinning and recognize the special needs of women that stemmed from a history of explicit and covert discrimination and from the likelihood that they would combine parenting with wage labor. In other words, they demanded a new family wage—or, as Dorothy Sue Cobble calls it, a degendered family wage—that promised economic independence to women.[55]

In August 1973, Dorothy Haener announced that NOW would launch "The New Action," a "multi-faceted venture aimed at improving women's economic lot." A full-scale lobbying and publicity effort, which would include "a rip-roaring advertising campaign . . . to raise public consciousness toward women's economic plight," the New Action included a call for full employment along with an expanded minimum wage, equal pay for equal work, welfare reform, job upgrading for "female ghetto jobs," and affordable quality child care.[56] Haener was an appropriate spokeswoman for the New Action. A longtime activist in the United Auto Workers and head of that union's Women's Department, a founding member of NOW and Women's Action Equity League, and one of the first chairs of NOW's Women in Poverty Task Force, she served as a liaison between feminist organizations, labor unions, and low-income women's groups.[57] By the 1970s, each of these groups had come to see full employment as a necessary, though not sufficient, foundation for women's economic advancement.

Access to good jobs had been a long-standing and central feminist and civil rights demand, and federally mandated full employment seemed even more critical by the mid-1970s, as rising unemployment rates began erasing recently won labor market victories.[58] Even before the 1963 March on Washington for Jobs and Freedom and campaigns during the 1960s for the National Urban League's Domestic Marshall Plan and the A. Philip Randolph Institute's Freedom Budget for All Americans, African American labor and civil rights activists and their liberal allies demanded access to jobs as an essential companion to equal opportunity efforts. Feminists, too, recognized early on that without universal access to employment, "women and minorities are brought into conflict with white male workers whose own jobs are threatened," and "workers are turned against workers in the fight for equal opportunity."[59] Heated political and judicial battles over affirmative action during the 1970s merely confirmed for both feminist and minority activists the need to step up the campaign for full employment.

Feminists had an additional impetus to emphasize access to employment: the rapid erosion of the male-breadwinner household. Of course, the family wage ideal had never been an option for most American women, particularly immigrant, working-class, and nonwhite women. In the early twentieth century, working-class "industrial feminists" and their middle-class allies protested women's low wages and the presumed dependent status that justified them, and African-American women built community institutions to help them combine their dual role of parenting and wage earning.[60] During and after World War II, as the proportion of married women and mothers in the labor market began to increase and policymakers and employers became more interested in using the nation's "womanpower," working-class women pressured their unions and lawmakers to recognize their financial role as providers through equal pay for comparable work and access to maternity benefits and affordable child care. Despite these challenges, though, the family wage model continued to structure the country's labor market and welfare state and remained a powerful and widely held cultural ideal. After the 1960s, though, as male wages stagnated, unemployment spread, and divorce rates soared, the family wage bargain had begun visibly to fall apart.[61]

One consequence of America's commitment to the male-breadwinner family ideal had always been higher rates of female poverty, a problem that gained increasing attention by the late 1970s, as feminist researchers began to document what sociologist Diana Pearce labeled the "feminization of poverty." It turned out that the country's longest economic boom along with a burgeoning welfare state had not improved Americans' economic status equally. Women—and especially single mothers—benefited little from a significant decline in poverty rates. Between 1959 and 1967, the percentage of white, male-headed families in poverty dropped from 11.4 to 5.4 percent (the numbers for black male-headed families were an equally impressive 43.1 and 20.9 percent). In the same period, the number of female-headed families in poverty soared, doubling between 1959 and 1972. By 1976, women's poverty rate was 12.2 percent compared to men's 7 percent, and women made up 60 percent of the country's adult poor.[62] "As the number of families headed by women grows," a 1977 League of Women Voters booklet noted, "poverty will become increasingly a women's problem."[63] Welfare rights leaders and a handful of antipoverty feminists pressured mainstream liberal and feminist organizations to attend to the plight of poor women, particularly poor single mothers, and, increasingly, feminists across the class spectrum spoke of poverty and welfare as key "women's issues."[64]

Welfare rights, feminist, and traditional women's organizations saw jobs as a significant part of the solution to women's poverty and as an opportunity to ensure for all American women "the right to live in dignity, without deprivation and free from dependence for economic reasons on any other person."[65] So in the beginning, women's organizations joined the full employment campaign with gusto, participating in coalitions, task forces, and demonstrations. Yet as early as 1975, NOW leaders complained that the full employment campaign was failing to address "the needs and problems of women workers." Sara Nelson and Lynn Darcy urged NOW members to join Coalition of Labor Union Women (CLUW) members at a union-sponsored "Jobs Now!" rally with signs reading "Unemployment Twice as High for Women than Men," "Women and Blacks Hit Hardest," and "NOW Fights for All Women Workers."[66] The organization saw it as "most critical to expose and publicize the seriously deteriorating status of women in the economy, particularly in the context of the current national debate over full employment."[67] The YWCA, which had extensive experience providing women with job counseling, training, and child care services, concurred. In a 1978 speech titled "Full Employment as a Women's Issue," the YWCA's Helen Parolla insisted that her organization had "learned the hard way that without a concerted effort, a concerted push, women [and] minorities . . . are going to be forgotten."[68]

Such concerns were not unfounded. Outside of promising to reduce overall unemployment rates, the bill left a race- and sex-segregated labor market largely as is. In its very definition of unemployment, for example, the bill favored the labor market's most privileged workers, white men. By aiming for a 3 percent overall unemployment rate, the bill would likely leave rates for minorities and women much higher, particularly given these groups' disproportionate representation among "discouraged workers." New York Congresswoman Bella Abzug showed Congress exactly what such discrepancies meant: a 5.1 percent unemployment rate for men, she noted, coincided with a 7.5 percent rate for white women and a 10 percent rate for black women.[69] Progressive women urged lawmakers to set "specific goals" for full employment for different groups of workers and to institute "planning to achieve them."[70] Without targeting specific groups, disproportionate unemployment rates would continue to afflict nonwhite and female workers.

Feminists across the class spectrum also warned that without aggressive antidiscrimination measures and efforts to dismantle occupational segregation, full employment legislation would merely perpetuate inequality in the labor market. These concerns conflicted with the optimistic predictions of many liberals, who declared that under full employment, "women—especially minority women—will be liberated from systematic and pervasive discrimination on the job market" and that "if you have full employment, you cannot

have discrimination."[71] Feminists instead saw full employment as a necessary *but not sufficient* solution to women's economic disadvantage. They
demanded that full employment legislation include rigorous antidiscrimination measures, affirmative action guidelines, and far-reaching measures to
employ women in "non-traditional" (meaning traditionally male, well-paid)
occupations.[72] Attacking the bill's assumption that "there would be no market
imperfections if the economy were moving," representatives of NOW, along
with nearly every other women's organization to testify on the bill, demanded
that the federal government work to combat the "dual labor markets for
so-called 'male' and 'female' jobs," which "resulted in artificially depressed
wage rates for most women workers." Without a massive reconstruction of
the gendered labor market, women's economic inequality and higher rates
of poverty "would simply be perpetuated."[73]

As the bill transformed over three years from the Equal Opportunity and
Full Employment Act to the Full Employment and Balanced Growth Act,
its job guarantee contracted in ways that further disadvantaged women. Although the original legislation promised a public service job to anyone who
wanted work but could not find it in the private sector, subsequent revisions
imposed eligibility criteria that, Bella Abzug insisted, would be "devastating" for women.[74] Lawmakers instructed Public Service Employment (PSE)
administrators to consider household income and the number of workers in
a household when allocating what was becoming a limited resource—public
service jobs. Married women with wage-earning husbands would be rendered
virtually ineligible. Feminists balked at this violation of the bill's original intent, which was, first and foremost, to achieve full employment, not to combat
household poverty. Marriage and a husband's income, insisted Coretta Scott
King, were "irrelevant to a woman's right to shape her life according to her
own values or goals."[75] To feminists who saw employment as the key to "each
individual's . . . claim to the right to be an individual, to develop one's own
personhood, to grow and become a complete human being," as Wellesley
economist Carolyn Shaw Bell put it, limiting jobs to one per household ne-
gated married women's individualism and right to gainful employment.[76] It
also evoked the specter of Depression era restrictions on a married woman's
right to hold a job. "Women want to be independent parts of the American
economy," insisted Audrey Cohen, chair of the Federal Task Force on Women,
Work, and Education, but the bill's restrictions reflected the "feeling, hidden
just below the surface today, that in times of high unemployment, equity
means one job per family, and that job ought to go to the man."[77]

While a handful of feminists noted that this "depression level mentality" violated liberal feminist principles, a majority targeted the restriction's

anachronistic family model.[78] "Does Congress adhere to the myth that each family contains a single breadwinner who needs a job? " they demanded.[79] Women continued to be "regarded as 'secondary' workers, working only to supplement the family earnings of some man," complained a YWCA representative. In reality, she continued, "many of us are primary wage earners," and "many of us work to maintain family standards in inflationary times."[80] Excluding married women from the job guarantee would "reinforce the myth that married women do not work," complained representatives of NOW, and "assumes, incorrectly, that married women are well taken care of throughout their lives."[81] In addition to a commitment to self-determination, then, feminist attention to three important trends convinced them to oppose such eligibility restrictions: the growing problem of "displaced homemakers"—women whose lack of paid work experience left them financially devastated when divorced or widowed; families' growing reliance on the income of two adult wage earners; and the plight of poor single mothers highlighted in welfare reform debates and welfare rights activism. "The truth is, *even* if you believed in the desirability of the traditional patriarchal family," declared NOW's Wilma Scott Heide, "(and *we* reject the idea and that economic support and/or maleness means head of household status), *most* poverty is visited on women and children without *any* man *available* for support."[82]

Those women without a man available for economic support—particularly AFDC recipients—would also find themselves largely excluded from the bill's job guarantee. The bill gave priority for public service employment to the short-term unemployed and failed to consider welfare mothers a priority group. Given that as many as 94 percent of AFDC mothers had been officially unemployed for more than a year, Women's Lobby's Carol Burris pointed out, the "duration of employment" criterion was merely "a way of excluding low income, low skill women and homemakers long absent from the labor force in favor of men with long work histories who are temporarily unemployed solely due to economic downturn."[83] In other words, Helen Ginsberg of the Friends Committee on National Legislation argued, eligibility criteria would serve to "limit the employment programs to some variety of 'worthy' unemployed," a group that consisted largely of those white, male, blue-collar workers featured in journalistic treatments of the mid-1970s recession.[84]

The indirect exclusion of welfare mothers was particularly devastating to welfare rights activists, who hoped that full employment legislation would help them "move into the mainstream . . . and live a dignified life above the level of poverty," as a representative from the Muskegon (Michigan) County Welfare Rights Organization wrote in a letter to Augustus Hawkins.[85] From its origins in the mid-1960s, the welfare rights movement had asserted a basic "right to live" expressed in demands for both "jobs and income." Before social-ist feminists began campaigning for "wages for housework," AFDC mothers argued in welfare rights literature, press conferences, demonstrations, and testimony before various official bodies that society should value women's unpaid household and child rearing labor with adequate, nonstigmatized welfare grants.[86] At the same time, though, both local welfare rights groups and the National Welfare Rights Organization, which reached its peak influ-ence during the first Nixon administration, demanded the education, train-ing, jobs, and child care that would enable poor single mothers to leave a penurious and stigmatizing welfare system and achieve the American Dream of economic self-sufficiency.[87]

Before the 1970s, most antipoverty warriors saw economic self-sufficiency in family terms and focused their efforts on male breadwinners. Federal policymakers who designed the Johnson administration's War on Poverty; civil rights leaders such as Martin Luther King Jr. and Whitney Young; black nationalists; and the religious, civic, and women's organizations that made up the labor-liberal lobby of the 1960s all sought to shore up black men's economic position in the job market and the family. Drawing on a long his-tory of sociological literature on the urban black family in America, liberals and radicals committed to fighting poverty and advancing racial equality blamed a host of social and psychological problems or "pathologies" among an emerging "underclass" on the higher incidence of female-headed house-holds among urban African Americans—a "matriarchal family structure" that itself resulted from lack of opportunities for black men. Seeking to en-able African American men to become proper family providers, antipoverty planners and advocates lobbied for jobs and job training for black men. In debates about welfare in the 1960s and early 1970s, poor people and their liberal allies generally viewed jobs for black men as the solution to the poverty of black women and children.[88]

A handful of witnesses during full employment debate explicitly adhered to this older model of antipoverty policy. Sometimes the emphasis was subtle, as when the A. Philip Randolph Institute's Norman Hill identified "the in-crease in joblessness among the male heads of two-parent black families" as "particularly damaging."[89] Sometimes, the focus on black male employment was more explicit. During the full employment hearings in 1975, for example, Percy Green of a St. Louis, Missouri, direct-action group called ACTION, lauded full employment as a way to provide "more and better paying jobs for black men" so that "they can become true breadwinners of their families."[90] The Reverend Buck Jones of the United Church of Christ likewise saw full employment as a way to provide jobs to black fathers and thereby prevent family breakup, while liberal economist Leon Keyserling hoped that full employment "would . . . reduce the conditions which force so many mothers to work instead of staying home with their children," a situation that "has grave social consequences."[91] That such analyses—so dominant as recently as the late 1960s—only occasionally cropped up during full employment debates is a measure of how influential feminist analysis and rhetoric was in the 1970s. That the full employment bill itself contained implicit favoritism toward male-breadwinner families is a measure of how far feminists had to go.

By the mid-1970s, female welfare rights activists and their allies in self-defined feminist and traditional women's organizations explicitly rejected what National Women's Political Caucus (NWPC) and Women's Lobby called the "trickle-down theory which presumes that women receive economic benefits as a result of men's expanded opportunities" and had come to see employment as the best remedy to women's economic disadvantage.[92] Drawing on years of work with welfare mothers in San Antonio, Texas, Lupe Anguiano insisted that AFDC recipients themselves "*saw employment as the only true viable alternative to assist them and their families [to] become self-sufficient.*" Anguiano worked with the Women's Bureau, NOW, Women's Lobby, and several welfare rights organizations to get poor women's recommendations for combating rising rates of female poverty. "The message from these women was the same," Anguiano reported, "the majority of women on welfare want to work and be self-supporting."[93] Maya Miller, a white academic-turned activist who had become a tireless ally of welfare rights activists in Nevada and who directed a Women, Work, and Welfare Project for NOW and Women's Lobby, attributed her organizations' interest in full employment to their "ongoing study of legislation related to welfare mothers." Reporting on a week-long study session with low-income women, Miller reported that "all of them said in effect, 'We want jobs, just like everybody else. Take back your degrading welfare with its harassments, and just give us jobs.'" Participants "got excited about the idea of full employment," but Miller's analysis of the bill left her "worried" that the legislation would leave AFDC recipients out in the cold.

Welfare mothers had nearly twenty years' experience with the male-breadwinner bias of federal training and jobs programs, and they had little reason to expect that the full employment bill would work any differently. The bill placed administration of public service employment with the U.S. Labor Department, which had a long history of "rampant sex discrimination," including tracking women into low-wage jobs and favoring male- over female-headed households.[94] In fact, "extensive experience" demonstrated that "government officials tend to ignore the problems of women and minorities unless they are specifically directed to concern themselves with these problems."[95] Participants in the Women's Bureau's Low Income Women Project, a series of consultations with poor women designed to identify the major barriers to employment, blasted administrators of the Comprehensive Education and Training Act, the Work Incentive Program (WIN), and the Manpower Development and Training Act for treating poor single mothers as "temporarily without husbands" and channeling them into low-wage "female" jobs.[96] According to reports such as the 1974 U.S. Commission on Civil Rights hearings, government jobs programs suffered from pervasive sex and race discrimination.[97] Even in WIN, which was designed to move AFDC recipients into the labor market, "men are placed and hired first," prompting a NOW-sponsored sex discrimination lawsuit.[98] There is little wonder why welfare rights activists testifying on full employment blasted what a New York City welfare rights organization called "government programs designed to combat unemployment" by "focus[ing] on male heads of household, leaving women to fend for themselves."[99]

Ruby Duncan, an African American AFDC recipient, mother of seven, and welfare rights activist and community organizer in Las Vegas, Nevada, eloquently expressed to Congress poor women's hopes and fears regarding full employment legislation. Testifying before a Senate subcommittee, Duncan reiterated the welfare rights movement's emphasis on a "right to live" and on the value of poor women's mothering when she demanded adequate grants to "compensate women who work in the home raising children." The majority of her statement, however, emphasized the full employment bill's potential to ensure a better life for poor single mothers and their children. Welfare mothers, like all poor people, wanted "a piece of the American pie" in the form of "jobs that will provide our families with a decent life."

Like women in feminist and traditional women's organizations, though, Duncan educated Congress on the ways in which the bill would exclude women such as herself. By targeting the officially and short-term unemployed, public service employment excluded many women, particularly AFDC recipients. She joined other feminists in critiquing the bill's list of priority areas for job creation, which focused on high-technology occupations at the expense of human service positions that were both desperately needed and more likely to fit the qualifications of poor women.[100] Poor women were "eager to do traditional 'women's work,'" Duncan assured lawmakers, "if it pays well." She critiqued the male-breadwinner bias of existing federal job programs: "traditional qualifications of white and male," Duncan noted, "exclude me."[101]

Duncan advised lawmakers to target welfare recipients and other poor mothers, to give "priority to those disadvantaged Americans who are working

day and night to enter the mainstream of American life." At the least, Carol
Burris added, the two million women already registered for the WIN program
must be counted as unemployed "or as a priority group for employment."[102]
To Dorothy Bolden of the National Domestic Workers of America, the "unemployment and underemployment which minority women face in the job
market today" was reason enough to target them in job creation efforts; so was
their sole responsibility for children. In addition to calling for jobs that suited
the skills of low-income women, Duncan joined other feminists in demanding
access to "nontraditional" employment, the kinds of well-paid, unionized jobs
that typically enabled men with little education to escape poverty. "Garbage
collectors are paid well," for example, "and enjoy universal respect." Like many
women who testified on the bill, Duncan acknowledged the particular needs
of mothers. "Abandoning my children in the street is not reasonable," she
noted. "A job must provide a decent wage so that child care and health care are
possible."[103] Carol Burris, who appeared with Duncan, also emphasized that
poor single mothers "have special needs for child care services to enter and
continue in the labor force . . . flexible hours and permanent part-time jobs to
fulfill their family needs."[104] Rejecting a national discourse that defined AFDC
mothers as lazy, promiscuous, and neglectful mothers who enjoyed living off
the public dole, Duncan assured Congress that she and her peers subscribed
to the "bootstrap theory." However, "it is a cruel jest to tell a bootless person
to pick herself up by her own bootstraps." Full employment legislation could
help provide those bootstraps, Duncan insisted, but "so far all the proposals
for full employment have not included *us*."

In 1977, the League of Women Voters summarized the agenda that welfare rights activists, union women, and feminists articulated during the full
employment campaign. In "To Promote the General Welfare—Unfinished
Agenda," the league noted with dismay increasing poverty rates among
women and children and the erosion of AFDC benefits, but their proposals
tackled the deeper problem behind women's economic disadvantage. Full
employment was one answer, the league insisted, but it must be accompanied
by "concerted efforts to eliminate race and sex discrimination in the mar-
ketplace, as well as in job training programs and vocational education"—in
other words, a reconstruction of the race- and sex-segregated labor market that kept women's earnings consistently lower than men's. Affordable
and accessible child care and health insurance, too, would be necessary to
combat women's economic vulnerability.[105] In other words, the league—and
the larger coalition of women's organizations and activists—demanded that
federal policymakers reject, once and for all, the male-breadwinner family
ideal. Instead, federal policy should help create a labor market and social

support system that would enable one parent, including a female parent, the opportunity to raise children in economic security. Only with this new kind of family wage, available to all adults, would the nation combat the poverty of single mothers and ensure women's economic independence.

If the full employment bill that passed did little for women in general or poor single mothers in particular, it did little for anyone else, either. In the end, the Carter administration and other powerful Democrats had little stomach for interfering in the "free market," even for deserving male-breadwinner families.[106] Instead, Congress instituted and expanded compensatory welfare programs to aid the "working poor," programs such as food stamps and the Earned Income Tax Credit. Meanwhile, the Carter administration embarked on a comprehensive welfare reform plan that would have redistributed welfare dollars from single mother families to male-breadwinner families. Feminists argued, again, that not only would such a strategy prove ineffective, given men's declining real wages and rising rates of divorce and single motherhood, but that it would further institutionalize women's economic dependence on men.[107] The only just and effective response would be "a new family wage"— the assurance that women, as well as men, had access to the jobs and social supports that would enable them to raise children out of poverty.

Women's activism during the full employment campaign helps to complicate the standard narrative of second-wave feminism by pointing to consensus across class barriers. As the historian Nancy MacLean recently noted, "much has been said about the class and race biases of second-wave feminism," but "when the focus of inquiry turns from the youthful women's liberation activists . . . to the usually older working women who mobilized around issues of employment and focused on changing public policy," the feminist movement "looks more diverse and more attentive to bread-and-butter needs."[108] Likewise, Dorothy Sue Cobble's analysis of working-class "labor feminist" campaigns for pay equity and an improved "social wage" and Susan Hartmann's attention to antipoverty activism outside self-defined feminist organizations have broadened our understanding of the second wave.[109] Women's activism during the full employment campaign provides further evidence that, despite conflicts and disagreements stemming from class and race differences, women committed to gender equity as part of a broader progressive program could, and did, develop analyses that addressed economic disadvantage among the country's poorest women. In a political climate increasingly hostile to workers' rights and government social supports, the new consensus was not an unambiguous step forward. Lost was an earlier recognition of the value of women's caregiving labor, and feminist emphasis on female breadwinning ultimately muted liberal opposition to punitive workfare programs. In the end, then, this shift in thinking about women's poverty contributed to the eventual repeal of AFDC in 1996, absent the restructured family wage that feminists demanded.[110] However, this was not the intended outcome. From welfare mothers and labor union feminists to middle-class women's organizations, these activists demanded a restructuring of the country's labor market and social support system that would enable women's economic independence.

What feminists faced on their own side of the aisle (among liberals) was an attempt to rebuild the New Deal coalition, to get back to some good old liberalism that could unify diverse constituencies—far from the identity politics that supposedly cannibalized the Left in the 1970s. In fact, the full employment campaign suggests that identity politics never dominated the political Left; if anything, the most established and powerful forces—Democratic politicians and strategists; organized labor; foundations; and a plethora of civil rights, religious, social welfare, women's, and civic organizations—pursued an opposite strategy.

Feminists *were* practicing some kind of politics of recognition in the full employment campaign. They did so because the very class politics that liberals appealed to was itself inherently gendered. Historians have illustrated that modern American liberalism, from the New Deal through the War on Poverty, always assumed the primacy of the male-breadwinner family; this assumption continues to structure the country's welfare state and labor market. Paeans to some mythical common good class politics aside, feminists recognized that without attention to the special circumstances of women—their relegation to a pink-collar ghetto, their primary responsibility for child rearing, and so forth—a supposedly "universal" program would continue to favor men. This would leave women economically dependent and, more and more often, impoverished. Given that liberal proposals such as full employment rested on an outmoded family wage model, then, women's only hope for accessing resources was by gaining recognition.

## Notes

The author thanks Nancy MacLean, Cynthia Harrison, Stephanie Gilmore, Susan Hartmann, Dorothy Sue Cobble, participants in the 2005 Berkshire Conference on the History of Women panel on Women, Work, and Welfare, and colleagues at Oregon State University for thoughtful comments on previous versions of this chapter. Some research was funded by a grant from the Arthur and Elizabeth Schlesinger Library on the History of Women in America at Radcliffe and a Clarke Chambers travel fellowship from the Social Welfare History Archive at the University of Minnesota.

The first epigraph is from Herrington J. Bryce, Joint Center for Political Studies, "Toward

Full Employment: Minorities and the Cities," presented to the National Conference on Public Service Employment, Academy for Contemporary Problems, Columbus, Ohio, November 1, 1974, in Congress, House, Subcommittee on Equal Opportunities of the Committee on Education and Labor, *Hearing on H.R. 50: Equal Opportunity and Full Employment,* 94th Cong., 1st sess., March 18, 1975, 55.

1. Congress, Senate, Subcommittee on Employment, Poverty, and Migratory Labor of the Committee on Labor and Public Welfare, *Hearing on S. 50 and S. 472: Full Employment and Balanced Growth Act, 1976,* 94th Cong., 2nd sess., May 1976, 615.

2. Congress, House of Representatives, Subcommittee on Equal Opportunities of the Committee on Education and Labor, *Hearing on H.R. 50: Equal Opportunity and Full Employment,* 94th Cong., 1st sess., October 14, 1975, 205.

3. Congress, Senate, Subcommittee on Employment, Poverty, and Migratory Labor of the Committee on Labor and Public Welfare, *Hearing on S. 50 and S. 472: Full Employment and Balanced Growth Act, 1976,* 94th Cong., 2nd sess., May 1976, 619.

4. Ibid, 617.

5. Premilla Nadasen, *Welfare Warriors: The Welfare Rights Movement in the United States* (New York: Routledge: 2005); Premilla Nadasen, "Expanding the Boundaries of the Women's Movement: Black Feminism and the Struggle for Welfare Rights," *Feminist Studies* 28, no. 2 (2002): 271–301; Martha Davis, "Welfare Rights and Women's Rights in the 1960s," *Journal of Policy History* 8, no. 1 (1996): 144–65; Guida West, *The National Welfare Rights Movement: The Social Protest of Poor Women* (New York: Praeger Publishers, 1981). An exception, Annelise Orleck's analysis of welfare rights activism in Las Vegas highlights some successful efforts to build coalitions between poor and middle-class women, including feminists. Annelise Orleck, *Storming Caesars Palace: How Black Mothers Fought Their Own War on Poverty* (Boston: Beacon Press, 2005).

6. Nancy Fraser, "From Redistribution to Recognition? Dilemmas of Justice in a 'Post-Socialist' Age," *New Left Review* 212 (July/August 1995): 68.

7. Thomas Furguson and Joel Rogers, *Right Turn: The Decline of the Democrats and the Future of American Politics* (New York: Hill and Wang, 1986).

8. Philip Jenkins, *Decade of Nightmares: The End of the Sixties and the Making of Eighties America* (New York: Oxford University Press, 2006); Bruce Schulman, *The Seventies: The Great Shift in American Culture, Society, and Politics* (New York: Free Press, 2001); David Frum, *How We Got Here: The '70s, the Decade That Brought You Modern Life (For Better or Worse)* (New York: Basic Books, 2000); Beth Bailey and David Farber, eds., *America in the Seventies* (Lawrence: University Press of Kansas, 2004). For historical treatments that locate the disintegration of the New Deal coalition in the racial and economic conflicts of America's postwar industrial cities, see Thomas J. Sugrue, *The Origins of the Urban Crisis: Race and Inequality in Postwar Detroit* (Princeton, N.J.: Princeton University Press, 1996); Arnold R. Hirsch, *Making the Second Ghetto: Race and Housing in Chicago, 1940–1960* (New York: Cambridge University Press, 1983); Robert O. Self, *American Babylon: Race and the Struggle for Postwar Oakland* (Princeton, N.J.: Princeton University Press, 2003); and Kenneth D. Durr, *Behind the Backlash: White Working-Class Politics in Baltimore, 1940–1980* (Chapel Hill: University of North Carolina Press, 2003). For a discussion of the racial implications of white Americans' emerging understanding of "rights," see Matthew D. Lassiter, "The Suburban Origins of 'Color-Blind Conservatism,'" *Journal of Urban History* 29, no. 10 (2004). For other works that emphasize race as the key wedge in the

New Deal coalition, see Dan T. Carter, *The Politics of Rage: George Wallace, the Origins of the New Conservatism, and the Transformation of American Politics* (New York: Simon and Schuster, 1995) and *From George Wallace to Newt Gingrich: Race in the Conservative Counterrevolution, 1963–1994* (Baton Rouge: Louisiana State University Press, 1996); Thomas Byrne Edsall with Mary D. Edsall, *Chain Reaction: The Impact of Race, Rights, and Taxes on American Politics* (New York: W. W. Norton, 1992). For works that emphasize the political mobilization of business interests, see Furguson and Rogers, *Right Turn* and Thomas Byrne Edsall, *The New Politics of Inequality* (New York: W. W. Norton and Company, 1984). H. W. Brands emphasizes foreign policy, particularly the decline of the cold war, for ending liberal dominance, in *The Strange Death of American Liberalism* (New Haven, Conn.: Yale University Press, 2001). James Davison Hunter argued for the centrality of cultural issues, particularly those involving sexuality and gender roles, in *Culture Wars: The Struggle to Define America* (New York: Basic Books, 1991).

9. Todd Gitlin, *The Twilight of Common Dreams: Why America is Wracked by Culture Wars* (New York: Henry Holt & Company, 1995), 30, 35.

10. Adolph Reed Jr. and Julian Bond provide a good summary and critique of this argument in a review of Thomas and Mary Edsall's *Chain Reaction: The Impact of Race, Rights, and Taxes on American Politics* (New York: Norton, 1991). They focus much more on black demands than on feminism, which tends to be emphasized more by conservative authors. Adolph Reed Jr. and Julian Bond, "Equality: Why We Can't Wait," *Nation* 253, no. 20 (December 9, 1991), 733. The list of works that blames liberals' supposedly exclusive attention to minorities and the poor in the 1960s and 1970s and the accompanying alienation of the white working and middle classes is long. It includes William C. Berman, *America's Right Turn: From Nixon to Clinton* (Baltimore: The Johns Hopkins University Press, 1998); Steven F. Hayward, *The Age of Reagan: The Fall of the Old Liberal Order, 1964–1980* (Roseville, Calif.: Prima Publishing, 2001); Frum, *How We Got Here*; Schulman, *The Seventies*; Hugh Davis Graham, "Legacies of the 1960s: The American 'Rights Revolution' in an Era of Divided Governance," *Journal of Policy History* 10, no. 3 (1998): 267–88.

11. Sean Wilentz, *Chants Democratic: New York City and the Rise of the American Working Class, 1788–1850* (New York: Oxford University Press, 1984); Ileen DeVault, *United Apart: Gender and the Rise of Craft Unionism* (Ithaca, N.Y.: Cornell University Press, 2004); Laura Hapke, *Daughters of the Great Depression: Women, Work, and Fiction in the American 1930s* (Athens: the University of Georgia Press, 1995).

12. Cobble, *The Other Women's Movement*; Nancy MacLean, *Freedom is Not Enough: The Opening of the American Workplace* (Cambridge, Mass.: Harvard University Press, 2006); Dennis Deslippe, *Rights, Not Roses: Unions and the Rise of Working-Class Feminism, 1945–80* (Urbana: University of Illinois Press, 2000); Nancy Gabin, *Feminism in the Labor Movement: Women and the United Auto Workers, 1935–1975* (Ithaca, N.Y.: Cornell University Press, 1991); Nancy MacLean, "The Hidden History of Affirmative Action: Working Women's Struggles in the 1970s and the Gender of Class," *Feminist Studies* 25, no. 1 (Spring 1999): 43–78; Nadasen, *Welfare Warriors*.

13. Statement of Elaine Day Latourell, Lynne Darcy, Mary Jo Binder, and Sara Nelson of the National Organization for Women, Congress, Senate, Subcommittee on Employment, Poverty, and Migratory Labor of the Committee on Labor and Public Welfare, *Hearing*

on *S. 50 and S. 472: Full Employment and Balanced Growth Act of 1976,* 94th Cong., 2nd sess., May 19, 1976, 598.

14. National Committee on Full Employment, "First Full Employment Conference," *The Full Employment News Reporter,* September/October 1975, box 17, folder 18, vertical files, RG98–002, the George Meany Memorial Archives (hereafter Meany Archives).

15. "National Coalition Begins Full Employment Week: Action Planned in 75 Cities September 4–10," *Full Employment Advocate,* Labor Day 1977, and "Millions Turn Out for Full Employment Week," *Full Employment Advocate,* October 1977, both in box 17, folder 18, RG98–002, vertical file, Meany Archives.

16. National Committee for Full Employment Membership List, n.d., box 79, folder 39, AFSCME President's Office–Jerry Wurf papers, Walter P. Reuther Library, Wayne State University, Detroit, Michigan.

17. Henry M. Jackson, "Full Employment: The Key to All Goals," *The American Federationist,* August 1971, Meany Archives, 16.

18. Too numerous to list, the literature of the Full Employment Action Council, journalistic coverage of the full employment campaign, and the congressional testimony of a wide range of witnesses cite these various reasons for supporting full employment.

19. Stanley H. Ruttenberg, "The Union Member Speaks," *Blue-Collar Workers: A Symposium on Middle America,* ed. Sar A. Levitan (New York: McGraw-Hill, 1971), 154.

20. Books, collections, and articles include Louise Kapp Howe, ed., *The White Majority: Between Poverty and Affluence* (New York: Random House, 1970); Andrew Levison, *The Working Class Majority* (New York: Coward, McCann and Geoghegan, Inc., 1974); Sar A. Levitan, ed., *Blue-Collar Workers: A Symposium on Middle America* (New York: McGraw Hill, 1971); Irving M. Levine, "A Strategy for White Ethnic America," June 1968, suppl. 2, box 47, folder "Ethnicity Conference, May 3–5, 1970," National Federation of Settlements papers, Social Welfare History Archives, University of Minnesota, Minneapolis; Arthur B. Shostack, *Blue-Collar Life* (New York: Random House, 1969); Basil Whiting, *The Suddenly Remembered American* (New York: Ford Foundation, 1970); Kenneth Lasson, *The Workers: Portraits of Nine American Jobholders* (New York: The Center for the Study of Responsive Law, 1971); Richard Sennett and Jonathan Cobb, *The Hidden Injuries of Class* (New York: W. W. Norton, 1972); Michael Lavelle, ed., *Red, White, and Blue-Collar Views: A Steelworker Speaks His Mind about America* (New York: Saturday Review Press, 1974); Richard F. Hamilton, *Class and Politics in the United States* (New York: John Wiley and Sons, Inc., 1972); E. E. LeMasters, *Blue-Collar Aristocrats: Lifestyles at a Working-Class Tavern* (Madison: University of Wisconsin Press, 1975). Some of the organizations that held conferences on the blue-collar backlash were the Ford Foundation, the National Federation of Settlements, the National Conference on Social Welfare, the AJC, and the Nixon administration's Labor Department.

21. Peter Schrag, "The Forgotten American," *Harper's,* August 1969, 27–35.

22. Levine, "A Strategy for White Ethnic America," 1; Brendan Sexton, "Workers and Liberals: Closing the Gap" in Howe, *The White Majority,* 236; George Wiley, "Building a New Majority: The Movement for Economic Justice," July 6, 1973, box 41, folder 4, George Wiley papers, State Historical Society of Wisconsin, Madison, Wisconsin (hereafter Wiley papers), 1.

23. The Coalition for Human Needs and Budget Priorities boasted over one hundred

national organizations. Much of the coalition's literature can be found in box 40, folder 4, Wiley papers.

24. John Gardner created Common Cause, an outgrowth of the Urban Coalition Action Council, as a "'citizens' lobby'—concerned *not* with the advancement of special interests but with the well-being of the nation." John W. Gardner to Friend, n.d., box 188, folder 25, AFSCME President's Office Files–Jerry Wurf, Walter Reuther Library, Wayne State University, Detroit, Michigan (hereafter Reuther Library). See also John W. Gardner, "Common Cause: A New Citizens' Lobby," *Current,* November 1970, 308, and Harry J. Sievers, "Common Cause: Citizens' Lobby in the Public Interest," *America,* September 5, 1970, 109.

25. The Full Employment Action Council was cochaired by Murray H. Finlay, President of the Amalgamated Clothing and Textile Workers and Coretta Scott King of the Martin Luther King Jr. Center for Social Change. Its board of directors represented a virtual who's who of 1970s liberalism, including leaders of labor unions; civil rights organizations; and women's, civic, religious, and social welfare organizations. NOW President Karen De-Crow, Coalition of Labor Union Women Olga Madar, League of Women Voters Executive Director Peggy Lampl, and *Ms.* magazine editor Gloria Steinem were all on the board.

26. Levine, "A Strategy for White Ethnic America," 12.

27. George Wiley to Welfare Rights Leaders, Members, Friends, and Supporters, December 15, 1972, box 41, folder 4, Wiley papers, 3–4; "Movement for Economic Justice Fundraising Letter," n.d., box 40, folder 11, Wiley papers, 2; "Testimony by George Wiley before the Senate Ad Hoc Committee on the Budget Versus Human Needs," June 14, 1973, box 41, folder 4, Wiley papers, 1.

28. Jordan delivered this warning at the tenth anniversary of the 1963 March on Washington. Vernon E. Jordan Jr., "Blacks and the Nixon Administration," *Vital Speeches of the Day,* May 1, 1973, 420. Similar advice issued from other black leaders. For example, one contributor reminded readers of the NAACP's *Crisis* that "the greatest gains by blacks have come from public policy measures enacted to achieve economic advancement for all people," while Jesse Jackson warned of the fight against federal budget cuts that "the one thing we cannot do is allow this to become a black issue." Vivian H. Henderson, "Race, Economics, and Public Policy," *The Crisis,* February 1975, 52; Austin Scott, "Right Forces Map Fight on Budget Slashes," *Washington Post,* March 12, 1973 (reprint), box 40, folder 4, Wiley papers.

29. Bayard Rustin to Leadership Conference on Civil Rights Subcommittee on Annual Meeting, July 18, 1979, pp. 2–3, box 18, folder 13, Bayard Rustin papers, Library of Congress, Washington, D.C. (hereafter Rustin papers).

30. Sociologist Charles Hamilton coined the term to describe the majority of African American families consisting of a married couple with children and employed fathers—a contrast, in other words, to the underclass of female-headed households. "The Moynihan Memo and Civil Rights," *America,* March 14, 1970, 262.

31. Ibid.

32. Frances Fox Piven and Richard A. Cloward, *Regulating the Poor: The Functions of Public Welfare,* updated ed. (New York: Vintage Books, 1993), 183–99; James T. Patterson, *America's Struggle against Poverty, 1900–1994* (Cambridge, Mass.: Harvard University Press, 1994), 171–84; Michael B. Katz, *In the Shadow of the Poorhouse: A Social History of*

*Welfare in America* (New York: Basic Books, 1986), 251–73; Nadasen, *Welfare Warriors*, 4–13.

33. West, *The National Welfare Rights Movement*, 211–29; Nadasen, *Welfare Warriors*, 71–72.

34. Quoted in Jack Rosenthal, "The 'Female-Headed Household,'" *New York Times*, July 29, 1971, 16.

35. Levison, *The Working Class Majority*, 45, 153; Lee Rainwater, "Making the Good Life: Working-Class Family and Lifestyles," in Levitan, ed., *Blue-Collar Workers*, 207, 209.

36. Worth Bateman and Jodie Allen, "Income Maintenance: Who Gains and Who Pays?" in Levitan, ed., *Blue-Collar Workers*, 288.

37. See, for example, Congress, House of Representatives, Subcommittee on Equal Opportunities of the Committee on Education and Labor, *Hearing on H.R. 50: Equal Opportunity and Full Employment*, 94th Cong., 2nd sess., March 16, 1976, 309, 332; "Why Recovering Economies—A Radical Change in Political Economics," *Business Week*, cited in ibid., 333; Congress, House of Representatives, Subcommittee on Manpower, Compensation and Health and Safety of the Committee on Education and Labor, *Hearing on H.R. 50: Full Employment and Balanced Growth Act of 1976*, 94th Cong., 2nd sess., April 8, 1976, 189.

38. Congress, Senate, Committee on Banking, Housing, and Urban Affairs, *Hearing on S. 50: Full Employment and Balanced Growth Act of 1976*, 94th Cong., 2nd sess., May 21, 1976, 111.

39. Quoted in Helen Ginsberg, "Full Employment: The Necessary Ingredient," *Do It NOW* 9, no. 7 (1976): 11, Arthur and Elizabeth Schlesinger Library on the History of Women in America, Radcliffe Institute for Advanced Study, Harvard University, Cambridge, Mass. (hereafter Schlesinger Library).

40. Congress, House of Representatives, Subcommittee on Manpower, Compensation, and Health and Safety of the Committee on Education and Labor, *Hearing on H.R. 50: Full Employment and Balanced Growth Act of 1976*, 94th Cong., 2nd sess., April 14, 1976, 437; Congress, Senate, Subcommittee on Employment, Poverty, and Migratory Labor of the Committee on Labor and Public Welfare, *Hearing on H.R. 50 and S. 472: Full Employment and Balanced Growth Act of 1976*, 94th Cong., 2nd sess., May 19, 1976, 572; Congress, Senate, Committee on Banking, Housing, and Urban Affairs, *Hearing on S. 50: Full Employment and Balanced Growth Act of 1976*, 94th Cong., 2nd sess., May 20, 1976, 3.

41. Congress, House of Representatives, Subcommittee on Equal Opportunities of the Committee on Education and Labor, *Hearing on H.R. 50: Equal Opportunity and Full Employment*, 94th Cong., 2nd sess., March 16, 1976, 302; Congress, House of Representatives, Subcommittee on Equal Opportunities of the Committee on Education and Labor, *Hearing on H.R. 50: Equal Opportunity and Full Employment*, 94th Cong., 1st sess., March 18, 1975, 35–36; Congress, Senate, Committee on Banking, Housing, and Urban Affairs, *Hearing on S. 50: Full Employment and Balanced Growth Act of 1976*, 94th Cong., 2nd sess., May 20, 1976, 54–55.

42. Congress, House of Representatives, Subcommittee on Equal Opportunities of the Committee on Education and Labor, *Hearing on H.R. 50: Equal Opportunity and Full Employment*, 94th Cong., 1st sess., February 25, 1975, 68.

43. Congress, House of Representatives, Subcommittee on Equal Opportunities of the Committee on Education and Labor, *Hearing on H.R. 50, H.R. 2276, H.R. 5937,* 94th Cong., 1st sess., May 5, 1975, 3.

44. Congress, House of Representatives, Subcommittee on Equal Opportunities of the Committee on Education and Labor, *Hearing on H.R. 50: Equal Opportunity and Full Employment,* 94th Cong., 1st sess., February 25, 1975, 107.

45. Daryl Michael Scott, *Contempt and Pity: Social Policy and the Image of the Damaged Black Psyche, 1880–1996* (Chapel Hill: The University of North Carolina Press, 1997); Alice O'Connor, *Poverty Knowledge: Social Science, Social Policy, and the Poor in Twentieth Century United States History* (Princeton, N.J.: Princeton University Press, 2001), 74–84, 195–209; Marisa Chappell, "From Welfare Rights to Welfare Reform: The Politics of AFDC, 1964–1984" (PhD diss., Northwestern University, 2005).

46. Congress, House of Representatives, Subcommittee on Equal Opportunities of the Committee on Education and Labor, *Hearing on H.R. 50: Equal Opportunity and Full Employment,* 94th Cong., 1st sess., March 24, 1975, 16.

47. Congress, Senate, Committee on Banking, Housing, and Urban Affairs, *Hearing on S. 50: Full Employment and Balanced Growth Act of 1976,* 94th Cong., 2nd sess., May 25, 1976, 352.

48. Liebow quoted in Congress, Senate, Subcommittee on Employment, Poverty, and Migratory Labor of the Committee on Labor and Public Welfare, *Hearing on S. 50 and S. 472: Full Employment and Balanced Growth Act,* 94th Cong., 2nd sess., May 1976, 726. Elliot Liebow, *Tally's Corners: A Study of Negro Streetcorner Men* (Boston: Little, Brown, 1967).

49. Testimony of Sister Regina Williams of Milwaukee's Justice and Peace Center, Congress, House of Representatives, Subcommittee on Equal Opportunities of the Committee on Education and Labor, *Hearing on H.R. 50: Equal Opportunity and Full Employment,* 94th Cong., 1st sess., October 13, 1975, 16.

50. Congress, House of Representatives, Subcommittee on Equal Opportunities of the Committee on Education and Labor, *Hearing on H.R. 50: Equal Opportunity and Full Employment,* 94th Cong., 2nd sess., February 13, 1976, 17.

51. Congress, House, Subcommittee on Manpower, Compensation, and Health and Safety of the Committee on Education and Labor, *Hearing on H.R. 50: Full Employment and Balanced Growth Act of 1976,* 94th Cong., 2nd sess., April 2, 1976, 99.

52. Bayard Rustin, "Black Rage, White Fear: The Full Employment Answer," speech to Bricklayers, Masons, and Plasterers International Union, [1970], RG98-002, vertical file, box 6, folder 7, Meany Archives.

53. Carol Burris to Olya Margolis, June 4, 1976, box 318, folder "Employment-Full, Correspondence, 1974–77," National Council of Jewish Women Washington Office papers, Library of Congress (hereafter NCJW Washington Office papers), 2.

54. Carolyn Shaw Bell, "Full Employment—For Women?" June 12, 1976, box 318, folder "Employment—Full, Correspondence, 1974–77," NCJW Washington Office papers, 1.

55. Dorothy Sue Cobble, *The Other Women's Movement: Workplace Justice and Social Rights in Modern America* (Princeton, N.J.: Princeton University Press, 2004).

56. Eileen Foley, "NOW Takes Aim at Economics," *Detroit Free Press,* August 23, 1973 (reprint), and NOW flyer, n.d., box 23, folder 4, United Auto Workers Women's Department: Dorothy Haener papers, Reuther Library (hereafter Haener papers).

57. Dorothy Haener, "What Do Women's Groups Want?," August 18, 1972, box 8, folder 49, Haener papers.

58. Nancy MacLean places the struggle for jobs at the center of both the black freedom and feminist movements. Nancy MacLean, *Freedom Is Not Enough: The Opening of the American Workplace* (New York: Russell Sage Foundation, 2006).

59. Mary-Jean Collins-Robson (National Organization for Women), Congress, Joint Economic Committee, *Hearing on Jobs and Prices in Chicago,* 94th Cong., 1st sess., October 20, 1975, 30.

60. Annelise Orleck, *Common Sense and a Little Fire: Women and Working-Class Politics in the United States, 1900–1965* (Chapel Hill: The University of North Carolina Press, 1995); Linda Gordon, "Black and White Visions of Welfare: Women's Welfare Activism, 1890–1945," *Journal of American History* 78 (September 1999): 559–90; Eileen Boris, "The Power of Motherhood: Black and White Activist Women Redefine the 'Political,'" in *Mothers of a New World: Maternalist Politics and the Origins of Welfare States,* ed. Seth Koven and Sonya Michel (New York: Routledge, 1993), 213–45.

61. Barbara Bergmann, *The Economic Emergence of Women* (New York: Basic Books, 1986); Nancy MacLean, "Postwar Women's History: From the 'Second Wave' to the End of the Family Wage?" in *A Companion to Post-1945 America,* ed. Roy Rosenzweig and Jean-Cristophe Agnew (London: Blackwell, 2002); Lynn Weiner, *From Working Girl to Working Mother: The Female Labor Force in the United States, 1820–1985* (Chapel Hill: The University of North Carolina Press, 1985).

62. Two contemporary discussions of the feminization of poverty are Women's Work Force Project of Wider Opportunities for Women, Inc., "The Feminization of Poverty: Issue Brief," December 1981, box 10, folder "Mobil Action-Minutes and Meeting Correspondence," Downtown Welfare Advocacy Center Records, Social Welfare History Archives, University of Minnesota (hereafter DWAC papers), and Kathleen Riordan (Women's Bureau), "Women and Work, Women and Poverty: A Look at a Women's Bureau Project" in SCAN Manuscripts, 105th Annual Forum—Los Angeles, [1978], suppl. 1, box 26, National Conference on Social Welfare papers, Social Welfare History Archives, University of Minnesota (hereafter NCSW papers).

63. "To Promote the General Welfare—Unfinished Agenda," 1977, Series IV, League of Women Voters papers, Library of Congress, Washington, D.C. (hereafter LWV Papers).

64. Susan Hartmann detailed the efforts of feminists in liberal organizations such as the American Civil Liberties Union, the National Council of Churches, and the Ford Foundation to channel resources toward addressing women's poverty and concludes that these women were more attentive to the needs of poor and minority women than were feminists in "feminist organizations." Susan Hartmann, *The Other Feminists: Activists in the Liberal Establishment* (New Haven, Conn.: Yale University Press, 1998). Nancy MacLean described the efforts of feminist activists to address women's poverty through campaigns for affirmative action and nontraditional jobs. "Saying good riddance to both the old family-wage system and the privations and humiliations of AFDC, [these efforts] aimed at a new model, a model in which women could build families from positions of autonomy and power, heading or coheading households while being recognized as full citizens at the same time." Nancy MacLean, "The Hidden History of Affirmative Action," 62.

65. Testimony of Lynn Darcy and Mary Jo Binder of NOW, Congress, House of Representatives, Subcommittee on Equal Opportunities of the Committee on Education and

Labor, *Hearing on H.R. 50: Equal Opportunity and Full Employment,* 94th Cong., 1st sess., March 18, 1975, 14.

66. NOW Women and Poverty Task Force, *Commonwealth,* [1975], box 210, folder 47, National Organization for Women papers, Schlesinger Library, Cambridge, Mass. (hereafter NOW papers), 10.

67. Congress, Senate, Subcommittee on Employment, Poverty, and Migratory Labor of the Committee on Labor and Public Welfare, *Hearing on S. 50 and S. 472: Full Employment and Balanced Growth Act,* 94th Cong., 2nd sess., May 1976, 606.

68. Helen Parolla, "Full Employment as a Women's Issue" (speech delivered at the National Women's Agenda Coalition Conference, Washington, D.C., March 17, 1978), p. 4, box 318, folder "Employment—Full, Miscellany, 1974–76," NCJW Washington Office papers.

69. Congress, House of Representatives, Subcommittee on Manpower, Compensation, and Health and Safety of the Committee on Education and Labor, *Hearing on H.R. 50: Full Employment and Balanced Growth Act of 1976,* 94th Cong., 2nd sess., April 14, 1976, 483–84.

70. Statement of Elaine Day Latourell, Lynne Darcy, Mary Jo Binder, and Sara Nelson (NOW), Congress, Senate, Subcommittee on Employment, Poverty, and Migratory Labor of the Committee on Labor and Public Welfare, *Hearing on S. 50 and S. 472: Full Employment and Balanced Growth Act of 1976,* 94th Cong., 2nd sess., May 19, 1976, 589. Some women suggested a "women's amendment" to the bill, and others called for a Women's Policy Bureau to be added to the proposed National Institute for Full Employment. Carol Burrs to Olya Margolis, June 4, 1976, box 318, folder "Employment—Full, Correspondence, 1974–77," NCJW Washington Office papers, 2; Statement of Marie W. Novak (Missouri Women's Political Caucus), Congress, House of Representatives, Subcommittee on Equal Opportunities of the Committee on Education and Labor, *Hearing on H.R. 50: Equal Opportunity and Full Employment,* 94th Cong., 1st sess., October 14, 1975, 186.

71. Statement of Carl Reinstein, Local 157, United Auto Workers, Detroit Michigan in Congress, House of Representatives, Subcommittee on Equal Opportunities of the Committee on Education and Labor, *Hearing on H.R. 50: Equal Opportunity and Full Employment,* 94th Cong., 1st sess., April 4, 1975, 337; Statement of Leon Keyserling, Congress, House of Representatives, Subcommittee on Equal Opportunities of the Committee on Education and Labor, *Hearing on H.R. 50: Equal Opportunity and Full Employment,* 94th Cong., 2nd sess., March 15, 1976, 272.

72. See Coalition of Labor Union Women Statement of Purpose, adopted at the founding conference, March, 23–24, 1974, RG98–002, vertical file, box 6, folder 10, Meany Archives. Demands for access to nontraditional jobs are too numerous to cite—they appear in most feminist statements on full employment.

73. Congress, Senate, Subcommittee on Employment, Poverty, and Migratory Labor of the Committee on Labor and Public Welfare, *Hearing on S. 50 and S. 472: Full Employment and Balanced Growth Act of 1976,* 94th Cong., 2nd sess., May 1976, 594.

74. Congress, House of Representatives, Subcommittee on Manpower, Compensation, and Health and Safety of the Committee on Education and Labor, *Hearing on H.R. 50: Full Employment and Balanced Growth Act of 1976,* 94th Cong., 2nd sess., April 14, 1976, 486.

75. Congress, Senate, Subcommittee on Employment, Poverty, and Migratory Labor of the Committee on Labor and Public Welfare, *Hearing on H.R. 50 and S. 472: Full Employment and Balanced Growth Act of 1976*, 94th Cong., 2nd sess., May 1976, 641.

76. Carolyn Shaw Bell, "Full Employment Without Inflation—For Whom?" A paper presented at the Full Employment Without Inflation Conference, Academy for Contemporary Problems, Columbus, Ohio, November 1974, quoted in Congress, Senate, Subcommittee on Employment, Poverty, and Migratory Labor of the Committee on Labor and Public Welfare, *Hearing on H.R. 50 and S. 472: Full Employment and Balanced Growth Act of 1976*, 94th Cong., 2nd sess., 400.

77. Congress, Senate, Subcommittee on Employment, Poverty, and Migratory Labor of the Committee on Labor and Public Welfare, *Hearing on S. 50 and S. 472: Full Employment and Balanced Growth Act*, 94th Cong., 2nd sess., May 1976, 674.

78. Testimony of Carol Burris (Women's Lobby), ibid., 618.

79. Congress, Senate, Subcommittee on Employment, Poverty, and Migratory Labor of the Committee on Labor and Public Welfare, *Hearing on H.R. 50 and S. 472: Full Employment and Balanced Growth Act of 1976*, 94th Cong., 2nd sess., May 18, 1976, 381.

80. Parolla, "Full Employment as a Women's Issue," 1, 4.

81. Congress, Senate, Subcommittee on Employment, Poverty, and Migratory Labor of the Committee on Labor and Public Welfare, *Hearing on S. 50 and S. 472: Full Employment and Balanced Growth Act of 1976*, 94th Cong., 2nd sess., May 19, 1976, 600.

82. "A Feminist Manifesto: H.R. 11167, Employment and Manpower [*sic*] Act of 1972: Testimony of Wilma Scott Heide, President of NOW, the National Organization for Women, Inc.," p. 3, series XLIII, box 201, folder 5, NOW papers.

83. Congress, Senate, Subcommittee on Employment, Poverty, and Migratory Labor of the Committee on Labor and Public Welfare, *Hearing on H.R. 50 and S. 472: Full Employment and Balanced Growth Act of 1976*, 94th Cong., 2nd sess., May 19, 1976, 626.

84. Ibid., 716.

85. Evelyn Sims to Augustus Hawkins in Congress, House of Representatives, Subcommittee on Equal Opportunities of the Committee on Education and Labor, *Hearing on H.R. 50: Equal Opportunity and Full Employment*, 94th Cong., 1st sess., 332.

86. In 1975, women in Brooklyn, New York, attending an International Wages for Housework Campaign conference in London, formed Black Women for Wages for Housework. The organization saw itself as carrying on a legacy pioneered by welfare rights activists. *SAFIRE* (newsletter of Black Women for Wages for Housework, USA), Fall 1977, box 1, folder 7, Minorities Collection, Sophia Smith Collection, Smith College, Northampton, Mass.

87. Premilla Nadasen presents this seeming tension within welfare rights between demanding the right to stay-at-home motherhood and demanding access to good jobs as part of welfare rights activists' "unique brand of feminism" located in African American women's experiences. Nadasen, "Expanding the Boundaries of the Women's Movement." There were still some welfare rights activists who rejected or at least cautioned against this increasing focus on jobs. Although not opposed to job opportunities for welfare mothers, experience led them to worry that any jobs emphasis would merely result in punitive policies; instead, they insisted that the movement prioritize the demand for a guaranteed income. See, for example, DWAC to All Welfare Coalition Folks Who Attended the April

5th Working Meeting for May 11th Action, n.d., box 12, folder "Misc. Actions 1978–82," DWAC papers.

88. See note 43.

89. Norman Hill, "Civil Rights and Full Employment," *American Federationist,* May 1977 (reprint), pp. 2–3, RG98–002, vertical file, box 7, folder 7, Meany Archives.

90. Congress, House of Representatives, Subcommittee on Equal Opportunities of the Committee on Education and Labor, *Hearing on H.R. 50: Equal Opportunity and Full Employment,* 94th Cong., 1st sess., 167.

91. Ibid., 179; Congress, House of Representatives, Subcommittee on Equal Opportunities of the Committee on Education and Labor, *Hearing on H.R. 50: Equal Opportunity and Full Employment,* 94th Cong., 2nd sess., March 15, 1976, 167.

92. National Women's Political Caucus and Women's Lobby to Democratic Platform Committee 1976, 1.

93. Statement of the NWPC by Ms. Lupe Anguiano, Chairperson, Welfare Reform Task Force to Welfare Reform Subcommittee, House of Representatives, on "Better Jobs and Income Act—H.R. 9030," October 31, 1977, box WE-4, general subject file, Jimmy Carter Library and Museum, Atlanta, Ga. (hereafter Carter Library). On the Low Income Women Project, see also numerous documents in box 6, folder "Low Income Women, 4/77–10/77," Staff Offices–Costanza Files, Carter Library.

94. Nearly every feminist (whether from a welfare rights, a liberal, or a feminist organization) testifying on full employment pointed to the failure of government job and training programs to serve women. It was a major complaint of the poor women who participated in the Women's Bureau Low Income Women's Project, as well. The phrase "rampant sex discrimination" was used by NOW's Lynne Darcy and Mary Jo Binder to describe the findings of a Government Accounting Office study of federal job and training programs. Congress, House, Subcommittee on Equal Opportunities of the Committee on Education and Labor, *Hearing on H.R. 50: Equal Opportunity and Full Employment,* 94th Cong., 1st sess., March 18, 1975, 15.

95. Ibid., 598.

96. Kathleen Riordan, "Women and Work, Women and Poverty: A Look at a Women's Bureau Project," SCAN Manuscripts, 105th Annual Forum—Los Angeles, [1978], suppl. 1, p. 11, box 26, NCSW papers. Feminists made this point repeatedly in debates over full employment and welfare reform legislation. For more information on the Low Income Women Project, see multiple documents in Staff Offices–Midge Costanza, box 6, Carter Library.

97. Congress, House of Representatives, Subcommittee on Manpower, Compensation and Health and Safety of the Committee on Education and Labor, *Hearing on H.R. 50: Full Employment and Balanced Growth Act of 1976,* 94th Cong., 2nd sess., April 14, 1976, 499; "Rights Panel Charges Programs to Help Women Actually Hurt Them," *New York Times,* June 20, 1974, 44.

98. Congress, Senate, Subcommittee on Employment, Poverty, and Migratory Labor of the Committee on Labor and Public Welfare, *Hearing on S. 50 and S. 472: Full Employment and Balanced Growth Act, 1976,* 94th Cong., 2nd sess., May 1976, 623. For the successful suit challenging AFDC-UP's exclusion of unemployed mothers, see Abigail McCarthy, "The Ideal and the Issue: Facing Reality in Helping Families," *Commonweal,* April 25, 1983,

233; Linda Greenhouse, "High Court Holds Jobless Mother Equal to Father on Welfare Right," *New York Times,* June 26, 1979, 9; Susan K. Blumenthal, "Court Extends AFDC Benefits in Westcott Decision," *National NOW Times,* August 1979, p. 3, NOW papers.

99. "Proposal, Downtown Welfare Advocate Center, January 1982," pp. 2–3, box 5, folder "Proposals 1982," DWAC papers.

100. See, for example, Congress, House of Representatives, Subcommittee on Equal Opportunities of the Committee on Education and Labor, *Hearing on H.R. 50: Equal Opportunity and Full Employment,* 94th Cong., 2nd sess., March 24, 1975, and Burris to Margolis, June 4, 1976, 1–2.

101. Statement of Ruby Duncan, president, Clarke County Welfare Rights Organization, Subcommittee on Poverty, Labor, and Public Welfare Committee, U.S. Senate, Full Employment and Balanced Growth Act, May 19, 1976, pp. 1–3, box 15, folder 18, Haener papers. Duncan's life and activism are chronicled in Annelise Orleck, *Storming Ceasars Palace.*

102. Burris to Margolis, June 4, 1976, 1.

103. Other feminists testifying on full employment noted that without adequate and affordable child care, many women would have difficulty taking advantage of the "resultant opportunities." Addie Wyatt of CLUW, Congress, House of Representatives, Subcommittee on Equal Opportunities of the Committee on Education and Labor, *Hearing on H.R. 50: Equal Opportunity and Full Employment,* 94th Cong., 1st sess., October 14, 1975, 157.

104. Congress, Senate, Subcommittee on Employment, Poverty, and Migratory Labor of the Committee on Labor and Public Welfare, *Hearing on S. 50 and S. 472: Full Employment and Balanced Growth Act, 1976,* 94th Cong., 2nd sess., May 1976, 618.

105. "To promote the General Welfare—Unfinished Agenda," [1977].

106. For an example of the administration's political calculations regarding full employment legislation, see James T. McIntyre Jr. to President, October 24, 1977, Presidential Handwriting file, "10/25/77[1]," Carter Library.

107. For a good example of feminist critique of the Carter welfare reform plan along these lines, see National Council on Women, Work, and Welfare statement, September 16, 1977 and "Welfare Reform is a Women's Issue," *Women's Agenda* (journal of the Women's Action Alliance, Inc.), March 1978, series 4, box 595, folder "Welfare Reform—Position Statements—Welfare 77–78," LWV papers.

108. MacLean, *Freedom Is Not Enough,* 118. See also 142–43.

109. Cobble, *The Other Women's Movement;* Susan Hartmann, *The Other Feminists: Activists in the Liberal Establishment* (New Haven, Conn.: Yale University Press, 1998).

110. Gwendolyn Mink, a welfare scholar and activist, notes that feminists who mobilized to oppose the 1996 Welfare Reform Act "were far from united behind a common vision of welfare justice. Although we could all agree on the urgency of childcare and health care and jobs, we were less certain about what social policy should say to single mothers who want to or need to care for their own children in their own homes." Mink insists, contrary to the more widely held feminist emphasis on employment, that an equitable welfare system should be based on the notion that "poor single women who give care to their children are mothers whose caregiving is work." Gwendolyn Mink, "Feminists, Welfare Reform, and Welfare Justice," *Social Justice* 25, no. 1 (1998): 153. Felicia Kornbluh also discusses the tensions within feminist circles about the appropriate remedy for single

mothers' poverty. Felicia Kornbluh, "Feminists and the Welfare Debate," *Dollars & Sense,* November-December 1996, 24–29. Mimi Abramovitz describes some recent feminist approaches to welfare, some of which emphasize employment, others of which insist on what Nancy Fraser called "caregiver parity," an allowance to compensate women for their caregiving labor. Mimi Abramovitz, *Under Attack, Fighting Back: Women and Welfare in the United States* (New York: Monthly Review Press, 1996).

# 13. Learning from Coalitions

## Intersections and New Directions in Activism and Scholarship

### ELIZABETH KAMINSKI

Social movement scholarship turns our attention to the rise and fall of movement activism, and often it emphasizes fragmentation and decline.[1] Although we have much to learn from examining the points where movements fall apart, this emphasis on fragmentation limits our ability to fully understand movement outcomes, transformations, and genuine attempts to include differences. A focus on feminist coalitions shifts our focus, however, and brings to light the various opportunities, negotiations, struggles, and successes enacted by people who come together across different points of view and backgrounds to pursue a common goal. Along with documenting recent U.S. feminist history, the scholarship in this book provides us with conceptual tools for understanding any social movement from the standpoint of various disciplines—including history, sociology, and political science. The coalitions that feminists created point us as scholars in new directions—specifically, they direct us to do a similar type of coalition work in our scholarship.

Two long-standing traditions in social movement scholarship are resource mobilization and political process theories, which call attention to the emergence and survival of social movements. Together, these theories suggest that social movements are viable only when activists have access to resources, particularly money, and to political opportunities that are conducive to protest, such as elites who are sympathetic to the movement or elites who are divided, weak, and therefore susceptible to replacement.[2] From these perspectives, the resources and opportunities crucial to movement emergence and success are often seen as related to broad structural transformations in politics and the economy and, therefore, beyond the control of activists. Moreover, as adherents to these perspectives explain, social movement organizations that emerge to take advantage of new opportunities often find themselves in competition with one another over available resources. The ensuing division and fragmentation within a movement can lead to its collapse, as can the narrowing of political opportunities.[3] Similar to much prior scholarship on the feminist movement, resource mobilization and political process theories tend to emphasize fragmentation and decline over cooperation.

Training our eye on coalitions, feminist and otherwise, can move us beyond these limitations. By providing empirical evidence of activists coming together across difference and working in coalitions, scholars have documented moments that have been overlooked in prior work and have pushed us to advance our theories of social movements. From such work, we can begin to explicate how, when, and why movement activism can lead to coalitions instead of collapse. Maria Bevacqua uses the term *bridge issues* to describe shared needs and goals that activists see as pressing enough that they come together across their differences. When, as Bevacqua describes, liberal and radical and black and white feminists (not mutually exclusive categories) prioritized the needs of rape survivors over their own differences, a powerful coalition was formed. Differences strengthened, rather than weakened the antirape movement: liberal strategies of reforming the system and radical strategies of creating alternative institutions overlapped to ensure that rape victims had improved legal protections and access to services. Moreover, that feminist organizers included white women and women of color meant that rape crisis centers would be more welcoming for a greater diversity of survivors.

We have similar evidence of coalitions forming around pressing needs and goals that bridge differences in ideology, strategy, and identity. Quoting one member of the National Organization for Women, Emily Zuckerman notes that coalitions formed around such "bread and butter issues" as women's employment. Access to adequate health care brought together the authors of *Our Bodies, Ourselves* and connected them with their readers, even when they clashed with one another over the content and means of publishing of the book. Access to health care also united welfare rights and abortion rights activists in Washington, D.C., as Anne Valk suggests. Along with health care and employment, access to essential social services also worked as bridge issues for the women whose activism is documented in this collection. The lack of adequate financial support and the lack of dignity with which they were treated by caseworkers and administrators led Aid to Families with Dependent Children (AFDC) recipients to come together for mutual support and establish welfare rights organizations. When cutbacks in city funding led to the closing of schools, hospitals, and police and fire stations in their neighborhoods, women in Brooklyn came together in interracial, grassroots community organizations to protect their children. Similarly, the desire to protect children from violence and war led Women Strike for Peace to radicalize their image and form coalitions with black power and New Left organizations.

As women came together across differences and worked toward a common goal, they left evidence that differences need not fragment a movement. In addition, they show that when activists work in coalition, they create new frameworks for analyzing social problems, altering the cultural and political terrain in which they worked. For example, by working with other neighborhood women, Brooklyn activists in the National Congress of Neighborhood Women (NCNW) gained an understanding of one another's lives. They were aware of their racial differences but they also identified similar problems, such as experiences of domestic violence, and common values, including the desire to protect children and improve their neighborhood. Identifying commonalities *and* differences allowed them to develop a structural analysis of their personal problems and to see race, class, and gender as interlocking systems of oppression long before scholars gave us the theoretical language to discuss it. Through coalition work, these women identified the sources of their oppression and saw differences in race, class, and gender as facilitating rather than impeding ongoing alliances.

Other women constructed new analyses of social problems through their coalition work. By working in coalitions, the largely middle-class and white women of Women Strike for Peace understood racism and poverty as linked to violence and war. This new analysis facilitated their increased radicalism and activism around numerous, interrelated social problems, creating in the process allies we might consider to be "strange bedfellows." Similarly, antirape activists came to see rape as connected to racism, sexism, and poverty. In the context of the civil rights and black power movements, welfare recipients of various races identified their oppression as a type of structural and institutionalized racism. Welfare rights activists and reproductive rights activists in Washington D.C. began to frame the abortion debate in terms of the need to provide everyone, regardless of race and economic standing, with equal access to health care. Church Women United, whose work on peace and ecumenical coalitions led them to develop an antiracist and feminist ideology, began to see their work on social justice as mandated by the Christian identity because, as Caryn Neumann notes, "that was what Jesus would do." Women's feminist coalition work led them to construct frameworks for understanding social problems that then became arguments *in support of* their continued activism rather than the cause of their activism's decline.

Although much work in the tradition of political process theory focuses on opportunities within the formal political system, scholars have begun to highlight the cultural context in which social movements operate.[4] Widely held norms, values, and beliefs can both constrain and enable social protest.[5] Feminist coalitions illustrate how social movement activists alter the cultural terrain while creating new and different opportunities for future social movement mobilization. Rather than waiting for opportunities to emerge, feminist activists working in coalitions, reframed issues and their own activism in ways that created an oppositional consciousness that justified further activism on a range of other social problems. Moreover, activists made strategic use of the media, including publications such as *Ms.* magazine and *Our Bodies, Ourselves* to spread these new oppositional frameworks to others. The creators of *Ms.* made use of the glossy magazine format to bring a feminist analysis into popular culture and thereby alter the political and cultural context surrounding their activism.

The new analyses generated within coalitions not only drew more resources—in the form of people—into their direct action and civil disobedience campaigns, it also created cultural justifications and opportunities for future activists, highlighting the connections between feminist coalitions and later waves of activism. For example, participants in the Midwest Academy, a crucial training space for feminist activists involved in the *Sears* case, went on to participate in diverse types of social justice activism including environmental, antirape, and civil rights movements. Some coalitions such as the one around the *Sears* case were short-lived, but others, such as the grassroots neighborhood and public housing coalition in Brooklyn's NCNW, have lasted for decades and still exist today. As Bernice Johnson Reagon has stated, activists entered coalitions for survival,[6] but working in coalition sustains the possibility not only for survival but also for generating meaningful social change and creating opportunities for further social justice activism.

Attention to feminist coalitions contributes to the growing body of literature that examines the cultural outcomes, processes, and opportunities of social movements. Much prior scholarship on the cultural aspects of social movements has emphasized that activists are not only resource-gathering, opportunity-taking individuals, but groups of people that come together around a shared identity or "sense of we" termed *collective identity*.[7] Numerous scholars have shown the necessity of collective identity in a wide range of movements and have documented the ongoing process of constructing a collective identity.[8] Because collective identity involves drawing a boundary around a group and defining who is "us" and who is "them," it also creates a dilemma for movements. It is at once both crucial to mobilization and prone to creating conflict and fragmentation that may lead to the disintegration of a movement.[9]

But by seeking to learn from coalition building, scholars can advance our conceptualization of collective identity. Coalition work underscores that *solidarity* is essential to social movement organizing. However, it also illustrates that solidarity is not always based on a static or singular identity. Activists in the women's movement were acutely aware of their differences from one another—liberal, radical, and socialist feminists; women of color and white women; poor and middle-class women; young and old activists; and women of different religious faiths. In such coalitions, these differences were not ignored or glossed over to construct a cohesive group identity. Rather, they were articulated, defined, and grappled with in ongoing discussions. Welfare rights activists, for example, were keen to such differences, as were the women who sought to see themselves reflected in the sisterhood promised by *Ms.* magazine. A sense of sisterhood was created through these discussions and debates, even though there was not always a consensus about its contours and boundaries. Moreover, the identity projected by a social movement organization may not necessarily be the authentic, personal identity of the activists, but a strategic construct used to tap into a cultural ideal. Such was the case for many in Women Strike for Peace who used the middle-class, mother and homemaker image as a defense strategy—the same image that welfare recipients appealed to in defending their right to bear and raise their children.

In some instances, the debates surrounding identity and difference were conflict-ridden and led the coalitions to weaken over time. The Women Strike for Peace activists, for example, conflicted over "issue and image" and this became a source of tension. Similarly, the coalition between welfare rights activists and reproductive rights activists weakened over time as the abortion rights movement began to frame abortion as a matter of choice rather than a matter of equal access to health care, which distanced predominantly white abortion rights activists from the needs and identities of poor women of color. Attention to coalitions need not minimize the difficulties, conflicts, and fragmentation that may result when people of varying class, race, gender, or religious identities work together to pursue social change. However, while noting the problems, such historical alliances also provide concrete examples in which difference and debate can strengthen a movement. Many coalitions, past and present, have been successful in resonating with large numbers of people, advancing structural analyses of social problems, and in many instances, gaining concrete outcomes—rape crisis centers, education and job training programs, federal grants for public housing, and changes in legislation. Through empirical examples, we can assess varying outcomes

made by activists who are fully aware of their differences and do not share
a common, singular identity yet nonetheless construct a sense of solidarity
and work toward common goals.

Coalitions, then, form not around a shared, singular, or static identity,
but around common needs, goals, and frameworks for understanding social
problems. In many cases, they also emerge around shared *emotions,* which
become a vital source of solidarity and a significant reason why diverse activists pool resources. Johnnie Tillman poignantly stated that hunger is a
feeling that crosses racial divides. Although hunger is a sensation and not
an emotion, her observation conveys the importance of shared experiences
and a sense of empathy in building coalitions. Other coalitions underscore
the significance of empathy, but also love, fear, anger, shame, and a range of
other emotions in building coalitions. For example, *Ms.* magazine served as
a "lifeline" or "life saver" for women who felt isolated in their hometowns
that may not have had a strong feminist community. Through the letters
to the editor, women shared feelings of shame surrounding such experiences as abortion and also shared their joy at connecting with one another
through the magazine. Shame and isolation were also significant to building
coalitions around welfare rights and reproductive rights. The experiences of
white and black welfare recipients, for example, differed because of racialized
stereotypes of welfare recipients and because caseworkers and administrators
often applied rules differentially to exclude black women from services and
opportunities. However, white, black, Latino, and Native American women
who received AFDC were all affected by the shame-inducing public rhetoric
and were united in their anger toward an unjust system. D.C.-based activists
in the welfare and reproductive rights coalitions also joined forces around
shared feelings of shame and humiliation caused by the way that health care
workers treated poor women and a sense of rage toward an inadequate health
care system. Although not necessarily protesting angrily in front of a hospital,
women who wrote or read *Our Bodies, Ourselves* also shared a sense of rage
about the health care delivery system that made light of women's needs and
concerns. Like *Ms.* magazine, the book created a space in which women
could share their stories of fear and anger and enact empathy. The authors
of the book also describe their collective as intimate and loving, even during
times of conflict. Church Women United activists, likewise, saw themselves
as "instruments of reconciling love," suggesting that emotions could bridge
divides; rape, for example, was a "bridge issue" precisely because it conjures
up such strong emotions for—and as—survivors.

Coalition work draws our attention to the significance of emotions in
social protest. Prior work in this area suggests that some emotions, such as

anger, are conducive to protest, but others, including fear or shame, might deter individuals from engaging in activism.[10] However, emotions can not only motivate individuals to participate in social movements, but also bring people together across differences and sustain coalitions. The emotion work of articulating and sharing personal experiences and feelings is essential to coalition building and to building diverse activist communities, even if for a short while.[11]

In many cases, shared emotions may result from similar experiences based on an "outsider status," even when the outsiders do not share a single identity. For example, white women who received AFDC felt they could understand racism and, in a sense, experienced what it felt like because of their own marginalized status as women on welfare. Neighborhood activists in Brooklyn point out that women often recognized their common emotions when discussing personal experiences in the context of consciousness raising. Feminists used consciousness-raising sessions deliberately to generate solidarity among NCNW activists. In addition to the face-to-face meetings common in many feminist organizations, consciousness-raising can also occur in the print media, as was, and is, the case with *Ms.* magazine and *Our Bodies, Ourselves* since both provide a forum for women to share experiences and emotions. Given the feminist movement's widespread utilization of consciousness-raising as a key tactic in promoting change, feminist organizations may be particularly conducive to coalition building. Nonetheless, scholars of any social movement and activists pursuing social change should take note of the documented importance of emotions in building coalitions and of how the force of emotion can help mobilize resources and create political and cultural opportunities.

Coalition work, especially that of feminist coalitions, extends our theories and conceptual tools by illustrating the attempts to work together across differences to bring about social change. Such activism not only documents fascinating and previously overlooked aspects of the feminist movement, but it also pushes us to change the way we look at movements and helps us understand how activists come together through shared emotions and reshape the political and cultural terrain, pool resources, and construct new frameworks for understanding social problems. These processes are essential in understanding historical and current forms of activism, particularly in the context of globalization in which people from across the world are coming together to pursue social change regarding such issues as peace, environmental protection, human rights, and the World Trade Organization. As scholars, we have much to learn by building scholarly coalitions across our disciplines and theories.

## Notes

1. On social movement fragmentation and decline, see, for example, Barbara Epstein, "What Happened to the Women's Movement?" *Monthly Review* 53 (May 2001); Joshua Gamson, "Must Identity Movements Self-Destruct? A Queer Dilemma," *Social Problems* 42 (1995): 792–811; Todd Gitlin, *The Whole World is Watching* (Berkeley: University of California Press, 1980); Doug McAdam, *Political Process and the Development of Black Insurgency, 1930–1970* (Chicago: University of Chicago Press, 1982); Arlene Stein, *Sex and Sensibility: Stories of a Lesbian Generation* (Berkeley: University of California Press, 1997); Lori Waite, "Divided Consciousness: The Impact of Black Elite Consciousness on the 1966 Chicago Freedom Movment," in *Oppositional Consciousness: The Subjective Roots of Social Protest,* ed. Jane Mansbridge and Aldon Morris (Chicago: University of Chicago Press, 2001), 170–203.

2. See, for example, J. Craig Jenkins and Charles Perrow, "Insurgency of the Powerless: Farm Worker Movements (1946–1972)," *American Sociological Review* 42 (1977): 249–68; McAdam, *Political Process and the Development of Black Insurgency;* John D. McCarthy and Mayer N. Zald, "Resource Mobilization and Social Movements: A Partial Theory," *American Journal of Sociology* 82 (1973): 1212–41; Sidney Tarrow, *Power in Movement* (Cambridge: Cambridge University Press, 1998); Charles Tilly, *From Mobilization to Revolution* (Reading, Mass.: Addison-Wesley, 1978).

3. See, for example, McAdam, *Political Process and the Development of Black Insurgency;* Patricia Cayo Sexton, *The War on Labor and the Left* (Boulder, Colo.: Westview Press, 1992).

4. See for example, Rachel L. Einwohner, "Practices, Opportunity, and Protest Effectiveness: Illustrations from Four Animal Rights Campaigns," *Social Problems* 46 (1999): 169–86; Hank Johnston and Bert Klandermans, eds., *Social Movements and Culture* (Minneapolis: University of Minnesota Press, 1995).

5. Ann Swidler, "Culture in Action: Symbols and Strategies," *American Sociological Review* 51 (1986): 273–86; Ann Swidler, "Cultural Power and Social Movements," in *Social Movements and Culture,* ed. Hank Johnston and Bert Klandermans (Minneapolis: University of Minnesota Press, 1995), 25–40.

6. Bernice Johnson Reagon, "Coalition Politics: Turning the Century," in *Home Girls: A Black Feminist Anthology,* ed. Barbara Smith (New York: Kitchen Table: Women of Color Press, 1983), 356–57.

7. Verta Taylor and Nancy Whittier, "Collective Identity in Social Movement Communities: Lesbian Feminist Mobilization," in *Frontiers in Social Movement Theory,* ed. Aldon Morris and Carol McClurg Mueller (New Haven, Conn.: Yale University Press, 1992), 104–30.

8. See, for example, Mary Bernstein, "Celebration and Suppression: Strategic Uses of Identity by the Lesbian and Gay Movement," *American Journal of Sociology* 103 (1997): 531–65; Stephanie Gilmore and Elizabeth Kaminski, "A Part and Apart: Lesbian and Straight Feminist Activists Negotiate Identity in a Second-Wave Organization," *Journal of History of Sexuality* 16, no. 1 (January 2007): 95–113; Alberto Melucci, *Nomads of the Present: Social Movements and Individual Needs in Contemporary Society* (Philadelphia: Temple University Press, 1986); Taylor and Whittier, "Collective Identity in Social Move-

ment Communities"; Jo Reger, Dan Meyer, and Rachel Einwohner, eds., *Identity Work* (Minneapolis: University of Minnesota Press, forthcoming); Sheldon Stryker, Timothy J. Owens, and Robert W. White, eds., *Self, Identity, and Social Movements* (Minneapolis: University of Minnesota Press, 2000); Steve Valocchi, "The Class-Inflected Nature of Gay Identity," *Social Problems* 46 (1999): 207–24.

9. Joshua Gamson, "Must Identity Movements Self-Destruct?"

10. On the importance of emotions in social movements, see, for example, Jeff Goodwin, James M. Jasper, and Francesca Polletta, eds., *Passionate Politics: Emotions and Social Movements* (Chicago: University of Chicago Press, 2001); Verta Taylor, "Watching for Vibes: Bringing Emotions into the Study of Feminist Organizations," in *Feminist Organizations: Harvest of the New Women's Movement,* ed. Myra Marx Ferree and Patricia Yancey Martin (Philadelphia: Temple University Press, 1995); and Verta Taylor and Leila J. Rupp, "Loving Internationalism: The Emotion Culture of Transnational Women's Organizations, 1888–1945," *Mobilization* 7 (2002): 125–44.

11. For other examples of how people bridge divides in social movement contexts, see Elizabeth Kaminski and Verta Taylor. "'I Want You to Feel . . . With Me': Music, Emotions, and Identity Work in Drag Performances," unpublished paper; and Stephanie Gilmore and Elizabeth Kaminski, "A Part and Apart."

# Acknowledgments

Coalition building is hard work, Bernice Johnson Reagon reminded us in her 1981 performance at the West Coast Womens Music Festival. Building feminist coalitions and pursuing feminist change in the face of internal and external opposition is no easy task; it never has been. Feminists worked across differences in race, politics, income, geography, religion, sexual identity, and perspective not only to create change but also to survive. The women whose lives are recounted in this book are survivors, veterans of feminist wars for reproductive rights, economic justice, welfare, antirape legislation, sexual autonomy, antiracism, health, and so much more. Their work reminds us of the potentials and pitfalls of coalition building, and that in spite of—and because of—our differences, we can, indeed, must work together. Their lives compelled the authors to collect and write histories that illuminate the breadth and depth of this movement; so my first debt is to the women who came together in these feminist coalitions, and who inspired *Feminist Coalitions*.

The origins of this particular book are in the 2002 meeting of the Organization of American Historians. After our panel on political history in the 1970s, Marisa Chappell and I walked and talked with Wendy Kline and Marjorie Spruill; in doing so, we all realized that our work overlapped in compelling ways, namely in the ways that feminists came together across differences to create feminist change. We commented on how that happened in the context of welfare legislation, the women's health movement, the formation of the International Women's Year agenda and meetings, and in local chapters of the National Organization for Women. It seemed to defy what we were supposed to know about the women's movement, namely that feminists could never bridge divides of race, class, sexuality, politics, religion, and so forth. I suggested that we should put together a book about it, and so the idea was born.

If I'm completely honest, though, I've been thinking about feminist co-alitions for some time. I've long known through instinct, experience, and research that feminists in the women's movement never fit into neat and discrete categories. But I've also been strongly influenced by feminists who speak about coalition politics and feminist activism, especially by Bernice Johnson Reagon. I have never met her, but I want to acknowledge the impact her words have had on my life as an activist and an academic and for living a life that illustrates how these two identities are not mutually exclusive.

Many feminists in my world remind me that academia and activism are synonymous, even necessarily so. The women who made women's history a possibility prove this point, and many of us have followed in their footsteps. The contributors to this volume, the majority of whom are newly minted PhDs, assistant professors, or just-tenured associate professors, inhabit an academic world in which the legitimacy of women's history is not challenged in ways that it was forty years ago. (Of course, that is not to say that there are no longer challenges to our field.) To these pioneering women's historians, I am grateful beyond words, and I am honored to continue the work of women's history.

One of these outstanding feminist scholars is Sara Evans, to whom I offer a special note of gratitude. Sara has been one of my strongest advocates, encouraging me while I completed my MA in Memphis and my PhD in Columbus. Because of the tremendous impact she has made on the field of women's history and because she continues to insist that second-wave feminism is a legitimate historical subject, I asked her to write the foreword to this book. She eagerly accepted and has been a fan of this project since its inception. She has also been a friend and colleague, generous toward and supportive of me at every personal and professional turn.

The scholars who joined this project are simply tremendous. They entered this project willingly, believing, as I did, that it was important to address some of the oversimplifications and (mis)interpretations of second-wave feminist activism in the United States. After reading a sketch of a proposal, they followed Marisa and Wendy and signed on to the project. They agreed to write original essays and adhered to my time frame for completed drafts! They labored through my tedious edits with what I now realize is characteristic attention to detail and a collective sense of humor. More than colleagues who present on academic conference panels with me, they are also friends who supported me when life threatened to slow progress on this project. They cheered when I completed my dissertation and took a tenure-track job; they offered unwavering support when I left that job a year later and returned home to teach and write. I acknowledge them for their participation on the project and their presence in my life. So my heartfelt thanks to

Cynthia, Amy, Wendy, Andrea, Caryn, Anne, Maria, Premilla, Tamar, Emily, Marisa, and Elizabeth.

Along the way, a number of people read proposals and chapters, listened to conference papers, and offered unyielding support. This project started when I was a graduate student at Ohio State University, and many of my graduate student colleagues and professors thought I must be nuts to propose a book while completing my dissertation. They were right, but I pursued anyway. Susan Freeman, Heather Lee Miller, Basia Nowak, Charlotte Weber, and Anne Collinson read the first drafts of the proposal and gave important initial feedback. Susan Hartmann read the final proposal and gave constructive criticism along with her praise and support; her generosity motivated me to pursue a contract. Over the years, various friends also nurtured this project by nurturing me over good food, strong drink, and deep conversation. For this, I thank Steve and Maggie Adair, Tamar Carroll, Marisa Chappell, Anne Collinson, Mary Erdmans and Tim Black, Andrea Estepa, Judith Ezekiel, Susan Freeman, Laura Gates, Elizabeth Kaminski, Kathleen Laughlin, Nancy MacLean, John O'Connor, Leila Rupp and Verta Taylor, Jan and Charlie Sherman, Kitty Sklar and Tom Dublin, Annie Valk and Leslie Brown, and Steve Valocchi and Laz Papanikolaou.

To say that Laurie Matheson has been my editor at the University of Illinois Press is accurate, but over the years she has also become a friend. She read my proposal, sent it out for review, and issued a contract within two months; since then, she has prodded gently, listened at great length, and offered guidance and sound advice. She took a chance on a young scholar with no real publishing record; I hope she knows how much I appreciate her critical eye, generous kindness, and unstinting support.

In spring 2005, I asked my graduate "feminar" on women and twentieth-century U.S. social movements to read the chapters and create and justify a table of contents. Amanda Dennison, Christine Eisel, Shirley Green, and Stephanie Shook took me through their thought processes, elaborating on why this chapter belonged with that one and how the book made the most sense. After two hours of physically reorganizing chapters on one of the tables at Beaner's coffee house and thrashing out ideas that these chapters raised, I walked away with a table of contents completely different from the one I originally proposed but one that makes so much more sense. I'm rather pleased that students organized the book in a way that was logical to them, and I am grateful for their help with this project and for being the joy in my first (and last) year at the University of Toledo.

My colleagues and students at Trinity College continue to inspire me to be a better writer, teacher, and activist. For their unwavering support and enthusiasm for my research during my time as a visiting assistant professor,

I thank Zayde Antrim, Rob Corber, Luis Figueroa, Cheryl Greenberg, Joan Hedrick, Kathleen Kete, Lou Masur, Susan Pennybacker, Gary Reger, Nancy Rossi, Barbara Sicherman, Gigi St. Peter, and Steve Valocchi. I am especially grateful for the open doors and righteous rage of my "sister visitors" Emily Musil and Manuella Meyer; both remind me that it is not only acceptable but also imperative to laugh within the walls of the ivory tower. Laura Lockwood and Karla Spurlock-Evans deserve special mention because they helped me see what really matters and, when others seek to discourage, they encourage me to keep on keepin' on. My students at Trinity College are truly amazing and give me hope for progressive coalitions in the future. They know I mean it when I tell them that they are my people.

We are in fact sisters by blood, but Suzanne Gilmore is my sister in every sense of the word. When we were little, she was sick with a cancer that should have killed her. Alas, she—nor I—did not know she could die. During the two years she was homebound, a tutor came to our house to teach her. Suzanne in turn taught me to read, write, spell, and add. As we grew from those little girls playing school into women (one of whom has yet to surrender school!), we fought, shared secrets, laughed, and loved. Over the years, especially the last six or seven, she has been and remains a pillar of strength and fortitude. For teaching me the real meaning of sisterhood, I thank Suzanne and dedicate this book to her.

When I first conceptualized this book, my advisor (and so much more) Leila Rupp thought I was onto something with the idea but encouraged me, as an advisor should, to focus on my dissertation. When I moved forward with *Feminist Coalitions* anyway, she shook her head and then gave me a big hug. Over the course of working on this book and my dissertation, in life in general and in our time together in Columbus, Key West, and Santa Barbara, she and Verta have taught me, by example, much about careful writing, passionate activism, and kindness. They have also opened their homes and hearts to me. When I needed to pursue a different professional course, they not only understood but also offered terrific advice and absolute support. They—and Sister Sledge—said it best: We are family.

Betsy Kaminski has read and listened to every single word of the countless drafts and final version of the proposal and the chapters; I am particularly grateful for her careful attention to detail and her thoughtful analytical perspective. More than a coauthor, though, she is also my partner in life and love. Completing this book without her would have been an impossible task because she cooked when necessary, walked our dogs, Fred and Raleigh, while I wrote, and offered only unconditional support. Her laugh is contagious, her love is limitless, and her smile still makes me pause and think about how very lucky I am.

# Contributors

MARIA BEVACQUA is associate professor and chair of the department of women's studies at Minnesota State University, Mankato. Her activist work includes rape crisis advocacy; abortion clinic defense; and gay, lesbian, and bisexual rights work. She is the author of *Rape on the Public Agenda: Feminism and the Politics of Sexual Assault* (Northeastern University Press, 2000). She holds a PhD in Women's Studies from Emory University.

TAMAR CARROLL is the Eisenberg Postdoctoral Fellow at the University of Michigan, where she studies and teaches post–World War II U.S. political and gender history. She is currently revising her manuscript, "Grassroots Feminism: Direct Action Organizing and Coalition Building in New York City." She has conducted more than fifty oral history interviews with grassroots activists.

MARISA CHAPPELL is assistant professor of history at Oregon State University. Her book, *From Welfare Rights to Welfare Reform: The Politics of AFDC, 1964–1984,* forthcoming from the University of Pennsylvania Press, analyzes debates about welfare, family, and economic justice in the late twentieth century United States.

ANDREA ESTEPA is a PhD candidate at Rutgers University, where she is completing her dissertation on the relationship between maternalism and feminism as motivations for women's social activism since 1960. She is currently a visiting instructor of history at Oberlin College and has also taught at Juniata College and Rutgers.

SARA M. EVANS is Distinguished McKnight Professor of History at the University of Minnesota. Her pioneering historical studies of second-wave feminism include such books as *Personal Politics: The Roots of Women's Liberation in the Civil Rights Movement and the New Left* and *Tidal Wave: How Women Changed America at Century's End*. She is also the recipient of numerous distinguished awards and grants, including those from the American Council of Learned Societies, MacArthur Foundation, and the Rockefeller Foundation.

AMY FARRELL teaches at Dickinson College in the departments of American studies and women's studies. She is the author of *Yours in Sisterhood: Ms. Magazine and the Promise of Popular Feminism*. She is currently working on a history of fatness and the fat acceptance movements in the United States.

STEPHANIE GILMORE is assistant professor of women's studies at Dickinson College. She has published articles on feminist activism, sex and sexuality, the National Organization for Women, and remains committed to teaching, writing about, and doing feminist, antiracist, and social justice activism.

CYNTHIA HARRISON is associate professor of history, women's studies, and public policy at George Washington University. She is the author of *On Account of Sex: The Politics of Women's Issues, 1945–1968* and articles on women, politics, and policy. She is currently at work on an examination of the way in which feminist organizations influenced policymaking concerning poor and minority women. She is also a member of the D.C. Commission for Women.

ELIZABETH KAMINSKI is assistant professor of sociology at Central Connecticut State University. Her current research focuses on the role of music in mobilizing and sustaining social movement activism and identity and on how music elicits emotional responses.

WENDY KLINE is associate professor of history at the University of Cincinnati. She is the author of *Building a Better Race: Gender, Sexuality, and Eugenics from the Turn of the Century to the Baby Boom*. She is currently finishing a book manuscript on the women's health movement in the United States.

PREMILLA NADASEN is associate professor of history at Queens College, City University of New York. She is the author of *Welfare Warriors: The Welfare Rights Movement in the United States*, which was awarded the John Hope Franklin Prize. She is currently writing a book about the history of domestic worker organizing.

CARYN NEUMANN is visiting assistant professor and special assistant to the dean for community relations at Miami University of Ohio at Middletown. She completed her dissertation on women's organizations in the post-1945 era at Ohio State University in 2006.

ANNE M. VALK is the associate director for programs at the John Nihcolas Brown Center at Brown University. She received her PhD in history from Duke University. Her research focuses on grassroots political activism, and she just completed a book about women's movements in Washington, D.C., in the 1960s-1970s entitled, *Radical Sisters: Second-Wave Feminism and Black Liberation in Washington, D.C.* She is currently engaged in a collaborative book project examining African American life in the Jim Crow South.

EMILY ZUCKERMAN is a PhD candidate in U.S. history at Rutgers University, where she is writing a dissertation on legal developments affecting women in the workplace during the 1970s and 1980s.

# Index

## Women in American History

The University of Illinois Press
is a founding member of the
Association of American University Presses.

_____

University of Illinois Press
1325 South Oak Street
Champaign, IL 61820-6903
www.press.uillinois.edu